ROBERT LEY

Hitler's Labor Front Leader

RONALD SMELSER

Robert Ley

Hitler's Labor Front Leader

BERG

Oxford / New York / Hamburg

Distributed exclusively in the US and Canada by
St. Martin's Press, New York

First published in 1988 by
Berg Publishers Limited
77 Morrell Avenue, Oxford OX4 1NQ, UK
175 Fifth Avenue/Room 400, New York, NY 10010, USA
Nordalbingerweg 14, 2000 Hamburg 61, FRG

British Library Cataloguing in Publication Data

Smelser, Ronald
Ronald Ley: Hitler's labor front leader.
1. Ley, Robert 2. National socialists—
Biography
I. Title
943.086′092′4 HD8453.L49

ISBN 0–85496–161–5

Library of Congress Cataloging-in-Publication Data

Smelser, Ronald, 1942—
Robert Ley, Hitler's labor front leader.
Bibliography: p.
Includes index.
I. Ley, Robert, 1890–1945. 2. Deutsche Arbeitsfront.
3. Labor and laboring classes—Germany—History—20th century.
4. National socialists—Biography. I. Title.
HD8453.L49S64 1988 331′.092′4 [B] 87–20960
ISBN 0–85496–161–5

Printed in Great Britain by A.Wheaton & Co. Ltd., Exeter

Contents

Illustrations

(between pages 160 and 161)

Acknowledgments

A number of institutions and individuals have been of great assistance in the preparation of this book. My thanks go in particular to the Council for International Exchange of Scholars and to the University of Utah Research Committee for their generous funding of my research.

The individuals to whom I am indebted are too numerous to mention. Special thanks are due to Dr John Mendelsohn and Robert Wolfe of the National Archives; Dr Heinz Boberach and the staff of the Bundesarchiv, Koblenz; Dr Hans-Jürgen Krüger of the Landeshauptarchiv Rheinland-Pfalz, Koblenz; Dr Michael Schneider of the Friedrich Ebert Stiftung, Bonn; Dr Agnes Peterson of the Hoover Institution, Stanford; Dr Jürgen Förster of the Militärgeschichtliches Forschungsamt, Freiburg, as well as to the staffs of the Berlin Document Center, the Institut für Zeitgeschichte, Munich, the Centre de Documentation Juive Contemporaine, Paris, and the Universitätsarchiv Münster. I also wish to acknowledge my debt to individuals who provided me with written information pertaining to Robert Ley and his political and private life. They include Ambassador John E. Dolibois, Julius Cieslik, Dieter Corbach, Wolfgang Corsten, Tom Doch, Wilhelm Heuser, K.H. Pampus, and Helmo Roth-Seefrid. Dr Molly Harrower and Dr Walter Reichert were very helpful in sorting out the medical factors in Ley's career. Special thanks go to Dr Marion Berghahn of Berg Publishers for her skill, patience, and kindness.

Finally, I wish to thank my wife, Ruth, whose emotional support and good humor have sustained me over many months. This book is dedicated affectionately to her.

Ronald Smelser
Salt Lake City, March 1988

Abbreviations

ADGB	Allgemeiner Deutscher Gewerkschaftsbund
AOG	Arbeitsordnungsgesetz, *or* Gesetz zur Ordnung der nationalen Arbeit
AWI	Arbeitswissenschaftliches Institut
BdA	Bank der deutschen Arbeit
DAF	Deutsche Arbeitsfront
Datsch	Deutscher Ausschuss für das Technische Schulwesen
Dinta	Deutsches Institut für Technische Arbeitsschulung
DVSTB	Deutschvölkischer Schutz-und Trutzbund
KdF	Kraft durch Freude
KPD	Kommunistische Partei Deutschlands
LBB	Leistungsertüchtigung, Berufserziehung und Betriebsführung
NSBO	Nationalsozialistische Betriebszellenorganisation
NSFP	Nationalsozialistische Freiheitspartei
NS-Hago	Nationalsozialistische Handels-und Gewerbeorganisation
OgW	Organisation der gewerblichen Wirtschaft
Promi	Reichspropagandaministerium
RAM	Reichsarbeitsministerium
RGI	Reichsgruppe Industrie
ROL	Reichsorganisationsleitung
RWM	Reichswirtschaftsministerium
SA	Sturmabteilung
SdA	Schönheit der Arbeit
SOPADE	Sozialdemokratische Partei Deutschlands
SPD	Sozialdemokratische Partei Deutschlands
SS	Schutzstaffel
Uschla	Untersuchungs- und Schlichtungsausschuss
VB	*Völkischer Beobachter*
WB	*Westdeutscher Beobachter*

Introduction

Although he was commonly regarded during the Third Reich as one of the top five Nazi leaders, a man of great power and a member of that select group who formed Hitler's immediate entourage, Robert Ley has yet to receive biographical treatment. The lives of the other chief Nazi leaders have been exhaustively examined (Himmler, Goebbels, Göring) and even second- and third-echelon figures have found their biographers (Streicher, Neurath). Ley, however, although he appears prominently in many general studies of Nazi Germany, has not been accorded the detailed investigation his notorious career deserves.

There are several possible reasons for this omission. For one thing, Ley's chief activity during the Third Reich was to run the German Labor Front, that mammoth bureaucracy which kept the workers under control through a combination of surveillance, discipline, and services. This organization itself has, curiously, received little attention, with a concomitant neglect of its leader. For another, there was little coherence to Ley's personal empire. He spread himself thinly across the power structure of the Third Reich with his fingers in numerous pies. Thus, the fragmented nature of Ley's own power position has likely discouraged scholars from putting the pieces of his career together. Thirdly, although Ley was a household word in Germany during Hitler's twelve years, he was little known abroad at the time. As one American observer noted, "It is extraordinary how powerful Dr Ley is in Germany and how little known he is outside the country." The Nuremberg war-crimes trials would have given Ley the international notoriety he deserved, for he was indicted as one of the major war criminals. His suicide, however, in October 1945, on the eve of the trials, consigned him and his career to relative oblivion.

Ley's role in the Third Reich was too important, however, to allow him to remain obscure. His career is a perfect example of the qualities which brought the Nazis such sustained success in agitating their way into power and which caused the regime then to be run so sloppily after the *Machtergreifung*. His multiple offices and his interminable battles with government ministries and other Nazi chieftains alike illustrate dramatically the bureaucratic nature of the Nazi regime. The limitations imposed by Hitler on Ley's role as Reichsorganisationsleiter of the party demonstrate clearly Hitler's policy of refusing to tolerate potential rivals at the organizational head of the NSDAP, even at the price of eternal confusion at the top levels of the party. Ley's position as the head of the Nazi Labor Front crystallizes the critical interpretive question with respect to the Third Reich: to what extent did the regime succeed in integrating the worker into society? And finally, the fact that the Nazi regime did provide many benefits for the German worker, many of them through organizations under Ley's control, demonstrates the aspirations which many Nazi idealists had (and Ley was arguably the chief idealist in the upper echelons of the party), aspirations which were in the end cruelly destroyed by the criminal nature of the regime. Robert Ley's career is, then, worth detailed examination.

After the war, a number of surviving Nazi leaders, many of whom had for years been among the bitterest opponents of Ley, sought to diminish his importance and portray him essentially as a harmless windbag and drunkard. Schwerin von Krosigk, for example, the former Minister of Finance, called Ley "the bullfrog of the party, who pumped himself up so much and let loose with such a voice, that one was to believe he was a great beast." Walther Darré, head of the Nazi Farmers' League, the Reichsnährstand, who for years had fought Ley's rural organizers, now reduced his former rival to a "laughable bugaboo." Albert Speer, whose job it had been to organize the Nazi economy for total war, called Ley a "vulgar drunkard," while Karl Wahl, former Gauleiter of Swabia, characterized Ley as an "eccentric idealist." Alfred Rosenberg, the Nazis' chief ideologist and least successful political infighter, pointed to Ley's "organizational gigantomania" as his greatest weakness. Otto Dietrich, former press spokesman for the regime, characterized Ley as a "geistloser Schwätzer" (mindless bullshitter).

But those who were observing him in his heyday took a somewhat different view. Stephen Roberts, an American journalist, quoted a German saying during the Third Reich which went: "When Ley comes, others make way." William Shirer, US correspondent in Berlin at the time, said that Ley was "a tough, hard-drinking, able administrator, fanatically loyal to his chief." This study will seek to demonstrate that Robert Ley, for all his failings, and they were numerous, nevertheless was an important, hitherto neglected force to be reckoned with during the Third Reich. More importantly, Ley was an important prototype of a certain Nazi — one whose fanaticism, idealism, and commitment to Hitler and the movement, made him an ideal "old fighter" but whose inadequacies in the management of power, whose inability to gauge means to ends, would cripple the effectiveness of the regime and eventually lead it to its destruction.

What was Robert Ley like as a man? He was rough and tough, uninhibited, given to emotional outbursts, venal and corrupt, and astonishingly lacking in good judgment. He was also a notorious womanizer who drank too much. At the same time, he was an intelligent man who had real organizational ability and a knack for choosing talented subordinates, at least in the upper echelons of his agencies, to run things for him during his frequent inspection tours across Germany. He was also exceedingly ambitious with a need to be "somebody." Above all, he was slavishly devoted to Adolf Hitler as a God-figure. Physically, he was of small stature (only 5 ft 4 in.), portly, with a florid complexion, which partly reflected his frequent state of high emotion, partly the quantities of alcohol he imbibed. But he stood out in a crowd, because he had a constant need to transfer his ideological fanaticism and emotional commitment into words.

Ley was, like his master, primarily an orator. His speeches were stuttering, stammering affairs, a rush of sentence fragments — but capable of stirring emotions and moving crowds. It was as a Nazi rabble-rouser that he had won his district in the Rhineland in the mid-1920s and it was as a constant speech-maker that he hoped to capture the allegiance of the workers for the new regime after 1933. A great many of those workers, especially older ones who had been schooled in the tradition of social democracy and the free-trade-union movement, found him too absurd to be taken seriously. But a lot of younger, politically indifferent or politically immature workers who had never been integrated into the socialist movement, were apparently impressed by the openness and bonhomie of the man who kept appearing in the factories and plants. Even the Social Democrats in exile reluctantly and with some puzzlement, concluded that: "Remarkably, in the circle of indifferent workers hope is being placed in Dr Ley, who, because of this or that word of encouragement, is provisionally being taken for a well-wisher who is being hindered by malevolent forces." (Sopade 1934: 429). Despite the frequent hyperbole in his public utterances ("The only person still leading a private life in Germany today is someone who sleeps") and the absurdity of many of his remarks uttered in the heat of political passion ("A scientist considers himself fortunate if he comes across one germ in the whole of his life, while a dustman uproots thousands of them with each sweep of his broom" — a remarkable quote for someone with a PhD in chemistry), Hitler nevertheless considered Ley "my greatest idealist" and entrusted him with a great deal of power. And Ley's lack of judgment and political astuteness aside, he did have as grandiose a vision of what the National Socialist regime should do for the German people as any Nazi leader.

"The brown collectivist," von Krosigk called him once, and the term was applicable. In his vision of a totalitarian welfare state with cradle-to-grave socialism for those who qualified as members of the *Volksgemeinschaft*, Ley seemed to be a combination of Nazi and Communist. His organizations would "take care of" (*betreuen*) the German people: would provide decent, healthy housing, adequate medical care, organized recreational activity, the consumer goods of industrial society as well as life insurance and old-age benefits. To this end he put his propensity for bureaucratic over-organization and gigantomania to work, collecting those empty titles which Hitler was more than ready to dispense to his faithful paladins, on the assumption that any man worth his salt would flesh out those titles with resolute action. Whether as leader of the German Labor Front, Commissar for Residential Building, head of the "Strength through Joy" (Kraft durch Freude) leisure-time organization, or eager collector of the working man's subscriptions to the new people's car, the Volkswagen, Ley seemed to stretch the concept of *Betreuung* to its maximum extent. Not content to speak only of the people's car, Ley also talked of other "people's" products such as the people's refrigerator (*Volkskühlschrank*).

In the end Ley found himself both beneficiary and loser in Hitler's political system, which combined overlapping jurisdictions, duplication of function, cut-throat competition, and a large measure of duplicity and intrigue in what amounted to a bureaucratic jungle. Ley did inherit, to be sure, the political organization of the party which Gregor Strasser had built into an effective political instrument prior to 1932; but it was an organization circumscribed in its powers and rivaled by the new office of Führer's Deputy (Stellvertreter des Führers), held by Rudolf Hess, and by the creation of a group of Reichsleiter at the top of the party, whose powers were equally shadowy. Ley did become head of the mammoth Labor Front, but he was never able to make it into the tool of social policy he wanted, and when during the war Hitler created the office of Plenipotentiary for the Mobilization of Labor, he gave that office to Gauleiter Sauckel and not to the eager Ley. Ley also became Reich Commissar for Social Residential Building but soon found his dreams for a bungalow for each German family thwarted by several government ministries and by the exigencies of war. By the same token, his assignment to create an insurance and retirement system for all Germans encountered the usual resistance of an entrenched bureaucracy.

On balance, he was, like several other top Nazis, a loser. His own emotional instability, lack of sound judgment, and inability to intrigue played an important role in his lack of success — as did the war, which undercut many of the social programs he espoused. Critical also was the rise of Martin Bormann, the sinister "Secretary," whose control of access to Hitler blocked the schemes of many a Nazi aspirant.

But in his very dreams, Ley did leave a legacy behind, as did, in a sense, the Nazi regime itself. The Weimar regime was light years away from being a welfare state. In its propaganda, the Nazi regime posed a vision of what government should do for the little people which, however unfulfilled at the time, took it a step beyond Weimar and built a bridge to the Federal Republic today. For stripped of the ludicrous qualifying criteria of the *Volksgemeinschaft* and the smothering terror apparatus of the totalitarian state, what the Nazi regime offered (or at least promised to offer) the German people formed much of the agenda of postwar planning. And Robert Ley's frustrated dreams were an important part of that agenda.

CHAPTER 1

The Making of a Nazi

East of Cologne and the Rhine, bordered by the rivers Ruhr and Sieg, lies the Bergisch Land. It is part of the German Central Uplands and takes its name from the counts of Berg, who for centuries resided in Burg on the Wupper. From 1824 to 1945 this area was part of the Prussian Rhine province. Topographically, Bergisch Land is a high plateau furrowed by valleys formed by the rush of many streams. Some of these valleys have historical significance. One is the Neanderthal, where the remains of one of man's early ancestors were discovered in the nineteenth century. Another is the Wupper, site of Barmen, home of Frederick Engels. Near the center of this Bergisch Land lies the Oberbergischer Kreis. It too would have some historical significance — of a tragic sort. For it was here on February 15, 1890 in the village of Niederbreidenbach that Robert Ley was born.[1]

For centuries the area has been a poor one. People farmed here, but the soil was poor and rocky and parsimonious in bestowing the fruits of nature. Farms remained, for the most part, quite small, "dwarf holdings" really and even early in this century out of a total of nearly 7,500 small holdings 7,200 were only between 0.5 and 20 hectares in size.

Because of the poor soil, already in the late middle ages, locals were availing themselves of the particular nature of the area to dig ore from the ground and process it into iron in smelters powered by the numerous streams. By the nineteenth century, paper and leather had joined iron as Oberbergisch industries. But even here, the area proved to be less than fortunate. The growth of the enormous German industrial plant in the Ruhr Valley to the northeast pro-

1. See Walter Marsden, *The Rhineland* (New York, Hastings House, 1973), pp. 64ff.

vided competition which the smaller, older industry of the upper highlands could not meet. At the point of Ley's birth, then, the local area was undergoing a painful transition, both in its industry and its agriculture.[2]

Given the general penury of the area, Robert Ley came into this world virtually privileged.[3] There was some considerable wealth on both sides of his family. His father, Friedrich Ley, inherited one of the better farms in the area from his father, Johannes Ley, who through hard work and rigid parsimony had become an affluent man. Friedrich, in turn, had married well. His wife, Emilie née Wald, inherited, along with her brother, a thriving lime quarry and kiln, which their father had had the foresight to build at precisely the time when a swiftly changing economy raised great demands for a product used both in construction and in artificial fertilizer. It was said that when Emilie and Friedrich married, her father was able to provide a dowry of 10,000 Taler in addition to the usual linen and household implements.

Life had much promise, then, for the young Robert, who was born the seventh of eleven children. Unfortunately, Ley's father was not able to hang on to the considerable fortune which he had inherited. Apparently, the very quality which had led to the amassing of the wealth in the first place — the grandfather's parsimony — now indirectly led to its dissipation. Friedrich Ley had been kept on a very tight financial leash by his father; even as a young husband and father, Friedrich had to content himself with the not munificent sum of 50 pfennigs spending money on Sundays. He was thus totally unprepared to handle money in large quantities. His inexperience led him to get into a number of business enterprises over his head, including horse trading. To cover his losses he took out mortgages

2. See NSDAP Kreisleitung, *Buch des oberbergischen Kreises* (Westdeustcher Beobachter, Oberberg Kreis, 1039), pp. 179–80; also Franz Petri and Georg Droege, *Handbuch der historischen Stätten Deutschlands*, vol. VIII, *Nordrhein-Westfalen*, p. 273 which describes Gummersbach, the nearest town and county seat.
3. Most of the following material on Ley's early life has been drawn from his own 74-page written autobiographical statement composed in his cell at Nuremberg just before his suicide on October 25, 1945. He entitled it "Bauernschicksal" (Peasant's Fate) and it will subsequently be cited as such. This document along with several others is located in the US National Archives, RG 238 Collection of World War Two Crimes, Justice Jackson file. Other biographical material on his youth can be found in his "Lebenslauf," Berlin Document Center, file Ley; and from Walter Kiehl, *Mann an der Fahne: Kameraden erzählen von Dr Ley* (Munich, Zentralverlag der NSDAP, 1938). As a model for combining psychology and politics I am grateful for the study by William Carr, *Hitler: A Study in Personality and Politics* (London, Edward Arnold, 1978).

— and then lost that money as well. As a last resort, Friedrich apparently torched his own farm in order to collect the insurance money. Discovered, he was arrested, tried and sentenced to a prison term of four years.

Young Robert was $6\frac{1}{2}$ years old at the time and the experience marked him for life. Suddenly the family was plunged into poverty. Its possessions and land were sold at auction for a fraction of their value. The older siblings scattered to find work while Robert and his youngest sister remained with their mother as she tried to eke out a living on a tiny, run-down farm in Mildsiefen which she purchased from a money-lender, who in turn, demanded the maid services of one of her daughters as the first mortgage installment.

Even at a distance of more than a half century, near the end of his life, Ley could still feel the pain and humiliation of having been "uprooted, impoverished and humiliated" at such a vulnerable age. "It was the first serious suffering that entered my young life. Home and father lost. Plunged into poverty and shame. . . . Fate had ordained that I should not become a farmer."[4] If there is anything more painful than being born into poverty, it is being plunged into it from a position of relative affluence. And for this to happen at such a young age must have scarred Ley; indeed, he would always be extremely sensitive about his social position and would develop a fierce desire to "be somebody", a desire which characterized a number of the top Nazi leaders. He would also try on several occasions to establish himself on an agricultural enterprise, in part to compensate for the father's failure, in part because Nazi ideology would honor those with roots in the soil.

With farm and money gone, young Ley had only one means of getting ahead — through education. And here his own fierce ambition was enhanced by the encouragement of his mother and several of his teachers, as well as by the increased opportunities of the late Wilheminian period. The fact that Ley was also very small in physical stature may also have prompted him to excel by way of compensation. Ley entered elementary school in March 1898 in the village of Grunewald. Here he remained for five years before transferring in 1903 to nearby Rupprechterroth so that he could study French in addition to the other subjects. For a time he was also enrolled in the Catholic *Rektoratschule* at Waldbröl, where he took Latin. In some subjects he was at the top of his class: history,

4. "Bauernschicksal," p. 20.

German, geography and the natural sciences. In modern languages, however, he did poorly. This variety of educational opportunities came as a result of the efforts of one of his teachers, Moritz Hardt, who encouraged him, arranged his transfer among the several schools, and convinced his somewhat reluctant parents (the father had meanwhile returned home when Robert was eleven) to allow Ley to continue his formal schooling beyond the point where a boy of his age and circumstances would normally have stopped. It was Hardt who arranged, finally, for Ley to attend *Realschule* and then *Oberrealeschule* in Elberfeld.[5] During these difficult years, Ley earned his way through a combination of tutoring, odd jobs, and doing book-keeping for his brothers, with whom he lived periodically. On February 7, 1910, he completed his *Abitur* — the key to admission to the university.

Apparently, Ley's family expected him to settle for the lower levels of the civil service, perhaps a modest position with the Post Office or Railroad. Thus they were surprised when he expressed the intention of going to the university. Nevertheless, with his mother's strong encouragement (if not his father's) he went off to the university almost immediately after completing his *Abitur* in 1910.

Following his academic strengths, Ley enrolled in the Natural Science Faculty, first at the University of Jena, where he spent five semesters, then at Bonn for two semesters, and finally at Münster, where he majored in chemistry. Although Ley must have been strapped for money, despite occasional help from his family (including siblings) and his own efforts on the side to support himself — which included tutoring and acting as a *Hauslehrer* (home tutor) in Bad Godesberg – Ley did not miss out on the more convivial side of traditional German student life and spent the first few semesters in the time-honored customs of drinking and frivolous behavior. At Jena he joined a fraternity (the Sängerschaft St Paulus, or Glee Club fraternity). In later life he would praise fraternity life, despite the fact that these traditional student associations were closed down by the Nazi regime for being "breeding nests of class arrogance". He felt that the discipline and stylized rituals of the frat house gave him a social polish entirely missing from his youth as well as "an education in good breeding, responsibility, sense of manhood and a

5. Hardt wrote in the school record under Ley's name in 1902: "Schulbesuch recht gut. Fortschritte sehr gut" (Good attendance. Very good progress). Quoted in Kiehl, *Mann an der Fahne*, p. 17.

full life in youthful, natural, genuine romanticism."[6]

By the time he got to Bonn and Münster, however, he had dedicated himself to serious studies. At Münster he found as his mentor Professor Bömer, with whom he studied chemistry with minor fields in physics and botany. It was at this point, in August 1914, as Ley was preparing for his state examination and already working on his dissertation research, that the First World War broke out.

Up to this point in his life, Ley had demonstrated considerable drive and ambition, fostered by help and encouragement in critical moments. It was an impressive performance but not strikingly unusual, for in late Wilhelminian Germany many a young man of modest means could and did move up the social scale. Students of lower-middle-class background already constituted nearly 50 percent of the German university population. Nor were fraternities as exclusive as they had once been; nearly 50 percent of male students were *Couleurtragende*, and while the Corps and *Burschenschaften* were still bastions of the upper classes, a singing fraternity would likely have demonstrated a predominance of lower-middle-class members.[7] Nor should we forget that, despite Ley's youthful poverty, his origins were those of a locally once-affluent family, with the expectations which would be raised by people (especially his mother) who had a taste of affluence and local respect. Yet, as with millions of others, the promising academic career of Robert Ley would now be interrupted by the cataclysm of total war, a war which would change the young man in fundamental ways and point him to a far different future than he surely envisioned for himself during that last, hauntingly beautiful prewar summer of 1914 (see Plate 1).

On August 6, 1914, following the lead of virtually an entire generation, Robert Ley enthusiastically volunteered for the colors.[8]

6. "Bauernschicksal", p. 30. For his later admission of having been a fraternity student and a careful defense of them, see his speech on the occasion of a DAF special course in July 1935 in US National Archives, Microcopy T-81, Roll 75, Frames 86582–87.
7. See Konrad Jarausch, "German Students in the First World War," *Central European History*, vol. XVII, no. 4 (Dec. 1984), pp. 312–13; see also John E. Craig, "Higher Education and Social Mobility in Germany," in Konrad Jarausch, *The Transformation of Higher Learning 1860–1930* (Chicago, University of Chicago Press, 1983), pp. 219–44. Craig argues that those who suffered real or imagined deprivation in the wake of societal transformation at the time — especially artisans, shopkeepers and peasants — sought university admission at a rate $2\frac{1}{2}$ times higher than other groups in the population.
8. Ley relates his war experiences in "Bauernschicksal," pp. 32–67; also in a long

He hiked to Strassburg in Lorraine, where he joined up with the Foot Artillery Regiment No. 10. His unit underwent six weeks of basic training at Wolfsheim then joined the 7th Battery of the regiment under the command of Captain von Perbandt. Almost immediately Ley's unit was engaged in battle, first north of the Peronne in front of St Albert, and then by Furcourt and Mannetz where the battle for Hill 110 was in full swing. It was Ley's baptism of fire, as he manned with his comrades a 15-cm howitzer.

Early in 1915, while fierce fighting continued between the French, who had once again gone over to the attack, and the Germans, whose lines were temporarily stretched thin by action in the East, Ley joined the 2nd Battery of the newly formed Reserve Foot Artillery Regiment No. 10. He saw considerable action, first in the Vosges Mountains, then at Ripont and Ripontmühle in the Champagne. For the first time he was exposed to the awesome destructiveness of the engines of twentieth-century war; saw the enormous casualties which machine-gun fire and concentrated artillery could produce; suffered the debilitating psychological wounds of those who live for months on end with violent death. Looking back on the first encounters with the enemy in the Champagne, Ley remembered: "at one stroke we lost the whole battery, only the battery officer, the medic and I remained. There must scarcely be a patch of earth that has drunk so much human blood as the lonesome, depopulated Champagne."[9] These early battles represented an attempt by the French commander, General Joffre, to exploit a temporary German weakness by attacking in the Artois, the Champagne, and the Vosges. Casualties were heavy on both sides, but the French suffered the greater number and a clear loss of morale. The fighting was especially difficult in the Champagne, where the chalky soil and undulating terrain covered with scant pine growth soon turned into a sea of mud under heavy rains. In the Vosges, the French threw in their best men, including the experienced mountain troops, the

---

article in WB, no. 96, April 25, 1931, p. 1, in which he defends his record against claims by his political enemies. See also Ludwig C.M. Koch, *Geschichte des Fußartillerie-Bataillons Nr. 56 im Weltkriege* (Berlin, Oldenbourg, 1926). I am grateful to Dr. Jürgen Förster of the Militärgeschichtliches Forschungsamt, Freiburg for aiding me in confirming the factual validity of some of Ley's description of his experience. Letter to the author of March 1, 1985.

9. "Bauernschicksal," p. 38. For a brief but clear background on the fighting in the Champagne and Vosges, see Christian de St Julien, "The Vosges Offensive," in Brig. Peter Young (ed.), *The Marshall Cavendish Illustrated History of World War One* (New York, London, Toronto, Marshall Cavendish, 1984), vol. III, pp. 661–9 (hereafter *World War One*).

Chasseurs Alpines, nicknamed the "Blue Devils" but only succeeded in demonstrating that frontal attack, even where carried out with great élan, would have little effect in what was rapidly becoming a new form of warfare dominated by trenches, machine-guns, and barbed wire. In the meantime, Ley was learning, along with the German high command, the value of fixed fortified defensive positions and modern heavy artillery.

In early May the French attacked once again, in part to relieve the pressure on their hard-pressed Russian allies, but Ley missed this offensive. His unit, now part of the 10th Corps of the 11th Army had been sent to the East to take part in a major German and Austrian offensive in Galicia.[10] Already in mid-April 1915 the Germans were preparing for a decisive action in the East; hundreds of trains brought division after division to the Carpathian front. Focal point of the offensive was the plain around the city of Gorlice on the Russian southwestern flank. The main thrust was to be undertaken by the German 11th Army under August von Mackensen. The attack was to commence on the first of May, but was delayed by one day until the German 10th Corps, to which Ley's unit was attached, was in place. The German and Austrian formations enjoyed a decided superiority in men and equipment and within a week the Russians were in retreat over a 300-km-long front. The Germans, confident that Russian offensive power could be broken permanently, pushed on to the San and Dniester rivers. Now, Ley's outfit joined a number of units regrouped under the rubric Army Group Mackensen. On the morning of June 13, 1915, the German 11th Army, supported by the Austrian 4th Army on their left, opened up a renewed offensive preceded by heavy salvos from over 300 guns. One of them was Ley's. This successful offensive, which witnessed Ley fighting on the Lubaszovka, a tributary of the San, soon had the Russians in full retreat once again and led to the fall of the important city of Lemberg on June 22. This put the German and Russian lines back where they had been at the outbreak of the war and nullified all the Russian gains of the prior ten months. The Germans were flush with victory. Their only complaint was about their Austrian allies, who, demoralized and lethargic, often had to be prodded to act. Ley himself complained that the German left flank, where he was fighting, had been endangered when the Austrians failed to ad-

10. For background see Kurt Peball, "Gorlice: Turning Point on the Eastern Front," in Young, *World War One*, vol. III, pp. 929–35.

vance in tandem with the Germans.

By fall 1915, as the eastern front stabilized in the wake of German victories, Ley was once again, after a brief respite, transferred to France, once again fighting in the Champagne. But two (much greater) actions were about to unfold, battles which became watchwords for the senseless slaughter of the First World War and in both of which Ley would participate: Verdun and the Somme.

In Verdun the German War Minister von Falkenhayn had picked an old fortress city which the French, for reasons of prestige, could not abandon, even though it was located in a salient which tactical wisdom would have dictated reducing. The German goal was to "bleed the French to death" by forcing them to fight to the end for the fortress salient. In April and May 1916 Ley's battery was present at two crucial engagements in the struggle to reduce the salient: the German attack on the dominant heights of the west bank of the River Meuse, the "Mort Homme" (Dead Man's Ridge) and Hill 304. Ley was part of the murderous artillery barrage which both sides inflicted on one another in this engagement. At one point there were nearly 4,000 guns in the salient and they took as their toll hundreds of thousands of casualties. The Germans concentrated the fire of over 500 guns on Hill 304 alone along a front less than a mile wide. The result was 10,000 French dead. The German crown prince, watching the assault on Dead Man's Ridge noted, "Mort Homme flamed like a volcano, and the air and the earth alike trembled at the shock of thousands of thousands of bursting shells". Indeed, the artillery was master of the battlefield and as troops approached the scene of action, they heard sounds "like a gigantic forge that never stopped, day or night."[11]

With this scene of carnage before him, and about to witness more at the Somme, it cannot have escaped Ley's attention at this point that a much more salubrious and quiet vista of the battle could be had far above the trenches. Indeed, under their inspired ace, Oswald Boelcke, the Germans had just acquired control of the air above Verdun. The ever-ambitous Ley began considering transfer to the air corps.

But before he did so, he was to take part in one more major engagement: the defense against the combined British–French offensive on the Somme. Once again artillery was trump — or

11. Quoted in Alistair Horne, "Verdun: Nivelle Takes Over," in Young, *World War One*, vol. V, pp. 1358–9; for a more exhaustive account of the battle, Horne's *The Price of Glory: Verdun 1916* (New York, Penguin, 1962) is excellent.

seemed to be initially. In the week prior to the attack the British and French amassed over 1,300 heavy guns and fired nearly 2 million shells at the German lines. But despite this horrendous bombardment, the Germans, who were extremely well dug in, managed on the first day of the offensive to impose the worst one-day casualty rate ever suffered by the British Army: 57,000 British officers and men fell on July 1, 1916 at the Somme, inaugurating what for them was to become 'the' battle of the war (as Verdun would be for the French). Just three days later, Ley, who was still in the Verdun sector, was promoted from Vizefeldwebel der Reserve to lieutenant. At the end of July, in part as a response to the British offensive, Ley's unit was transferred to the Somme and saw action at Peronne and St Christ, not far from where Ley had first had his baptism of fire at the beginning of the war. The Germans were now counter-attacking in order to reverse the modest British gains. It was, as one official history put it: "A period of fighting when hardly any ground was gained and the struggle became more than ever a grim test of endurance".[12] It was a particularly trying hour for Ley, since the British had a temporary superiority in artillery and their counter-battery fire could be lethal. The overall battle dragged on into September, when it petered out, both sides exhausted.

It was after weeks and months of this sort of action that Ley finally applied for transfer to the flying corps. He subsequently explained his move by suggesting that it represented an opportunity "first, to get to know this weapon and second, to bring a change to my monotonous skills of war".[13] He might well have added that, after months of inconclusive slaughter, the prospect of observing the trenches from the air must have appeared very appealing.

Ley's timing, at any rate, was good. The spring of 1916 had witnessed the high point of what had been heralded by the press of both sides, warningly by the Allies, triumphantly by the Germans, as the "Fokker scourge." Thanks to an invention by the Dutch aircraft pioneer Anthony Fokker, a gear synchronizing device which

12. See Ward Rutherford, "The Somme: Bloody and Futile", in Young, *World War One*, vol. V, p. 1608; also useful in the same volume are Brig. Anthony Farrar-Hockley, "The Somme Barrage," pp. 1493–501 and Leo Kahn, "July 1, 1916—a Generation Sacrificed," pp. 1502–10; the best account of the Somme is Lyn Macdonald, *Somme* (London, Michael Joseph, 1983).
13. "Bauernschicksal," p.47. For background on this aspect of the war, see D.B. Tubbs, "The Air War: Tactics and Technology" and "Aircraft: Higher, Faster, Lighter," in Young, *World War One*, vol. V, pp. 1440–51 and vol. VI, pp. 1860–70, respectively.

enabled them to fire through their propellers, the Germans had been able to dominate the air. As a result, a new kind of hero emerged in the otherwise mass, industrial war, a throwback to a more chivalrous era: the "ace". In Germany Boelcke and his pupil, Max Immelmann, both recipients of the "Pour le Mérite," Germany's highest decoration, had become national heroes, fêted by the press. Less well known and dramatic in their exploits than the aces, but no less important, were the flyers who functioned as artillery spotters and observers. It was to this group that Ley would be assigned.

After being sent for a six-week training period at Stolp in Pomerania, where he learned Morse code, Ley transferred to Warsaw for observer training. (Years later he could not refrain from mentioning that the training school had been in Lubinski Park at the former palace of August the Strong).

His training completed, Ley was assigned to Fliegerabteilung 202 and sent to a position in Marle south of Cambrai as artillery observer. His commander was Captain Wentscher. It was here, while flying experimentally in a new 220 h.p. Albatross CV, that Ley crashed for the first time. The pilot was killed, and Ley lay unconscious for several hours. He was not seriously injured, although the psychological impact must have been great.[14] His luck, however, was not to last long.

On July 29, 1917, Ley took off with his new pilot, an inexperienced 20 year old named Emil Mäulen, on what was destined to be his last mission.[15] The mission — to fly behind the lines spotting artillery — was dangerous under any circumstances (Ley called it "suicidal"). Poor light forced the pilot to maintain a low altitude of only 1,100 ft, which compounded the danger. Moreover, the two other planes which were to fly protective cover fell behind, exposing Ley's plane to the full fury of enemy fighters. Finally, the Germans were greatly outnumbered in planes in this sector, as the Allies were covering preparations for the battle of Passchendaele, which was to begin in four days. When the inevitable dogfight began, Ley's machine-gun jammed. Within moments he was wounded — shot

14. Although his next crash would cause far greater physical damage, one should not underestimate the psychological damage of this first one. The plane plunged over 8,000 feet before levelling off, a time when Ley could do nothing but await his death. On the impact of this kind of experience, see Alan Clark, *Aces High: The War in the Air over the Western Front 1914–1918* (New York, Putnam's Sons, 1973), esp. Ch. 4, entitled "Death."

15. He describes this mission and its aftermath in detail in "Bauernschicksal," pp. 53ff.

through the thigh. Only the quick action of Mäulen, who went into a diving spiral, recovering just yards above the ground, saved their lives. The plane crash landed — but behind French lines. Shot down by a British pilot, Ley now fell into French captivity. He was seriously injured. The thigh wound almost cost him his leg — to keep it he had to endure six operations while in captivity. In the course of one of them he had a cardiac arrest and came close enough to death to have had an out-of-body experience.[16] Moreover, upon impact Ley suffered frontal lobe damage which would become chronically worse over the years, leaving him with a stammer and an alcohol problem. The severe trauma of these experiences — being wounded and crashing, undergoing multiple operations under the primitive conditions of the time, plus brain damage which would represent a chronic problem — would be a lasting legacy for Ley and would in many ways have a strong conditioning influence on his future career in politics. In another sense, as well, being wounded and falling into captivity foreshadowed his later career. By his own admission, it was during the several years in French prison camps that he first became aware of, and exercised, his organizational and speaking skills. It was not at all uncommon during the First World War, both behind the lines and in officer POW camps, to organize *Etappenhochschulen*, a kind of continuing education for student-soldiers.[17] The purpose was to combat boredom and to enable a generation of students who had volunteered en masse for service to make up some of the lost time. It was Ley's claim to have organized one of these at the officer's camp at Chateauroux, where a number of subjects, including mathematics, philosophy, languages, and history were offered. In addition, Ley claimed to have made his first speech in connection with a boycott of the camp's overpriced canteen.

At the end of January 1920, after two and a half years in captivity, Ley returned home to a Germany dissolving into political and social chaos with little more than physical and emotional scars and an Iron Cross, Second Class, to show for his nearly six-year absence.

After his return from the war, Ley was able, in contrast to so many of his generation, to reintegrate into society apparently with astonishing ease. Returning to Münster and his old mentor, Professor Bömer, he picked up his studies where he had left off and quickly finished the doctorate. Already on June 5, 1920, he completed his defense of the dissertation — which had been two-thirds completed

16. See ibid., p. 61, for a description of this experience.
17. See Jarausch, "German Students," p. 319.

before the war broke out — on the theme of mixed glycerides in butter fat, which qualified him as an expert in the field of food chemistry. Through the influence of Bömer, part of Ley's dissertation appeared in the *Zeitschrift für Nahrungsmittel-Untersuchung.*[18]

His education complete, Ley now embarked on what for all intents and purposes was a secure, upper-middle-class existence. He obtained a well-paid position with a branch of the giant chemical trust, IG Farben at Leverkusen; bought a substantial home in nearby Wiesdorf, got engaged, married, and soon became a father. As he himself later put it, "So I had now finally after a restless life of thirty years found a secure harbor, and it seemed as if my life would now proceed as a veritable model of all secure, bourgeois existences."[19]

And yet within three years Ley would find himself in a very different role — as a fanatic, politicized National Socialist, an emotional rabble-rouser, a tireless servant of Adolf Hitler, whose life-style would part company dramatically from any sort of "bourgeois model." Eventually, he would cut virtually all ties with his "respectable" past, including giving up — when confronted with a choice — his secure, well-paying position in industry.

All of this raises the question of how such a man, one who had already established prewar roots, who had on the surface, at least, accomplished the task of returning to normal life, could now deviate so dramatically from the course which he had set out for himself in life. His social origins, youthful experiences and personality make-up all suggest clues to what might have predisposed him to such a dramatic change and, in fact, did trigger such a change in a man in his early thirties: clues to the making of a Nazi.

To have been born in a relatively secure, affluent environment, then suddenly to be plunged at a quite impressionable age into a situation of great material, emotional, and social insecurity must have been a quite traumatic experience. A sufficient trauma both to spur the boy and young man on to upward mobility — after all, the motivation and the mother's expectations were clearly present — but also to create in him a terrible fear of experiencing the fall once again. Indeed, there is clear evidence throughout Ley's life of a

18. Material from Universitäts-Archiv Münster, Philosophische Fakultät Prom.: 2231, including cover page and abstract of the dissertation; note from Prof. Bömer on Ley's progress; Ley's request to be admitted to the oral part of the examination and a brief personal history.
19. "Bauernschicksal," p. 67.

terrible social insecurity, a fear of falling back into a social abyss. It is evidenced in part in his frequent remarks about social worthlessness. "There is nothing more degrading and humiliating for someone", he once said in a speech, "than when he recognizes that he is without value in human society." It is also shown by Ley's often barely suppressed loathing for the real "upper classes" in Germany. In the wake of the July 20, 1944, officers' plot against the life of Hitler, Ley published a vicious diatribe against the nobility in Germany, one so vitriolic that it had to be suppressed by a regime which itself had no love for the Junker class.[20] By the same token, Ley, in his early years in politics, liked to distance himself from his university-trained colleagues and, not unlike Hitler, surround himself with cronies of lower-class or classless social standing: chauffeurs, roughnecks, artisans, and so on. Men who, in a kind of wonderment at having a PhD in their ranks, referred to Ley in comradely affection as "our doctor." Men, also, who represented no social threat to Ley, unlike his IG Farben colleagues who, he felt, laughed at him.[21]

This extreme social insecurity comes out most clearly in a short episode which he described in his last writings in his cell, an episode which happened to him just after he had established that postwar "bourgeois existence." He was strolling around the streets of Wiesdorf, to which he had just moved and was suddenly confronted with a mob of strikers and political demonstrators:

> This parade was led by a wildly gesticulating woman with black disheveled hair. Otherwise the street was empty of people; only I, naïve fool, stared at this hateful picture as if frozen in place. Then the woman caught a glimpse of me and cried out in inarticulate sounds: a bourgeois, a bourgeois. . . .
>
> Whereupon the head of the column plunged up to me with the intent of striking me down. I took to my heels, which was the only thing I could do under the circumstances.[22]

20. Ley wrote in his paper *Angriff* the following words: "Degenerate to their very bones, blue-blooded to the point of idiocy, nauseatingly corrupt, and cowardly like all nasty creatures — such is the aristocratic clique which the Jew has sicked onto National Socialism. . . . We must exterminate this filth, extirpate it root and branch." Quoted in Albert Speer, *Inside the Third Reich* (New York, Macmillan, 1970), p. 390n.; his remarks on worthlessness were made at the 1934 *Reichsparteitag* in Nuremburg.
21. See Kiehl, *Mann an der Fahne*, p. 83.
22. "Bauernschicksal," pp. 68–9.

In light of the fact that Ley's final scribblings are a revelation of the major traumas of his life, this brief anecdote — whether actually literally true or allegorical — takes on some importance in its demonstration of Ley's social angst.

For Ley, then, consumed by ambition and stricken by fear of social decline, the Nazi movement, as a spiritual home, as an organization in which one could lose oneself in the pursuit of a higher purpose, seemed to offer the paradoxical promise of achievement and security. One could hope for success, not as an isolated atom in a highly individualistic society, where failure or bad luck could bring precipitate social destruction, but rather as an integral part of a dynamic organization reaching out in an almost chiliastic fashion for total transformation of the world. For Ley, then, the movement, the party, became a sort of psychological "safe harbor," where all the rules and sanctions and risks of liberal society were suspended and where one was insulated by the brown shirt from the social decline which even a secure bourgeois existence could not prevent in a chaotic, disrupted society. Ley, whose speeches often revealed stunning personal revelations amongst the ideological nonsense, allowed as much in remarks made years later at an Arbeitsfront meeting when he said:

> The party is our religious order, our home. Without it we cannot live, my friend! Consider, if someone were to take off your brown shirt! It is so wonderful to be in this party. And so wonderful to be able to go around in the brown shirt. But it would be difficult to the same degree and perhaps much more frightful, if someone would take that brown shirt away. For then you will be destroyed, at least you who has been an honest Nazi.[23]

But it was far more than social anxiety which drove Ley to join the Nazi movement. Combined in his mind with angst was a strong streak of romantic idealism; indeed, Hitler would later call him "my greatest idealist."[24] Throughout Ley's career a pronounced rage born of social fear and resentment (and perhaps exacerbated by the unresolved relationship with his father) coexisted with a naïvely utopian romantic idealism. Ley could, at the same time, inveigh in the most vulgar, brutal street language against Jews and Commu-

23. His remarks were made at an *Arbeits- und Schulungstagung* of the DAF in December 1935 quoted in Robert Ley, *Deutschland ist schöner geworden* (Berlin, Mehden-Verlag, 1936), p. 255.
24. See Otto Dietrich, *Zwölf Jahre mit Hitler* (Munich, 1955), p. 259.

nists, while waxing eloquent about a myriad of social schemes — insurance and retirement plans, suburban resettlement and housing plans, leisure-time opportunities, and so on — which were supposed to make life infinitely better for the German people. Indeed, from this perspective, he was the perfect representative for a regime which would confront the German people with an iron fist in a velvet glove: surveillance and social control backed by terror mixed with solicitous attention (*Betreuung*).

The utopian strain in his make-up was central to Ley himself. Near the end of his life, while trying to explain why ultimately he had joined Hitler, he resorted to quoting from his favorite author, Willi Vesper. Vesper, who came from the same region as Ley, was a rather popular writer of short stories, poems, and dramas aimed particularly at youth. He represented the *völkisch* point of view but refracted through romantic, medieval settings and imagery. It was his book *Parzifal* which Ley cited as providing the clue to his motivation. *Parzifal* deals with the pursuit of the Holy Grail. For Ley, pursuit of a racial populist utopia became his Holy Grail.[25]

This romantic idealism of Ley's was enormously intensified by the fact that the Nazi movement was far more than just a radical political phenomenon on the right; it was at its core even more a secular, surrogate religion, a twentieth-century millenarian movement charged with messianic zeal and in pursuit of apocalyptic goals.[26] Like medieval Christian millenarian movements, National Socialism appeared during a time of economic and social upheaval; it produced a charismatic leader who claimed to have a "special knowledge" of the world and who posited for himself and his followers the task of literally setting up the "kingdom," that is the racial community (*Volksgemeinschaft*), here on earth. Like its medi-

25. Ley was reading this book in his cell at the end and quotes from p. 56 of it: "But the voice of his blood drove him with its dark power as it always does those of nobility. All those who are called by fate, know this voice, which frightens them out of their reverie and effortlessly invades their lives in order that they suffer, struggle and grow to the charge which they have to fulfill." "Bauernschicksal," p. 69.
26. This critical aspect of National Socialism was recognized by Norman Cohn, *The Pursuit of the Millenium: Revolutionary Messianism in Medieval and Reformation Europe and Its Bearing on Modern Totalitarian Movements*, 2nd edn (New York, Harper Torchbooks, 1961); as well as by Eric Voegelin in *The New Science of Politics* (Chicago, University of Chicago Press, 1952) and *Science, Politics and Gnosticism: Two Essays* (Chicago, Regnary Gateway, 1968). Most recently the theme has been developed at length by James M. Rhodes, *The Hitler Movement: A Modern Millenarian Revolution* (Stanford, Hoover Institution, 1980). See especially Chapter 2 where Rhodes lays out a set of symptoms characteristic of millennial consciousness to which Ley's own consciousness corresponds very closely.

eval counterparts, Nazism also had its devil figure — in fact the same one — the Jew. Like the Christian followers of leaders like Joachim of Fiore or Thomas Müntzer, the followers of Hitler viewed themselves as special initiates, men who had been victims of great disasters but who had been blessed with the revelation of who the enemy was and how he could be combated in order to achieve the millenium. The political scientist Michael Barkun has developed a definition of millenarian movements which virtually describes the essence of National Socialism, or at least the Nazism which Robert Ley found so attractive. They are:

> social movements which expect immediate, collective total, this-worldly salvation. They anticipate the complete destruction of the existing social, political and economic order, which is to be superseded by a new and perfect society. They frequently couple this anticipation with an active desire to speed the inevitable result, often through violent, revolutionary means. The old must be totally destroyed before a new and perfect society can be established in its place. This type of utopianism implies the potential for violent confrontation, with room for neither bargaining nor compromising.

Barkun's model also fits the behavior and attitudes of individual Nazis like Ley, who joined the movement as a panacea. It encompasses

> intense emotional expression; aims so sweepingly comprehensive that outsiders regard them as impossible to attain; claims to esoteric knowledge and some measure of control of basic social and historical processes; dependence upon charismatic leadership; blanket condemnation of the existing social and political order, coupled with a total renunciation of its claims to legitimacy; association with periods of disaster, change and social upheaval; breach of accepted norms, laws and taboos, high risk-taking; and withdrawal from conventional social, political, religious and economic relationships.[27]

As we later observe Ley's behavior as Nazi orator, organizer, and brawler in the Rhineland, we will see all of these factors coming into play.

This millenarian aspect of National Socialism must have been immensely attractive to Robert Ley, and many times over the length of his political career he revealed his quasi-religious motives for joining the movement.

27. *Disaster and the Millenium* (New Haven, Yale University Press, 1974), pp. 18–19.

> As I went off to war, I was a godless man. . . . As the war ended. . . . I came home a godless man. I was still more hopeless. . . . Today I believe in a God in heaven, over me and in me, who leads and steers me, who has me in his protection every day and hour and minute. This knowledge of a God, this faith in a God I did not receive through the church, but alone through Adolf Hitler. . . . On this earth I believe only in Adolf Hitler. I believe that there is a Lord God who loves us and who blesses Adolf Hitler's work with success.[28]

For Ley the Nazi movement provided meaning, purpose, and context for his life. This point he was aware of and gave expression to many times. None more revealingly than in a 1935 speech:

> Then we recognize our holy mission. Then I know that I am not in this world just to live a petty life of 50, 60, 70 or 80 years; then I know that this small life is only a drop, a tiny little drop in the gigantic sea of the history of German blood. Then I know that my life has worth and that I am no longer wandering around the world useless and worthless, but rather that my work and my spirit, my insight and my reason are important in order that the history of Germany not be broken off.[29]

And there is little doubt that, for Ley, Hitler was the German messiah who would build the German utopia. Hitler's impact on Ley personally was not dissimilar to that on many other Nazi leaders. As one of Ley's old comrades reported: "As he [Ley] stood before the Führer for the first time, he said to me literally: 'I cannot speak about it.'" A contemporary Nazi account of Ley's career noted: "His home village could not make a pastor out of him. Now his faith in Hitler has made of him a preacher."[30] Indeed, Ley's speeches were often more like emotional sermons than anything else. Contrasts between two contending worlds saturate his public speeches, one good and one evil. Sometimes it is the contrast between the world of power and that of reason which he draws; sometimes between one which is a vale of tears and one which is life affirming; occasionally a liberal or Marxist world versus a National Socialist one; often — indeed most frequently in his speeches — a world of chaos stands opposite one of order, an image which once

28. Quoted from Robert Ley, *Soldaten der Arbeit* (Munich, Zentralverlag der NSDAP, 1938), p. 112.
29. From a speech in Leipzig in December 1935 at a DAF meeting in Robert Ley, *Deutschland ist schöner geworden*, p. 197.
30. Both quotes are from Kiehl, *Mann an der Fahne*, the first from Karl Maletz, p. 77; the other, p. 16.

again reflects Ley's basic fears and aspirations.[31] Nor did Ley hesitate, like Goebbels in Berlin, to create martyrs for the movement. If Goebbels created the myth of Horst Wessel on a national scale, then Ley's equivalent in the Rheinland was Wilhelm Wilhelmi, shot during a riot in Rastätten in 1927.[32]

Closely related to Ley's being drawn to National Socialism was his attraction to Hitler as an authority figure, ultimately a messiah figure to replace the missing and discredited father. Again and again in his autobiographical statement, Ley betrays, often unconsciously, just how much he loved and valued his mother — and how little, despite some perfunctory compliments, his father really meant to him.

As he speaks of his early youth and of the incident which altered his life dramatically at the age of 6, although he admits that he really was never completely certain about his father's guilt in insurance fraud, it is clear from his description that he implicitly believes so. He writes about money going to his father's head and how a sizable sum "melted like butter in the sun." It is also clear that the father became, through his crime and punishment, the agent of the beloved mother's shame and pain. "She often had to go to court and endure humiliation," Ley wrote, " Then she would cry bitterly and we children would console her."[33] He clearly developed a tremendous admiration for the mother's strength and ability to cope, and when the father finally did come home when Ley was 11, his reappearance was duly noted but scarcely heralded. "We children had hardly missed him," Ley wrote later, "Mother never spoke of him . . . So the return of the father was like an everyday event."[34] Similarly, when Ley recollected the various stages of his education, when the decision had to be made whether to continue or not, it was always the mother who was supportive and the father who scoffed. As Ley was contemplating transferring to the *Realschule*, the father "mumbled something in his beard about 'megalomania,'" while the mother "beamed."[35] Sometime later, when Ley announced that he

31. This black–white contrast appears in most Ley speeches. Samples include: *Deutschland ist schöner geworden*, pp. 12–13, 19–21, 168, 189–90; also *Soldaten der Arbeit*, pp. 37–8, 94–5; as well as *Wir alle helfen dem Führer* (Berlin, 1937), p. 12; also in Kiehl, *Mann an der Fahne*, p. 139. The first three volumes appear under Ley's name.
32. See below, Chapter 2, p. 48.
33. "Bauernschicksal," p. 19 and p. 22 respectively. For a discussion of the medical aspects of Ley's case, see p. 309.
34. Ibid., pp. 22–3.
35. Ibid., p. 24.

wanted to study at the university, "my mother looked up and asked anxiously how long it would last and how much it would cost, whereby she gave to understand, that she liked the idea. By contrast, my father growled: 'Yeah, if it was up to you' — turning to the mother — 'he'd become a government minister.' 'Yes, he should,' replied the mother." Looking back, Ley took a perverse pride in having confounded his father, by pointing out that he had become a government minister after all.[36] A surviving snapshot from the First World War shows a young Ley in uniform on home leave — standing beside his mother. The father is nowhere in sight.[37] And, more symbolically, Ley draws in a number of speeches the parallel between the Weimar Republic and an unkind father who encourages discord among his own children. Speaking in Leipzig in 1935, Ley said, "The Weimar system appeared to me like a father who locks his little boys in a room and stirs them up against one another and says: 'Beat each other up as much as you want. That's the ideal'".[38]

It also emerges from Ley's autobiographical statement, although he never says so in as many words, that a number of men played the role of surrogate father to him, a role which the real father could not play. The awe with which Ley refers to several of his teachers — one is reminded of a young athlete today looking up to a coach — suggests such a relationship.[39] So does his description of Major Scholz, one of his officers in the war, whom Ley remembers with something bordering on hero worship, despite Scholz having temporarily unjustly demoted Ley on one occasion. "I belonged to his staff and he liked to see me suffer — I don't know why. Once I was suddenly and arbitrarily degraded, then two weeks later, as he saw his mistake, restored in rank . . . But that in no way lessened the regard which I had for this blameless officer."[40]

The rejection of the father and the heroization of other authority

36. Ibid., p. 26–7.
37. The picture is in Kiehl, *Mann an der Fahne*. Apparently, Ley also tended to view other women in his life, even his very much younger second wife as mother replacements. In an imagined conversation with Inge, his second wife, in his cell at Nuremberg, Ley said: "I see you standing before me in your beauty. You laugh kindly and knowingly like the experienced mother to her child. Despite your youth you always called me little Bobby (Bobjie). You know how comforting that always was to me." See "Zwiegespräch," in US National Archives, RG 238 Collection of World War Two Crimes, Justice Jackson File.
38. Quoted in Ley, *Deutschland ist schöner geworden*, p. 118.
39. "Bauernschicksal," pp. 23–6; he refered to these rural teachers as "real heroes" (p. 23).
40. Ibid., p. 43.

figures which emerges in Ley's remembrances suggests strongly a longstanding serious void — arising perhaps from a lack of personal autonomy and ego strength — which ultimately Adolf Hitler would fill for the remainder of Ley's life (as Hitler would do for a number of other top Nazis like Himmler, Goebbels, and Göring, who, although terribly ambitious, also betrayed a similar lack of personal sovereignty). Ley's last written words, in fact, betray both his sense of apocalypse and of Hitler as his father-messiah, whose death took all the meaning from his life:

> I am deeply convinced that in this, the greatest of revolutions, of which an American said, that it would not end until the year 2500, in this struggle for the recognition of races and their survival in the eternal quest for the true nature of humanity and thereby the establishment of a just socialism, *the nordic man* — whether German, English or American — will remain the victor. Germany pays for its glory with the most terrible suffering, Adolf Hitler pays with death and we his disciples will follow him. The fate of everything great.[41]

To recognize, however, a number of factors in Ley's life — including the ambition to "be somebody," fear of social decline, romantic idealism, and lack of personal autonomy — which *predisposed* him to become a Nazi, still does not explain what actually *triggered* his disengagement from private existence and his re-engagement into a quasi-religious political movement at the age of 33. What, indeed, would cause a man, who had had the intelligence to complete the highest degree in a difficult natural science, to give himself to an irrational political movement in whose service he was capable of uttering the following social comparison: "A roadsweeper sweeps a thousand microbes into the gutter with one brush stroke; a

41. Ibid., pp. 73–4. Ley's father complex and his relationship to strong personalities may help to explain what one early observer termed a "subaltern nature". Kurt Ludecke recalled a reception early on at the Propaganda Ministry: "After the speeches, Dr. Ley and I strolled out to help ourselves to drinks. Göring, as we passed him, beckoned to Ley as one would signal a waiter. And Ley, subaltern that he was, trotted meekly over and listened as though Göring were the Almighty himself," in *I Knew Hitler* (London, Jarrolds, 1938), p. 393.

scientist preens himself on describing a single microbe in the whole of his lifetime."[42] For this we must turn to some of the insights which psychologists and psychiatrists have developed to explain the reciprocal relationship between trauma and stress, both individual and societal, and the emergence of millenarian movements.

Certainly, childhood trauma is one factor that needs to be taken into account. The dramatic events which struck Ley at the age of 6, depriving him of a secure emotional as well as material environment, surely created the insecurities which made Hitler and National Socialism so attractive later. But one cannot stop at that. Childhood experiences did not lead in a direct line to political activism. As Fred Weinstein has pointed out, "We cannot infer the ability to engage in socially useful activity in the Nazi era nor the willingness to participate in the Nazi movement, much less the willingness to participate in the Holocaust, from systematic child-rearing experiences in a particular familial context."[43]

What is important and more direct, though, is the propensity of later tragedy, or series of traumatic experiences, to, in a sense, revive the earlier trauma and greatly exacerbate it. Peter Loewenberg has referred to the phenomenon of regression, whereby childhood traumas come back to haunt us when we suffer a different kind of trauma later in adult life.[44] Loewenberg has focused on the Hitler Youth, for whom the early traumas came during the First World War in the form of hunger, loss of father, collapse of norms, and so on. Later, the Great Depression — for these young men the trauma of their adulthood — triggered regressive behavior in the form of externalized violence and a yearning for a father figure.

Ley, to be sure, was a generation older than the Hitler Youth cohort; but his experiences, in a different time-frame, are analogous. His childhood crisis came many years before the war; but the loss of father, and material want and a loss of norms (sudden shame and ostracism) must surely be considered a similar experience. The First World War, then, is for an adult Ley what the Depression is for the Hitler Youth generation: the adult trauma which conjures up the earlier trauma and generates violent, asocial behavior.

42. Quoted in Richard Grunberger, *The Twelve Year Reich: A Social History of Nazi Germany 1933–1945* (New York, Holt, Rinehart, & Winston, 1971), p. 310.
43. *The Dynamics of Nazism: Leadership Ideology, and the Holocaust* (New York, Academic Press, 1980), p. 107.
44. In his important article "The Psychohistorical Origins of the Nazi Youth Cohort," in *American Historical Review*, vol. 76, no. 5 (Dec. 1971), 1457–502.

It is the combination of disasters that leaves Ley with insufficient ego strength to deal for long with the vagaries of life in chaotic Weimar and causes him to disengage within a very few years from that life and re-engage in Hitler's millenarian movement. In childhood, at a time when his ego was weak and undeveloped, he experienced the wrenching change of losing his father, suffering acute social status loss and material want. Later came the shock of war, injury, invasive surgery, deprivation of victory (hence the loss of a sense of socially useful work, i.e. soldiering) and imprisonment. The combination was deadly. Moreover, as Anthony Wallace has noted, it is not only one traumatic shock, but chronic stress, such as four years in the trenches would have engendered, which often causes people to undergo a complex set of physiological changes, which, in turn, lead them to change personality and to redefine entirely their cultural surroundings, as Ley did after 1923.[45]

After Ley had broken sharply with the past and joined Hitler's millenarian movement, he became one of the most notorious Nazi rabble rousers and brawlers. His speeches were very emotional affairs, characterized by the expression of a blind faith in Hitler and blind hatred of the Jews, by rejection of the current order and dedication to Germany's rebirth; by a spirit of intense brotherhood with those who would join him in this task; veritable torrents of words and images which were uttered, often in a broken, stammering style, from a kind of ecstasy. This should not surprise us, for such behavior has been characterized both as abreactive to great disaster experiences as well as typical of those who join millenarian movements.

As Barkun has pointed out, disaster "may involve grief through the loss of loved ones, guilt at being a survivor, shame at lowered social status, or fear that the disaster will return" (all of these apply in one form or another to Ley). Conversion to a millenarian sect adds a new dimension, for it demands of its followers that they sever all loyalties to their past, a demand which cannot but be guilt producing. Ecstatic behavior effectively purges these emotions, "whether through wild dancing, *the response of crowds to oratory* (em-

45. See his "Stress and Rapid Personality Changes," in *International Journal of Medicine*, no. 169 (1956), pp. 761–4. Joachim Fest asserts in connection with the Nazi leadership that "a considerable number, among them Goebbels, Göring, Ley, Himmler and not the least Hitler himself were in a narrow clinical sense sick." See *Das Gesicht des Dritten Reiches. Profile einer totalitären Herrschaft* (Munich, Piper, 1980), p. 396.

phasis added), or physical trembling" (in Ley's case perhaps also stuttering).

Not only does this ecstatic behavior salve guilt, it also facilitates the break with the past. As Barkun continues:

> Through ecstatic experiences they mobilize energy for personal transformation. The experiences themselves, to the extent that they also violate conventional norms [brawling and street fighting] constitute the most vivid kind of release from former values and obligations. To the extent that participants are bound together by common experiences and common guilt, they rapidly become socialized to a new kind of community.[46]

Moreover, as Peter Worsley has pointed out, millenarians sound themes which indicate a totally new environment: renunciation, rejection, defiance, fraternity, dedication, and rebirth.[47] All of these themes were sounded again and again in Ley's speeches. One, which he made at a DAF *Kreistag* in Rüstringen-Wilhelmshafen in August 1935, contains many of them and can be regarded as symptomatic:

> In the year 1924, as I began to fight for Adolf Hitler, we had neither money, nor power, not even newspapers! I had a group of young people around me, pupils and workers, loyal people. But the people understood us. We hadn't visited any public speaking schools, the others were more clever speakers. They had money and political newspapers. We didn't have any of that. Many didn't want to have anything to do with us! My good colleagues of yore looked down on me with pity; he's a decent fellow, too bad about him! Look, we all had that experience. . . . Yes, it was a terrible time. And yet so wonderfully sublime! It was a time of comradeship and loyalty. One knew each and every comrade. . . . It was brutal and difficult, but we still conquered Germany. . . . And now those same gentlemen, who in those days were not in a position as elevated, respected, all-powerful party and union leaders to triumph over us, want to pretend to us that they had the same will and fanatic faith as we? And they want to bring us to heel today? They're crazy, they're crazy and criminal at the same time. We couldn't care less if some little nobody (*Dahergelaufener*) yelps and barks. But we cannot be indifferent if he tries to prevent the people from helping in the building of a new Germany. That we won't tolerate, always at the right moment we'll grab a hold.[48]

46. Barkun, *Disaster*, pp. 156–7, 160; see also William Sargant, *Battle for the Mind* (Baltimore, Penguin, 1961), pp. 52–4.
47. *The Trumpet Shall Sound: A Study of 'Cargo' Cults in Melanesia* 2nd edn (New York, Schocken, 1968), pp. 249–51.
48. Quoted in *Deutschland ist schöner geworden*, pp. 24–6.

But despite the importance of National Socialism to Ley as a religious movement, we must not neglect finally the role of Nazi ideology *per se* in his life, not only as an expression of missionary zeal but as a world-view to integrate his thought, action, and social position into what for him was a satisfactory whole. There was a specific content to National Socialism which had for Ley a programmatic meaning. However illogical, however far from reality NS ideology might appear in retrospect, Ley believed quite sincerely in its promise, as we shall see in the chapter on the ideological dream. Weinstein, in his attempt to integrate psychiatry and sociology, points out that it is not only childhood experiences or libidinal strivings which cause people to act dramatically as adults, but any disruptive social conflict can produce the same result. Normally, society exists for most people as what Weinstein calls a "background of safety"; that is, there are no serious incongruities between society in its various realms and the ideological view of the world that makes society understandable to people and legitimizes their day-to-day activities within that society. When disruptive social conflict occurs, however, the adaptive activities of many people suddenly do not cope adequately with the new situation nor do their ideological constructs give an adequate explanation of what is happening. This produces an intense emotional reaction consisting to varying degrees of futility, desperation, helplessness, and rage. This was certainly the case in Weimar Germany where "people lived with a sense of failure, of weakness; they were afraid that they would not be able to achieve goals, aims, and ideals (e.g. to be competent and competitive, to be active, masculine, admirable), that present difficulties could not be surmounted, no matter what one did."[49] These feelings were certainly aroused in those who faced unemployment or some other kind of grim situation — but was not limited to them. Even someone in an economically sound position, as Ley was, needed to have their day-to-day activities legitimated in their own mind; that is, they needed an ideological position that was adequate to explain the surrounding society and their role in it. Prior to joining the Nazi movement, Ley lacked precisely that explanation and legitimization. The movement provided him with both, even at the expense of his "bourgeois existence", for as Weinstein again asserts, " people will go to the most extraordinary lengths to sustain or impose an ideological orientation that legitimizes valued activity. And if they

49. Weinstein, *Dynamics*, pp. 58, 107.

cannot justify this in terms of objective or "true" connections, they will not hesitate to fabricate false ones."[50] For Ley the myths of Jewish conspirators and November criminals, as well as Hitler's divinely inspired leadership and the vision of a future German utopia became the ideological orientation which allowed him once again to integrate ideology, social reality, and his own activities into a coherent whole.

But one might argue that at the age of 33, Ley was already too formed for many of the above-mentioned psychological mechanisms to come into play. Here one final contributing factor must be added, which not only functioned as a triggering mechanism to cause Ley to disengage from bourgeois life and re-engage with the Nazi movement, but also helps to explain many of his more bizarre statements and behavior patterns throughout his political career. This factor is the serious — and chronic — frontal lobe injury which he suffered as a result of his plane crash in 1917 and which got gradually worse over his lifetime, probably exacerbated by drinking and by an automobile accident in 1930, which again injured his head. Several sources agree that Ley emerged from the crash, which left him unconscious for many hours, with a pronounced stutter and often severe background noise, which only alcohol could relieve.[51] His consumption of alcohol did become legendary during the Third Reich, earning him the nickname "*Reichstrunkenbold*" (Reich Lush), but was never as severe as many thought. It did not impair his activities to the degree which many of his competitors assumed, and his emotional, stuttering, stammering outbursts during occasions of public speaking had much more to do with his frontal lobe injury than with his alcohol intake. His injury and its probable consequences were confirmed after the war both by Rorschach tests and by pathological examination. Nuremberg psychiatrist Douglas Kelley wrote of Ley's Rorschach test:

> The Rorschach record of Dr Robert Ley was perhaps the most interesting because a diagnosis of frontal lobe damage was suggested from the record alone. . . . Meticulous studies made after the Rorschach record had been taken demonstrated evidence of euphoria, emotional instability with marked lability, extremely poor judgement and some memory

50. Ibid., p. 119.
51. Several Nazi sources spoke of a "schwere Sprachlähmung" or "Sprechstörung". See VB of February 15, 1940, and DAF Informationsdienst No. 38 of February 15, 1934, in BA NSD 51/10. The 1930 crash occurred when his chauffeur, Alfons Balette, fell asleep at the wheel and hit a tree. See Kiehl, *Mann an der Fahne*, p. 71.

> loss . . . . The over-all picture of Robert Ley's Rorschach record is definitely that of an individual suffering from damage to his frontal lobes.[52]

This Rorschach evaluation was confirmed by pathological examination, both at the autopsy and later when Ley's brain was flown to the United States for examination by the Army Institute of Pathology. The autopsy already noted "mild degenerative changes" in Ley's brain. The later microscopic examination confirmed a condition known as "chronic [diffuse] encephalopathy" which was "of sufficient duration and degree to have impaired Dr Ley's mental and emotional faculties and could well account for his alleged aberrations in conduct and feelings."[53]

It is very important to take this condition into account, for it helps to explain not only Ley's decision to break with traditional life and his often inept political infighting (lack of judgment) but also his ecstatic displays of fanaticism (manic behavior) and occasional aberrant personal behavior (emotional instability). The condition exaggerated and reinforced tendencies that were already there. There is a close link in Ley between disruptive social environment, conversion to a millenarian movement, and ecstatic behavior, a link which is reinforced by disease-related judgmental problems and consumption of alcohol. Barkun, for one, sees conversion and ecstasy as closely related phenomena, and views among other things, "alcoholic spirits, hypnotic suggestions, hyperventilation and drugs" as "ecstasy inducing techniques".[54]

As we consider Ley's entry into politics during the *Kampfjahre* of the 1920s, we see with increasing frequency the interaction between his mental state and his political action. As Ley admitted to his interrogators at Nuremberg: "An inner voice drove me forward like hunted game. Though my mind told me differently and my wife and family repeatedly told me to stop my activities and return to civil and normal life, the voice inside me commanded 'you must; you must'."[55]

52. See Douglas Kelley, "Preliminary Studies of the Rorschach Records of the Nazi War Criminals," *Rorschach Research Exchange*, vol. X, no. 2 (June 1946), p. 46.
53. See "Dr Robert Ley's Brain", *Medical Record*, vol. 159 (1946), p. 188.
54. *Disaster*, pp. 156–7.
55. See Douglas Kelley, *Twenty-Two Cells at Nuremberg* (New York, Greenberg, 1947), p. 153. Here, as well, Kelley confirms the link between Ley's pathology and his public behavior. "His bluntness and lack of tact, his lack of concern for the opinions of others, his uninhibited reaction to a situation and subsequent dismissal of the unpleasant, his totally bad judgment, are all typical findings in individuals suffering frontal lobe damage or excision" (p. 157).

CHAPTER 2

The Years of Struggle

Robert Ley's political activity in the Rhineland began against the background of unprecedented social and political turmoil. Imperial Germany and its Kaiser, once the focus of German nationalism, were gone, mourned nostagically by large segments of the German middle class. In power was a republican form of government, the birth of which had been attended by revolution, defeat, and national disgrace. The Weimar Republic would not become for many Germans the focus of national identity and patriotism that the old Germany had been. Moreover, the country seemed beset by conflict between radical left, feared by many as a harbinger of bolshevism, and the radical right, struggling in a myriad of forms to find a new base for German nationalism. Economically, the country labored under the burden of lost markets and territory, tremendous dislocation, inflation engendered by the war — which in 1923 would become hyperinflation — burdensome reparations payments as well as millions of discharged veterans clogging the labor market. The Rhineland itself smarted particularly under the odious terms of the peace settlement; demilitarized, it was supposed to endure continuing French occupation for fifteen years and would be a storm center in 1923, when the French marched further into Germany and occupied the Ruhr industrial area in order to exact reparations. But perhaps the heaviest burden was psychological: the once mightiest nation in Europe, stronger than any other two powers, had to the disbelieving despair of her population not only succumbed on the battlefield but had been saddled by her victorious enemies with the moral blame for causing the entire conflict in the first place. So great was the psychological blow that many Germans availed themselves of a growing national myth — that of the stab in the back — in order to cope with developments that simply did not make sense.[1]

1. See Gordon Craig, *Germany 1866–1945* (New York, Oxford University Press, 1978),

It was in this environment that Robert Ley found National Socialism. According to Ley himself, he first became aware of the existence of Hitler and the Nazi Party by reading of Hitler's trial for treason in early 1924. As Ley put it:

> I read about a man whom I had never seen. I read Adolf Hitler's words in the Munich trial. 'I stepped into this courtroom not in order to deny anything or to shirk responsibility. I protest that anyone else take responsibility. I SHOULDER THE RESPONSIBILITY ALL ALONE. I cannot plead guilty. BUT I ADMIT TO THE DEED. There is no high treason against the traitors of 1918. It is impossible that I should have committed high treason. I do not feel myself to be a traitor, BUT A GERMAN WHO WANTED THE BEST FOR HIS PEOPLE.' These words gripped me tremendously . . . . I'll never forget the moment when I read them in my bourgeois newspaper. What is that? It doesn't fit in with these times. WHAT KIND OF A MAN IS THIS? WHAT DOES HE WANT, WHAT'S HE TALKING ABOUT, WHAT'S GOING ON IN MUNICH? I was seized by something new and hitherto unknown to me.[2]

These words, uttered in retrospect, may have been, as with Hitler's description of how he became politicized, mere self-dramatization. But Ley's behavior lends credibility to the words as does the testimony of those who worked with him in the early years. One of them recalled Ley's first appearance among the early Nazis in Cologne in late spring 1924: "We all sit up and take notice. A genuine academic is something new in our ranks. Dr Ley has an explosive impact. He is still little known and has no 'achievements' yet in the eyes of our group. He takes the floor immediately and calls passionately for a fight." Josef Grohé, who was Gau business leader, decided on the spot to send Ley to Ehrenfeld, a Communist bastion.[3]

But the Nazi party that Ley joined in the Rhineland in 1924 bore little resemblance to the mass movement he would help it eventually to become. The Nazi Party in the Rhineland emerged from the broadly based, amorphous *völkisch* movement which assumed great

---

Ch. 11; also Joachim Fest, *Hitler* (New York, Vintage, 1975) Ch. 2.

2. Quoted from Walter Kiehl, *Mann an der Fahne, Kameraden erzählen von Dr Ley* (Munich, Zentralverlag der NSDAP, 1938), pp. 12–13. This is a very tendentious Nazi publication, but does offer some useful information.
3. Remark is from Richard Schaller, later deputy Gauleiter and Gauobmann of the DAF, in Kiehl, *Mann an der Fahre*, p. 99.

importance in Germany directly after the First World War. It was a right-wing political phenomenon which was intensely nationalistic, anti-semitic, anti-republican, anti-Marxist and took a myriad of organizational forms. One of them — the direct predecessor to the NSDAP — was the Deutschvölkischer Schutz- und Trutzbund (DVSTB, German Populist League for Defense and Defiance).[4] Most of the men who would work with Ley before and after 1933 belonged originally to the DVSTB and included Josef Grohé and Heinz Haake, both Gauleiters of the party in the Rhineland; Rudolf and Eduard Schmeer, who would help to organize the city of Aachen for Ley, as well as a number of others. The DVSTB, which appeared under different names after being periodically banned by occupation authorities, came to be linked with like-minded groups, including Julius Streicher's German Social Party in Nuremberg and, in early 1920, with Hitler's infant party in Munich. In fact, Egon Lützeler, who was Gauführer of the DVSTB in Cologne, met Hitler in Munich in February 1921 at the Sterneckerbräu, one of the popular beerhalls for Hitler's burgeoning activities. The two men were introduced by the notorious Captain Ehrhard, whose free-booter unit had been at the center of the abortive Kapp putsch to overthrow the Republic just two years before. Lützeler was so impressed with Hitler that he agreed to publish Hitler's 25-point program once he had returned to Cologne. The NSDAP in the Rhineland, then, emerged out of the Cologne branch of the DVSTB. Lützeler himself, under pressure from the occupation authorities, hesitated to formally proclaim the establishment of the new party. Instead, a master cabinet-maker named Hermann Breuer did so in August 1921.[5]

For the next year or so the Rhenish branch of the Nazi Party languished in obscurity. Headquarters in Munich did not even take cognizance of it until March 1922, when one of Hitler's lieutenants, Hermann Esser, formally "founded" the party with locals at Cologne and Dortmund. The police agreed that the party was hardly attracting adherents in large numbers. A report from April 1922 noted:

> For quite a while this party has been unable to create a basis for its

4. For a general background on the NS movement in the Rhenish area, see Wilfried Böhnke, *Die NSDAP im Ruhrgebiet 1920–1933* (Bonn and Bad Godesberg, Neue Gesellschaft, 1974); a contemporary Nazi account is P. Schmidt, *Zwanzig Jahre Soldat Adolf Hitlers* (Cologne, Westdeutscher Beobachter, 1941).
5. See Grohé, *Soldat*, pp. 40ff.

> activity in Cologne. The number of its adherents has been very small. Only on March 3 of this year was there a general membership meeting at which a board of directors was elected . . . . Despite active propaganda the party has only grown to 56 members, including six women and ten youths.

To make matters worse, in November the party was banned by decree in Prussia, an order to which Breuer acquiesced, while Grohé and Haake refused.[6]

January witnessed a series of events which would make 1923 the most difficult year the new republic would have to face and present the Nazi Party with its first opportunity to contemplate seizing power on a national level. The Germans having been declared in arrears on their reparations payments, the French (and Belgians) marched into the Ruhr industrial area to force acquiescence. The German government, in turn, declared a policy of passive resistance and much of the Rhineland turned into the site of urban guerilla warfare with sabotage, sniping, taking of hostages, and general violence. The Communists saw their opportunity to fish in troubled waters and began their own revolt.[7] It was an ideal opportunity for the Nazis in the Rhineland to achieve notoriety by playing the patriotic card of resistance to both foreign occupier and the radical left. Indeed, a number of local Nazis did exactly that. Both Grohé in Cologne and Rudolph Schmeer in Aachen busied themselves blowing up railroad tracks, an activity which earned Schmeer a fifteen-year sentence at the hands of a Belgian military court (which he never served) and which forced Grohé to flee the area altogether. But these were individual efforts and did not redound to the benefit of the Nazi Party *per se*, largely because Hitler, determined that his party not disappear against the background of the general right

6. Ibid., pp. 44–5. Grohé was born in 1902 in Gemünden Hunsrück ninth of thirteen children of a Catholic small businessman. Too young to have fought in the war, he went to Cologne in May 1919 as a volunteer looking for action. Until 1925 he worked intermittently as a salesman for an iron dealer, while becoming very active in *völkisch* politics, joining first the DVSTB, then the Nazi Party. The older Haake, born in 1892 and the son of a Cologne architect, was a bank teller. He fought in the war and was wounded severely four times. Returning in 1918 to Cologne, he too became politically active, first in the DVSTB and then the Nazi Party. He was the first Nazi Gauleiter of the Rhineland. See BDC: File Grohé and Haake; also Albrecht Tyrell, "Führergedanke und Gauleiterwechsel: Die Teilung des Gaues Rheinland der NSDAP 1931," *Vierteljahrshefte für Zeitgeschichte*, vol. 5, no. 4 (1975), pp. 357–8; a summary of Haake's party experience can be found in NSDAP Hauptarchiv, Reel 56, Folder 1347.
7. For the events of 1923, see Craig, *Germany*, Ch. 12.

wing, forbade such activity. For him, overthrowing the Weimar Republic took precedence over expelling the French.[8]

Thus, the focus of Nazi activity in 1923 was not on the Rhine and Ruhr but rather on Munich, where on November 9 Hitler attempted his abortive putsch. The coup attempt failed ignominiously. But the subsequent trial for treason, in which Hitler boldly took full responsibility and postured as a true German patriot, achieved for him ironically something that the coup itself had not, namely, it had put him and his regional party in the national spotlight. It was there, of course, where Ley first became aware of his future leader's existence.

With Hitler in jail the Nazi Party splintered into often quarreling factions. In the south a number of Hitler's older followers, such as Max Amann, future publishing czar; Julius Streicher, already an infamous Jew-baiter in Nuremberg; and Franz-Xavier Schwarz, future treasurer of the Nazi Party, reconstituted the movement under the rubric of the "Grossdeutsche Volksgemeinschaft." In the north the movement took the form of the National Socialist Freedom Party and was led by younger men, many of them veterans, such as Gregor Strasser, perhaps the party's best organizer, and Josef Goebbels, future Gauleiter of Berlin and party propagandist. To add to the confusion, there was a certain amount of periodic name changing and general organizational confusion which arose out of electoral alliances with other *völkisch* groups and deserters from the Conservative Party . In the Rhineland, for example, directly after the putsch, the party was reorganized by Grohé and Haake as the "Deutschvölkischer Wahlverein," which in March 1924 became the "Völkisch-sozialer Block" and in August was rechristened the "National Socialist Freedom Movement".[9]

Despite the confusion of nomenclature, the Nazi–*völkisch* alliance did surprisingly well in the Reichstag elections of May 1924, garnering 6.5 percent of the vote and thirty-two seats. Later in the year, however, despite having co-opted the wartime leader General Ludendorff to their cause, the alliance faltered at the polls, falling to 3 percent of the vote and only fourteen seats in parliament. It was some indication of the Nazis' weakness in the Rhineland, however, that the May election which brought in 6.5 percent nationwide only

8. See Fest, *Hitler*, pp. 163–4; also Tyrell, "Führergedanke," p. 358.
9. On the post-putsch Nazi Party, see Dietrich Orlow, *The History of the Nazi Party, 1919–1933* (Pittsburgh, University of Pittsburgh Press, 1969), pp. 46–75. On the permutations in the Rhineland, see Grohé, *Soldat*, pp. 63–4; also Böhnke, *Ruhrgebiet*, Ch. 1.

produced 1.5 percent and 1.3 percent, respectively, in the two electoral districts in which Ley would soon begin his activities — Cologne-Aachen and Koblenz-Trier.[10] Ley had his work cut out for him.

Among his first assignments was to help prepare for the elections to the Reichstag and Prussian Diet on December 7, 1924. Grohé had been sufficiently impressed by Ley's speaking ability, in fact, to propose him as leading candidate in the two districts. It was on the occasion of this electoral campaign that Ley made the first of many appearances in his home district. On November 29 he gave a speech at Rosbach. As a result of the elections, which did not turn out well for the nascent Nazi movement, Haake went to the Diet; Ley would have to wait several years.[11] For Ley and the others the year 1924, not an auspicious one for the movement, did end on a positive note. On December 12 the ban on the Nazi Party in Prussia was lifted, paving the way for the release of Hitler from prison on December 24.

Hitler had announced that he would not simply take over the reins of the National Socialist Freedom Movement after he was released from prison; rather, he expressed the intention of re-founding the Nazi Party on his own terms. Although this caused some resentment and ruffled feathers among many *völkisch* people, it certainly caused no trouble for a loyalist like Ley. Indeed, Haake was already in touch with Hitler through Gregor Strasser and knew of Hitler's intent. As he wrote to Grohé in mid-January, "So I'll inform you privately and confidentially that Adolf Hitler will probably draw up his old NSDAP. Work quietly but carefully to that end."[12] On February 26, 1925, Hitler's paper the *Völkischer Beobachter* appeared once again. In the meantime, Hitler had already turned to one of his most effective organizers, Gregor Strasser, and given him *carte blanche* to organize the party in the industrial north. The energetic Strasser, a veteran who had been active since 1919 in *völkisch* politics, commander of the SA in Lower Bavaria, member of the Bavarian Diet in 1924 as candidate of the "Völkisch Bloc" and Reichstag deputy from the NSFP since the December 1924 elections, quickly went to work. His ideas differed significantly from those of Hitler — he advocated nationalization of industry under worker control and an alliance with the Soviet Union, for example — and he

10. Böhnke, *Ruhrgebeit*, p. 70.
11. Kiehl, *Mann an der Fahne*, p. 107; see also *Aus der Geschichte Waldbröls*, Heft 11, 1985, published by Raiffeisenbank, Waldbröl, p. 8.
12. Quoted in Grohé, *Soldat*, pp. 64–5.

would soon rebel against the influence of some of the Munich people around Hitler, but there was never any question as to his loyalty to Hitler himself.[13]

In the course of 1925, Strasser would organize no less than ninety-one meetings. One of the most important came at the beginning. On February 21–2, he chaired a conference in Hamm of northern and western Nazi leaders. Over 100 district leaders of the NSFB appeared and went over to the newly reconstituted NSDAP. Among them was Heinz Haake from Cologne, who was invested with the title of *Gauführer* of Rhineland-South.[14] It is an interesting commentary on how little control Munich had over its gaus and locals, that Haake was actually elected to the post by local and district representatives less than two weeks later and was "confirmed" in that post by Hitler on March 27. More often than not Munich responded to *faits accomplis* rather than actively initiate action in the Gaus, as Robert Ley's accession to the Gauleiter post less than three months later would illustrate.[15] Hitler's reconstituted party did enjoy some advantages. The alliance with the various *völkisch* groups was broken and the NSDAP could now stand alone, unhampered and uncompromised by the kind of ties which had trapped Hitler in 1923. It was also rapidly becoming a national party rather than a regional Bavarian one, as locals were formed in the north and west.

With the departure of the French from the Ruhr in July 1925, the party also had more freedom of action in that area. But it also faced immense difficulties. If Hitler had been swimming with the stream of economic decline, disastrous inflation, and political chaos prior to 1924, now he had to move against the stream. By 1925 the foundations had been laid for the five "good" years of Weimar. The end of Ruhr occupation, the reform of the mark, the influx of American dollars as a result of the Dawes Plan, the Locarno pacts, and membership in the League of Nations, all of these pointed to a Germany with restored prosperity, enhanced social and political stability, and international respectability. This would not be to the advantage of the Nazis in the Rhineland as elsewhere. The brief

13. The best study on Strasser to date is Udo Kissenkoetter, *Gregor Strasser und die NSDAP* (Stuttgart, Deutsche Verlagsanstalt, 1978).
14. See Kissenkoetter, *Strasser*, p. 70; also Grohé to Max Amann of March 2, 1925, in US National Archives Microcopy T-580, Roll 23, Ordner 203.
15. On the independence of local leaders in the early days, see Peter Hüttenberger, *Die Gauleiter. Studie zum Wandel des Machtgefüges in der NSDAP* (Stuttgart, Deutsche Verlagsanstalt, 1969), particularly pp. 9–26.

increase in membership, for example, that followed in the euphoria of French departure in July 1925, was followed by membership decline, ill-attended meetings, and general lack of public interest. Nor did it help that the party's leader, Hitler, was deprived of using the greatest recruiting tool it had — his voice — as a result of being silenced by many German states, including Prussia. In some states the ban would last well into 1928. This made Hitler quite dependent on his local leaders for their organizational and oratorical skills. Men like Ley became invaluable to him.[16]

The other side of the coin of this dependence was the striking degree of independence of local and regional leaders, who often did just what they pleased, ignoring instructions from Munich. This was an advantage in one sense. In the absence of a well-organized party bureaucracy — something which Strasser would create in the next few years — a largely independent collection of locals, each responding to the specific needs of the area, taking on the color of the immediate environment, perhaps represented the best way to keep the movement alive. On the other hand, that same independence made it difficult to establish a coherent party line, to keep track of the membership and, above all, to establish some kind of reliable financial base. There often seemed to be a multiplicity of Nazi parties — some socialist in orientation, some anti-semitic, some petit bourgeois, depending on where one happened to look—and few could be relied upon either to report accurate accounts of their activities or to remit promptly the membership dues. In this respect Ley would be little different in his practices from the rest.[17]

Add to all these difficulties what seemed to be an incipient revolt in the party during 1925–6. The northern people, especially Strasser and his radical protégé, Goebbels, were increasingly unhappy at the Munich branch of the party. They were operating in the proletarian north, where a much more "leftist" appeal was necessary, and resented the bourgeois cast which many of the men ("calcified big shots" as they were called) around Hitler were giving the party. As a result, during the fall of 1925, the northerners took both the organi-

16. See Boehnke, *Ruhrgebiet*, pp 98–105; dates for the speaking ban on Hitler in the various states are listed in Tyrell, "Führergedanke," pp.107–8.
17. This fact is illustrated in the correspondence between the gau and the party headquarters. See Bundesarchiv Koblenz (hereafter BAK), Schumacher Sammlung, 203; also Hüttenberger, *Gauleiter*, p. 24 and Albrecht Tyrell (ed.), *Führer befiehl . . . Selbstzeugnisse aus der 'Kampfzeit' der NSDAP: Dokumentation und Analyse* (Düsseldorf, Droste Verlag, 1969), pp. 105, 139, 231, 233.

zational and ideological initiative.

Under Strasser's leadership, they formed the task force (*Arbeitsgemeinschaft*) of the northern and western Gaus and established a fortnightly review, *Nationalsozialistiche Briefe* (National Socialist Letters) to attack the Munich line and give expression to their more urban, radical, anti-capitalist views. The revolt crystallized quickly. The committee was formed at a meeting in Hagen on September 10. By November 22 at a meeting in Hanover, the radicals had developed their program and launched an attack on the "pope in Munich." In December, Strasser actually distributed a draft of his program among the members, one which was to replace the original 25-point program of the party. Here was a direct challenge to Hitler, for Strasser advocated getting away from the "legal" approach and preparing for violence in a "politics of catastrophe." This sort of thing threatened Hitler's parole, and he resolved to take action in 1926. In the meantime, there was a groundswell of support for Strasser in the north. At the December meeting of twenty-five people who took part in the discussion of Strasser's plan, only one came out openly in support of Hitler. It was Robert Ley, who for five months had been Gauleiter of Rhineland-South.[18]

Ley, who had been functioning as deputy Gau leader, had both inspiration and opportunity to move into the Gauleiter post. The inspiration came from Hitler. In his closing words at a meeting of regional party representatives at Plauen on June 12, 1925, Hitler had once again reinforced the commitments of those for whom the party was a millenarian movement:[19]

> Above all believe one thing: whatever I do happens according to the best knowledge and conscience I have. *I love the movement: it is my life's work*! I am not one of those politicians who is here today and gone tomorrow. The movement — *that* is my task. *With this task I shall live and die and fall! I do not want to be anything else*! Please help me in this.

The opportunity came from the Gauleiter Heinz Haake. Haake's job as deputy in the Diet in Berlin left him little time to administer his Gau. Pain from his war wounds often left him out of commission

18. Generally on the 'revolt of the north,' see Kissenkoetter, *Strasser*, 25ff.; Fest, *Hitler*, p. 233; Hüttenberger, *Gauleiter*, pp.26–38; Joseph Nyomarkay, *Charisma and Factionalism in the Nazi Party* (Minneapolis, University of Minnesota Press, 1967), pp. 71–110; Orlow, *Nazi Party*, pp 66–72. On Ley's support of Hitler, see Konrad Heiden, *Der Fuehrer: Hitler's Rise to Power* (Boston, Beacon, 1969), p. 287.
19. Quoted in Tyrell, *Führer befiehl*, p. 109.

anyway. Moreover, the ambitious Gau business director, Grohé, whom Haake felt to be indispensable, would not take orders all the way from Berlin. As a result, Haake wrote his Du-friend (my dear Robert) on June 1, 1925, saying:

> Given my frequent absences from the Rhineland, it is simply impossible for me to continue leading the Gau in a way necessary for the movement without the energetic help of a rather independent business leader. For this reason I ask you to take over the post of gau leader in my stead . . . You just have to accept, for you are the only man suitable. Otherwise the movement in the Rhineland will go to the dogs.[20]

Ley accepted and quickly sent a copy of Haake's letter along with one of his own to Hitler. The letter (and the resulting exchange) is instructive.[21] Already at this early date, when most Nazi leaders were addressing Hitler in letters as "Herr Hitler", Ley uses the salutation "Verehrter Führer" (revered leader!). He announces the change in leadership and requests that Hitler confirm him as Gauleiter. He then goes on to reveal what poor financial shape the Gau is in. They had to give up the business office in Cologne; it is now functioning out of Ley's home in Wiesdorf. The Gau also has 800 marks debt left from the elections. Morever, he also sketches a dark picture of the privations which the party comrades have to bear in order to function at all in the French and Belgian occupied zones. Then he comes to the point. The NSFB, he points out, was freed from the burden of remitting its dues; Strasser had accorded the same privilege to Haake temporarily. Could he (Ley) now have the same privilege, so that dues could be used locally to pay debts?

He concludes with another request. To bolster the morale of the Rhinelanders, Ley proposes a "thousand-year celebration of the NSDAP" to be held at unoccupied Caub on the Rhine in September and begs Hitler to be present, whether he can speak publicly or not.

Here is vintage Ley; the way he will appear from now on. Slavishly devoted to Hitler, while at the same time ambitious for himself. Using hyperbole in order to get financial advantage. Full of grandiose, if impracticable, ideas, particularly in the realm of public displays. And not loath to shaving the truth if it is to his benefit. Although the new Gauleiter, Ley was not yet the powerful Reichsor-

20. BAK, Schumacher Sammlung, 203.
21. Ibid. Ley to Bouhler, June 7, 1925; Bouhler to Ley, June 16; Ley to Bouhler, June 23; Bouhler to Ley, July 2.

ganisationsleiter of later years. Back from Munich came the reply from party headquarters. Pending Hitler's final decision, Ley was left provisionally in office. As to his request to keep dues, here the answer was a clear No. Whatever Strasser might have promised, headquarters "can in no way be in agreement with such a measure." Munich had more important financial obligations of its own to meet and therefore had to insist that Ley send 1 mark for each application form filed as well as 10 pfennigs per month per member, whether the members had in fact paid their dues or not. The letter concluded: "At the same time we ask urgently that you send us the application forms of your Gau in order that we can send you the membership cards and finally get a clear picture of the state of the movement."

Ley replied that he would send in the money as soon as possible; meanwhile, he needed the support of headquarters in disciplining those who would question his leadership. He was, he asserted, alone responsible to Hitler for his Gau. Headquarters answered that it would, of course, oblige as best it could and expressed agreement with Ley's leadership philosophy. In the meantime, it looked forward to receiving the money. Soon thereafter, Ley received a certificate dated July 14 and signed by Hitler recognizing that Ley had replaced Haake and stated that Ley was "confirmed by me as responsible leader of this Gau until a future final disposition."[22]

There was a tentativeness about the whole matter which reflected the situation of flux in which the movement found itself in the early years. Ley tentatively agreed to send the money. Headquarters tentatively supported his authority. Hitler tentatively confirmed him as Gauleiter. (Only in September 1928 would Hitler formally appoint Ley to office.) What all this meant was that Ley, like his counterparts in other Gaus, would have to "conquer" his area for Hitler and the movement. And conquest was measured in successful propaganda resulting in well-attended public meetings, resulting in turn in new members (and their dues) and new locals. It would not be an easy task.

The Gau Rhineland-South was composed of the electoral districts of Cologne-Aachen and Koblenz-Trier plus Birkenfeld. It was not a coherent area socially. The northern part of the Gau was heavily urban working class, the southern part rural and thinly settled. Both parts were overwhelmingly Catholic. The political consequences of

22. BAK, NS26/ 144. This represents the first Gauleiter change in the history of the Nazi party. Tyrell, "Führergedanke," p. 359.

this social pattern for the Nazis were that they faced strong entrenched resistance from both the Socialist and Communist Parties as well as the Center Party.[23]

The Gau, then, would be among the weaker ones. Despite Ley's strenuous efforts, the number of members only increased from 335 to 868 between August and December 1925, with 400 more to be added by August 1926. Even in the Depression year 1931, the Gau had considerably under 10,000 members (by comparison, Silesia had 40,000 and Berlin 20,000). In the Reichstag elections of 1928 and 1930 in both Koblenz-Trier and Cologne-Aachen, the Nazi Party garnered lower percentages that it did in the Reich as a whole.[24]

But despite the apparent obstacles, Ley went to work with a vengeance. Although he was still employed full-time with Bayer-Leverkusen, Ley tried to be everywhere — speaking, organizing, cajoling, threatening. He tightened up the very loose Gau structure by dividing it into seven districts, each with a district leader with initially a total of 60 locals. He reorganized Cologne and put in his man, Wilhelm Becker, as Ortsgruppenleiter. It was a choice he would soon regret. He confirmed the dynamic and often independent Josef Grohé as Gau business manager. He revived the nearly moribund Gau newspaper, the *Westdeutscher Beobachter* and by September was requesting that it be recognized as an official organ of the party. He increased the number and kinds of meetings: youth days followed change of season celebrations. He tried to hold weekly discussion evenings (*Sprechabende*) in each local. He attempted to found locals far and wide in the Gau. Already in August he commissioned the first local in Trier. In November he held the first meeting in Birkenfeld. He was especially active in organizing his own home area of Bergisch-Land. It was of particular importance to him to goad the Red enemy; to this purpose, he tried especially hard to found locals in Red areas.[25]

This, of course, resulted in brawling, something else from which Ley did not shrink. In towns like Leverkusen, Opladen, Schlebusch, Wald, Solingen, Remscheid, Mermelskirchen, Dünnwald, Mülheim,

23. For a good contemporary description of the Gau and problems in organizing it, see Gustav Simon to Strasser, March 14, 1931, in BA NS22/1056. A valuable study which focuses on Cologne is Wolfgang Corsten, "Die NSDAP im Raum Köln (1925–1933)," unpublished Magisterarbeit, University of Cologne, 1984, see esp. pp. 3–8, 85–6.
24. These figures are in Tyrell, "Führergedanke," p. 361.
25. See Ley's "Tätigkeitsbericht des Gaues Rheinland-Süd" of August 23, 1925 in BAK, Schumacher Sammlung, 203.

Cologne, Koblenz, and Rastätten, Ley became notorious for the beer hall brawls (*Saalschlachten*) which he incited. Ley's activities on behalf of the NSDAP were, then, all-encompassing. One *Altkämpfer*, looking back on those days, noted that "Dr Ley was at the time not just Ortsgruppenleiter of Wiesdorf, but also Gauleiter, Treasurer, SA leader, in short, he was so to speak 'jack of all trades.'"[26] By early 1926, Gottfried Feder, one of the founders of the movement, suggested that Ley could rival Goebbels and (Karl) Kaufmann (Gauleiter of the Ruhr) as "champion of the National Socialist idea in the Rhineland."[27]

But none of this initial success came without a heavy price in terms of arbitrariness and heavy-handedness. Ley made enemies in his Gau by arbitrarily expelling people from the party and reorganizing without consultation. One letter from an active former member to Hitler accused Ley of turning on his own man in Cologne, Becker, expelling him from the party, and defaming his name by accusing him publicly of being a spy for the Center Party. The complainant also accused Ley of expelling or driving away over 100 members since January 1926 alone. He also accused Ley of withholding an accurate membership list from Munich. Even Becker, an Ortsgruppenleiter, had not been carried officially on the books. Nor did Ley endear himself with HQ in Munich through his chronic reluctance to remit dues and accurate membership lists.[28] Despite frequent dunning notices from Bouhler, the executive secretary, and Schwarz, the treasurer, Ley was constantly in arrears. Owing to difficulties in organizing a Gau which had, until recently, been under occupation, Munich even made concessions to Ley. He was forgiven the 1925 dues. He was even forgiven the 1926 ones, but HQ insisted on the 1-mark initiation fee per new member and an accurate list of members. It seldom got these either.

A letter from the Reichsleitung to Ley in May 1926 summarized the grievances against him.[29] He redivided Cologne organization-

26. See Kiehl, *Mann an der Fahne*, pp. 55, 73, 107; see also "Chronik der Ortsgruppe Trier-Mitte," quoted in Franz Josef Heyen, *Nationalsozialismus im Alltag, Quellen zur Geschichte des Nationalsozialismus vornehmlich im Raum Mainz-Koblenz-Trier* (Boppard, Harald Boldt Verlag, 1967), pp. 77–81.
27. See Feder to Heinemann, May 2, 1926, in Tyrell, *Führer befiehl*, p. 127.
28. Fritz Jejeune to Hitler, May 10, 1926; also Grohé's letter of April 4 to headquarters defending Ley's actions (there must have been other, earlier complaints) in BAK, Schumacher Sammlung, 203.
29. BAK, Schumacher Sammlung, 203; it was commonplace for local Nazi officials to send in misleading reports so that they would not have to remit their dues. See

ally without permission; he maintained a Gau business director, despite the fact that the low membership did not justify this expense; he was not turning in his dues; he had expelled Becker from the party illegitimately — there had been no arbitration meeting nor had Becker even been informed in writing of his expulsion; Ley had exceeded his authority as Gauleiter, as had Grohé, in not responding to the Reichsleitung in the Becker case.

But despite these complaints, Ley did not change. Indeed, his behavior became worse in subsequent years, resulting in several indictments against him and Grohé by the party court. But his position as Gauleiter was not threatened. Hitler kept him on the job. He did so for several reasons.

First of all, Ley was doing precisely what Hitler wanted. He was taking a set of party locals notorious for their "*Vereinsmeierei*" (clubbiness) and welding them into a powerful propaganda and agitation organization. To do this, heads had to roll. Hitler himself noted that the party was not a school for girls but a *Kampfbewegung*.[30]

Secondly, Ley had an ability which was sadly lacking in the party in those days — he was a good speaker, not in the traditional sense of fluid oratory, his stuttering and stammering did not permit that, but rather in the new Nazi style of emotional rabble-rousing. This was especially important in light of Hitler's being banned in many states. Just a week after the letter of complaint from the *Reichsleitung* to Ley went out, Hitler was privately addressing a general membership meeting in Munich and underscoring the value he placed on good popular speakers: "I know what it means to speak really rapturously and enraptured; know, that it cannot be learned, but is an inborn blessing. Every first-class, really good popular speaker will always be irreplaceable for our movement. We must be glad when more and more such fellows peel off from the mass of our party comrades."[31] Given this priority, Hitler was willing to overlook a great deal from his regional chieftains, as long as they were successful on the hustings.

Thirdly, and most importantly, Hitler was willing to grant Ley a great deal of latitude in his behavior because he could be sure of

---

John Toland, *Adolf Hitler* (New York, Doubleday, 1976), p. 220; but Bouhler and Schwarz were determined to collect dues and issue membership cards themselves. See Orlow, *Nazi Party*, pp. 60–1 and specifically a dunning note to Ley of January 20, 1926, in BAK, Schumacher Sammlung, 203.

30. On "clubbiness," see Orlow, *Nazi Party*, p. 104.
31. Quoted in Tyrell, *Führer befiehl*, p. 133.

Ley's total loyalty. This Ley had proven, and was still proving, in the factional struggle which beset the party in 1925 and 1926. From the very beginning of the revolt of the northern leaders against the Munich leadership, Ley had sided completely with Hitler. Already at the organizational meeting of the *Arbeitsgemeinschaft* at Hagen on September 10, 1925, Ley had dissented from the majority, as Goebbels noted annoyed in his diary: "Yesterday at Hagen. . . . We got all we wanted. The North-Gau and West-Gau will be merged. United leadership (Strasser). United office (Elberfeld) United management (moi). Publication of a fortnightly newsletter . . . In other words, as we wanted it. Everyone agreed. Only Dr Ley, Cologne, felt called upon to make mischief."[32]

Ley continued to make mischief. On September 30 Goebbels noted again in his diary: "Perhaps the battle will flare up very soon. The task force protects our rear. . . . Dr Ley is a fool and perhaps an intriguer. He will have to get out of the task force."[33]

In December, as the northern leaders debated Strasser's program, of the twenty-five participants in the debate, only Ley came out openly for Hitler.

In February 1926 Hitler went over to the attack. He gathered a group of the northern leaders at Bamberg on the 14th, making sure that the meeting was packed with his own adherents, including Ley. In a five-hour speech he tore into Strasser's program point by point. Again the millenarian nature of the movement became apparent when Hitler called the original program "the Founding Charter of our religion, our philosophy. To deviate from it would imply a betrayal of those who died for their faith in our ideas." Goebbels was appalled. "Horrible! Program suffices. Content with it. Feder nods. Ley nods. Streicher nods. It hurts my soul when I see you in this company!"[34]

But Hitler worked his magic on the rebels.In April he invited Goebbels to Munich and overwhelmed him. Goebbels was his from that point on. But Hitler left no doubt who his real allies had been. Goebbels recorded Hitler's dressing down of several northern leaders: "Why then scold me? And then a veritable hodgepodge of accusations. . . . Dr Ley and Bauschen have intrigued. Strasser and I come off badly. Every unconsidered word is warmed up. Lord,

32. Helmut Heiber (ed.), *The Early Goebbels Diaries: The Journal of Joseph Goebbels from 1925–1926* (London, Weidenfeld, 1962), p. 32.
33. Ibid.
34. Fest, *Hitler*, p. 239; Heiber, *Diaries*, entry of February 15, 1926.

these swine! Working community, Gau Ruhr, everything is brought up. In the end unity. Hitler is great."[35] The revolt was over, and Ley had been on the right side from the outset. It was a loyalty that Hitler would not forget. And, as he faced the difficulties of "conquering" his Gau during the Indian summer of Weimar, Ley would need Hitler's backing.

The years 1927 and 1928 were the best years the Weimar Republic would experience, years which witnessed growing political stability based on economic prosperity. Conversely, they were dry years for the Nazi Party, as attested to by the results of the Reichstag election of May 20, 1928, in which the NSDAP received 2.6 percent of the vote and twelve seats. This made the Nazis a fringe phenomenon in a country where even many recalcitrant conservatives were becoming *Vernunftrepublikaner* (republicans by reason).

It was perhaps the frustration of being a voice in the wilderness that made Ley's political activity more and more strident in these years. His public meetings evolved from true discussion evenings, where even political opponents might have a say, to rabble-rousing propaganda displays accompanied by frequent violence. The Gau's newspaper, never known for its restraint, became increasingly an organ for gutter journalism, vilifying Republican politicians and Jews in terms which often brought slander suits. Ley's arbitrary behavior created for him additional enemies within the ranks of his own Gau. His financial entanglements became ever more Byzantine, as he skirted the edges of criminal behavior. More and more, even the Munich headquarters threatened disciplinary action against him. All of which simply seemed to increase Ley's fanaticism and drive him further from the last traces of a normal "bourgeois" existence — his job. Finally, even that went at the end of 1927.

Ley became notorious for his rowdy meetings, which he held with increased frequency. It would serve no purpose to mention them all here. One example, however, will serve to make the point. It is an important one, for it comes early and begins a pattern which will become increasingly clear as the depression set in several years later. It also creates the first Nazi martyr in the Rhineland and illustrates the degree both of Ley's anti-semitic fanaticism and of Hitler's support for his actions.[36]

35. Ibid., entry of April 13, 1926.
36. The following description is based on the March 7, 1927, report of the Koblenz police commissioner and the text of the police questioning of Robert Ley in Landeshauptarchiv Koblenz (hereafter LHAK), 403/13381, pp. 763–89.

On March 5, 1927, it was brought to Ley's attention that a meeting would be held in the town of Rastätten with the theme "The true Face of National Socialism or the Danger of the Völkisch Movement." The meeting was called by the local hotel owner, supposedly a Jew, and was to consist of a panel discussion among a rabbi and two pastors. Ley immediately saw the tentacles of the Jewish conspiracy reaching out to strike at the movement and quickly decided to act. He called out SA and SS units from Cologne and from areas as far away as Koblenz and Wiesbaden with the intent of going to Rastätten, holding his own meeting, and spreading propaganda in the streets. Around 4.00 p.m. on March 6 over 125 Nazis converged in trucks on the small town; the other meeting had already concluded. Ley determined to speak in the local hall, but it was soon overflowing and had to be cleared. He thereupon climbed upon a truck bed on the main square and began to harangue the crowd which gathered. In his speech he stressed the dangers which Jews represented to the local peasants, who, if they weren't careful, might lose their farms. While Ley spoke, his men fanned out, marching about the streets shouting SA slogans like "Clear the streets" and selling Nazi propaganda. In the meantime, the mayor asked Ley to clear the square. While the two were conferring, things got out of hand. Stormtroopers, hearing that there were Jews in the hotel, smashed their way in and started beating up a young man. The undermanned rural gendarmes, of whom there were only several, tried to intervene. They too were set upon by the stormtroopers. One officer was knocked down and trampled. To save him, another drew his pistol and fired what was supposed to be a warning shot. But in the mêlée the shot went into the crowd and between the eyes of one of Ley's young followers, one Wilhelm Wilhelmi, who died instantly.

This effectively stopped the riot. The remaining officers, fearing a lynching, fled into the hotel. Ley got his men under control again and formed them into columns. They took the body to the mortuary, got into their trucks, and headed out of town. At the edge of town, they shouted at a Jewish-looking young woman with her baby in arms that they would return and "cut the throats of the Jews." On the way home the Nazis stopped at a tavern in Braubach to slake the thirst undoubtedly generated by their violent activities. Shortly after, as they were about to cross the Rhine bridge at Lahnstein, they were apprehended by larger police units.

The incident had immediate consequences. The dissolution of the larger locals (Cologne and Koblenz) along with several smaller ones (including Ley's own of Wiesdorf) was ordered by the civilian authorities. The Cologne ban would last for nearly a year, thanks to Ley's frequently provocative behavior. At the same time, the *Westdeutscher Beobachter* was also temporarily banned.[37]

Ley took a defiant stance. Meeting with his people in Cologne shortly after the banning, he decided to put the members of the dissolved locals directly under Gau authority (some suggested they be put directly under the Reichsleitung in Munich, but Ley refused. He would thereby lose control over both dues and membership cards).[38] He also embarked on a series of speeches in which he blamed the whole incident on provocative Jewish behavior and again raised the spectacle of the Jews as the main threat to the Nazi movement. At the same time, he initiated a personal vendetta with Cologne Police Chief Bauknecht, one which would rival that between Goebbels and Vice Police-president Weiss in Berlin. Ley directed a letter of protest at Bauknecht in which he accused him of violating the civil rights of the Nazis and undermining the very state which he was supposed to uphold "with an energy and ruthless singlemindedness beside which even Metternich's police methods would pale." Ley concluded: "You can be sure, that the struggle for the Third Reich will progress without stumbling over police decrees." From this point on the "Bauknechtpolizei" would be a favorite target in Ley's paper.[39]

In the meantime, Ley sent Grohé to Munich to see if Hitler approved of his methods and actions. Hitler replied, in Grohé's words, "that he considered all the measures to be correct and was happy to have such fighters in the Rhineland."[40] Ley clearly had a green light for his future activities. It should not be a surprise that Hitler approved Ley's rough and ready tactics; they corresponded with an official change in Hitler's own stance that had been a

37. Ley appeared frequently in public places, particularly taverns, and gave political speeches despite the ban. He also ridiculed and goaded the police detectives who had been assigned to keep him under surveillance and occasionally engaged in materially destructive behavior. See following reports in LHAK, 403: report of mayor of Wiesdorf to the Düsseldorf Regierungspräsident of September 17, 1927 (pp. 391–4); report of the Düsseldorf Regierungspräsident to Minister of the Interior of October 3, 1927 (pp. 375–89).
38. See report of the Düsseldorf Regierungspräsident to the Koblenz Regierungspräsident of April 22, 1927, with enclosures LHAK 403/13381, pp. 826–45.
39. Ley to Bauknecht, April 8, 1927, in LHAK, 403/13381, pp. 819–23.
40. See police report of April 9, 1927, as enclosure in Düsseldorf Regierungspräsident to Koblenz Oberpräsident, April 22, 1927, in LHAK, 403, p. 839.

product of the party day at Weimar the previous August. Prior to that the Nazis had worked more quietly than openly, concentrating on developing propaganda directives and extending their network of locals. After Weimar much more stress was to be laid on public agitation. Now the Nazis often shouted the slogan "Wir prügeln uns gross" (We'll become great through brawling). It was a slogan to which Ley could subscribe with relish.[41]

The Rastätten incident is interesting for two further reasons. It provided the pretext for one of the first Nazi martyrs — a kind of prototype for Horst Wessel several years later. Wilhelmi, the young man who was shot at Rastätten, became a martyred saint for the Rhenish branch of the movement. Adulatory poems about this young ruffian appeared regularly in Ley's paper. Regular pilgrimages were conducted to his flower-bedecked grave. His name was regularly invoked to inspire the "party comrades" to greater sacrifices.

Finally, the Rastätten incident also illustrates some of the depth of Robert Ley's anti-semitism and its links both to his past and to his social insecurity. Ley, like several other prominent Nazis (Heydrich, Eichmann, or even Hitler himself) was particularly sensitive about any possible link between himself and the Jews. With the others it was the fear of the possible taint of Jewish blood. With Ley, it was having to live with frequent accusations by his enemies in the party that he himself was a Jew. These unfounded accusations rested in part on his name (his real name is Levy and he just dropped the "v" they said), partly on his appearance (his receding hairline and facial appearance could fit the Nazi stereotype of the Jew) and partly on his place of work (IG Farben was considered by Nazi propagandists to be a "Jewish" firm because of the presence of prominent Jews on its board of directors and was frequently referred to as "IG Farben and IG Moloch"). Ley was sufficiently concerned about these accusations to have a party investigation launched, which cleared him of any such allegations. But investigation or not, it was a subject about which Ley was very nervous, given his extreme insecurity and the potentially lethal danger of being drummed out of the movement and consigned to the forces of evil.[42] Given his very labile personality, exacerbated by the frontal lobe

41. See police report of July 15, 1927, in BAK, R134/51, p. 95.
42. On the fears of Hitler see Alan Bullock, *Hitler: A Study in Tyranny* (Harper & Bros., London, 1952), p. 24. On IG Farben as a "Jewish" company, see Joseph Borkin, *The Crime and Punishment of I.G. Farben* (New York, 1978), p. 54. The report clearing Ley is from Dr G. at NS Auskunft to Buch at USCHLA of

injury, it took very little to set Ley off on his anti-semitic tirades. Thus the news of the "Jewish" meeting at Rastätten — and one to be chaired by a rabbi named "Levy" at that — triggered Ley's precipitate decision to go there with his stormtroopers. Nor was his brief speech to the peasants in Rastätten entirely a calculated appeal to widespread resentments in the countryside to Jewish traders. Ley said, "Peasant, if the Jew even looks into your farmyard, you've already lost five marks; if he comes in, you've lost 50 marks; if you throw in with him, then you've lost the entire farm. So, peasant, protect yourself and drive him away."[43] In the urgency of Ley's remarks one can hear the echoes of the traumatic incident in his youth when his father lost the farm. Always unsure about his father's true guilt, it was an easy transference to shift the guilt for all such incidents onto the Jew.

But it was not just the "Devil" whom Ley felt he had to contend with; there was also the devilish infighting within the party itself. In any party like the Nazi Party, which depended on a great deal of grass-roots initiative to grow, there was bound to be a great deal of rivalry, as strong people jockeyed for power and influence. Hitler's own belief in a competitive Social Darwinistic approach, combined with his inability to do much more than to confirm local *faits accomplis* in the early days of the party, only compounded this tendency toward intraparty strife. Moreover, there was a built-in source of conflict in the Gaue that lay in the tension between the political leadership as vested in the Gauleiter and the SA organization, which jealousy guarded its independence and jurisdictions. Ley's own proclivity for arbitrary and precipitous behavior toward his rivals only exacerbated the strife within his own Gau.

A major squabble in the Rhineland Gau ensued between Ley and the SA and SS leaders, especially in Cologne. Already at a general membership meeting early in 1927 Ley complained that the Cologne local had been his "troubled child" (*Schmerzenskind*) and that the SA organization there "was still in baby shoes."[44] Things had not

---

September 3, 1932; accusations continued to haunt Ley even after he was in power. See letter to the editor of *Stürmer* of June 27, 1933, in Berlin Document Center (hereafter BDC): File Ley. The rumor persisted after the war. See also statement by Father Adolf Bormann (son of Martin) of September 25, 1958, asserting that Ley was a "full Jew": Institut für Zeitgeschichte, Munich; Aktennotiz Buchheim ZS/1701.

43. From 7 March 7, 1927, report of Ley interrogation in LHAK, 403/13381, p. 777.
44. See "Bericht über die Generalmitgliederversammlung der NSDAP," January 25, 1927, in LHAK, 403/13381, pp. 629–35.

changed that much by the end of the year. At a leadership conference Ley attacked directly the Gau leader, Dr Hans (coincidentally also a chemist) and his adjutant Sitt. Ley pointed to the "exceedingly sad state of the Cologne local" and underscored strongly the fact that the SA activities had come to a standstill. Activism and discipline alike in the SA were down drastically, said Ley. "Anyone can open his yap and wear a uniform," he went on, what was needed was deeds and not just words.[45]

In the wake of this attack upon them, Hans and Sitt established during the course of 1928 a faction against Ley in the party, which included Hermann Schmitz, Gau SS leader as well as Willi Kaiser, Gau Hitler Youth Leader, and a number of others.[46] By summer the feud had taken on such proportions that Hitler issued instructions banning any public display on the occasion of the annual midsummer festival in Caub, lest the factionalism spread into the streets. In fact, the Führer forbade any large rallies in the Rhine Gau until the differences between Hans and Ley should be settled.[47]

By fall Ley had decided to expel the whole lot from the party and got the agreement of the SA leadership in Munich to dismiss them from the SA as well. As new SS leader, Ley installed his old friend and predecessor, Haake, also with Munich's permission.[48]

The excluded members did not hesitate to take their case both to the party court and to the public. They accused Ley of being a half-Jew named Levy, of embezzling party funds for personal purposes, and (this accusation included Grohé as well) of printing sensationalistic articles in the paper, which defamed the party.

The party court rejected their accusations for lack of evidence. [49] They had more success initially with SA leader Pfeffer von Salomon, whom Hans visited in Munich. The expelled members were put directly under the Reichsleitung, but no actions were taken against Ley or Grohé for fear of weakening the party itself. The official status

45. Report of Cologne Regierungspräsident to Koblenz Oberpräsident of December 9, 1927, in LHAK, 403/13382, pp. 523–6.
46. See later report from Cologne Polizeipräsident to Cologne Regierungspräsident of January 12, 1929, in LHAK, 403/16744, pp. 221–7.
47. See Hitler *Verfügung* of June 8, 1928, in Institut für Zeitgeschichte, Munich, Fa 223/52; also Grohé to Reichsleitung, July 6, 1928, in BDC: File Grohé.
48. See OSAF, Munich to SSVM, Cologne of October 1, 1928, in LHAK, 403/16743, p. 831; also report from the Cologne Polizeipräsident to the Cologne Regierungspräsident of October 9, 1928, ibid., pp. 825–9.
49. In its reply to Hans, USCHLA rejected the charges as unfounded. Letter of November 8, 1928, in Institut für Zeitgeschichte, Munich, Fa 223/52.

of the *Westdeutscher Beobachter* was however temporarily revoked in recognition of their complaints about Grohé's hate articles.[50]

Not satisfied with this, the opposition also began to leak information to the left-wing press, including the Communist *Socialist Republic* and the Socialist *Volksstimme*. One article had Ley frequenting a brothel in Cologne. On one occasion, allegedly, he could not pay his bill and had to leave his swastika-bedecked jacket behind as collateral only to be dunned later for the money.[51]

These articles, in turn, led to a round of accusations, counter-accusations, and law suits. Ley attacked his tormenters on the pages of his paper (despite Hitler's injunction that intraparty battles not be fought out in the party press), while they retorted in printed flyers. Former SS leader Schmitz attacked Ley on the street with a horsewhip, while Grohé, taken to court by Sitt on charges of perjury, beat up Sitt on the street with a wrench. It was a kind of rivalry which would beset the Gau from this time forward and ultimately lead to the division of the Gau in 1931.[52]

From the first the struggle had taken on a generational cast, with some of the younger, more radical leaders, like Grohé, asserting their right to indulge in any form of behavior which might advance the movement, while older members still found certain forms of behavior offensive under any circumstances. One striking case involved Grohé's article in the *Westdeutcher Beobachter* castigating public officials in the most scurrilous terms. Particularly at issue were articles by both Grohé and Ley which amounted to a campaign of vilification against Koblenz police inspector Lehnhoff in particular and the city administration in general. The campaign was, once again, a spin-off of the infamous Rastätten incident of early 1927. It had been the Koblenz police alone among local authorities who had been willing to apprehend Ley and his fleeing stormtroopers after

50. Report of Cologne Polizeipräsident to Cologne Regierungspräsident of January 12, 1929, in LHAK, 403/16744, p. 223.
51. Ibid., p. 225. See also article entitled "There's a Crackling in the NSDAP Timbers," *Volksstimme*, no. 163, September 11, 1928; a less reliable source had Ley trying to get one of his men to seduce a factory owner's wife, so that Ley could then blackmail her. See Paul Friedrich Merker, *Deutschland, sein oder nicht sein?* (Mexico City, El libra libre, 1944, vol. II, p. 335.
52. See footnote 50 above. For Hitler's order of September 17, 1928, which appeared in all party papers, see BAK, Schumacher Sammlung, 350. For remarks on the factionalism in the Koblenz local, see police report from Koblenz to the Regierungspräsident in Koblenz of March 25, 1929, in LHAK, 403/16745, pp. 251–7. For a detailed discussion of the rivalries in the Cologne local among SS, SA, and political leadership see Corsten, "NSDAP," pp. 32–44.

the incident and Koblenz officials who had most effectively and rigorously enforced the resulting ban on the Nazi Party. Grohé and Ley hated this and determined to destroy the career of Lehnhoff and, if possible, of Mayor Russel as well. In addition to calling these gentlemen "vermin and upstarts" (*Schädlinge und Emporkömmlinge*) in their paper, they also accused Lehnhoff, who headed the vice squad, of moral infractions.[53] This brought not only a libel suit against the two but complaints to the party central in Munich as well. The head of the party court, aging retired major Heinemann, apparently sympathized with the complaint, for he received an impatient defense of the articles from Grohé based on the right of youth to do whatever was necessary to advance the goals of the movement.

> One particular reason why I have taken up the case of Lehnhoff lies in the fact that the police authorities in Koblenz have been combating our movement with methods which we have not experienced in other cities. If we succeed in toppling Lehnhoff, then we will not only appear to the public as champions for purity in public life [*sic*], but will have dealt police Chief Dr Biesten a blow which will redound to our benefit. . . . In our struggle it is not incumbent upon us to ask whether some old gentleman is in agreement, or whether he is pleased or not when we make an old acquaintance the target of our fight, but rather to ask what serves the progress of our movement. . . . As a National Socialist young in years I would ask you, Herr Major, to make the effort to understand the youthful world.[54]

But it was not only the police officials in Koblenz who made trouble for Ley (and vice versa), the town was also the center of a putative revolt of party members who complained bitterly to Munich about Ley's corruption and unreliable leadership. One such complaint pointed to conditions in Koblenz which threatened to spill over into other parts of the Gau. Ley had violated the trust put in him by the membership. Ley covers up by conveying a rosy picture in his reports and then tells anyone who dissents to shut up. Everything is "ship shape" (*in bester Ordnung*) in Koblenz, Ley insists, while in reality older, knowledgeable comrades are incensed

53. For an extensive report on Nazi attacks against the Koblenz municipal administration, see Koblenz Oberbürgermeister to Koblenz Regierungspräsident of October 12, 1928, in LHAK 403/16743, pp. 673–97.
54. Grohé's letter to USCHLA of January 21, 1928, quoted in Tyrell, *Führer befiehl*, pp. 287–8.

about Ley's supporters, whom the writer characterizes as "half-educated hangers-on," "obtrusive scum," and "job hunters" who are on the "lowest step of morality." Thanks to these people the movement in Koblenz lacks "content," "intellectual depth," and "comradely solidarity." Moreover, Ley's own behavior there had been "damaging to the party," particularly his financial reports, which are a "heavy-handed swindle." Suspicions abound that party moneys are being diverted into Ley's own newspaper accounts.[55]

In fact, the suspicions about Ley's mismanagement of money in connection with his newspaper endeavors were not unfounded. Nor were the comments about the abysmally low intellectual content of the paper. Given the fact that much of Ley's later work with the DAF would have to do with "educating" the workers, and that the DAF itself would become a veritable swamp of corruption, it behooves us at this point to look more closely at the antecedents of both Ley's press propaganda and his venality during the *Kampfzeit*, for the two are not unrelated.

From the very beginning, "conquering" a Gau meant reaching and mobilizing the public — in an age before the modern electronic media, primarily through speeches and the press. The Nazi Party leadership laid a great stress on both approaches. In terms of style and content both tended toward rather crude sensationalism. As Goebbels, the premier Nazi propagandist put it: "It was not our intent to found an information sheet, which would replace the daily paper for our followers. . . . Our goal was not to inform, but to egg on, to fire up, to urge on. The organ that we founded should in a sense act as a whip to wake the dilatory sleeper from his slumber and to drive him forward to restless action."[56]

In whatever Gau Nazi papers happened to appear, they had several things in common: their crude and vituperative language coupled with frequent suspensions; the fact that they were most often local products, founded through the initiative of the Gau Leader and Kreisleiter; and that they usually began as weekly newspapers between 1925 and 1930, then converted to dailies after 1930. Most found themselves often in financial trouble. As one analyst described them, "no capital, no regular subscribers, no advertising; the office established in one or two rooms with borrowed furniture; a

55. See Oskar Dönch to Reichsleitung, August 8, 1928, in BDC: File Ley.
56. Joseph Goebbels, *Kampf um Berlin* (Berlin, Munich, Franz Eher Verlag, 1938), p. 188.

single telephone connection, and a printing contract with any sympathizers who would extend credit." They also shared the goal of seeking recognition from party headquarters as officially designated party organs. There were thirty-one officially recognized publications, nineteen of which had the additional honor of being designated official organs. These papers were entitled to use the swastika on their letterhead. One of them was the *Westdeutscher Beobachter*, official voice of the Nazi Party in the Rhineland and Roberts Ley's voice in print.[57]

Not long after taking over as Gauleiter, Ley announced the publication of the *Westdeutscher Beobachter* and requested that the Reichsleitung recognize it as an official organ of the party. Headquarters complied. Initially, the paper remained property of the Gau with Joseph Grohé as editor and publisher. In 1928, however, Ley himself took possession of the *Westdeutscher Beobachter* and became publisher.[58]

From the first the *Westdeutscher Beobachter* was a scandal sheet; a sensationalist paper that thrived on vilifying Communists, Socialist, Jews, the Republic and its politicians. A typical issue of the paper would include a provocative headline to grab the eye of the potential reader, often alluding to local scandal. Some examples: "Merry Barhopping by Police Captain Oberdorfer"; "Sex Crime in the House of Tietz" (large department store chain founded by the Jew Hermann Tietz); "The Jew Hirsch Seduces a Nine-year-old Girl"; "Police Orgies in a Brothel"; "Violator of Women Lichtenstein. Jewish Sadism".[59] Like our own sensational rags of today the story following the headline would often turn out to be full of lies, distortions, or innuendo, which resulted in many suits for slander or defamation of character. Also on the front page would appear a light article by some prominent Nazi leader, often the Gauleiter. Then in the following pages came the features, which included: "Aus der

57. See Oron J. Hale, *The Captive Press in the Third Reich* (Princeton, Princeton University Press, 1964), pp. 41, 46–7, 50–1. There were conditions for official recognition. Editors had to observe the party line and follow directives from the propaganda office; they were subject to reprimand for breach of party regulations; they had to include, gratis, announcements emanating from party headquarters,and they were forbidden to accept advertisements from Jewish firms.
58. Ley to *Reichsleitung*, September 28, 1925, in BAK Schumacher Sammlung, 203. The first issue of the *Westdeutscher Beobachter* bearing Ley's name on the masthead was March 4, 1928.
59. Headlines are from the following dates in 1928: September 2, September 9, September 23, November 25.

Bewegung" (From the Movement), a calendar of events; "Das schwarze Brett" (The Bulletin Board), which brought stories from individual towns in the Gau; "Family Mammon," which specialized in stories about Jewish influence; "We Demand," which posed Nazi demands on the Gau and one feature on Nazi activities throughout Germany which hadn't found their way into other newspapers termed *Journaille* — a combination of journalism and canaille, indicating what the Nazis, who were in a position to know, would term "gutter journalism."

Using these attention-grabbing techniques, the paper was boasting a circulation of 14,000 per week by early 1927, which encouraged its editor, Grohé, to claim that it had developed "alongside the SA into a feared weapon on behalf of the Adolf Hitler idea in the Rhineland."[60]

It was in keeping with the Nazi movement as a millenarian phenomenon, that its press would seek to develop objective enemies, devil figures as focus of attack. One, who has already been mentioned, was Polizeipräsident Bauknecht of Cologne, who was regularly enlisted in the columns of the *Westdeutscher Beobachter* on the side of evil. As a police observer recorded the words of Haake during one rally, "He emphasized that in the current struggle the Cologne police president and Dr Ley stood opposite one another. Even if police-president Bauknecht had all the means at his disposal, Ley could be assured that the idealism of his followers stood behind him."[61] On the heels of the Rastätten incident, for example, Bauknecht had banned the Cologne branch of the party. When the local was reconstituted in different form, Bauknecht wrote Ley a letter "to avoid any doubt" that he was aware of the trick. Ley responded in an insulting public letter on the front page of the *Westdeutscher Beobachter*: "'To avoid any doubt' you feel compelled once again to remind us of your ban. Do you believe that in doing so you are being more effective? The opposite is the case! You run more the risk of appearing ridiculous. The louder the dog barks, the less he is inclined to bite." Then Ley goes on to contrast Bauknecht, the former worker, with his aristocratic predecessors:

> You have taken on the social manners and the mindless repressive techniques of your monarchical predecessors, but you lack their courage

60. See "Bericht über die Generalmitgliederversammlung der NSDAP," January 25, 1927, in LHAK, 403/13381, p. 633.
61. Police report from Wiesdorf of April 9, 1927, in LHAK, 403/13381, p. 843.

> and their capability to carry out the duties of their high office effectively. "To avoid any doubt", we are informing you that we will tirelessly exercise our constitutional right in word and in print to spread the National Socialist idea. Morally, constitutionally and legally the bans are wrong. Go ahead and ban, we shall work! . . . Herr Police President, resign. The hour belongs to young Germany! [62]

Other similar targets included Police Inspector Lehnhoff in Koblenz, who was, as we have noted, a particular target of Grohé, as well as the Lord Mayor of Cologne, Konrad Adenauer, whom the Nazi press accused of fostering an independence movement in the Rhineland during the French occupation. Adenauer, with his high cheekbones and drawn skin also presented a racial target; he was often cast in the role of a Jew by exaggerating his "Mongolian" features.

Ley could also launch major campaigns against political parties. The Communists and Socialist were, of course, daily fare. But he was also capable of attacking the Catholic Center Party, a risky enterprise in the Catholic Rhineland, when the opportunity presented itself. In early 1931, for example, during the battle over the Young Plan, Ley launched a series of sharp attacks against the Center Party, whose man Brüning was Chancellor. The usual headlines followed: "Dr Ley Proclaims: Destroy the Center, the Patron of Bolshevism"; "Incitement to Murder by the Enslavement Parties"; "Millions in Tax Money for Dirty Spying on the NSDAP"; "The Center Prefers Bolshevism to a Drop of National Pride"; "Black Treason! Center County Official Drinks with Polacks".[63]

One specialty of the *Westdeutscher Beobachter* was finding (or inventing) local scandals with which to titillate its readers, often for weeks on end. One such occasion involved a restaurant chain in Cologne owned by the family Katz-Rosenthal. On April 24, 1928, an amateur boxer named Jack Domgörgen was eating in the restaurant when he allegedly found a cooked mouse under the meat on his plate. Confronting the wife of the owner, he soon found himself in a wrangle with restaurant employees, during the course of which the evidence disappeared down a toilet. The upshot was that the boxer sued the restaurant, while the restaurant countersued for libel and theft (presumably Domgörgen was reluctant to pay for his meal).

62. *Westdeutscher Beobachter*, November 6, 1927, p. 1.
63. Headlines are from January 31, February 21, February 22, March 4, and March 11, 1928, respectively.

Ley leaped on the incident and tried to create a local *cause célèbre*, linking the "Jewish" restaurant with the sale of rotten meat. It was an ideal opportunity to play on real local resentments, not only on the part of consumers but also German restaurateurs. The *Westdeutscher Beobachter* editorialized: " The firm Katz-Rosenthal is well known as a firm which is trying with all available means to open outlets and restaurants in all parts of the city, thereby driving out small businesses."[64] The various law suits provided the opportunity to drag out the scandal for months. But the tactic worked; circulation of the *Westdeutscher Beobachter* went from 10,000 to 40,000 during the campaign against Katz-Rosenthal.

By far the most frequent target of Ley and his paper were the Jews, either on a grand scale (Weimar as "Jewish Republic") or, as in the case of the Katz-Rosenthal family, on a local basis. Nowhere does Ley's vituperative hatred for the Jews as devil figures come out more clearly than in the headlines of his paper. He never missed an opportunity to castigate them in every manner possible with insouciant disregard for the consequences. Already in October 1925 Ley was arrested for defaming the murdered Foreign Minister, Walter Rathenau. In late 1927 he was fined 300 marks (or sentenced to one month in jail) for referring to the Republic in print as "Dirty Jew Republic." Such official rebukes, however, only fired Ley's fanaticism.[65]

Among Ley's favorite Jewish targets was the Tietz department store chain. Here he was able to play on widespread resentments on the part of artisans and small retailers against the large firm whose mass marketing techniques seemed so threatening. As the mayor of the town noted, this sort of attack went over very well in Koblenz:

> The paper draws all the more attention because Koblenz is a middle-sized town in which sensationalist papers by their very nature cause a greater sensation than in large cities. Add to that the fact that wide circles of the populace here, who were prosperous pensioners before the war, are now impoverished and dissatisfied and, further, that numerous business-

64. See *Westdeutscher Beobachter*, May 20 and May 27, 1928; it was a campaign which local Nazis remembered fondly for years to come. Kiehl, *Mann an der Fahne*, pp. 126–30. On *Westdeutscher Beobachter* circulation, see Corsten, "NSDAP", p. 25.
65. See report from Koblenz Bürgermeister to Regierungspräsident of October 12, 1928, in LHAK, 403/16743, pp. 683–4; also Düsseldorf Regierungspräsident to Koblenz Oberpräsident, February 10, 1928; and *Westdeutscher Beobachter*, November 13, 1927.

> men, who before the war had a rich source of income from the strong German garrison and the large number of retirees, are now struggling for their existence and are angry. The *Westdeutscher Beobachter* cleverly exploits this mood and foments dissatisfaction in evey way. So it is that certain business circles, which are against Jewish businesses and feel threatened particularly by the powerful expansion of the Tietz department store, support the paper and reach greedily for it.[66]

Nor did Ley hesitate, quite in the spirit of Julius Streicher's scurrilous anti-semitic rag, *Der Stürmer*, to use a pornographic approach to titillate as well as to enflame his readers. A regular theme in *Westdeutscher Beobachter* was the lustful Jew seducing or raping the innocent German girl. One issue headlined: "How the Jewish Furniture Store Owner Ravished a German Woman. The Blonde Soija and the Alien. Blood and Body contaminated." Another story about a rape commented: "The Asiatic scoundrel, schooled in the Talmud as a violator of girls also raped his father's maid."[67]. Occasionally, he would combine the social and sexual themes and have the rape occur at the hands of a Tietz manager.

But by far the most lethal anti-semitic theme pursued by Ley, one that got him in trouble both with the law and with his own party, was that of ritual murder. It was a theme which obsessed him, even to the point where he read in the Talmud for quotes to support his contention that orthodox Jews found it necessary as part of their religious practice to slit the throats of young Christian males and to drink their blood. It was one of those myths about the Jews deeply embedded in Western popular Christianity and Ley's embracing of it indicated the power it still had even in the twentieth century.

The unsolved murder of a young high school student in March 1928 provided Ley with the opportunity to sensationalize his beliefs about ritual murder. The boy's body had allegedly been left in front of his home, castrated, and drained of blood. The initial suspect, a classmate, had demonstrated his innocence. No other suspect was at hand. That vacuum drew in the *Westdeutscher Beobachter* on October 28 with the headline: "Daube Murdered by Jews." The article which followed alleged that the boy had really been taken to a synagogue and ritually murdered for his blood, after which he had been mutilated to simulate a sexual crime and throw the police off the

66. Koblenz Bürgermeister to Regierungspräsident, Koblenz, October 12, 1928 in LHAK, 403/16743, p. 675.
67. *Westdeutscher Beobachter* issues of May 5, 1929, and May 13, 1928, respectively.

trail. An accompanying picture on the front page illustrated graphically the inside of a synagogue where a number of Jews are holding a naked figure over a container and slitting his throat.

The authorities acted immediately. The issue was confiscated and Ley was charged by the states attorney with insulting the Jewish religion, incitement to violence, and gross misdemeanor. Undeterred, Ley went on—in a somewhat more pseudo-scholarly vein—to defend his accusation of ritual murder in an article entitled "Ritual Murder. A Study in Race." The case was sufficiently serious that the Prussian Diet, in which Ley sat as a deputy of the Nazi Party, voted to suspend his parliamentary immunity in order that he be prosecuted. On July 21, 1929, he was convicted and fined 1,000 marks.[68]

The very next evening, Ley appeared before a public meeting and repeated in an hour-and-a-half speech his accusations of ritual murder, quoting at length from the Talmud. His method and conclusions were frightening, and full of foreboding: a pseudo-scholarly attempt to create a devil, which, in turn, had to be destroyed. His concluding words, as recorded by the police observer, could not have been clearer in light of later events:

> Dr Ley then expanded on the race problem, which he tried to substantiate scientifically. In doing so he characterized the Jews as parasites, whose extermination (*Ausrottung*) was the duty of every racially aware person. He concluded his remarks with the words of the Cologne rabbi, Dr Rosenthal, who is supposed to have said, "now the National Socialists are becoming dangerous, for Dr Ley is beginning to substantiate his teachings scientifically." It is good that the Jews are coming to this realization, for the National Socialist doctrine should definitely be dangerous to them. All Jews would have to die so that Germany might live. (*All Juda müsse sterben, damit Deutschland leben könne.*)[69]

Even some segments of the party were appalled at the gutter anti-semitism of Ley's paper. A number of members complained to the party court, which itself took action against Ley on November

68. See *Westdeutscher Beobachter*, November 11, 1928, and August 4, 1929; also report of July 29, 1929, from Cologne Polizeipräsident (Bauknecht) to Cologne Regierungspräsident in LHAK, 403/16746, pp. 527–9, respectively; see also *Kölner Jüdisches Wochenblatt* of July 21 and August 2, 1929, for description and commentary on trial. The latter article made note of Ley's stammering and lisping in court.
69. Ibid., report of July 27, 1929, p. 517.

11, 1928. Noting that the tone of the paper had changed since Ley took over as editor, Walter Buch, chair of the court, wrote in his report: "While before there was nothing in the content to find fault with, from that point on [i.e. Ley's takeover] the tone of the paper got worse and worse. It became a purely anti-semitic rag (*Radaublatt*), which occupied itself with the most evil things. This tone is simply not compatible with the symbol of the party on its masthead." Buch went on to mention other incidents, including the story of Ley in the brothel and concluded: "Because of all these incidents Uschla feels compelled to propose that for several months at least the *Westdeutscher Beobachter* lose its right to carry the official party emblem." It tells us something about the intensity of Robert Ley's fanaticism and his lack of judgment that even high officials of his own, avowedly anti-semitic party should have felt that he had gone too far. Fortunately for Ley, his Führer was as fanatical as he was, and the Uschla order was quashed.[70]

Ley's dangerous apocalyptic demagoguery did not just achieve expression in occasional remarks and articles in his newspaper. It was also institutionalized in courses which Ley and Grohé set up to train neophyte Nazi speakers. Here they tried to anticipate questions which the public might raise about Nazi ideology and give the proper response. As to the question, aren't Jews people too? Ley encouraged the response: "Sure the Jew is also a person. None of us has ever denied that. But the flea is also an animal — only not a very pleasant one. And since the flea is not a pleasant animal we don't see it as our duty to watch over and protect it, to allow it to flourish so that it can stick and pain and torture us, rather we must render it harmless. And so it is with the Jews." Nor was there any doubt in these courses that Ley regarded the movement as anything else but a quasi-religious one: "Our task can only be to soften up the enemy. We must rob him of his faith in his panacea. Then he will soon regard us as the bringers of a new evangelism. A public gathering is like a sermon, after which even the just fall seven times a day."[71]

A major thrust, then, of Ley's activities as a leading Nazi during the *Kampfzeit* was to "educate" people both through the press and through a variety of courses. He had a powerful, built-in drive to

70. See USCHLA report in letter Buch to Ley of November 8, 1928; also warning letter of October 29 in BDC: File Ley.

71. Text of a "politischer Schulungskurs für Führer" included in report of Polizeipräsident Bauknecht dated June 20, 1928. In LHAK, 403/16743, pp. 227 and 245, respectively.

proselytize. This drive continued after Hitler came to power, as Ley developed the DAF into a major organization to integrate the worker into the new Germany through "educating" him in a wide variety of ways. Nor did Ley abandon his newspaper; the *Westdeutscher Beobachter* became after 1933, with the exception of the *Völkischer Beobachter*, the most widely circulated of all Nazi daily papers.[72]

None of Ley's multifarious activities in spreading the Nazi faith came cheaply though. Newspapers cost money to run; public meetings and rallies were expensive to promote. And party headquarters in Munich, itself on a tight budget, was not providing the capital; it all had to be raised locally. This fund-raising provided both a challenge and a temptation. And Ley's response on the Gau level would foreshadow his later activities during the Third Reich, when he would have access to funds on such a massive scale that they would dwarf the amounts of the *Kampfzeit*.

Once the Nazi Party had transformed itself under the impact of the deepening Depression from a fringe sect to a mass movement —from about the summer of 1930—it proved quite successful at generating large amounts of money. Taking their cue from the Socialists, the Nazis' party organizers created a system of party books with stamps to record the payment of regular dues. Before long quite large amounts of money were flowing regularly from bottom to top, providing the party at the national level with extraordinary financial autonomy and allowing it to compete with the much larger Social Democratic Party. Ley's Gau was particularly successful in this regard, and its ability to generate funds was higher than the Reich average. One police report from September 1930 noted that for the month of August alone, the Rhineland Gau had sent 45,800 marks to the treasury in Munich. "With receipts like that," the report concluded, "it won't be difficult for the NSDAP to pay its speakers well and besides that to spend a considerable amount for propaganda purposes too." But during the lean years between 1925 and 1930 it had not been that way, and even in the better years which were now dawning the locals and the Gaus still had to look out for themselves, since most of the money was going to headquarters. Given Ley's organizational megalomania, which was already becoming evident in these early years, the paucity of funds at the local level meant trouble.[73]

72. Hale, *Captive Press*, p. 53; additional material on the *Westdeutscher Beobachter* can be found in NSDAP Hauptarchiv, Roll 49, Folder 1155.

73. Report of Polizeipräsident Winkler, Cologne, to Regierungspräsident, Cologne,

But Ley had an additional financial problem. As of January 1, 1928, he was discharged from his lucrative position at Bayer-Leverkusen. The firm's management had demonstrated a good deal of patience and tolerance for Ley's extracurricular political activities during the prior two years, including the incident at Rastätten and the increasingly shrill anti-semitic utterances.

The last straw, however, was apparently when Ley, in one of his speeches insulted Max Warburg, a member of the IG Farben board of directors. Warburg turned to Herrmann Bücher, who belonged to Farben's economic council (Wirtschaftsbeirat) as well as to the main representative organization of German industry (Reichsverband der Industrie). Bücher induced the Bayer management to demand an apology from Ley.

Ley communicated this demand to Hitler on the occasion of the Gauleiter meeting at Weimar on November 27, 1927, and sought the Führer's advice. Hitler advised him not to apologize but rather to ask the firm "what ethical and moral right they had to make such a demand." Ley did so and was confronted with the choice: either cease his public appearances or lose his job. Ley decided to leave. As he wrote to Hitler on December 27:

> Now I am free. It is good that way. Of what use is the nicest and most secure position when Germany is going under. I also said that to management. I'll buy myself a little farm in order to sustain my family, however modestly. As for me, I will now dedicate myself completely to the party, in particular to my Gau and the *Westdeutscher Beobachter*, the editorship of which I have taken over. Within a year I hope to show you a Gau which belongs to the best. The foundations are already there."[74]

Now Ley had disengaged entirely from the bourgeois life and belonged entirely to the Nazi movement, and part of his dedication was expressed in the intent to build a Gau press empire. The problem was, with what financial means? Ley was now unemployed and had to live on the modest salary of a Gauleiter. He did, for

of September 18, 1930, in LHAK, 403/16753, p. 11. For an excellent study on the self-financing of the Nazi Party, based on the financial records of the Rhineland Gau, see Horst Matzerath and Henry Turner, "Die Selbsfinanzierung der NSDAP," *Geschichte und Gesellschaft*, vol. 3 (1977), pp. 59–92 and particularly their conclusions on p. 70.

74. See Grohé to Reichsleitung of December 21, 1927, and Ley to Hitler of same date in BAK NS26, vorl. 1356a and 1358a. Even the radical Grohé had to admit that the firm "had comported itself relatively decently."

a while, have the additional income of a Landtag deputy, but even this had been cut by the stingy party treasurer, Schwarz. Ley supposedly received a very generous severance allowance of 36,000 marks, enough to live on for quite a while by the standards of the time; but, as he explained to Hitler in his letter, he intended to use that to establish himself in agriculture—apparently the vision of the failed father still haunted him. But that turned out to be a very short-lived and unsuccessful endeavor. Just three months later the Gau was requesting that the Reichsleitung in its candidate list revert to referring to Ley's occupation as "chemist." "Pg. Dr Ley tried a while ago to establish himself in agriculture, but was not successful. As before he is now again a chemist, even if without a position." Not only had he lost his job, his house was gone too. By August 1928 he was sharing a room with a fellow Nazi while his wife and daughter stayed with relatives in neighboring Rupichteroth.[75]

How then was he going to secure the means to establish his newspaper empire? He needed a benefactor. He soon found one in the person of Friedrich Christian, Prince of Schaumburg-Lippe. The Prince, scion of a well-to-do noble family with its family seat at Bückeberg, had already been drawn to the Nazi movement through his acquaintance with Baldur von Schirach, the future Hitler Youth leader. Through the efforts of Rudolf Hess, future Deputy Führer, Lippe now came into contact with some of the Rhenish Nazis, among them Robert Ley. Ley, sensing an opportunity, invited Lippe for a meeting at the hotel "Bergischer Hof" in Bonn and regaled the prince with his vision. Lippe later recalled:

> The rather small, bull-necked, stuttering man at first made a disastrous impression on me. In the course of the conversation [however] I began to admire his energy and his apparent organizational talent. He wanted to know if I were interested in working for his press — and at the same time to invest my money in it. He reckoned up that I could earn a lot of money and would have a very interesting task.[76]

Sensing success, Ley went on to unfold for the prince his grandiose plans. "We'll build up a newspaper concern the likes of which Europe has never seen! Without a penny I've already established

75. See Grohé to Frick of April 3, 1928, in NSDAP Hauptarchiv, Roll 56, Folder 1356a; also report of Landrat in Opladen of October 9, 1928, in LHAK, 403/16743, p. 2, and *Westdeutscher Beobachter* of August 19, 1928, p. 3.
76. The account is from Schaumburg-Lippe, *Zwischen Krone und Kerker* (Wiesbaden, Limes Verlag, 1952), p. 95.

three papers, just with my work and my courage." But the empire was not to end with the press. Ley had even bigger ideas, ones in which we can already ascertain the beginnings of the jurisdictional omnicompetence, egotistical grasping for titles and dreams of a social utopia which would characterize Ley in the later Third Reich. "Dear Prince," he went on, "stick with me. I'll make my Rhineland into a social state which the world will scarcely find possible. Through my measures here I'll become so beloved that some day they'll call me the Duke of the Rhineland and everyone will find that completely natural!" The prince, always a very suggestible man, was bowled over. He later recalled: "He [Ley] pleaded his cause with such force of conviction, yes credibility, that it left me speechless. I said to myself: no wonder that Hitler supports this man."[77]

With the trusting prince's considerable funds at his disposal, augmented by what was left of his own money and loans from friends, Ley now went to work establishing his Westmark Verlag publishing operation. In order to publish not only his *Westdeutscher Beobachter* but also other papers in the Gau, which included the *Nationalblatt* in Koblenz and Trier (opened on June 1, 1930) as well as the *Westwacht* in Idar-Oberstein, all of them dailies, Ley purchased a large printing plant furnished with linotype machines, rotary presses, and other equipment. Not satisfied with this, Ley also paid 500,000 marks at the end of March 1929 for a stately building in Cologne, the so-called "Friesenpalast," which he hoped to completely renovate as his party headquarters, press center, and printing plant. To finance the renovation, he proposed issuing non-negotiable stocks at 100 marks each. Nor did he forget to tap the prince for an important status symbol for any Gau in those days — its own automobile. The prince donated a "Reo" to the Gau, which was reserved primarily for the use of Ley and his cronies.[78]

But things went wrong from the start. In his usual grandiose style,

77. Above quotes from Prince Schaumburg-Lippe, *Verdammte Pflicht und Schuldigkeit . . . Weg und Erlebnis 1914-1933* (Leoni, Druffel, 1966), pp. 169-171. The Prince's publications should be used with extreme caution, especially in the conclusions which he draws. In describing his business dealings with Ley, however, he is fairly accurate.

78. On Ley's press activities, see Ley to Bouhler, June 6, 1930, in BAK, Schumacher Sammlung, 203; also Hale, *Captive Press*, pp. 52–3; and Schaumburg-Lippe, *Zwischen*, pp. 95ff. On the Gau car, see Regierungspräsident, Koblenz to Oberpräsident, Koblenz, of September 23, 1930, in LHAK, 403/16759, p. 18; also Orlow, *Nazi Party*, vol. I, p. 94. On the Gau building plans, see report of Cologne Polizeipräsident to Cologne Regierungspräsident of May 6, 1929, with stock proposal attached in LHAK, 403/16745, pp. 369–75.

Ley had overreached himself. His management was poor. Characteristically, he had jumped prematurely into the operation without adequate attention to planning; six weeks was not a long enough gestation period for a publishing enterprise. Moreover, to save money, he had bought old typesetting machines, which turned out poor copy. He also hastily rented an inadequate building — on a ten-year lease! Papers were constantly late coming off the press and were poorly turned out.[79] What profits did come in were misused by cronies or funneled into party activities. Ley was never able to keep personal and political endeavors separate (another characteristic which would appear writ large during the Third Reich). The Prince, who played a sporadic managing role, tried to get other contracts for the press, but many potential customers, taking exception to Ley's politics, placed their orders elsewhere. Moreover, especially during election campaigns, Ley gave away large numbers of papers instead of selling them. The Prince, sinking deeper and deeper in the hole, could not escape Ley's requests. "If you don't contribute more at this point," Ley would say, "then you'll have lost everything."[80]

Ley, for his part, was trying everything to bring in money. Already several years before—in 1927—he'd stumbled on the technique of awarding copies of *Mein Kampf* along with autographed pictures of himself for multiple subscriptions. Now desperation became the mother of ever more inventive schemes. He sold stock in his Westmark Verlag to small businessmen and artisans, letting them believe that it was an official Nazi house. He also paid the clerical personnel of the Gau poor wages, while doing very well himself. In December 1930, for example, combining his salary as Gauleiter, his speaker honoraria, and his allowance as Landtag and Reichstag member, Ley was bringing in 2,350 marks per month. Office help got 200 marks on average, a disparity which led the police official who was reporting on the Nazi finances to comment laconically: "In any case, one can say that the leaders and functionaries of the national 'socialist' German 'workers' party seem to have understood how to completely solve the social question as far

79. This negative assessment came from Gustav Simon, who would be Ley's successor. See Simon Denkschrift to Strasser of March 12, 1931, in NS 22, vorl. 1056. It may be a bit exaggerated, but given Ley's tendencies, it is probably nearer to the truth than Hale's suggestion of a modern plant. Hale, *Captive Press*, p. 53.

80. Schaumburg-Lippe, *Zwischen*, p. 96: Ley had long been in the habit of distributing gratis copies of his *Westdeutscher Beobachter* at meetings. See report from Regierungspräsident, Trier, to Oberpräsident of September 4, 1929, in LHAK, 403/16747, p. 93.

as their own persons are concerned. It cannot however be demonstrated that they have shown any social understanding for the workers they hire as is demonstrated by the salaries and wages they are paid." Finally, in desperation, Ley sent his people literally begging for money. On one occasion it came to the attention of Munich headquarters that Ley had sent two men in a Nash car to make unauthorized collections, not only in the Gau, but outside as well.[81]

None of it was to any avail; Ley had overstretched himself. In March 1931, despite denials to that effect in the *Westdeutscher Beobachter*, the Westmark Verlag went bankrupt. The prince, who had complained in vain to Hitler, cut all financial ties to Ley, announcing his action in a rather lengthy and, for Ley, embarrassing newspaper advertisement. Ley responded in the *Westdeutscher Beobachter*, explaining his relationship with the prince in rather lame terms. Shortly thereafter, the Gau Uschla charged the prince with behavior damaging to the party, while the prince left his opulent villa in Bad Godesberg for a lengthy vacation in Austria. From Munich came a sharp rebuke from Strasser, who informed Ley that an investigation would be underway and that "It doesn't occur to anyone here to build party houses and that those kinds of collections, as you must know, are forbidden. There is a suspicion that the money collected is to be used for covering the debts of the Westmark Verlag and not for the announced purpose."[82]

As a final blow to Ley, he was picked up on March 27, 1931, by the police in order to serve a one-month sentence stemming from a 1929 conviction arising out of one of his newspaper articles. Three weeks later the Gau wrote to Munich requesting 1,500 marks to pay fines lest Ley face another three months behind bars; he was broke

81. For the autographed picture advertisement, see *Westdeutscher Beobachter*, July 31, 1927. On the sale of stock to locals, see *Auszug* of report of Cologne Polizeipräsident to Cologne Regierungspräsident of April 8, 1931, in BAK NS26, vorl. 1358a. On low-paid personnel, see report of Polizeipräsident to Regierungspräsident of December 20, 1930 in LHAK, 403/16733, p. 329. On unauthorized collections, see letter from Helle to Strasser of March 2, 1931, and Schwarz to Ley of March 10 in BDC: File Ley.

82. Strasser to Ley, March 10, 1931, in BDC: File Ley; also Ley to Strasser, March 17 in BA NS22, 1057, pp. 124–5. The prince printed a notice of his dissolving financial ties with Ley in the *Kölner Stadtanzeiger*, no. 137, April 4, 1931; see also *Westdeutscher Beobachter* January 19 and April 8, 1931; also Gau Uschla to Buch of April 10, 1931, in Helmuth Heiber, *Akten der Parteikanzlei der NSDAP* (Munich, Oldenbourg, 1983), 117/08758; also report from Bad Godesberg Bürgermeister to Cologne Polizeipräsident of October 1931, in NSDAP Hauptarchiv, Roll 56, Folder 1366.

and could not come up with the money.[83]

Ley was not the only Gauleiter to court financial disaster with a Gau publishing firm. Joseph Terboven skirted the edge of bankruptcy for years. But Ley's failure was the most spectacular and the one to which Hitler would point for years to come in warning against such enterprises. Too much party printing had to be done on faith and credit so that the usual profit calculations went out the window.[84]

In early 1931 then, just as the Nazi Party was rapidly developing into a mass movement nationwide, Robert Ley seemed to be in deep trouble. He had driven his Gau printing firm into bankruptcy. He had engaged in fund-raising practices which had incurred the wrath of the party treasurer and verged on embezzlement. He had created many enemies in his own ranks through his high-handedness and crude propaganda techniques. He had aroused the ire of the authorities through his vituperative attacks and had been sentenced at least four times since 1927 to stiff fines or jail sentences. He was now about to face — partly because of the above factors — the division of his Gau into two. In any other party with any other leader Ley would have been long gone. But it says something about the nature of the Nazi Party and its leader, Adolf Hitler, that instead of receiving an expulsion notice in his jail cell, Ley received instead the following message from his Führer: "I was grieved to learn that you were arrested right in the middle of your work and now have to serve a lengthy sentence. I know from personal experience how difficult something like that is to bear. I am sending my heartiest greetings to you for Easter and hope that you bear the burden and distress of incarceration well."[85]

In future weeks lay the losing struggle to keep his Gau intact. But it was a loss that would bring Ley to Munich and into the close proximity of his leader — and as such represented the opening of opportunities which would eclipse those available in the Rhineland. But that story is better told if we step back and put Ley within the larger context of the emergence of the Nazi Party as a major national political force in Germany.

83. Gau Rheinland to Kassenverwaltung Munich, April 21, 1931, in Institut für Zeitgeschichte, Munich Fa 223/52.

84. See Henry Picker, *Hitlers Tischgespräche im Führerhauptquartier 1941–1942* (Stuttgart, Seewald Verlag, 1965), p. 317.

85. Hitler to Ley on April 4, 1931, in Kiehl, *Mann an der Fahne*, opposite p. 113. Hitler sent this message the same day that he cracked down on the Stennes SA rebellion in Berlin. He must have been particularly grateful for completely loyal men like Ley.

CHAPTER 3

Cologne – Munich – Berlin

The Nazi Party was in reality two parties living symbiotically in one organization. The initial party, the one which Ley joined in 1924 and in which he always felt more at home, was the quasi-religious sect of initiates, men (and women) who had disengaged themselves from the surrounding society and re-engaged themselves as converts to a political religion which promised to change the world in apocalyptic ways. Characteristic of this earlier party was an intense personal relationship with the charismatic leader, the myth-person, Adolf Hitler.

The second party, which came later, was a mass movement, joined and supported by a wide variety of people for differing motives and characterized by a complex, impersonal bureaucracy, which pursued the goal of preparing to take power in a large, modern country. Ley did not feel quite so at home in this party, for he always made a far better evangelist than a business manager. This remained true even after 1933, when he preferred to be constantly underway, haranguing workers in factory after factory to managing the gigantic bureaucratic DAF empire.

It was the genius of Hitler, however, which brought these two very different parties together into one and successfully overcame the tensions between them. He remained the charismatic leader who embodied the movement in his own person, while at the same time institutionalizing himself through a complex party bureaucracy, which represented him and his will on a day-to-day basis. Thus he could control and manipulate what by 1930 had become a mass movement, while at the same time not losing his unique position as godlike figure who could at any time rise above his own bureaucratic structure and intervene personally — *deus ex machina* in a given situation. He had, in short, the best of both worlds.[1]

1. Important studies which emphasize this approach to the Nazi Party: Dietrich

His Gauleiters as derivative agents of Hitler's power and charisma, played an analogous role at the regional level. Initially, they enjoyed a very personal role as expressions of his will; later they had to combine this function with that of bureaucrat, seeing to it that membership records were kept, books balanced, and correspondence flowed smoothly. They had to transform themselves from retainers of a knight to organization men, a task which was not easy and which caused Ley many of the problems he confronted as Gauleiter between 1925 and 1931.

Early on, Hitler envisioned transforming his band of followers into a mighty mass movement and began to take the necessary bureaucratic steps to prepare for that development. As early as 1926, for example, he expanded the space which his Munich headquarters occupied by three times in one year. This already represented a bureaucratic organization too large for the modest membership at the time but represented a farsightedness on the part of Hitler, who, though he still preferred "a small, tough kernel of specialists in propaganda," which men like Ley represented, nevertheless anticipated the mass movement which would emerge after 1930.[2] Also in 1926 the party set up a speakers' school for the all-important task of training the vitally needed propagandists of the movement. This also proved to be a prescient move, for by 1932 6,000 speakers had been trained under its auspices. The best of them were rewarded with the title Reichsredner (Reich speaker) and were reserved for meetings where from 100 to 1,000 people were expected to attend. Ley was one of those Reichsredner.[3]

By the time of the Nuremberg party day celebration in August 1927, Hitler's efforts had borne sufficient fruit that it was no longer possible for the dedicated members to differentiate Hitler the person from Hitler the Reichsleitung of the party; the bureaucratization of the Führer and of the party was well underway. And Hitler took the occasion to reward his Gauleiters, who had been busy welding their local organizations from chummy clubs into successful propaganda

---

Orlow, *The History of the Nazi Party, 1919–1933* (Pittsburgh, University of Pittsburgh Press, 1969), particularly his introduction; Albrecht Tyrell (ed.), *Führer befiehl. . . Selbstzeugnisse aus der 'Kampfzeit' der NSDAP, Dokumentation und Analysie* (Düsseldorf, Droste Verlag, 1969), especially his analyses preceding each documentation section; more recently, Michael Kater, *The Nazi Party: A Social Profile of Its Members and Leaders, 1919–1945* (Cambridge, Harvard University Press, 1983).

2. See Joachim Fest, *Hitler* (New York, Vintage, 1975), pp. 247–8.
3. See Orlow, *Nazi Party*, pp. 159ff.; also Fest, *Hitler*, p. 252.

tools, by giving them the power to appoint the lower-level leaders, who until then had still been elected.[4]

By the beginning of 1928, party membership had grown to over 80,000, and the organization question became paramount. Hitler, however, was not the one to do the formal day-to-day work of running a bureaucratic party. To do so would have undermined his status as a charismatic leader. Besides, Hitler throughout his career found administrative tasks mundane and boring and preferred to leave them to those more disposed to do that kind of work. He found the ideal person in the extremely talented and energetic Gregor Strasser. Strasser, who had led the revolt of the northern Gauleiter against the clique of Munich people surrounding Hitler in 1925–6, had long since succumbed to Hitler's charisma and now lent himself as a dedicated bureaucratic tool (although he still had some very pronounced differences with Hitler over the nature and direction of the party, which would erupt seriously in late 1932). On January 2, 1928, Hitler formally invested Strasser with the title of Reichsorganisationsleiter (Reich Organizational Director, ROL).[5] In the coming several years Strasser would take steps to thoroughly bureaucratize the Nazi Party vertically and horizontally and to transfer control of the movement to the Reichsleitung in Munich. With the cooperation of the parsimonious party treasurer, Schwarz, Strasser gradually got financial control of the Gaue, forcing them to adapt standard bookkeeping techniques and remit their funds to Munich on a regular basis. He also put the Gauleiter themselves on salary, thus making them more dependent. Moreover, he put pressure on the Gauleiter to transfer his own reforms to their administrative level, compelling them to bureaucratize the Gaue, introducing such functionaries as business managers. In the Rhineland, Grohé would fulfill this function for Ley. Gradually, the Gauleiter began to resemble more and more the "division managers" of a large corporation.

In addition, Strasser began increasingly to use Gauleiter and other high party functionaries as candidates for deputies, both in state assemblies and then in the Reichstag itself. This move, in turn, led to the redrawing of Gau boundaries to make them contiguous with Reichstag electoral districts. It was this kind of rationalization which led to the division of Ley's Gau in early 1931.

4. Orlow, *Nazi Party*, pp. 112ff.
5. An excellent study of Strasser which details his reforms is Udo Kissenkoetter, *Gregor Strasser und die NSDAP*, Schriftenreihe der Vierteljahrshefte für Zeitgeschichte no. 37 (Stuttgart, Deutsche Verlagsanstalt, 1978), esp. pp. 31ff.

Finally, Hitler also refurbished the Uschla, the party court, retiring the aging Major Heinemann in 1928 and replacing him with the younger Walter Buch. The Uschla thus became a more effective mechanism for control and arbitration and could serve as a screen by taking heat for some of Hitler's and Strasser's less popular decisions. Given the stresses and strains of the bureaucratization process, particularly among the older Gauleiter like Ley, the Uschla became a very handy tool indeed, as we have seen in looking at the many tensions (press scandals, financial irregularities, intraparty strife) which resulted from Ley's attempts during these years to adjust to what one author has called the "bureaucratized romanticism" of the Nazi Party.[6] Another important tool was bestowing — or witholding — a visit to a Gau by the Führer himself, a reward offered to those Gauleiter whose house was in order.

Parallel to the organizational reforms in the Nazi Party during and after 1928 ran a change in political direction as well. Prior to 1928, led by the dynamic northern Gauleiter, the Nazi Party, anxious to defeat the left and live up to its name as a "workers" party, had concentrated its efforts on winning over the proletariat in the cities with radical attacks on the depredations of capitalism and the promise of a coming "German socialism." Goebbels and Strasser had been especially dedicated to this approach. After the party day in August 1927, however, at the same time that Strasser was busy reorganizing the party, Hitler began to alter this approach and appeal instead more to frustrated middle-class nationalists and less to radicalized socialist workers. Now, instead of attacks on the capitalist system, Nazi propaganda began to focus more on Chancellor Stresemann's foreign policy, particularly on its attempts at rapprochement with France.[7] This shift was given impetus by surprising Nazi successes in the rural-protestant north in what otherwise were the disastrous Reichstag elections of May 20, 1928, in which the party nationwide only received 800,000 votes and twelve seats in the Reichstag. This shift in emphasis eventually enabled the Nazis to capture immense numbers of votes from a desperate and disechanted lower middle and middle class in Ger-

6. The phrase is Orlow's. See *Nazi Party*, p. 80, and generally on the reforms pp. 78–86 and 121ff. Hitler announced the Uschla reform in the *Völkischer Beobachter*, no. 99 of April 28, 1928, p. 3. Hitler threatened expulsion from the party for those who disobeyed the Uschla's orders, but many powerful Gauleiter, including Ley, regularly did so with impunity with Hitler's occasional backing.
7. On the change of political direction to the "rural-nationalist" emphasis, see Orlow, *Nazi Party*, pp. 117ff. and Ch. 5; also Tyrell, *Führer befiehl*, Ch. 6.

many once the Great Depression settled in two years later. In the meantime, it redounded very much to Robert Ley's benefit. His Gau was, after all, heavily populated by petits bourgeois and peasants, who would be vulnerable targets for the "rural-nationalist" plan.[8] Moreover, Ley had never sympathized with the northern Gauleiter and their approach from the beginning, being, despite his overt radicality, more business than labor oriented.[9] So Ley went along loyally in a political shift which created quite a few conscience pangs for some of the Gauleiter, and his loyalty did not go unnoticed in Munich. Just a month after the leadership conference in Munich which confirmed the official switch in direction, Hitler rewarded Ley by officially appointing him Gauleiter of the Rhineland, an office which Ley had been filling since 1925 in an "acting" capacity.[10]

Participation in the national elections of 1928 had come only after some agonizing on Hitler's part and resulted not from great expectations of a landslide vote during this prosperous time, but rather from the advantages which the Nazi Party might derive from having at least some deputies in the Reichstag, as well as in the various state legislatures. Not the least of these advantages, apart from having a platform from which to disrupt the legislative process, lay in the fact that deputies received an emolument, a free railroad pass, and enjoyed parliamentary immunity from prosecution. Hitler indicated as early as 1926 that he was aware of these advantages. In his report to the general membership in May of that year he had said:

> For us the main thing is the deputy's railroad ticket. It offers the opportunity of sending agitators around, that is it serves, as does the *per diem* allowance, the party exclusively. The gentlemen who represent us in parliament, for example, do not ride to Berlin in order to deliver their ballot, but rather ride around uninterruptedly in the service of the

8. See Gustav Simon's comment on the occupational breakdown of the Gau in his position paper. Simon to Strasser, October 7, 1930, in BAK NS 22/1056; the main contributors to the party were also mainly businessmen, artisans, and landowners. See Horst Matzerath and Henry Turner, "Die Selbstfinanzierung der NSDAP," *Geschichte und Gesellschaft*, vol. 3, pp. 59–92.
9. Ley had rendered Hitler a valuable service during the time when Hitler was banned from speaking publicly by setting up private meetings with business executives in the Rhineland area. See, for example, the invitation to business leaders of November 21, 1926, signed by Ley, announcing a lecture by Hitler in Königswinter, NSDAP Hauptarchiv, Reel 54, Folder 1305.
10. See "Bestätigungsurkunde," September 29, 1928, in Walter Kiehl, *Mann an der Fahne. Kameraden eszählen von Dr Ley* (Munich, Zentralverlag der NSDAP, 1938), opposite p. 112.

movement. In part for that reason it was possible during the past year alone to have held over 2,370 mass gatherings in Germany.[11]

Goebbels, writing just a week after the 1928 elections, was even more succinct: "I am not a member of the Reichstag. I am a HOI. A Holder of Immunity. An HORP. A Holder of a Railroad Pass. What do we care about the Reichstag? We have been elected against the Reichstag, and we will exercize our mandate in the interests of our employer. . . . An HOI is allowed to call a dungheap a dungheap and does not have to use such euphemisms as 'government.'"[12]

Hitler made very good use of this opportunity. In early April 1928 the lists of Nazi candidates for the elections were announced. Of thirty-six Reichstag candidates, twelve were Gauleiter and another seven prominent national leaders (Ritter von Epp of Bavaria headed the list). Moreover, most of the other Gauleiter, SA leaders, and Reichsleitung executives found spots on the various state Landtag list. Many had their chances of election enhanced by being represented on lists in several districts. Robert Ley was a candidate both for the Reichstag and for the Prussian Landtag in the districts of Koblenz-Trier and Cologne-Aachen.[13]

He threw himself into the campaign with characteristic verve. Even before the campaign, he had been following an exhausting schedule of speeches and rallies, giving speeches on practically a daily basis. March's schedule, published in the WB, shows him giving major speeches on twenty-one of thirty-one days in such towns as Koblenz, Cologne, Nuremberg, Aachen, as well as in smaller villages in the rural areas.[14] With the campaign his schedule only intensified, and recently freed from the necessity of earning his daily bread (he had been fired on January 1), Ley now threw himself with reckless abandon into party agitation. No doubt this exclusive commitment to the party also had something to do with his failure at this time to establish himself on a farm, as he had wanted to do.

Though the elections generally turned out badly for the Nazis, Ley was rewarded for his efforts by being one of six Nazi deputies sent to the Prussian Landtag in Berlin. (The others were Haake,

11. Quoted in Tyrell, *Führer befiehl*, p. 132.
12. Quoted in Fest, *Hitler*, pp. 255–6.
13. See Orlow, *Nazi Party*, p. 126; see *Westdeutscher Beobachter*, April 15, 1928, for list of candidates.
14. See *Westdeutscher Beobachter*, February 5 and March 4, 1928. Other frequent speakers were Grohé, Kayser, and Schmeer.

Kaufmann, Lohse, Kerrl, and Kube, who was head of the delegation.) In the Diet Ley continued his tradition of crude outspokenness. As Kube put it, "He rages like a furious dervish on the Landtag platform."[15] Indeed, the record of Ley's speeches before that august body show him raving at the usual targets. Catholics will not be free until "the Center Party in Germany is destroyed"; or, "we recognize quite clearly that Jew-dom must one day be destroyed." On occasion, in his more lucid moments, he would attempt to use his position to actually help his constitutents, as he did, for example, in seeking financial aid from the government to ameliorate rural poverty around Trier. He also tried, along with the other NS deputies, to introduce resolutions lifting the ban on Hitler's public speaking in Prussia.[16]

It is some indication of Ley's importance to Hitler as a propagandist-organizer in the Rhineland that his frequent absences on speaking tours from areas in which he had agitated intensively prior to this time led to a decrease in NSDAP membership. A police report from Ley's former residence of Wiesdorf indicated such a decline and attributed it to Ley's new duties as Landtag deputy. "Dr Ley was up to now the soul of the whole movement. He understood in masterful fashion how to fascinate those surrounding him." The Landrat in Opladen observed similarly: "Presumably the decline has to do with the fact that the soul of the organization, Gau leader of the National Socialists and Landtag deputy Dr Ley, is not heard from so often. Even affiliates of the NSDAP have not been organized."[17] Even Uschla in Munich, which had its share of quarrels with Ley, recognized his importance as a radical agitator when it declined to support a petition from Cologne Nazis to open a party court proceedings against the Gauleiter. "The party is neither a circle of spinsters nor a league of decency," chairman Buch responded, "It is an organization of fighters for the future of the German people."[18]

In January 1929 Ley attended another leadership congress in Weimar at which the organizational and progammatic changes of

15. See Kube to Strasser of October 5, 1928, in BAK NS22/375.
16. See speeches of July 5 and October 24, 1929, respectively and Urantrag, no. 53, June 13, 1928, all in NSDAP Hauptarchiv, Reel 30, Folder 571.
17. Police report is quoted within Landrat's report of October 9, 1928, in LHAK, 403/16743, 783.
18. Buch to Adolf Trumph of November 26, 1928, in BDC: File Ley.

the prior year were confirmed. Now Strasser's relentless bureaucratization was proceeding apace, with consequences for Ley and all the other Gauleiter. Increasingly in the coming year Ley, despite his inclinations, would have to fulfill the role of executive (although he would pawn off much of this activity on Grohé and on Erich Evertz, his Gau business director). Indeed, it would not be long until Ley himself would be sheltered by bureaucratic padding from the day-to-day interference of party comrades seeking favors, redress, and advancement.[19] But this only released Ley to do what he preferred most — haranguing possible converts to National Socialism. He had his chance beginning in the summer of 1929.

On July 9, a rightist coalition, including Hitler's party, launched a major campaign against the Weimar Republic, focusing on a hoped-for plebiscite to defeat the American-sponsored Young Plan. The plan, which was to put German reparations payments on a new and final schedule lasting until 1988, was viewed by the right as a symbol of foreign domination of Germany's finances. A successful plebiscite would have represented a serious defeat for the politicians of fulfillment in Germany and a devastating blow to the Republic itself.

Propaganda for the plebiscite and against the Young Plan lasted throughout the summer and fall of 1929 with the Nazis outpacing all the other right-wing groups in the intensity and ferocity of their propaganda. In a speech toward the end of November, Hitler said, "The time will come when those responsible for Germany's collapse will laugh out of the other side of their faces. Fear will grip them. Let them know that their judgment is on the way."[20]

Ley, not to be out-agitated even by his master, said on the occasion of a rally for the release of right-wing vigilante killers (*Fememörder*), "But the criminals [of November 9, 1918] could not have emerged if someone had stood them up against the wall in time. . . . Instead of hanging them from lamp posts, they made state secretaries out of them."[21] Occasionally, Ley's enthusiasm overcame his better judgment. In August and September he rented the large Messehalle in Cologne and had placards put up announcing Hitler's appearance. Hitler had other plans, which earned Ley a

19. See Rundschreiben from Evertz to Bezirks- Kreis-, and Ortsgruppenleiter of March 21, 1930, in LHAK, 403/16732, pp. 207–9.
20. See Fest, *Hitler*, p. 263.
21. See report of November 29, 1929, in Helmuth Heiber (ed.), *Akten der Portei-Kanzlei der NSDAP* (Munich, Oldenbourg, 1983), p. 26.

rebuke from Bouhler in Munich. But as always, Ley's usefulness to Hitler outweighed his blunders. This had been apparent most recently at the party day celebration in Nuremberg at the beginning of August. By and large the rallies went by smoothly and were successful as mass demonstrations of Hitler's drawing power. One controversial matter did surface though in the discussion sections, that of National Socialist unions. It was a sore point. Many radical, labor-oriented Nazis favored the establishment of Nazi unions as a tool for invading the factories and capturing workers' loyalties away from the socialist free trade unions. Hitler was ambivalent, but certainly must have feared that, given the bread and butter orientation of trade unions, a Nazi union might detract from the revolutionary thrust of his movement. A Nazi union of sorts — the NSBO (Nationalsozialistiche Betriebszellenorganisation, or National Socialist Organisation of Factory Cells) had been organized as a pilot project in Berlin and now its advocates at Nuremburg were anxious to establish the NSBO on a national basis. The session dealing with the topic, a session chaired by the NSBO founder, Johannes Engel, threatened to get out of hand. At that juncture, Hitler sent the loyal Ley to intervene: "I don't know why [all of you] wish to speak comrades. After all, we are not in a parliamentary gossip hut (*Schwatzbude*) here, with discussion, votes and agendas. You know you can't make decisions here. You came here to hear the opinion of the Führer; [and] I have told you that. Now act accordingly."[22]

Despite a well-financed and intensively pursued propaganda campaign, the plebiscite against the Young Plan lost in December. But it was a Pyrrhic victory for the hard-pressed Republic. Already early in the year the first signs of the Depression which would devastate Germany were apparent. Unemployment crept above 3 million for the first time. In the spring the number of business bankruptcies increased dramatically. Then, at the height of the campaign, two dramatic events signaled the death knell of the Weimar Republic. On October 12, Gustav Stresemann, former Chancellor and Foreign Minister and the embodiment of rapprochement with the West, died. A little more than two weeks later, on October 24, on Black Friday, the New York stock market crashed. The echo of the latter event particularly resonated quickly throughout the German eco-

22. Ley's advertisement announcing Hitler's visit appears in *Westdeutscher Beobachter*, September 29, 1929, p. 6. For Bouhler's remonstrance to Ley of September 23, 1929, see BA Schumacher Sammlung, 203; for the incident at Nuremberg, see Orlow, *Nazi Party*, p. 169.

nomy. Foreign short-term loans, which had been the basis for Weimar's short-lived prosperity, were called in by nervous creditors. Capital began to dry up, and with it investment possibilities. Germany had begun her long slide into economic depression.

Hitler did not hesitate long. He now broke with the rest of the right wing after the failure of the plebiscite and began his own independent attack on the Republic. It did not escape his attention that those who were the biggest losers in the growing crisis were the middle and lower middle classes and the peasants whom he had already targeted over a year before. He now refined and intensified his "rural-nationalist" plan. New techniques were developed such as saturating a single district with a barrage of speakers right down to the smallest hamlet. Individual communities would be bombarded with posters and leaflets. The SA and SS would stage a whole spectrum of events to get recruits, including "athletic events, living tableaus, plays, singing of songs, lectures by SA men, showing of the movie of the Party Rally."[23]

Nazi activities in Ley's Rhineland Gau during the early months of 1930 illustrate well the success of the new tactics, particularly with the targeted middle classes and peasants. Police observers were struck by the number of people from the "better elements" of society who had begun to attend Nazi meetings. From Trier came the observation: "It is remarkable that in the evening discussions (*Sprechabende*) more and more members of the middle class and the so-called better ranks are to be seen." Or as the Oberpräsident of the Rhine province reported to the Prussian Interior Minister:

> These numbers show clearly a growing favorable response to the movement among the urban populace. In this context it is remarkable that both the Regierungspräsident in Trier as well as police chiefs in Cologne and Koblenz, in contrast to former observations, have unanimously ascertained a stronger and stronger participation at Nazi meetings of the middle class and good bourgeois circles.

The report also reveals that Ley was using effectively the new tactics, including SA torchlight parades and concerts, summer solstice celebrations as well as en masse attendance in brown shirts of both Protestant and Catholic church services. In the heavily Catholic Rhineland, Ley liked to represent the party as protectors of

23. See Fest, *Hitler*, p. 267.

Christianity.[24]

As in other parts of Germany, the Nazis had made their initial inroads in Protestant areas but by 1930 were successfully penetrating Catholic strongholds as well. As one police report from the Koblenz area observed:

> The domain of the National Socialists is primarily in the Protestant villages Veldenz, Traben-Trarbach, Wolf, and Enkirch. The Protestants having nothing with which to counter Nazi agitation, whereas in the Catholic and Social Democratic localities counter agitation takes place. The fact is, though, that recently the Nazis are also pressing forward in Catholic locales, even though their success there is always dependent on the accretion of young people.[25]

Ley's success in breaking into the ranks of respectable society (for many of the élite it was no longer disreputable to belong to the Nazi Party) in the towns was mirrored by dramatic inroads among the peasants as well. Already in the fall of 1929 police observers noted that "If, as was stated up until recently the Nazis concentrated their work mainly on the towns, in the course of this year they have also systematically undertaken agitation on the land."[26] By early 1930 the Nazis were already registering dramatic successes in terms of the growth of membership and locals in rural areas. Nazi reports of a 64 percent increase in members and a 61 percent increase in locals between October 1929 and March 1930 were no exaggeration, noted the Oberpräsident in a report to the Prussian Interior Minister. The Nazi recruiting meetings "demonstrate a hitherto unprecedented across-the-board increase in participants not only in the towns but also indicate in the smaller rural communities a growing participation which is astonishingly high in relation to the size of the local population."[27]

Ley targeted two areas in particular. One was the Mosel area, where he found enthusiastic listeners among the discontented vintners. The other, as one might expect, was his own home territory of

24. See report of the Trier Regierungspräsident to the Oberpräsident of March 21, 1930 and report of Oberpräsident to Prussian Interior Minister of May 19, 1930, quoted in Franz Josef Heyen, *Nationalsozialismus im Alltag. Quellen zur Geschichte des Nationalsozialismus vornehmlich im Raum Mainz-Koblenz-Trier* (Boppard, Harald Boldt Verlag, 1967), pp. 93 and 33-4, respectively.
25. Report to the Koblenz Oberpräsident, April 9, 1930, in ibid., p. 24.
26. Oberpräsident of the Rhein province to Prussian Interior Minister, September 12, 1929, in LHAK, 403/16746, p. 99.
27. Report of May 19, 1930, in Heyen, *Alltag*, p. 30.

Oberbergisch Land. In both areas police ascertained on many occasions a pronounced gullibility on the part of locals when it came to believing the Nazi message. One police observer could not resist noting that "The vintners are easily influenced — like the inhabitants of the Oberbergisch Land. They believe the gospel of the Nazis uncritically."[28]

A series of rallies which Ley held in the heart of his home area, in the towns of Waldbröl, Gummersbach, and Berneustadt in late March 1930 to protest the Young Plan well illustrate a number of the factors now characteristic in the rapid growth of the Nazi Party: its new attraction for the middle classes despite (or rather because of) its radical stance; its new fashionability among the élites; the success of its intensive rural-nationalist thrust as well as its ability to politicize the hitherto innocently apolitical.

Posters in shops and advertisements in local newspapers announced the three-day propaganda blitz several days in advance. On the first day Ley arrived with a bevy of speakers and staged three parallel meetings in Waldbröl alone, all of which were well attended. His special guest speaker was His Royal Highness August Wilhelm Prince of Prussia (known as Auwi), former heir to the throne and recent convert to Hitler's movement. The presence of the prince helped to draw large numbers of people not only from the simple folk but, as the police observers noted, from the propertied classes as well. Ley, out of a combination of false social modesty and the desire to represent the Nazi Party as heir to the tradition of Frederick the Great, stood next to the prince on the platform and said: "The Prince of Prussia, next to whom I, poor peasant's son, have the honor to stand, embodies the old race, old Fritz. I, miserable peasant son, am standing next to the powerful spirit of Sanssouci."

Apparently the spirit of Sanssouci survived only in diluted form in the prince however. The prince addressed the crowds, to be sure, but his style and delivery were scarcely in keeping with the times, and Ley had to seize the floor after each speech to re-establish the mood. A police observer noted that:

> the ex-prince is supposed to have lost a great deal of his nimbus because of his feeble bearing in the Oberbergisch area. At first he excited the people present in the individual meetings by his very appearance, but didn't score any successes with his speeches because of his flat delivery. The applause was sparse. After each of the prince's speeches Dr Ley

28. Report to the Koblenz Oberpräsident, April 7, 1930, in ibid., p. 22.

seized the floor in order to heat up the cooled mood.

Through efforts like this the Nazis gained tremendous momentum in the course of 1930. They were aided by the deepening Depression, which brought them an increasing number of recruits and by the soldiers are there again and they demand power! We are telling you, on the day of accounting we will be brutal, ruthlessly brutal!"

Ley's barnstorming was a huge success, even in the eyes of the sceptical police observer from Cologne: "The Oberbergisch population is particularly easy to influence. Broad sections of it are convinced that the Third Reich will be founded in the foreseeable future. According to my officials on the scene, even the local police officers are in the grip of this psychosis."[29]

Through efforts like this the Nazis gained tremendous momentum in the course of 1930. They were aided by the deepening Depression, which brought them an increasing number of recruits and by the political disintegration of the Weimar Republic as a functioning parliamentary system. Already in March the Grand Coalition which had governed Weimar broke up in the wake of a conflict over unemployment benefits and would never be reassembled. The new Chancellor, Heinrich Brüning, was only able to govern at all through the use of emergency powers provided the President by Article 48 of the Weimar Constitution. Brüning, quickly dubbed the "Hunger Chancellor" because of his ruthless deflationary policy of cost cutting, only aggravated the crisis. In July he made what, in retrospect, seems to be a fatal mistake. He dissolved the Reichstag, which had been balking at his fiscal reform measures, and called new elections for September. Now, with Germany in economic destitution and in political disarray, the Nazis would have the opportunity to break like a thunderstorm onto the political scene at the national level.

Seizing their opportunity the Nazis now unleashed an unprecedented propaganda campaign, and in doing so reached new lows of vitriolic assault. "Throw the scum out!" Goebbels wrote, "'Tear the masks off their mugs! Take them by the scruff of the neck and kick them in their fat bellies on September 14, and sweep them out of the temple with trumpets and drums."[30] The party's main speakers,

29. The above account, including quotes, is from a report of the Polizeipräsident Cologne to the Cologne Regierungspräsident, March 24, 1930, in LHAK, 403/16740, pp. 83–103.

30. Fest, *Hitler*, p. 276.

including Ley, appeared everywhere. As the Prussian Interior Minister observed in a memorandum: "Meetings attended by between a thousand and five hundred persons are of daily occurrence in the larger cities. . . . Often, in fact, one or several parallel meetings have to be held because the previously selected halls cannot hold the number of persons wishing to attend."[31]

On September 14, 1930, the Germans went to the polls in what would be in retrospect a turning point in the history of the Weimar Republic. They went in record numbers, 35 million of them — 4 million more than in the previous election in 1928. And they dealt the Republic a devastating blow. The liberal parties were decimated. The Communists registered dramatic gains. But most ominously, the NSDAP won in a veritable landslide. No less than 6.4 million Germans cast their vote for Hitler; the Nazis would now have 107 deputies in the Reichstag as opposed to the previous twelve. Even the Nazis were unprepared for a victory of this magnitude. They had not even put up 107 candidates. But again, Hitler recovered quickly from this delightful surprise. On October 13, 107 Nazi deputies marched en masse into the Reichstag wearing their brown shirts — which was illegal.[32]

In the wake of the election victory the always bold Hitler decided to continue the attack. Though still publicly adhering to his oath of legality, he nevertheless exhorted his followers to become more vituperative in their attacks on the Republic. The two positions seemed contradictory, but most Nazis enjoyed the spectacle of Hitler skillfully walking the tightrope. At the trial of three young army officers charged with spreading Nazi propaganda, Hitler, called as a witness in late September, said: "I stand here under oath to God Almighty. I tell you that if I come to power legally, in my legal government I will set up state tribunals which will be empowered to pass sentences by law on those responsible for the misfortunes of our nation. Possibly, then, quite a few heads will roll legally."[33]

In the Rhineland Gau Ley took his cue. He had already contributed greatly to the Nazi vote there. In District 20 (Cologne-Aachen) the NSDAP had won 14.5 percent of the vote, slightly more than the Socialists and equal to the Communists. In District 21

31. Ibid., p. 277.
32. See Gordon Craig, *Germany 1866–1945* (New York, Oxford University Press, 1978), pp. 541–2; and Fest, *Hitler*, pp. 287ff.
33. See Fest, *Hitler*, p. 292.

(Koblenz-Trier) the party won 14.9 percent, significantly more than the Socialists and more than twice that of the Communists. In these very strongly Catholic areas, however, the Center Party continued to overshadow all the others with 36.4 percent and 46.8 percent of the vote, respectively.[34] Probably for this reason, Ley launched a particularly vicious attack on the Center in the first weeks of 1931.

The post-election propaganda continued to draw new members to the NSDAP in the Rhine Gau. In the last quarter of 1930 membership grew 20 percent (from 25,617 to 30,000); during the first quarter of 1931 another 20 percent (to 36,416). The number of locals also grew dramatically. Four rallies in January, at two of which Ley was the featured speaker, drew 5,200, 5,500, 1,000, and 2,600 visitors, respectively. At the end of the month, the Regierungspräsident in Aachen observed that: "the development of the party does not yet appear to have reached its apogee, which can be ascertained by the steadily growing number of members. . . . Interest in the NSDAP is growing demonstrably among the populace."[35]

On February 15, 1930, Robert Ley celebrated his forty-first birthday — as usual not in the bosom of his family but out on the hustings. He had done very well for his Führer. That is why the impending inner crises in his Gau and the division of the Gau itself would mean a step up rather than down for him. His successes as Gauleiter over a period of nearly six years, despite excesses, outrages, and often remarkably poor judgment, and above all his fanatical loyalty to Hitler, would mark him as a comer at a time when the NSDAP stood on the threshold of power in Germany.

It was probably inevitable that the Rhineland Gau be divided in two. Gregor Strasser's administrative reforms entailed making Gau boundaries coterminous with electoral districts, which meant logically that Cologne-Aachen should constitute one Gau and Koblenz-Trier another. In fact, by 1931 there remained only two exceptions to this rule: Silesia and the Rhineland. Ley was prepared to accept the division if it were absolutely necessary, but he obviously did not desire such a development. Even less did he desire a division if the impetus for doing so came — as it did — from within the Gau rather than from the Reichsleitung in Munich.

34. For the figures, see Albrecht Tyrell, "Führergedanke und Gauleiterwechsel," *Vierteljahrshefte für Zeitgeschichte*, vol. 5, p. 365, n. 113.

35. On the growth figures, see report of the Polizeipräsident of Cologne to the Oberpräsident, Koblenz, April 8, 1931, in LHAK, 403/16740, pp. 505–7; Regierungspräsident to Oberpräsident, Koblenz, January 31, 1930, ibid., pp. 383ff.

In 1929 Ley had appointed as one of five district leaders in his Gau a party veteran of long standing named Gustav Simon.[36] Simon, born in 1900 of a father who had worked his way up from manual laborer to Oberinspektor in the railroad service, was himself an ambitious man. After sampling various fields of study, including education, economics, and law, Simon finally earned a diploma as a business college teacher and had worked since 1927 in the French-occupied Saar as an apprentice teacher in a business college. In the meantime, he became active in the *völkisch* movement in 1922 while a student at the University of Frankfurt and in 1924 joined the National Socialist Freedom Movement and a year later, after its refounding by Hitler, the NSDAP.

In 1928 Ley put Simon in charge of the hitherto neglected area of Trier-Birkenfeld in the southern part of the Gau, and Simon soon showed a great deal of organizational talent. In 1929, largely through Simon's efforts, the NSDAP won 38.5 percent of the vote in Koblenz municipal elections, the largest total of any town in Prussia. After the September landslide of 1930 Simon went to the Reichstag as one of four elected representatives of District 21.

Relations had not always been smooth between Simon and his Gauleiter, however. Ley's often imperious ways combined with long periods of neglect must have given Simon food for thought, while at the same time, his own success as a Nazi agitator certainly fueled his ambition. Moreover, Ley's disastrous financial dealings revealed a side of the Gauleiter vulnerable to attack. In October 1930 Simon made his move.

In a seven-page memorandum to Gregor Strasser in Munich Simon made a strong case for dividing the Gau in two. Such a move would correspond to the general guidelines anyway, Simon began. Moreover, keeping the Rhineland Gau intact would be detrimental to the party. The Gau was much too large and unwieldy to allow party members to take part in a large range of activities necessary to the expansion of the movement. Meetings, parades, speaker exchange, telephone contact — all were expensive or impossible for members in his area to take part in if they were held in the northern part of the Gau. The result was a growing lack of cohesion. An additional reason for forming two Gaus out of one lay in the differing social structure of the population. The north was more urban with

36. See Albrecht Tyrell, "Führergedanke", pp. 563–4 for biographical information on Simon. Tyrell deals with the story of the division of the Gau in this excellent article, but in a different context.

an occupational profile of worker, middle class, and peasant and a relatively strong enemy in SPD and KPD. The south was more rural with predominantly farming, wine-making, and the tourist trade providing work. Here the enemy was the Catholic Center Party. Each area had to be addressed in different terms. Add to that, Simon continued, the fact that the Gau as now constituted was organized very loosely. "The Gau business office issued as good as no organizational directives." There was also a financial inbalance owing to the fact that the southern districts produced far more in revenue than was returned for administrative expenses. Simon concluded that both potential new Gaus were viable entities and requested the formation of a Gau Rhineland-South as soon as possible — and certainly before the upcoming elections for the Prussian Landtag.[37]

There appears to have been no initial reaction from Munich, and Ley himself seems to have been in the dark about Simon's intentions. That changed dramatically on January 6, 1931, however, when the two men met in Koblenz. Simon revealed to Ley his plans to push for a separate Gau in the south; he also indicated that as part of his independent activity he would start a weekly Gau newspaper as well. This was too much for Ley. To have one of his own district leaders plan the dissolution of his Gau was bad enough. But to add insult to injury, that same man now wanted to compete with his Gauleiter in the newspaper business at a time when Ley's enterprise was already near bankruptcy.

Ley stewed all the way back to Cologne in the train and then that very evening wrote an angry response to Simon. First he absolutely forbade him to establish a weekly. "I said to you," Ley wrote, " that I will not tolerate this under any conditions. That I would find it at this time not only damaging to the party, but also a disloyal attitude toward me." Turning to the Gau division, Ley indicated again that he was against the whole idea. "A reorganization only makes sense," he noted, "if it would enhance the striking power of the movement. Visible advantages for the party would have to come out of it; if not, then any reorganization would be damaging." Simon had given him no convincing reason why the Gau should be divided other than the fact that he (Simon) had ambitions to be a Gauleiter and that Ley had supposedly promised him that post. "Should the *Reichsleitung* someday generally decide, for reasons which have nothing to do with me, to make the Gaus smaller and embark upon a

37. Simon to the Reichsleitung, October 7, 1930, in BAK NS22/1056.

reorganisation on a nationwide basis, then, as I have always explained to you, I would not have a closed mind. As long as this is not the case and as long as you cannot produce any visible reasons for making the south Rhineland independent, I will resist these strivings." He concludes by saying that if Simon takes his case to Munich, as he indicated he would, then he would find a copy of this letter waiting for him there. But he should not have any illusions about any future collaboration between the two of them. Then Ley concluded, threateningly and, given his own vaulting ambition, somewhat hypocritically: "As much as I regret losing your valuable strength, I must also be alert that individual ambition, to the extent that it is healthy and furthers the movement, does not grow to the point where it endangers the party."[38]

Simon, undaunted by Ley's letter, turned to Munich anyway, contacting Strasser's deputy, Schulz. Strasser, who apparently had not yet decided when or if to complete his Gau reform, put Simon off. He indicated that there would be no division of the Gau at this time. Furthermore, he also refused to permit Simon to establish his weekly. What Simon should do was what he was told to by Ley. "I ask you particularly at this time in the interests of the unity of the movement to apply yourself with all your strength to the labors demanded by the Gauleitung."[39]

Shortly after this communication to Simon, Strasser was put out of commission for two months by a serious skiing accident. When he returned to the question of Gau Rhineland again it was early March. In the meantime, Simon had continued to agitate; enough so that Strasser's deputy, Schulz, had come to Cologne for an inspection and had talked to both men. Once again Simon had prepared a position paper on the issue.

On March 6, Strasser wrote to Ley indicating that, while the door was still open to preserving the status quo, a division of the Gau was more likely:

> The progress of the movement mandates carrying out the present organizational plans. A part of them is the organizational principle that a Gau should be coterminous with an electoral district. Up to now we have made exceptions either when membership strength forbade it or where

38. Ibid. Matzerath and Turner have pointed out that Ley's description in this letter of a lean administrative apparatus in the Gau was inaccurate. "Selbstfinanzierung," p. 66.
39. Strasser to Simon, January 17, 1931, in BAK NS22/1056.

> several electoral districts were combined to form a Gau because they represented legally a federal state. Westfalia has already been divided and with that Silesia and Rhineland are the sole remaining exceptions. I request that you make known the reasons why you are against the dividing of the Gau in order that I have recourse to them in my proposal to the Führer.

Then in a post-script Strasser concludes, "At the same time I request nonbinding suggestions on the nature of the division and on the filling of the new Gauleiter post."[40]

In all probability, Strasser was moving to the decision to divide Ley's Gau for precisely the reason he gave: it suited his general organizational schema to make electoral boundaries contiguous with Gau boundaries. A minor factor in the decision, however, might have had to do with Ley's growing financial problems. It was at precisely this time that Ley was receiving the admonitions from both Schwarz, the party treasurer, and from Strasser on several matters ranging from unauthorized fund-raising and building party houses to the deplorable financial condition of Ley's publishing house.[41]

Simon certainly used these troubles to advance his own cause. Writing to Strasser he revealed his frustration at having to sue various newspapers because of articles alleging corruption on the part of himself and Ley in the Koblenz district, articles which tarred the party with the brush of what was in reality in private matter — Ley's Westmark Publishing House. Moreover, he also revealed a lack of trust in Ley himself.

> Personally I find myself in a bad situation. On the one hand I lack trust in the Gauleitung in Cologne, and that cannot be replaced in the long run by the best discipline and subordination. On the other hand I cannot even consider leaving an area which is organizationally my work, where the majority of locals were founded by me personally. It would do irretrievable damage if I were to resign. I owe it to myself and to the movement not to sacrifice the organization created here and to request the only available way out here: the creation of a Gau Koblenz-Trier.

Simon also sent Strasser another position paper — his third — in which he once again reiterated his reasons for wanting a separate

40. BAK NS22/1057.
41. See Schwarz to Ley, March 12, 1931, in BDC: File Ley; and Strasser to Ley, March 10, 1931, in IfZ Fa 223/52.

Gau. This time, however, he was more direct and pointed in his criticism of Ley, dwelling on the collapse of Ley's publishing enterprise.[42]

Ley also wrote to Strasser, responding to the latter's request for a case against dividing the Gau. On objective grounds his case was weaker than that of Simon. He pointed out initially that dividing the Gau would dilute the party's efforts and destroy the unified newspaper organization he had built up. Then he made an appeal which is very revealing both about Ley's fears and his personal ambition as well as about the free-enterprise nature of the Nazi Party in the *Kampfzeit*:

> It is the purpose of any organization to provide those working within it the possibility of upward mobility. [!] Sound ambition is the driving force of achievement. . . . If a political leader, who has been in charge of a struggle for six years since its beginning, and, as I can maintain in my case, has brought a splendid organization to this struggle, is deprived of part of his command, that means the same as when a soldier is demoted. You say that it is happening in general and that all the Gaus are to encompass only electoral districts. Of course, I recognize this. But then, on the other hand, the organization would have to be extended so that a party comrade who has organized and led a larger area and who has proved himself should be afforded a further opportunity to rise. Either you should tell me that I don't have the strength to lead a Gau anymore, after you've been satisfied with me for six very difficult years, or you should give me the opportunity to display my strength and capabilities. . . . Therefore I should like to emphasize clearly once more that a division of my Gau without the kind of complete reorganization which I spoke to you about, would be nearly unbearable for me.[43]

One can almost sense in these lines a real fear and desperation. Ley has dedicated himself totally to Hitler and the movement. Having disengaged from the outside society, he has invested his entire social ego in advancing within the movement. The prospect of his Gau being divided posed for him the terrifying threat of having the rug pulled out from under his feet entirely — and at a time when he was about to be sent to jail. The thought of suffering his father's fate of incarceration without the legitimization of doing so for a higher purpose must have added the threat of an acutely remembered disgrace to the existing one of social decline.

42. Letter of March 14, 1931, in BAK NS22/1056.
43. Letter of March 17, 1931 in BAK NS22/1057, pp. 122–5.

Ley need not have worried. Hitler had plans for one of the most loyal and fanatical of his paladins. With the question of dividing the Rhineland Gau settled on principle, it was now a matter of carrying out the process and finding an important position for Ley — and in a way that would enable him to save face.

Strasser wrote to Ley on March 30, assuring him once again that when membership totals justified it, he would divide Gaus as a matter of principle, and personal pride or prestige played no role. He reminded Ley that Hanover, Westphalia, Mittelfranken, Brandenburg, and Ostmark had all been divided and the Gauleiters affected had not made it a matter of personal prestige — and neither should Ley.[44]

By now Ley had abandoned his opposition and now complained only about the manner in which the change had been handled. Writing for Ley, who in the meantime had begun to serve his sentence, Grohé confided to Strasser that what had made the division difficult for Ley was the fact that it had been discussed openly for months and that impetus had come from below (Simon) rather than from above. Moreover, Ley took umbrage at the fact that the announcement came not from him as Gauleiter but rather from Buch on the occasion of a Uschla meeting in Koblenz — just two days after Ley had gone to jail.[45]

Strasser evidently recognized the validity of Grohé's remarks, for he took pains to facilitate Ley's shift of position within the party. When informing Simon of the impending division, Strasser warned him to stop his agitating: "I expect of you until June 1 discipline under all circumstances; otherwise you will yourself destroy the possibility of my suggesting you to the Führer as Gauleiter of the new Gau."[46]

The party also saw to it that Ley's release from prison on April 27 was greeted by great hoopla. That evening, borne on the shoulders of SA men and surrounded by flowers, Ley addressed a rally of 5,000 at the Cologne Messehalle. Telegrams of greeting arrived from Hitler, Strasser, Goebbels, and other party luminaries. Ley also had the party to thank that he did not serve another three months behind bars. Given Ley's impecunious state, the Reichsleitung had paid the 1,500-mark fine which permitted Ley's release.[47]

44. Ibid., p. 112.
45. Letter of April 3, 1931, ibid., pp. 104–5.
46. Letter of March 23, 1931, BAK NS22/1056.
47. On the release, see Polizeipräsident of Cologne to Oberpräsident, Koblenz,

Ley also did his bit to smooth his own transition from Gauleiter to a higher duty which had not been exactly defined yet. In early May he wrote to Strasser actually requesting on grounds of overwork and other pressing duties that his Gau be divided. This letter was leaked to the press in an effort to convince the public that Ley himself was behind the move.[48]

On May 31 at a Gau-day celebration the public announcement was made. Everything had been arranged between Strasser and Ley in advance. Ley was honored for the contributions he had made toward building the movement in the Rhineland. Ley announced that the Gauleiter of the newly-created Gau Koblenz-Trier was Gustav Simon. Grohé would preside over the new Gau Cologne-Aachen as deputy Gauleiter (Hitler had not yet decided, given the conflicts in Cologne between the SA and the political leadership, whether or not to officially invest Grohé with the title of Gauleiter). As for Ley, he announced that he was taking a vacation and that on September 1, he would take over the post of Political Inspector for the party.[49]

Ley's departure on vacation coincided with the summer doldrums for the NSDAP as well. The party took a breather to consolidate after a year of dramatic growth. Hitler and Strasser needed the time to consider the next step in reorganizing the party and give the membership time to gather strength for the next onslaught in fall 1931. Ley, however, did not vacation for long. By late June he was back on the hustings again, giving the police additional opportunities to press charges. On June 28 at a rally in Dieringhausen in his home area, Ley incited the crowd against Prussian Prime Minister Braun and Ministers Severing and Hirtsiefer. He warned these men to resign before it was too late and that the people were demanding their heads.[50] Ley's continuing agitation may also have betrayed his nervousness at the fact that Hitler and Strasser were taking so long to make a final dispensation both of the Gau Cologne-Aachen and his position as Inspector. In mid-August he wrote to Strasser, noting the situation and requesting that by September 1 Grohé be made

---

April 29, 1931, in LHAK 403/13381, pp. 57–63; also *Westdeutscher Beobachter*, April 28, which headlined "Dr Ley Free Again!"; letter to Munich requesting payment of Ley's fine of April 21 is in IfZ Fa 223/52.

48. Letter of May 5, 1931, in BAK NS22/1057, p. 91.
49. See Ley to Strasser of June 12, 1931, in ibid., p. 84.
50. See report from Regierungspräsident, Cologne to Oberpräsident, Koblenz of July 7, 1931, in LHAK 403/16735, pp. 11–15.

Gauleiter and he receive his promised inspectorate.[51]

While Ley waited impatiently, Strasser continued to wrestle with the reorganization of a party which by now had become truly a mass movement whose members were impatiently thirsting for power. As the party organization had become increasingly large and complex, both at the level of the Reichsleitung in Munich and at the Gau level, it became more and more necessary to build in some kind of liaison to link the two levels more tightly. The masses of new members had to be gotten under control.[52]

Strasser himself was almost completely snowed under. In addition to his comprehensive organizational duties as Reichsorganisationsleiter he was also a delegate to the Reichstag, where he would make a number of important speeches and initiatives. Moreover, he was also developing a complex network of contacts across a wide political spectrum with such diverse groups as conservative nationalists, Catholic Centrists, and even trade-union leaders. He had appointed a deputy and chief of staff, Paul Schulz, in October 1930, but one man was scarcely enough to inspect thirty-six Gaus.[53]

In the early months of 1931, as Strasser was still groping for a solution and discussing various possibilities with a number of high party leaders, including Ley, who was already anticipating the division of his Gaus,[54] the solution appeared — by way of analogy. Ernst Röhm had just taken over command of the SA and was proceeding to re-establish centralized control over an organization whose power base had spread to the Gaus. One of his moves was to appoint an SA Inspector-General, von Ullrich, to travel constantly and report back to Röhm on conditions. Strasser now grasped that idea and began to consider appointing "Gau-inspectors", each with several Gaus under his authority, to act as liaison with Strasser in Munich.[55]

Ley was a natural to be one of them. He had the authority of a senior, experienced Gauleiter. As a parliamentary deputy he had the all-important railroad pass to facilitate his travels. And he would

51. See letter of August 17, 1931, in BAK NS22/1057, p. 47.
52. See Orlow, *Nazi Party*, Ch. 6.
53. See Peter Stachura, " 'Der Fall Strasser': Gregor Strasser, Hitler and National Socialism 1930-1932," in Peter Stachura (ed.), *The Shaping of the Nazi State* (New York, Barnes & Noble, 1978), p. 93; also Tyrell, "Führergedanke", p. 370.
54. See Ley to Strasser, March 17, 1931, in BAK NS22/1057, p. 124.
55. See Orlow, *Nazi Party*, p. 214.

soon need a job. Still, Strasser delayed making the appointment until the fall, partly because he needed time to find other potential Inspectors (e.g. Bernard Rust, Gauleiter of Hannover-Süd-Braunschweig), partly because he needed time to make up his mind whether, given the rifts in Cologne, Grohé really should become the new Gauleiter there and apparently, because he was seriously considering a trip to the United States to raise money. The swollen bureaucratic organization was becoming very expensive.[56]

By autumn the decision had been made. On October 21, Hitler formally appointed Grohé Gauleiter of Cologne-Aachen; at the same time he named Ley Reichsorganisations-Inspekteur of the party. Ley's duties were to travel to the various Gaus offering advice and guidance and reporting back to Strasser. He was also to draft various organizational documents for the party and otherwise carry out "organizational tasks of all kinds."[57]

The office was prestigious, but not very powerful. The following summer came another reorganization — Strasser's last and most ambitious. This time Strasser appointed two Reichsinspekteurs, each with several Landesinspekteurs under them. Reichsinspekteur I was Strasser's good friend Schulz, who had the northern and eastern areas under his control. Reichsinspekteur II was Ley, who got the west and south, including Austria. Ley himself was also a Landesinspekteur of Bavaria. He would keep both posts until the seizure of power in January 1933.[58]

In the meantime Ley was up to his old tricks. In Cologne in April he physically attacked the Social Democratic leader, Otto Wels, and the Cologne Police-President Bauknecht in a hotel. He had apparently been indulging in alcohol. As he entered the hotel a police official challenged him by saying, "Are you here again already?" Whereupon Ley retorted, "That's none of your damn business," and added the well-worn line from Götz von Berlichingen (Kiss my ass!). The incident earned Ley a three-month suspended sentence.[59] His shady financial dealings also continued to haunt him. His newspaper, the *Westdeutscher Beobachter,* had gotten hopelessly into debt during the expensive campaign of 1932. To partially cover

56. See Tyrell, "Führergedanke," p. 373.
57. Ibid. See also Orlow, *Nazi Party*, pp. 227–8; also VB, No. 100, October 27, 1931.
58. For details on the reorganization see ibid., pp. 256–62; also Kissenkoetter, *Strasser*, pp. 209–11 and 364–78.
59. See Kiehl, *Mann an der Fahne*, pp. 147–51, for a description of the incident; also *Westdeutscher Beobachter*, April 26, 1932.

these debts, Ley in fact swindled Simon and his Gau. Ley had arranged for someone to donate a carload of printing paper to the Gau; he told Simon, however, that the paper was being offered to the Gau at a discount. The unsuspecting Simon paid — but the money went into the coffers of the *Westdeutscher Beobachter* which was now registered in the name of Ley's and Grohé's wives. Simon found out about the swindle and tried to haul Ley before the Uschla. In the interests of not compromising an important party leader, Uschla convinced Simon to turn over his claim to a printing company, which would then sue Ley in civil court and thus remove the affair from the party entirely.[60]

But Ley's continuing antics did not obscure the fact that Ley was now without an independent power base. During the fateful year 1932, as the NSDAP was desperately seeking power in one national election after another, Ley appears to be in a kind of suspended animation. As Strasser's deputy he was overshadowed by the Reichsorganisationsleiter, who had to approve Ley's various visitations and was subject to any further organizational changes Strasser might want to implement. But this organizational dependence obscures a more important fact: that Ley was, in effect, Hitler's man in Strasser's growing bureaucratic empire. Although Strasser was virtually indispensable to Hitler, the Führer was becoming increasingly distrustful of him during 1932. Strasser was staffing his bureaucracy with men who were friends or at least loyal to him; Konstantin Hierl, for example, who was to be in charge of all the party affiliates. Moreover, Strasser seemed to be developing a strategy for the party which was at odds with Hitler's own. For Hitler the party was a weapon to secure total power for himself over Germany. Increasingly for Strasser the possibility of sole Nazi power in Germany was giving way to a vision of a broad coalition of national-minded groups which would cooperate to save Germany from the Great Depression. Although Strasser continued to be loyal to Hitler and share his ideas with him, tension between the two men increased, and as it did so, Ley became more and more important to Hitler as his eyes and ears in Strasser's organization.

The NSDAP reached its apogee in votes in the Reichstag election of July. In August Hitler once again demanded the Chancellorship — and was denied by President Hindenburg. In November, elec-

60. See Simon to Strasser, July 24, 1932 in BAK NS22/1056; also Peter Hüttenberger, *Die Gauleiter, Studie zum Wandel des Machtgefüges in der NSDAP* (Stuttgart, Deutsche Verlagsanstalt, 1969), p. 64.

tions were held again. This time the Nazis lost dramatically, as Strasser had feared and predicted. Now with the party broke and in disarray, the issue of coalition versus sole power became critical. Strasser, negotiating with such disparate leaders as the ex-Chancellor Brüning of the Center Party, soon-to-be-Chancellor General von Schleicher of the Reichswehr, and trade-union leaders from both the Christian and Socialist unions, hoped desperately to get the NSDAP into government on some basis before it disintegrated entirely. He was in a powerful position to do so. His organizational changes had given him an enormous power base. Indeed, it has been observed that he only lacked the title General Secretary to have been a kind of German Stalin. Moreover, although he was certainly not the God-figure Hitler was, he was very popular and had widespread support for his ideas in the party. Contemporary estimates had between sixty and 100 Reichstag deputies behind Strasser as well as a dozen Gauleiter. Certainly, other political circles in Germany would have looked favorably on a split in the Nazi Party which would have brought a somewhat less radical Strasser wing into the responsibilities of government.[61]

But Strasser was not about to split the party. Rather, after the NSDAP had lost 40 percent of its vote in provincial elections in Thuringia on December 4, he launched a last-ditch attempt to convince Hitler of the wisdom of his course of action. But Hitler, with his eyes on total power, refused once again. With that Strasser submitted his resignation as Reichsorganisationsleiter on December 8.[62]

The resignation came as a tremendous shock to Hitler, who was staying at the Hotel Kaiserhof in Berlin ("a bombshell," Goebbels called it). It came in the form of a secret letter to him from Strasser, but was leaked to the press the same day. For all Hitler knew it meant the beginning of a mass defection from the party and his own political ruin. He went into one of his deep depressions and walked about his room all through the night of December 8/9, mumbling that "if the party falls apart, it will take me just three minutes to end it all with a pistol."

It was at this point that his loyalists went into action. Hitler went to the home of Goebbels, continuing to imagine the worst. Ley met

61. On Strasser's political negotiations against the background of national politics, see Kissenkoetter, *Strasser*, pp. 162–71; also Stachura, "'Fall Strasser'", pp. 102–9.
62. Text of resignation is in Stachura, "'Fall Strasser'", pp. 113–16; the best description is in Kissenkoetter, pp. 172ff.

with a number of NS deputies in the Kaiserhof, trying to convince them that Hitler was right and Strasser wrong. He also telephoned the various Gaus to fathom what the mood was in the provinces. Finally, he called Hitler himself, informing him that the situation was becoming more acute from hour to hour and imploring him to emerge from the background and act, since he alone could rescue the situation.[63]

That did the trick. Hitler snapped out of his lethargy and took charge. He announced that Strasser had been allowed to take a three-week leave of absence on medical grounds. Then he took over the Reichsorganisationsleitung himself with Ley as his deputy. Ley now, in effect, replaced Strasser, but without his enormous powers. Hitler would never again give anyone the control over the party that Strasser had possessed. Next Hitler ordered his loyalists to go out and recapture wavering party members and prepare to win back the voters as well. Off to the Rhineland traveled Ley and Goebbels to address thousands of the party faithful in Essen and Düsseldorf. "The whole day was a roaring success," Goebbels wrote in his diary. "In twenty-four hours we succeeded in grasping 20,000 party officials."[64] Several weeks later provincial elections in the tiny state of Lippe provided the Nazis with an opportunity to once again grasp the initiative they had lost in November and regain their critical momentum. All the best party speakers were thrown in, including Ley, and the Nazis got 39.5 percent of the vote on January 15.[65] Hitler's tactic had worked and the impression of regained momentum would be invaluable in the behind-the-scenes negotiations which would surprisingly bring him the Chancellorship — and power — several weeks later.

In the meantime, back in Cologne, the local Jewish newspaper, the *Jüdisches Wochenblatt*, had headlined the Strasser crisis "The Nazi Curve Is Sinking. . . ." It noted with foreboding the replacement of Strasser, whom it regarded as somewhat more moderate, with Ley, whose anti-semitic tirades over the years were all too familiar:

63. For a description of Ley's role, see Konrad Heiden, *Der Fuehrer: Hitler's Rise to Power* (Boston, Beacon, 1969), pp. 505–6.
64. See Joseph Goebbels, *Vom Kaiserhof zur Reichskanzlei* (Munich, Zentralverlag der NSDAP. 1934), p. 226.
65. See Kiehl, *Mann an der Fahne*, opposite p. 159, which reproduces Ley's honorary citizenship for the town of Bösingfeld in Lippe, where he gave one of his speeches on January 4, 1933.

> We in Cologne can already picture for ourselves the further course of events, for we know that this Dr Ley, who has just been kicked upstairs, is an inferior, hate-filled psychopath, who has managed to create for himself even in right-wing circles a more than doubtful reputation for his lies about ritual murder. Here a development is becoming clear, which we regard with the greatest concern. Whatever ripples will be caused by this internal restructuring, we as Jews can be prepared for a change to a very different tune, although one asks oneself how the NSDAP could top itself with regard to Jew-baiting.

Despite this demonstration of concern, the article went on to anticipate that the responsible behavior of the current government could not help but lead to economic improvement, which, in turn, would deprive the Nazis of much of their support. Further elections, it opined, would bring further Nazi defeats. "All these things are interrelated and one must be hopeful that these times and what we have learned from them are harbingers of a more normal and quieter epoch, for us Jews as well."[66]

Six weeks later, on January 30, 1933, Adolf Hitler was named German Chancellor.

66. *Jüdisches Wochenblatt*, December 16, 1932. I am grateful to Dieter Corbach of Cologne for bringing this article to my attention.

CHAPTER 4

Wielding Power: The Substance and Style of Dictatorship

The Nazi seizure of power seemed to offer limitless possibilities to Robert Ley's vaulting ambitions. It gave him the opportunity to realize both his romantic social idealism as well as to indulge his limitless egotism and venality. Both were now to be magnified by Ley's access to enormous power and wealth and shaped by the singular nature of the emerging Nazi system.

Ultimately, Robert Ley wanted a German society which was conflict-free, a united, harmonious racial community. On one level this meant integrating the worker into society, for in National Socialist ideology the *sine qua non* of a healthy *Volksgemeinschaft* was ending the divisive differences between caste and class. On another level, it meant carrying out an apocalyptic struggle with world Jewry whose pervasive influence posed a possibly lethal threat to the autonomy Germany needed to create the healthy *Volk* community. The two levels were connected because only a Germany fully united and infused with National Socialist ideology would be capable of waging the titanic struggle against so lethal an international enemy with influence in so many countries. Here again Ley's embracing of Nazi ideology and his deepest psychological fears and aspirations reinforced one another; for only a healthy, secure *Volk* community could ultimately allay his fears of personal and social decline into chaos, and, at the same time, provide the context for his towering ambitions.

The main instrument in waging the great struggle which Ley envisioned lay in the Nazi Party and its affiliates. He meant to play a major personal role in the struggle, for he alone among the top Nazi leaders held an office which permitted him great control over the political cadres of the party (he was Reich Organizational Director (Reichsorganisationsleiter) of the NSDAP) while at the same time running one of its most important affiliates, the Deutsche Arbeitsfront, or German Labor Front.

Ley's strategy consisted in combining as closely as possible these two components of his personal empire and structuring them to fit his concept of exactly how the Nazi Party should best wage the struggle. His strategy was basically to view the Nazi Party as preacher/educator/*Betreuer* of the German people. Indeed, his favorite word was "*Betreuung*," which means quite literally "to take care of" in the sense that a Mafia godfather "takes care of" his people. The party then would be a gigantic propaganda school and welfare organization which would in a religious fashion inculcate National Socialist ideology in the minds of the German people, school them to regard themselves as a racial *Volk* community and then "take care of them," that is provide the material and psychological succor which would make them accept the regime and ultimately internalize its values.[1]

But there was a fly in the ointment. All this was not being done simply to make the lives of the Germans more comfortable, but rather to lay the groundwork for making enormous demands on them. Ley expected that the *Volksgemeinschaft*, the racial community, would also be a *Leistungsgesellschaft*, a performance-oriented society. Only a disciplined, obedient, hard-working, productive, efficient people could permit Germany to triumph in the apocalyptic struggle against the Jews. After all, viewed through Nazi lenses, life was not comfort — life was struggle. The benefits of *Betreuung* were not an end in themselves, but a means to an end.[2]

There was thus an unresolvable tension in Ley's concept, and indeed within National Socialism itself. It wanted at the same time to control the German people and to be loved by them. For the duration of the Third Reich, the Nazi Party and Ley would be torn between the love for power and the desire to be loved, and would constantly face falling between the stools as they approached the German people with the balm of butter and the challenge of guns.[3]

1. See Dietrich Orlow, *History of the Nazi Party: 1933–1945* (Pittsburgh, University of Pittsburgh Press, 1973), pp. 15f.
2. See Otto Marrenbach (ed.) *Fundamente des Sieges. Die Gesamtarbeit der Deutschen Arbeitsfront von 1933 bis 1940* (Berlin, Verlag der Deutschen Arbeitsfront) p. 17.
3. Orlow, *Nazi Party*, p. 261.

Ley's attitude toward the German people was characteristic for the Nazis. He viewed them as objects of paternalistic love; as targets for exhortation and quasi-religious conversion; and ultimately, as instruments for combat. But he never regarded them as full adults. He had little confidence in them if they remained untutored; no faith in their spontaneity (in fact he feared it); in short, no trust. They were children — to be watched, admonished, disciplined, and shaped into something other than that which they were, whether they wanted to be or not.

In one of his pamphlets, Ley complained about the difficulty of his task of setting a mass of 80 million people in motion, a mass which like any mass first obeyed the law of lethargy. "The people are children," he wrote, "stubborn, defiant, naughty, like children are wont to be. But also believing, loyal, and in need of love, the way children are. A people wants to be taken care of and must be taken care of. A people has the right to have care lavished on it by its leaders. It was the greatest foolishness of the democratic system to believe that a people can lead itself."[4]

In a speech before DAF functionaries in the fall of 1933 he said:

> Whereas the old state was a night watchman state, our state is an educational state, a pedagogue, a fatherly friend. From cradle to grave it doesn't let people go. . . . And so we begin already with the child of three years. As soon as it begins to think, it gets a little flag to carry. Then there follows school, Hitler youth, SA, military service. We don't let go of the person; and when all this is finished, then the Labor Front comes and picks him up and doesn't let him go until he dies, even if he resists it.[5]

To undertake such a gigantic task meant shouldering great responsibility; and those who do so often feel the need for great rewards. Ley, with his tremendous need to be somebody, demonstrated even more than some other Nazi bigwigs (with the possible exception of Göring) that he had indeed become somebody. Despite his efforts to appear just a "fellow worker" in his constant travels to factories and plants, Ley enjoyed the fruits of his high position, which included expensive villas, servants, a landed estate, high-powered automobiles, and the best cognac available. Hitler only encouraged such venality among his old followers and rewarded Ley

4. See *Arbeiter Bauern und Soldaten* (Berlin, Verlag der DAF, n.d.), p.16.
5. In "Was will die deutsche Arbeitsfront," published in September 1933 by the *Oberbergische Bote* (pamphlet is in the library of the Friedrich Ebert Stiftung, Bonn).

handsomely for his loyalty. Ley's attitudes spread to the party organizations which he led, particularly to the Labor Front, where corruption was rife and salary scales well above those of the private sector.

As Hitler took power then in January 1933, great vistas seemed open to Ley to realize his ambitions on a vast scale. He was never able to do so, however. Partly because the vision itself was fatally flawed; partly because Ley frequently was his own worst enemy. But primarily it was the nature of the Nazi system itself that constantly frustrated and ultimately thwarted Ley.

Robert Ley loved to draw up complex bureaucratic flow charts, the more complicated the better. For hours he could develop gigantic bureaucratic empires on paper, with logical areas of jurisdiction, exactly defined down to the last minor duty, with ever-increasing numbers of tasks which, in turn, added more lines to the flow chart, which then suggested even more tasks to be accomplished. It is ironic that he should have done so, because the Nazi regime was anything but a logical bureaucratic entity, smooth, efficient, jurisdictionally clear. Rather the opposite was the case. Nazi Germany was a labyrinthine nightmare, a "bureaucratic state of nature", where jurisdictions were never clear but overlapped in tangled thickets; where bureaucratic organizations — within the party, within the state apparatus, and between the two — became cancerous growths, constantly expanding and encroaching on each other; where top Nazis built giant personal empires like castles on a medieval landscape and fought with one another for turf, like Mafia families vying for gambling or prostitution rights in New Jersey. Indeed, in their time the Nazis were likened to gangsters — a not inappropriate analogy. The Nazi regime was thus a highly competitive enterprise in which, if one wanted to realize his goals, one had to be ruthless and cunning, able to sniff the wind, negotiate shifting alliances, keep one's nerve in tense situations and, above all, have access to the fount of all power — the Führer — for the ultimate weapon in the competitive struggle was an order from the Führer (*Führerbefehl*).[6]

6. The competitive nature of the regime has been amply demonstrated in the literature. See, for example, Ernst Fraenkel, *The Dual State* (New York, Oxford University Press, 1940) as the classical statement; more recently, see Gerhard Hirschfeld and Lothar Kettenacker (eds.), *Der 'Führerstaat': Mythos und Realität. Studies on The Structure and Politics of the Third Reich*, publications of the German Historical Institute, London (Stuttgart, Klett-Cotta, 1981), vol. 8. Most recently see Ian Kershaw's fine bibliographical study *The Nazi Dictatorship, Problems and Perspectives of Interpretation* (London, Edward Arnold, 1985), esp. Ch. 4.

Ley tried to fit this mold, and in many ways he did. He was certainly ruthless. He made a number of successful alliances in his time. He developed a large bureaucratic empire with enormous resources. And he remained to the end one of the Führer's inner circle. But he was also flawed. His psychological make-up caused him often to display poor judgment; to mistime moves; to make inappropriate remarks in public; to underestimate enemies and overestimate friends; above all, to overreach himself. And the alcohol did not help either, for it only magnified and reinforced these flaws. Indeed, the highly competitive Nazi system generated such intense pressures that many an aspirant to power was driven to the bottle. Ley's drinking problem got worse, not better, under these pressures.

The competition and confusion were rife everywhere. One finds it within the party and its affiliates, with the state apparatus and between state and party offices. It resulted in part from the fact that the Nazis had come to power "legally" and, therefore, had never needed to overthrow the state and step into its place. The state apparatus remained where it was, functioning as it always had. Next to it, searching for its own post-1933 role, stood the party. The relationship between the two was never clarified and remained unresolved during the Third Reich. Unlike fascist Italy, where the state wrestled the party under control, or the Soviet Union, where the party controlled the state, Nazi Germany preserved the ambiguity and out of that ambiguity ambitious men strove to carve power-empires.[7]

The competitive nightmare also resulted from Hitler's philosophy of power and how it should be wielded. As a convinced Social Darwinist, Hitler believed firmly in struggle. And so he encouraged competition in the faith that the best man would emerge and do the best job. As he once put it to one of his retinue, "As in nature the stronger prevails, so I see to it that personalities are able to prevail. I imagine myself to be a gardener, who looks over the fence at his garden and watches as the plants themselves struggle for their place in the light."[8] Indeed, Hitler virtually programmed competition into the system by such techniques as assigning the same task to two or

7. On the relationship between party and state, see Peter Diehl-Thiele, *Partei und Staat im Dritten Reich: Untersuchungen zum Verhältnis von NSDAP und allgemeiner innerer Staatsverwaltung 1933–1945*, 2nd edn (Munich, Beck Verlag, 1971).

8. See Institut für Zeitgeschichte Munich, unpublished ms, "Aufzeichnungen 1945–1948," by former Reichsbauernführer R. Walther Darré.

more subordinates, issuing vague or contradictory instructions, or bestowing grandiose titles on men who then tried to make something meaningful out of them. His purpose, of course, was clear. To keep himself unchallenged at the top, as the linchpin of the system, as the ultimate arbiter.

In this highly charged, competitive atmosphere the usual restraints on government, both ideological and institutional, broke down. Jurisdictional confusion created in individual Nazi power-aspirants a sense of omnicompetence, a sense that their organization could do everything, that their organization, indeed, embodied National Socialism and represented the model for its future development. Thus one had Himmler's vision of the SS state, Röhm's vision of the SA state, and a number of others competing with Ley's model.[9] Moreover, Hitler's contempt for legal niceties and his refusal to recognize any restraints on his own power infused the whole system, creating a pervading sense of normlessness, a sense that traditional values, legal norms, and institutional constraints no longer applied and that anything was possible. Finally, National Socialism as a millenarian movement also put its stamp on the regime. The various power aspirants, as we have seen with Ley, went about their work with a messianic fervor and intensity which underscored their firm belief that their tasks were not mundane ones but rather an integral part of an apocalyptic struggle between good and evil which, if they succeeded, would usher in the racial millenium. These characteristics gave the system an awesome dynamic but also caused it to behave in confusing, ill-organized, and ultimately, self-destructive ways, as Robert Ley's career amply demonstrates.

In a very real sense the problem lay in the fact that while many of the top Nazi leaders — and in a sense the party itself — found themselves prepared, during the years of struggle, for organizing successful political campaigns, when Hitler came to power it became apparent that they were ill prepared for the effective administration of a large, modern country. The same characteristics we have just noted as being integral to the regime — normlessness, omnicompetence, and messianic fervor — were qualities which had distinguished the party during the *Kampfjahre*. Its struggle against the Weimar Republic as a "system" put the NSDAP well outside the political norm of the Republic both in terms of concepts and beha-

9. On this point see Ronald Smelser, "Nazi Dynamics, German Foreign Policy and Appeasement," in Wolfgang Mommsen and Lothar Kettenacker (eds.), *The Fascist Challenge and the Policy of Appeasement* (London, Allen & Unwin, 1983), pp. 32–4.

vior. The fact that the Gauleiter in particular were jacks of all trades and carried out a number of unrelated tasks, such as speech-making, fund-raising, newspaper printing, and providing social services, developed in them early on a sense of omnicompetence. And the messianic fervor with which they had announced the coming of the Third Reich did not lessen on January 30, 1933, but rather took on new urgency. These qualities do not normally characterize a party in the seat of power, but in the case of the NSDAP there was really no willingness to alter the pre-*Machtergreifung* nature of the party. There was one other legacy of the years of struggle which has very much to do with our protagonist in this study. One might well ask oneself why a man such as Ley, an alcoholic, brain-damaged individual who, like the party itself, was very effective at pre-1933 activities, but ultimately a failure at wielding power, was allowed to rise so high in the regime and remain there to the bitter end. The answer lay in the fact that Hitler was almost neurotically attached to the loyal 'old comrades' who had been with him since the early days of the movement. They were, in almost a biblical sense, his disciples, and he seldom was able to part with any of them, just as he was unwilling to alter in any fundamental way the nature of the institution which had done so much to bring him to power. It was almost as if he had decided, superstitiously, somewhere in the recesses of his mind, that to change the ethos or personnel of the heroic age of struggle would spell his doom. In reality the opposite was true. Hitler's tenacity in hanging onto both the means and the men of the 1920s and early 1930s was a source of real weakness for the regime and ultimately contributed greatly to its demise.

With Hitler's takeover in January 1933 Ley soon found himself entangled in rivalries within the political organization of the party, with other affiliates of the party and with a number of government ministries. To the extent that he tried to resurrect Strasser's dominant position over the party organization, he found himself in trouble with Rudolf Hess. To the extent that he tried to increase the scope and jurisdiction of his Labor Front, he found himself in competition with other Nazi luminaries such as Alfred Rosenberg, the chief party ideologist, and R. Walther Darré, head of the party's agricultural affiliate. To the extent that he tried to determine social policy, he ran foul of the various government ministries. A running battle ensued which would be fought on a number of fronts simultaneously, now with one front blazing and another quiet, soon to be followed by a renewal of action in a hitherto quiet sector. Moreover, the battles also tended to overlap, as opponents made shifting alliances or staked out new territory. Since the main focus of this study is Ley's role as head of the Labor Front, we will tend to deal with a number of these struggles only peripherally as they relate to the main theme. In that way, one hopes to bring some order to what was essentially a very chaotic world.

Before turning to the Labor Front, however, it is necessary to look briefly at the rivalry within the party in connection with Ley's role as Reich Organization leader, in part because he tended to merge in his own mind and in terms of staffing the Political Organization of the party and the Labor Front, in part because his political enemies in the party, especially Hess, tried to use their party position as a springboard for wrestling control of the DAF from Ley.[10]

As we noted previously, the Strasser crisis of December 1932 persuaded Hitler never again to put so much control over the party into the hands of one man. As a result, he took over direct control of the party organization himself and fragmented what had been a unified structure. The agricultural affiliate of the party, the Office of Agrarian Policy, under Darré was made independent. A new office, the Political Central Commission, was created to make and carry out political decisions. What was left, which was considerable, fell under Ley's jurisdiction as Hitler's direct chief of staff. (Ley continued to use the title Reich Organization Director in the hope of restoring Strasser's former authority; his enemies kept trying to have it abolished for the opposite reason).[11]

Basically, Ley now controlled the personnel office, the organizational office, and the office for inservice-training of the party. The first he would use to try to control the political cadres; the second to restructure the party along the lines of his educational-ideological dream, and the third to train a corps of religious propagandists to carry out that dream. In addition, Ley inherited control over a number of professional, economic, and social-service offices in the party, the remnants of Strasser's attempt to create a new world in microcosm within the party which would then absorb and Nazify the larger society. These included the NS Factory Cell Organiza-

10. On the Ley–Hess rivalry, see Orlow, *Nazi Party*, pp. 15f., 70–9, 96–8, 102–5, 133–4, 151–3, 161–2, 182–92, 207–9, 215, 220–1, 266, 337–40, 420–3; Diehl-Thiele, *Partei und Staat*, pp. 201ff; Jochen von Lang, *The Secretary. Martin Bormann: The Man Who Manipulated Hitler* (New York, Random House, 1979), esp. pp. 68–71, 107–8, 189–91, 228–38, 315–16.
11. For an outline of the changes made after the Strasser affair, see Kissenkoetter, *Strasser*, pp. 364–70; also Orlow, *Nazi Party*, pp. 67–70.

tion, the Nazi union; the NS Hago, the Nazi Retailers Organization; the Nazi Women's Organization; the Nazi League of Public Officials; the Nazi League of Teachers; the Nazi Student Association; the Nazi Office for Municipal Politics; the Nazi Office for Technology; the Nazi Office for People's Charity; the Nazi Office for National Health; and the Nazi Office for War Victims. These organizations, in part, provided Ley potentially with the means of carrying out the second part of his dream: to "take care of" the German people.

But there were serious challenges to Ley's aspirations. As head of the Political Central Commission, Hitler appointed one of his oldest and most loyal associates, Rudolf Hess. Hess had been born in Alexandria, Egypt, fought in the First World War and then joined Hitler in the early days of the movement in Munich. He was involved with Hitler in the putsch attempt of November 1923 and was his cellmate in prison at Landsberg. It was Hess to whom Hitler dictated *Mein Kampf*. Hess, who continued as the Führer's personal secretary, was completely loyal to Hitler, closer to him than most 'old fighters' and was not nearly as dumb as contemporaries assumed. He represented formidable competition to Ley.[12] That competition would be even more formidable when Hess acquired as his own chief of staff, Martin Bormann. Bormann, relatively unknown to the public, had graduated from the right-wing vigilante in the early 1920s to chief of the party-owned insurance business. He also married the daughter of Walter Buch, head of the party court. But his real power position came from his relationship to Hitler. He ran Hitler's personal business affairs, was part of Hitler's inner sanctum and showed an uncanny talent for formulating Hitler's often vague wishes into clear bureaucratic directives. He was also a tireless worker and an implacable enemy of Robert Ley. Ultimately, after Hess's flight to England in 1941, Bormann would inherit his former chief's powers and become one of the most powerful men in the Third Reich as Hitler's "Secretary", by controlling the all important access to the Führer. In doing so he would become the nemesis of Robert Ley and a number of other top Nazis as well.[13] From the outset, then, the Hess–Bormann team would be a major rival to Ley in the party's political organization.

12. For a brief but useful portrait of Hess see Joachim Fest, *Das Gesicht des Dritten Reiches. Profile einer totalitären Herrschaft* (Munich, Piper, 1980), pp. 257–71.
13. Two useful studies of Bormann are James McGovern, *Martin Bormann* (London, Barker, 1968) and Lang, *Secretary*.

Ley's competitive position was not helped by the fact that soon after Hitler assumed power he gave Hess the title of "Deputy Führer" (*Stellvertreter des Fuhrers*, StdF for short) and made him head of a newly created Party Chancellory, whose task was to deal with relations between party and state. Thus Hess was in a position to monitor (and, he hoped, control) any impetus for legislation coming from the ranks of the party. Hitler, always the Social Darwinist, added to the confusion by also creating a new party rank, Reichsleiter, and bestowed it on sixteen top Nazis, including Ley, Himmler, and Göring. As always, it was not clear just what authority went along with the title, but it had potential since all sixteen were men who had that all-important direct access to Hitler. By fall 1933 Bormann was also appointed to the ranks of the Reichsleiter, which conferred two advantages on the Hess–Bormann team. It put Bormann on a par with Ley, since both were Reichsleiter; and, since Bormann was Hess's chief of staff, made Hess appear to be higher on the pecking order than Ley.[14] In the years after 1933, then, Ley's rivalry with Hess and Bormann would represent an important battle front, for it was both a jurisdictional struggle — with Ley and Hess basically contending to restore Strasser's old power position for themselves — and a battle of concepts. Ley envisioned the political wing of the party — in conjunction with his DAF — as a massive education-propagandistic machine, while Hess viewed the party as a command élite (see Plate 2).

While Hess and Bormann represented one kind of threat to Ley's plans, the party's parsimonious treasurer, Franz Xavier Schwarz, represented another. Ultimate power is the power of the purse, and Schwarz was more than willing to use that power in order to assert his own position and rein in those whose activities he felt to be detrimental to the party or whose ambition threatened to become overweening. Ley would conduct a running battle with Schwarz, in part to increase his share of annual allocations and also to retain exclusive control of the massive funds confiscated from the old trade unions. It did not help Ley's position that Schwarz did not think much of Ley's vision of the party as "educator", nor that Schwarz and Hess often cooperated with one another.[15]

Finally, one other set of power centers existed which could be both

14. See Orlow, *Nazi Party*, pp. 53–4, 56; Lang, *Secretary*, p. 69.
15. The best study on Schwarz as party treasurer is Ulf Lükemann, "Der Reichschatzmeister der NSDAP," dissertation, Free University of Berlin, 1963.

allies and antagonists of Ley in the party — the Gauleiters. These were the territorial chieftains of the party who had, almost in the manner of medieval dukes, complete political authority in the thirty-four Gaus. They owed allegiance to Hitler and to no one else; only he appointed them; only he could fire them — which he seldom did. They represented a useful counterweight to tendencies toward overcentralization of power in Berlin.[16]

Ley never gave up his struggle to wrestle the party's political wing under control; but increasingly — especially after Hess and Bormann began to make headway — Ley would devote less time to his position of Reich Organization Director and more time to the second leg of his empire, the DAF. The Labor Front held more promise: it was a brand new field of organization, it had immense wealth at its disposal; it represented a potentially powerful tool for social policy; and it represented the most challenging domestic task the regime faced — dealing with the German worker. It also represented a chance for Ley and those like him — parvenus, opportunists, social climbers — to enjoy the material emoluments of great power. The DAF would become notorious for its massive corruption, and its leader set the tone for the whole organization. However, before turning in the next chapter to the DAF, it is useful to consider briefly Ley's personal style of life as one of the prominent personalities of the Third Reich, for especially in the case of the parvenus at the top of Nazi Germany there is an important reciprocal relationship between the substance of power and the style of life which accompanied it. Nowhere better than in the private life of Robert Ley — one which made a mockery of the idea of *Volksgemeinschaft* — can one observe the old maxim at work: power tends to corrupt.

After the war, former German Finance Minister Schwerin von Krosigk remembered that Ley "used the wave of good fortune which had carried him up to enrich himself without restraint."[17] Krosigk was right. Ley's 1943 tax statement shows him earning the considerable salary of 3,920 marks per month (by comparison the average worker whom Ley was "taking care of" earned around 200 per month). Moreover, unlike almost all other Germans who were

16. See the somewhat outdated but still useful study of Peter Hüttenberger, *Die Gauleiter. Studie zum Wandel des Machtgefüges in der NSDAP*, Schriftenreihe der Vierteljahrshefte für Zeitgeschichte No. 19 (Stuttgart, Deutsche Verlagsanstalt, 1969).
17. See his unpublished "Politische Erinnerungen," located in the Institut für Zeitgeschichte Munich, ZS/A20 SvK vol. 12, p. 185.

subject to punishing deductions for various party purposes, Ley's statement shows no deductions for DAF and only occasional ones for Winter Relief. But his earnings were really considerably more than the tax statement would indicate.[18] His secretary, Hildegard Brueninghoff, when interrogated after the war, estimated his monthly income to be 7,100 marks (4,000 marks as head of DAF, 2,000 marks as ROL, 700 marks as Reichstag deputy, and 400 marks as Prussian Staatsrat).[19]

But this was just the tip of the iceberg. He also got huge royalties from his publications, including books and pamphlets. Although he did not advertise them publicly, he did insist that subtle pressures be put on the huge membership of the DAF through the organization itself to buy or subscribe to his publications. His secretary estimated that in a three-year period he earned 150,000 marks from his newspaper *Angriff* alone.[20]

And he had access to substantial sums of money from the former trade unions since, as DAF leader, he was given almost exclusive control of them. Since he had a tendency anyway to mix personal and institutional funds, one presumes that much of this money became discretionary money.

Most dramatically, Hitler also bestowed his financial blessings on the loyal paladin. In 1940 he gave Ley a one-time donation of one million marks![21]

This pecuniary cornucopia supported a grand life-style. Tendencies already present before the seizure of power to lead what one Berlin police report called a "loose life-style" became much more pronounced now that Ley's perennial financial difficulties were behind him.[22] He owned a number of villas throughout Germany, all of them in exclusive neighborhoods, and staffed them lavishly. In Berlin, his main seat of residence, the villa was located in fashionable Grunewald (Herthastrasse 13/15). Here his staff included a butler, a cook, two nannies for the children, a chambermaid, a

18. The tax forms are located in BA NS 26/1358a.
19. See "Private Life of Ley", a seventeen-page translation of her handwritten statement in US National Archives, RG 238 Collection of World War Crimes, Justice Jackson file (hereafter "Brueninghoff"), p. 13.
20. On advertising, see DAF Gauobmann to DAF Kreispresse- und Propagandawalter, Gau Bayerisch Ostmark of May 5, 1939, in US National Archives Microcopy T-81, Roll 66, Frame 76140; also "Brueninghoff", p. 13.
21. Ibid., p. 13; Schwerin von Krosigk puts the sum at 1.2 million marks, "Politische Erinnerungen," p. 185.
22. Report of Polizei-Präsidium Berlin, n.d. BA NS 26/1358a.

gardener, and a housekeeper. His home in a wealthy Munich suburb (Geiselgasteig 6) housed another housekeeper and two maids. And there was yet another home in the east at Saarow/Mark (Kronprinzendamm 27). A fourth home — in Bonn (Blücherstrasse) — he had turned over to his divorced wife and daughter. Up to 1938 the DAF paid for these homes. Thereafter they were paid for privately, but expensive entertainment costs caused Ley to make a special arrangement with the DAF in late 1939 whereby he would pay the DAF 1,000 marks monthly and the DAF would then take over all household accounts. There is little doubt as to who got the better part of that deal.[23]

Ley also had a number of cars, including a powerful Mercedes, and presented his second wife with two automobiles as gifts. In order to travel officially in style, he also had a railroad car refitted for himself and had access to several planes through the DAF with which he would frequently fly to his estate.[24]

He also dressed very expensively, as did his wife, and furnished their villas with expensive paintings and decor. His life-style, although not too different from a number of Nazi big-wigs, especially Göring, nevertheless attracted attention. Himmler, head of the SS once asked his masseur, Felix Kersten, somewhat caustically, "How do you think . . . Ley would take to monastic life? I would just like to see Ley's face if he was offered sour milk and black bread for nourishment and the Bhagavad-Gita to sustain his soul."[25]

Ley's corruption took on such dimensions that in 1938 the judge of the party court went to Hitler, laid out a voluminous file of material and demanded that Ley be cashiered. Hitler threw him out. Such legal niceties meant nothing to Hitler, who anyway feared making major changes at the top of his administration. It was also rumored that Hitler was quite taken by Ley's new, young wife. At any rate, after throwing out Buch, Hitler went to Ley's for tea.[26]

Access to such funds only increased Ley's propensity to gigantomania and magnified his already bad judgment. He got enthusiastic about every hare-brained scheme that came along and was

23. See "Brueninghoff," pp. 11–12.
24. For correspondence on the railroad car, see Lammers (Chief of the Reichskanzlei) to Bormann, August 24, 1941, in Heiber, *Parteikanzlei*, 101/08420–1. On the the cars and plane, see "Brueninghoff," p. 10; see also Albert Speer, *Inside the Third Reich* (New York, Macmillan, 1970), p. 217.
25. See *The Kersten Memoirs 1940–1945* (New York, Macmillan, 1957), p. 156.
26. See Darré, "Aufzeichnungen," vol. 1, 37; also Lang, *Secretary*, p. 122.

prepared to spend large amounts of money on the most impractical ideas. Once, as Hitler's architect, Albert Speer, was planning to open up large new boulevards in Berlin for development, Ley got the investment bug. "With some difficulty," Speer later related, "we restrained Dr Ley . . . from using the enormous funds he collected from workmen's contributions to buy up a fifth of the entire length of the boulevard for his own purposes. Even so, he obtained a block a thousand feet in length, which he planned to make into a large amusement area."[27]

On another occasion Ley and his wife accompanied Hermann Giessler, the architect whom Hitler had commissioned to redesign parts of Munich, to the showroom where models were set up. Ley indicated interest in building on one block. When asked what the purpose of his building would be he said: "A large fashion house. We'll determine all the fashions. My wife will take care of that end. We'll need the whole building for it. Lets! My wife and I will set the German fashions . . . . And . . . and . . . we'll need whores too! Lots of them, a whole house full, with the most modern furnishings. We'll take everything in hand; a few hundred millions for the building, that's nothing." As ridiculous as it sounds, Ley actually undertook negotiations with the Propaganda Ministry in Berlin in 1941 to jointly unify the fashion industry, purge it of Jews and, taking advantage of the eclipse of Paris, make Berlin into a world fashion leader. Always the educator, he also planned to have offices in the factories where working women could be advised sartorially. Ley was prepared to put up 1 million marks from DAF to hire and première 1,000 exemplary models.[28]

Access to power, wealth, and the good things of life was not without effect on Ley's family life. Apparently, he had been seeing a number of women since the seizure of power in 1933, but in 1935 he met and became infatuated with Inge Spilker, young, beautiful, and charming daughter of opera singer Max Spilker and herself a soprano. In 1938 Ley divorced his first wife and on August 20 married Inge. The birth of their first child, Lore, on November 6, suggests that the pregnancy precipitated the termination of the old union and the beginning of the new one. They were to have two more children, Wolf, born in 1940 and Gloria in 1941. Reports on

27. See *Inside*, p. 141–2.
28. Ibid., p. 142; for the negotiations, see internal memo, probably by Staatssekretär Gutterer, of the Reichspropagandaministerium of October 9, 1941, in BA R55/622, pp. 3–5.

Ley's relationship with his family contrast dramatically. After the war Ley's secretary testified that Ley was a good father to his children and remained impartial despite the fact that they came from several wives. He supposedly made good provision for his first wife and daughter and remained on friendly terms. Indeed, the secretary praised generally his attitude toward women, saying that he "behaved courteously, attentively, and gentlemanly toward [them]." As for his second wife, she appears to have been the love of his life. Brueninghoff remembered that "without a doubt, Inge was the woman whom Ley had loved. He gave in to any of her wishes."[29] Indeed, one of the documents Ley composed in his cell in 1945 was a reminiscence of her (in fact, he perceived her as being with him). Commenting on her beauty and character he wrote, "Your outward beauty was paired with a pure soul, a truthful character, a clever understanding and marvelous voice. Your pure soprano captivated everyone. You were a rare creation of our Lord God. Often one was tempted to believe in a trick of nature, so ethereally translucent was your skin."[30]

And yet there was another side to the picture. Ley could also be crude and cruel, if not to say downright tasteless. On one occasion von Krosigk was a guest at the Ley's for dinner. After the meal Ley went to an easel and with a flourish unveiled a portrait of his wife — naked from the waist up. The picture, probably painted by the President of the Reich Art Chamber, Ziegler (who bore the dubious title Reich Pubic Hair Painter (Reichsschamhaarmaler)), caused even old Nazis among the guests to catch their breath. As for the Finance Minister, he regretted that his wife had not attended: "She would have found something appropriate to say to this unveiling. Nothing occurred to me."[31] On another occasion, Ley apparently unveiled his own wife, tearing her clothes off so that guests could admire her lovely body. "He treats me outrageously," she said, "he'll end up killing me one day."[32] Indeed, on December 29, 1942, after a trivial quarrel with her husband, Inge Ley shot herself. Ley's secretary thought the suicide was occasioned by an alcohol and drug addiction problem which Inge could not master; she had had gall stones and an accident while carrying Gloria and had become

29. See "Brueninghoff," p. 8.
30. He entitled the document "Zwiegespräch" (Dialogue). US National Archives, RG 238 Collection of World War Two Crimes, Justice Jackson File, p. 1. The document is dated August 14, 1945.
31. "Politische Erinnerungen," p. 159.

addicted to her medication.[33] More likely she was the victim of her husband's alcohol problem, which was getting worse along with his brain disease. The dramatic contrasts in description of his family life are very suggestive of an alcoholic who can be alternately solicitous and cruel. Indeed, Brueninghoff noticed changes in Ley's public behavior which suggest the same thing. At various times, she testified, he would respond to petitions from all over Germany on such matters as housing, furniture, or air-raid victims, would stage annual Christmas parties for orphans, and provide housing for bombed-out families. On other occasions — indeed increasingly as the war went on — he showed a violent temper at the office and would behave badly to the very workers he was trying to court. Once he was visiting Telefunken in Berlin when an air raid commenced. Much to the resentment of the workers Ley immediately repaired to the nearest municipal shelter.[34]

Indeed, there many reports about Ley's drinking habits. Dr Kersten, Himmler's physician, refused to treat Ley after a month in which Kersten had not once found Ley sober when he made his house calls. Himmler prevailed upon Kersten to treat him anyway because of his loyalty to Hitler and his contribution to the party.[35] On one occasion, Ley and his drunken entourage caused a ruckus in Heidelberg when one of the Reich Organization Leaders' staff roughed up the Baden Minister President. A local party man complained to Hess, reminding him of a similar incident in Baden-Baden two years before, when police had to intervene. The complainant concluded with resignation, however, that nothing was done because of Ley's high office.[36] Perhaps the most embarrassing incident resulting from Ley's penchant for alcohol came in 1937. The Duke and Duchess of Windsor were visiting Germany, officially as guests of the DAF, which meant that Ley hosted them.

32. Quoted in Erich Bleuel, *Sex and Society in Nazi Germany* (New York, Bantam, 1973), p. 3.
33. "Brueninghoff," p. 8. Glenn Enfield, *Hitler's Secret Life* (New York, Stein & Day, 1979), p. 85 claims, without substantiating evidence, that Inge Ley comitted suicide because she was infatuated with Hitler and wanted to have sex with him but he refused. In fall 1943 Ley, who by his own admission "could not be without a woman," took up with a beautiful young Estonian girl, who remained with him to the end of the war ("Brueninghoff," p. 8).
34. "Brueninghoff," pp. 2–4.
35. See Achim Besgen, *Der stille Befehl, Medizialrat Kersten, Himmler und das Dritte Reich* (Munich, Nymphenburger Verlagshandlung, 1960), p. 183.
36. See Eduard Max Hofweber to Hess, January 25, 1935, in Heiber, NSDAP *Parteikanzlei*, 124 01494.

One of Ley's former aides later remembered what happened when an inebriated Ley insisted on chauffeuring the couple in his big Mercedes around workers' barracks at a factory on the outskirts of Munich. "He drove the car through the locked gates and then raced up and down at full speed between the barracks, scaring hell out of the workers and nearly running over several. The next day Hitler told Göring to take over the Duke's visit before Ley killed him."[37] It is some indication of the hypocrisy of the Nazi regime that the 1939 "keep-healthy-through-abstinence" campaign was launched by Ley, who proclaimed as the official slogan "Moderation is not enough! . . . We must also be radical in abstinence."[38] Ley did try to cut down on his drinking after a warning from Hitler, but the combination of high-pressure political competition and the perceived ameliorating effect of alcohol on his malady brought him back to the bottle again.

The real tangible symbol, though, of Ley's corruption and gigantomania, his aspirations to achieve social status, and his attempt to overcome childhood familial disaster and establish a place of permanent security was his landed estate, Rottland. Rottland is. in miniature, the story of Robert Ley and the Third Reich.

Rottland was an estate near the town of Waldbröl in Ley's home area. It had been acquired in 1924 by an evangelical congregation in Cologne and had served as a convalescent home. On December 1, 1935, Ley bought it for 150,000 marks.[39] Like so many of his social projects, Rottland contained the germ of a good idea, which was then spoiled by ideology, social pathology, and gross exaggeration. Initially, Ley spared no expense to make the estate productive. Swampy land was drained and brought into production, employing the best fertilizers and seeds. One of the first hay-drying machines was set up. A nursery was constructed. The estate was designated a *Lehrbetrieb* (school for apprentices). Soon there were 500 acres of barley, oats, rye, and wheat.[40]

37. Enfield, *Secret Life*, p. 114. The author interviewed one of Ley's former aides, Hans Sopple.
38. See Richard Grunberger, *The Twelve Year Reich: A Social History of Nazi Germany 1933-1945* (New York, Holt, Rinehart, & Winston, 1971) p. 65.
39. See Gottfried Corbach, *Geschichte von Waldbröl* (Cologne, Scriba, 1972), p. 527.
40. See unpublished manuscript by the former steward of the estate under Ley, Wilhelm Heuser, entitled "Hitler und sein Paladin," pp. 19–24; also letter to the author from Dieter Corbach of April 12, 1986. Corbach grew up near the estate and personally observed its condition during the Third Reich; the hay-drying machine was mentioned in a letter from local resident Tom Doch to author, March 23, 1986.

But then Ley's ideological side took over. All the buildings, some of them quite venerable half-timbered ones, were to be demolished. Ley brought in the architect Prof. Clemens Klotz, who designed the monumental and pretentious *Ordensburgen* ("order castles") for the party and whose specialty was turning Hitler's grandiose and limitless ideas into wood and stone. Up went a new set of buildings in a horseshoe-shaped design, with a long drive leading up to the manor house. Flanking the entrance stood two huge statues mounted in cement, one of a stormtrooper holding a swastika flag, the other a peasant sowing seed.[41] Inside, the house was finished lavishly. On its walls hung valuable paintings including a Kaulbach, a Corinth, two Menzel sketches, and Pesne's portrait of Frederick the Great. To set his new possesion firmly in a Nazi racial context, Ley had it declared an *Erbhof* — an hereditary-entailed estate (protected from foreclosure or forced sale and division, which only racially sound German farmers with so many generations on the soil could own).[42] Unfortunately, all the grandiose building got in the way of, and nearly ruined, that year's crop, which rotted in the rain for lack of a place for storage.

The estate steward, Wilhelm Heuser, with an eye to yields, had submitted a modest plan for improvements. Ley rejected them as far too modest. In a very revealing statement Ley told Heuser:

> Your suggestions are not bad and if I were still Ley the little man (*der kleine Ley*) they would have sufficed. But I'm not that anymore. Now I must have something beautiful constructed here; something archetectonically beautiful. One day the Führer will accompany me to view my possession. What would he say if I had operated in a narrow-minded, hidebound way and if I hadn't fashioned this reconstruction into a symbol of National Socialist power and greatness." In this same spirit, Ley refused to have his pasture fenced. "Little people build fences," he said, "great people don't."[43]

And on his estate Ley played the great man. Flying in from Berlin he would buzz the area to signal his arrival at the local airport. A chauffeur waited to drive him to Rottland. The whole staff right down to the stable boys would then have to stand at attention in

41. See Heuser, "Hitler und sein Paladin," p. 20.
42. See "Brueninghoff," pp. 6, 13.
43. See Heuser, "Hitler und sein Paladin," pp. 22–3; also interview with Heuser in the *Oberbergische Volkszeitung*, no. 169, July 23, 1980, p. 2.

front of the manor house as Ley's car pulled up. He was charitable to the locals — he periodically set up a beer tent and invited widows, children, and soldiers on leave — but in a self-consciously patronizing way. Speaking to several local farmers from his horse, he reminded one witness of Landvogt Gessler in Schiller's *William Tell*.[44] And a jovial lord-of-the-manor air could not disguise the acquisitiveness and fanaticism underneath. On one occasion he confiscated land from local people for one of his projects (land which they got back again after the war). On another, in early 1938, he allegedly ordered the expulsion of mentally retarded children from the local Lutheran home (probably in connection with the opening of a new Adolf Hitler school in Waldbröl); the children were sent first to a former Franciscan cloister in the Westerwald and were eventually sent to the notorious Hadamar institution, where they presumably perished.[45]

Nor did the exigencies of the war and its concomitant shortages deter Ley from improving his estate. In 1942 he wrote to Albert Speer, Hitler's then Plenipotentiary for regulating the building sector of the economy requesting materials to complete his pigsty.[46] Speer later recalled the incident. "Robert Ley fought for a pigsty on his model farm. This was actually a war priority, he argued, since his experiments in hog raising were of great importance for food production. I turned down this request in writing but took gleeful delight in addressing the letter: "To the Reich Organization Chief of the National Socialist Party and Chief of the German Labor Front. Subject: Your pigsty."[47]

In the end Rottland did not survive Ley or the war. At the end of March 1945 Ley had local Hitler Youth boys fill the buildings with combustibles and then sent an SS officer, Sturmführer Eisgruber, to torch it. Hitler had never come to visit after all. The best Ley had done was Baldur von Schirach, Nazi Youth Leader.[48] What was to have been the continuation of Ley's peasant roots, the expiation for his childhood shame, the grand manor house of the new racial aristocracy, the architectural expression of Nazi greatness disappeared with the man and the movement.

44. Remembrance of Dieter Corbach in letter to author of April 12, 1986.
45. Letter to author from Julius Cieslik of March 4, 1986. Cieslik worked at the Lutheran home at the time.
46. See Ley to Speer of April 14, 1942, in BA NS 26/1358a.
47. *Inside*, p. 216.
48. Corbach remembered the burning (letter to author); Schirach's visit mentioned in the *Oberbergische Volkszeitung* interview; "Brueninghoff" mentions the SS officer, p. 12.

CHAPTER 5

The Creation of the Deutsche Arbeitsfront

The Deutsche Arbeitsfront (DAF) was the most important institutional response to a vexing social problem facing the Nazi regime from its inception: how to integrate the German worker into the new Third Reich, or at least, to render him organizationally impotent. This appeared to be no easy task. After all, the working class had been the most impervious of all social groups to Nazi propaganda appeals during the years of struggle. The Nazis did succeed in attracting some young, unemployed workers, many of them into the SA, but for the most part, German labor remained immune to Nazi political appeals. Nazi attempts to penetrate the factories through their organization of factory cells (Nationalsozialistische Betriebszellenorganisation, or NSBO) had garnered only very limited success prior to 1932. Instead, non-communist worker organizations, especially the Social Democratic Party and the related free trade unions, had remained bastions of support for the Weimar Republic.[1]

As the Nazis reached for power, it was clear that worker political parties, like all other parties, would have to go. Hitler was not about to share his monopoly on political power. But what about trade unions? Here the Nazi leadership was ambivalent. On the one hand, it was reluctant to dismiss the whole idea of trade unions. That might have been premature and dangerous. The unions had done

1. There is general agreement on the Nazi failure to break into the ranks of the working class. The interpretation which emphasizes more strongly than the others Nazi successes in this regard is Max Kele, *Nazis and Workers: National Socialist Appeals to German Labor, 1919–1933* (Chapel Hill, University of North Carolina Press, 1972). The best study of the relationship between National Socialism and the German working class is Timothy Mason, *Sozialpolitik im Dritten Reich. Arbeiterklasse und Volksgemeinschaft*, 2nd edn (Opladen, Westdeutscher Verlag, 1978).

too much for the worker in the past, something even the Nazis reluctantly admitted. Moreover, there were many Nazis, particularly those who had been close to the Strasser wing of the party, who strongly supported the idea of a specifically "Nazi" trade union. These people clustered in significant numbers in the NSBO, which they hoped to transform into a super-union.[2] On the other hand, unions represented in the eyes of most Nazis, Marxist class struggle, something anathema to them and something they had promised to abolish. At the same time, the Nazis were very beholden to business for its support, financial and other, and business would dearly like to have seen the unions disappear. For a time, the Nazis contented themselves with propaganda on behalf of so-called "pure" trade unions, that is ones emptied of the concept of class struggle, but this point sounded increasingly hollow against the failure of the NSBO either to successfully infiltrate the working class on a large scale or to transform itself from a political combat organization designed for fighting Marxism in the plant to a genuine trade union. Soon after the seizure of power, then, if not before, it became clear to Hitler that the trade unions would have to be smashed whatever else was done. Earlier in his career Hitler seems to have harbored the notion that Nazi trade unions might well be possible, as passages in *Mein Kampf* indicated. By 1932 at the latest, however, he seems to have given up this idea. In discussions with a number of business leaders in May, he floated the idea of eliminating the unions; they gave it their full approval.[3]

During the several months after January 1933 developments conspired to lend a certain sense of urgency to getting rid of the unions. One was the startling passivity bordering on obsequiousness on the part of the union leadership vis-à-vis the Nazis. This was even the case with the large, socialist free trade unions which, demoralized by the deepening Depression, facing a membership composed of 44 percent unemployed, and led by tired, older men, cast about impotently for an effective strategy.[4] Already before Hitler's ap-

2. On the NSBO, see Jeremy Noakes, *The Nazi Party in Lower Saxony 1921–1933* (London, 1971), pp. 174–82; also Mason, *Arbeiterklasse*, pp. 66ff.
3. For Hitler's earlier ruminations on the union question, see *Mein Kampf*, 378–9 printing (Munich, NSDAP Zentralverlag, 1938), pp. 670–83. On Hitler's speech to businessmen, see Arthur Schweitzer, *Big Business in the Third Reich* (Bloomington, Indiana University Press, 1964), p. 359. For a contemporary background on the NSBO, see Gerhard Starcke, *NSBO und Deutsche Arbeitsfront* (Berlin, Reimar Hobbing, 1934).
4. See Helga Grebing, "Gewerkschaftliches Verhalten in der politischen Krise der

pointment as Chancellor, Theodor Leipart, president of the socialist umbrella trade union organization (the Allgemeiner Deutscher Gewerkschaftsbund, or ADGB), had agreed to reckon with any government, negotiate with any economics minister and, if necessary, "also go to the chancellor, whoever he might be."[5]

In the weeks after the Nazi takeover little more occurred to Leipart and his colleagues. Their abhorrence of violence prevented preparing for armed resistance, while fears of retribution from the regime and possible non-compliance on the part of the membership squelched the idea of a general strike. The already pronounced demoralization only deepened in the wake of the dramatic events of late February and early March. The Reichstag fire of February 28 led to a state of emergency and special powers for Hitler's regime, which only strengthened its position vis-à-vis any opposition. The elections of March 5, which gave the Nazi–Conservative coalition an absolute majority seemed, in turn, to legitimize the new regime and its measures. The result on the part of the unions was increasing accommodation, which took a number of forms.

More and more the socialist trade union leaders seemed to abandon their own principles and embrace at least the terminology of the new regime. In a speech, Leipart affirmed the *German* identity of the trade unions and the ideal of a specifically *German* socialism, which seemed to scuttle the old principle of international working-class solidarity.[6] The union leaders also applauded the Nazi goal of integrating the worker into the nation and expressed the timid hope that this task would not be carried out "through physical threats or moral constraint." They also thought they saw a more responsible Nazism now that Hitler was in power. "*National Socialism governing* would be better than a National Socialism on the attack," they vainly opined.[7]

As an additional self-protective measure, the ADGB cut off its longstanding connections with the political wing of socialism, the Social Democratic Party, and informed Hitler so on March 29.[8] If

Jahre 1930–1933," as addendum to the reprint of the *Gewerkschaftszeitung* 1933 (Berlin, Bonn, Dietz, 1983), pp. 7–47.

5. *Gewerkschaftszeitung*, no. 4, January 28, 1933, pp. 50ff.
6. See reference to Leipart's Bernau speech in ibid., p. 53.
7. Ibid., no. 13, April 1, 1933, p. 197.
8. See Dieter von Lölhöffel, "Die Umwandlung der Gewerkschaften in eine nationalsozialistiche Zwangsorganisation," in Ingeborg Esenwein-Rothe, *Die Wirtschaftsverbände von 1933 bis 1945,* Schriften des Vereins für Socialpolitik no. 37

Socialism as a political phenomenon had to go, they reasoned, there was perhaps a chance to save it as a social phenomenon, if only the trade unions could survive organizationally. Indeed, they really seemed to think that unions had become an indispensable part of the economic landscape.

This stubborn clinging to the organization, as if the ship could not go down in a storm, led the ADGB leadership to counsel the mass of trade-union members to caution, thus preventing any preparations for widespread resistance. At a national meeting the very day Hitler was appointed Chancellor, the leadership intoned the watchword: "Organisation — not demonstration. That's the slogan of the hour." That same day a proclamation to the workers read: "The vital interests of all the workers are at stake. In order effectively to fend off attacks against the constitution and people's rights, cool heads and prudence are the watchwords. Do not let yourselves be provoked into premature and therefore dangerous individual acts."[9] Even the Reichstag fire which foreshadowed a quick end to constitutional rights led to admonitions "to keep a cool head and not be diverted from a legal struggle against all dangers to constitutional freedoms."[10]

And, finally, the union leaders appealed to the President and other government ministers urging them to uphold legality. Hindenburg declined to give them an audience.[11]

Accommodation eventually went so far that the socialists seemed to be applauding the victory of their former, bitter enemies. On April 29, just three days before the Nazis smashed the unions, a younger union leader, Walther Pahl, wrote: "We really do not have to 'cave in' in order to confess that the victory of National Socialism, although it was won in a victory over a party which we recognized as the bearer of the socialist idea, is also our victory, in so far as today the socialist task is that of the whole nation."[12]

(Berlin, Duncker & Humbolt, 1965), pp. 152–3; also Hans Joachim Reichhardt, "Die deutsche Arbeitsfront. Ein Beitrag zur Geschichte des nationalsozialistichen Deutschlands und zur Struktur des totalitären Herrschaftssystems," unpublished dissertation, FU-Berlin, 1956, pp. 20–4.

9. *Gewerkschaftszeitung*, no. 5, February 4, 1933, pp. 65, 67.
10. Ibid., no. 9, March 4, 1933, p. 129.
11. Ibid., no. 5, February 4, 1933, p. 67; see also letters of March 10 and April 5 to Hindenburg detailing acts of violence against the unions and requesting that he take action to stop them in BA R43II/531, pp. 9–10 and 37–51, respectively.
12. Ibid., 17, April 29, 1933, p. 259. This was the last issue of the GZ; the Nazis later claimed that Leipart had approached them secretly before the *Gleichschaltung* in

And this statement was coming from one of the leaders of the largest and hitherto most militant trade-union organizations. The other unions, including the various white-collar organizations, as well as the Catholic and liberal (Hirsch-Duncker) unions showed even less resistance. After the coup against the socialist unions in May they would either go over to the Nazis entirely or voluntarily dissolve themselves.[13]

It is surely one of the greatest ironies of these initial months of the Third Reich that, while the socialists were doing their best to avoid even the appearance of violent resistance to the Nazis, Hitler was concerned (to a far greater extent than his Conservative allies) that precisely such an eventuality was possible — and, under certain circumstances, even likely. In his first Cabinet meeting, on January 30, while Hitler's Economics Minister, Alfred Hugenberg, was blithely recommending the suppression of the Communist Party so that a majority for an enabling Act could be obtained in the Reichstag, the new Chancellor exhibited considerable anxiety about the possibility of widespread social unrest. According to his experience, "the banning of parties had no purpose. He feared difficult domestic struggles and possibly a general strike as results of any banning of the [Communist Party]."[14] Clearly, Hitler at this point, like his paladin Roberty Ley, was still deeply under the influence of the stab-in-the-back myth. But he need not have worried in this instance, for the Nazi victory would be infinitely easier than he imagined, a fact which gradually dawned on him in the weeks after the *Machtergreifung*. And that coming victory was made even sweeter by a clever step contrived by Joseph Goebbels. May 1 was traditionally Labor Day in Europe, the day on which, since the 1880s, socialists had demonstrated for such goals as the eight-hour day and

---

May 1933 in the city of Danzig, where the Nazis had just got a majority and offered to negotiate a deal with Hitler, whereby they would subordinate themselves to the regime. The protocol of these negotiations supposedly disappeared, however, shortly after May 2 into one or another DAF office while it was on its way from Berlin to Hitler in Munich. See Hoffman (Gestapo) memorandum of May 7, 1935, in BAK, R58/447, p. 16.

13. See Lölhöffel, "Umwandlung," p. 154–5. The best study to date of the background to the events of April and May 1933 remains Hans-Gert Schumann, *Nationalsozialismus und Gewerkschaftsbewegung. Die Vernichtung der deutschen Gewerkschaften und der Aufbau der 'Deutschen Arbeitsfront'*, (Hannover, Frankfurt, Norddeutsche Verlagsanstalt, 1958).

14. See minutes (Ministerialrat Wienstein) of Cabinet meeting in BAK, R41I/1459, pp. 241–5.

better working conditions. During the Weimar years the socialists had attempted in vain to get the day recognized as a national holiday with pay. Now, on April 4, the Nazi regime announced publicly that May 1 would be proclaimed the "day of national labor," a national holiday. Seeing the Nazis co-opt their day, the trade-union leadership were now maneuvered into the position of applauding the step and urging their members to take part in the celebration, which they did on April 22.[15]

Thus the bankruptcy of the trade-union movement in Germany seemed to be complete, and the Nazis were fully aware of it. There seemed little prospect of any firm resistance to a plan which called for the elimination of such compliant unions. As Robert Ley put it later, "All of us who took part on the 2nd of May know how Herr Leipart and whatever their names were, were waiting for us to come."[16] It is crucial to stress this important factor of trade-union accommodation, not only as background to the events of May 2 but also to underscore that what success the DAF might have with the workers in the coming years in part derived from the failure of the trade-union leadership in 1933 and the resulting helplessness and demoralization on the part of the German working class.

Another development was even more important in inducing the regime to act against the trade unions when it did: the spontaneous and widespread wildcat action of various Nazi groups, especially the SA, on a grass-roots level against the unions, their personnel, and property. We must keep in mind that Hitler's appointment unleashed a veritable orgy of activity on the part of hundreds of thousands of Nazis, who, having fought for years for victory, now sought with messianic fervor to slake their thirst for revenge on their enemies and to acquire a place at the trough. The spring and summer of 1933 witnessed veritable chaos in the economy as a plethora of Nazi "commissars" were busy firing or replacing important businessmen from their positions as directors and board members of companies, from chambers of commerce, banks, and

15. See ADGB proclamation signed by Langner of April 27 in BAK, R58, 80; apparently many SPD locals were also seeing the handwriting on the wall and swiftly accommodating, something which disgusted and worried the Nazis. "It is downright shocking when one has to read about whole SPD locals going over to the NSDAP," deplored one Nazi newspaper, "When this change of position represented a change of conscience we'd be extraordinarily happy. Unfortunately, that is naturally not the case, and because of this, serious dangers are arising." *Der Deutsche*, no. 78, April 1, 1933 in BAK, NS26/282.

16. In *Deutschland ist schöner geworden* (Berlin, Mehden-Verlag, 1936), p. 259.

stock exchanges. Martin Mutschmann, Gauleiter of Saxony, even arrested and detained for a month the venerable president of the Saxon Staatsbank, Carl Degenhardt.[17] A special target was the trade unions, and in a very real sense it can be said that the actual destruction of the trade unions came from below weeks before the official government act of May 2.[18] Indeed, as was the case with the one day boycott against the Jews at the beginning of April, the May 2 blow against the trade unions came in part as an attempt at the top to head off and contain widespread, uncontrolled activities at the grass-roots level.

As one observer put it in retrospect, "The real bearers of the brown upheaval, the disinherited, the dispossessed, now presented their bill."[19] All over Germany, encouraged by the fact that the SA had been deputized to round up Communists, other Nazi organizations, particularly the NSBO, felt free to play vigilante against the trade unions. Union buildings were occupied or closed, often under the eyes of cooperative police. In countless factories NSBO commissars threw out the elected union representatives and took their places. What began tentatively turned into a wave after the March 5 elections. Starting on March 6, over 160 towns and cities reported such actions, including Berlin, Kiel, Kassel, Breslau, and Dresden. Bavaria and Saxony were especially hard hit. Even the ADGB school at Bernau was occupied. Unions protested in vain to Labor Minister Franz Seldte that elected factory councils all over the country were being prevented from carrying out their tasks.[20] That grass-roots Nazis could operate with such impunity was viewed in

17. See Willi Boelcke, *Die deutsche Wirtschaft 1930–1945. Interna des Reichswirtschaftsministeriums* (Düsseldorf, Droste Verlag, 1973), p. 68. Ley had to issue directives forbidding all kinds of deviant behavior, including the wearing of party badges to which the member was not entitled, establishing wildcat "race offices," attacking consumer co-ops, demanding the free use of cars from auto manufacturers, and attacking foreigners. See BAK, NS25/489.
18. See BAK R58/80 for numerous reports of attacks by wildcat Nazi units on union and SPD people. For example, Schlimme (ADGB) to Göring, March 8, and to Vice Chancellor Franz von Papen, April 5. In the latter he complains of beatings, break-ins, and so on, in thirty-nine cities. A number of scholars concur in this assessment. See, for example, Mason, *Sozialpolitik*, pp. 82ff; also Erich Matthias and Rudolf Morsey (eds.), *Das Ende der Parteien 1933* (Düsseldorf, Droste Verlag, 1960), pp. 171–5; also Geoffrey Pridham, *Hitler's Rise to Power: The Nazi Movement in Bavaria, 1923–1933* (London, Harper & Row, 1973), p. 311.
19. See Hans-Berndt Gisevius, *Adolf Hitler: Versuch einer Deutung* (Munich, Bertelsmann, 1973), vol. I, p. 121.
20. See reports from *Gewerkschaftszeitung*, no. 10, March 11, p. 145; no. 13, April 1, p. 205; and no. 14, April 8, p. 209.

Berlin with both alarm and satisfaction. It demonstrated that the unions could field little resistance beyond verbal protest against their tormentors. But it also demonstrated that the party was not in command of its rank and file. Even the normally radical Goebbels was afraid that things might get out of hand and contemplated very serious measures to restore discipline: "In the end we may not shrink back from the death penalty, for otherwise there is danger that the revolution, which is going on constantly, might slip out of the hands of the Führer."[21] Even the NSBO leadership complained that wildcat activities were only "throwing a club between the spokes" of the organization.[22]

The protests of the trade unions were, of course, ignored by a contemptuous regime; not so though those of big business, which feared that uncontrolled interference in the factories threatened property as well as law and order. On March 10, Gustav Krupp, speaking for the umbrella organization of German big industry (Reichsverband der deutschen Industrie) wrote to Interior Minister Wilhelm Frick appealing for order: "Numerous reports reveal growing tumult in many factories as a result of the recent events. We have faith that among the great majority of workers and employees there is goodwill on behalf of constructive work for people and state. It would be all the more disastrous if, out of a continuation of this unrest, activities should develop which would be detrimental to the recovery of our economic situation."[23] Hitler's response came that same day in the form of a decree which admonished SA and SS to preserve the "strictest discipline" and to refrain from individual actions.[24]

So great was the dynamic of wildcat activity, however, that this decree went largely unheeded and had to be followed by a number of others. On March 15, the party's Economic Commission forbade individual interference in the economy and began to send out Gau economic advisers. On March 20, the Cabinet decided on harsh punishments for "provocateurs who appear in uniform." On April 7 Rudolf Hess issued a directive in the name of the Political Commission of the party forbidding NSBO, SA, and SS members "to interfere in the inner workings of economic enterprises, industrial

21. In *Vom Kaiserhof zur Reichskanzlei*, p. 284.
22. See Reinhard Muchow (NSBO), circular letter of March 29, 1933, p. 2 in BAK, NS26/283.
23. See BAK, R43II/362, p. 15.
24. See Schumann, *NS and Gewerkschaftsbewegung*, p. 63.

plants, banks, etc., to take action against unions, to plan the removal [of officials] and similar activities."[25]

All these decrees and orders had somewhat of a dampening effect, but wildcat activities went on just the same. In the meantime, Hitler had already decided to act. In early April he commissioned Robert Ley with the task of smashing the trade unions.[26] Ley must have represented the obvious choice. First, he had a long record of absolute loyalty, and this was important at a time when the National Socialist revolution threatened to get out of hand. Secondly, Ley's leanings were more in sympathy with business than with labor, owing in part to his former relationship with IG Farben. Thirdly, the NSBO with its experience in the plants would be one party organization very useful in any coup against the unions; besides, many local NSBO people were already acting on their own and the coup presented the opportunity to get control of their activities. Since the NSBO came under the ROL, Ley was a logical choice to head the whole action. Moreover, Ley's general approach of education-propaganda-*Betreuung* offered an interesting alternative model of activity for an electoral-campaign-oriented party which had little raison d'être now that Hitler had been admitted to the corridors of power. To use a party organization as an experimental laboratory in which to work on the very social class furthest from integration into the Reich offered interesting possibilities for the future. Finally, Hitler could not have helped but remember how Ley had silenced the spirited discussion on Nazi unions at the party congress in 1929.

Hitler's choice coincided nicely with Ley's ambitions.To smash the unions successfully and then develop an alternative to them gave him a chance to strengthen his party position vis-à-vis the Hess–Bormann team. It also gave him a clear jurisdictional area at a time when many aspiring Nazis – Heinrich Himmler, for example – waited in vain for the call to play an important role in the new regime. Also, Ley now had a chance to try out his long-term concept of using education and *Betreuung* to create that conflict-free society he so yearned to live in. More than was the case with most Nazis, the utopian memory of a classless, party-less society of August 1914 and its contrast, the revolutionary, stab-in-the-back society of November 1918, haunted the imagination of Robert Ley. His concept might resurrect the first and preclude the second from ever happening

25. Ibid., pp. 64–5.
26. Ley mentions the commissions in *Deutschland ist schöner geworden*, p. 258.

again: "We do not want the same thing to happen to us," Ley said on the day of the takeover, "that happened in 1918 to the SPD and the Weimar parties. We know exactly that our enemy, Marxism, is only playing dead, but in fact is not yet dead . . . . We will not let ourselves be fooled by our opponents like the Weimar parties did in 1918."[27] Last but not least, the challenge of smashing the unions opened up the possibility of acquiring access to vast wealth, for the union properties and, above all, membership dues, represented, even in the depths of the Depression, significant sources of income.

Despite his general concept of how to approach the German people in general, and the worker in particular, Ley had no specific model in his own mind as to what exactly to do beyond directing an illegal, nationwide act of violence against the trade unions. Organized violence was something, after all, at which he had had considerable experience. As he admitted later, "I arrived as a bloody layman, and I believe that I myself was most mystified as to why I was entrusted with this task. It was not the case that we had a completed plan which we could haul out and on the basis of this plan build up the Labor Front. Rather, I received from the Führer instructions to take over the unions and then I had to see what I would make out of that."[28]

It was both fortunate and unfortunate for Ley that to carry out his task he had to avail himself of the help of people who *did* have a very clear idea of what they wanted to build on the ruins of the trade-union movement in Germany. This was fortunate in that Ley did not have to operate his way into a vacuum; however, it was unfortunate in that the vision posited by Ley's helpers ran counter to what much of the party, the business world, and Hitler himself wanted. Sometime during the first two weeks of April, Ley appointed a so-called "Action Committee for the Protection of German Labor," another one of those euphemisms which the regime would become so adept at using. The committee had the task of working out the details of the nationwide takeover of the unions. Ley chaired the

27. See *Der Deutsche*, no. 102, May 2, 1933; see also Mason, *Sozialpolitik*, pp. 26, 32, 71.

28. From Ley's speech on the occasion of the fifth anniversary of the DAF, given at the 1937 Nuremberg Party Day celebration in "Der Parteitag der Arbeit vom 6. bis 7. September 1937," *Offizieller Bericht über den Verlauf des Reichsparteitages mit sämtlichen Kongreßreden* (Munich Zentralverlag des NSDAP, 1938) pp. 264ff. Like so many of Ley's speeches, this one is an astonishing combination of crude lies and admissions of truth.

committee, but the real work was done by one Reinhard Muchow and his associates on the committee. And herein lay the rub.[29]

For some years Muchow had been the visionary and driving force behind the NSBO, the Nazi factory cell organization.[30] Of Berlin working-class origins, Muchow joined the Nazi movement there in 1925 at the tender age of 21 and a year later became a propaganda assistant to the newly arrived Gauleiter, Joseph Goebbels. Recognizing the nature of "Red Berlin," Muchow became adept at appealing to the working class using the language, techniques, and organizational models of the Communists. After the formation of the NSBO in Berlin in 1928, Muchow joined up and by 1932 was its undisputed driving force, trying to lead it in the direction of industrial trade unionism. He took the lead in supporting strikes, ranging from that of the Berlin metalworkers in 1930 to the famous Berlin transport workers' strike of November 1932, when Nazis and Communists collaborated. With the slogan "Keine Arbeitsstelle ohne Nazi-Zelle" (No workplace without a Nazi cell), Muchow was instrumental in the growth of the NSBO during 1932 and early 1933. With Hitler in power, Muchow was determined to create a truly Nazi trade union and, using the fashionable but outmoded corporativist (*ständisch*) concepts of the day, to unite that union with various other professional and economic groups to create a social umbrella organization which would decisively shape the social policy of the Third Reich. His ambitions emerge clearly in a circular letter toward the end of March: "We desire not only to infuse the German labor force with a new spirit, but to reshape the extraordinarily complicated social-political machinery of the state and the economy according to our National Socialist ideology." Anticipating the mushroom growth of his organization, Muchow ordered that all local membership prohibitions be lifted:

> We won't be satisfied with 17 million National Socialists, it must rather be 20, 25, and 30 million, and finally the whole German people. That is absolutely correct. Naturally we can win these millions who still stand aside by means of ceaseless propaganda, but certain portions must also be

29. On the constitution of the action committee, see Ley (PO *Stabsleiter*) circular letter no. 6/33 of April 21, 1933, in BAK, Schumacher Sammlung, 235.
30. For details on Muchow, see Berlin Document Center (BDC): File Muchow; also Kele, *Nazis and Workers*, pp. 149–50, 171–3, 199; Schumann, *NS und Gewerkschaft*, pp. 34–5; Starcke, *NSBO*, pp. 12–17.

> grasped *organizationally*. We must chain them to our organization so that they can really become agents of our will.[31]

Here, then, was the initial vision of what would become the German Labor Front: a gigantic organization which would encompass virtually all Germans, working class and otherwise, and make a major imprint on the nature of the emerging Third Reich and its social and economic policy. The gigantomania would fit in well with Ley's proclivities. The union format was something else again.

Muchow had plenty of support for his concept, because most of the other eight members of the action committee were old associates of his. Among them was Walter Schumann, also a Berliner of working-class backgound, a war veteran, who came to the Nazi Party in 1925 via the free corps Bund Oberland.[32] At 27 he became leader of the NSDAP branch in Berlin-Neukölln and in 1930 became part of the Nazi Reichstag delegation. Although he joined the NSBO rather late, by 1931 he advanced to organizational director and Reich leader of that organization. Together, he and Muchow made an effective ideological and organizational team. In the wake of May 2, Schumann was scheduled to become commissar of the unions which had been under the ADGB (see Plate 3).

His counterpart as commissar in charge of the white-collar employee unions, which were organized under the umbrella of the Allgemeiner Freien Angestelltenbund (AFA-Bund) was Karl Ludwig Peppler, also a veteran of the war and several free corps. Peppler, a former bank and insurance company employee had made his way to the Nazis via his white-collar union and had joined the NSBO as editor of its bi-monthly paper *Arbeitertum*.[33]

Another member of the committee, an old friend of Muchow was Hans Biallas.[34] A graphic designer by trade, Biallas also gravitated to the NSDAP in 1925, after having served in *völkisch* organizations since he was 19. In 1926 he joined Muchow in Berlin propaganda work and also joined the editorial staff of the *Arbeitertum* at Muchow's behest. On May 2, he was to handle the press and propaganda part of the operation.

Two other members of the committee, Bank Director Müller and Brinkmann, had the largely technical job of seizing the various bank

31. March 29, 1933, in BAK, NS26/283.
32. On Schumann, see BDC: File Schumann; also Starcke, *NSBO*, pp. 185–7.
33. On Peppler, see BDC: File Peppler; also Starcke, p. 229.
34. On Biallas, see BDC: File Biallas; also Starcke, pp. 216–20.

accounts of the unions (see Plate 3).

The only committee member who was really Ley's man was Rudolf Schmeer.[35] An old Ley crony from the Rhineland, Schmeer had been in the Aachen branch of the party since 1923 and a Reichsredner since 1926. As Ley rose he took Schmeer with him. A Reichstag deputy since 1930 and deputy Gauleiter of Köln-Aachen during 1931–2, Schmeer was appointed to the Reichsinspektion by Ley in 1932. Ley obviously needed the experience of Muchow and his associates; Schmeer was there to watch them for the boss.

As he was about to carry out his Führer's orders, then, Ley found himself in a bit of a trap. He needed the NSBO people both for the decisive strike against the unions on May 2 and for an organizational concept of what would replace them as a Nazi home for the working class. The problem was that their concept smacked too much of the very kind of worker representation which Hitler was trying to eliminate, while their revolutionary zeal to restructure German *Sozialpolitik* made the business and government community, whose support Hitler needed, very nervous indeed. Even a Nazi trade union, after all, still gave off a fishy odor of class conflict, despite being wrapped in the brown paper of quasi-medieval estate packaging. No sooner would the free trade unions be eliminated when an organizational and conceptual struggle would ensue over just how the working class and the idealized *Volksgemeinschaft* might be reconciled with one another.

In the meantime, Hitler issued further marching orders. On April 16 at the Obersalzburg, he let Goebbels in on what was to happen. The Propaganda Minister was eager to take part. He confided to his diary:

> We shall turn the first of May into a grandiose display of the will of the German people. Then on May 2 the union buildings will be occupied. *Gleichschaltung* in this area too. There might be a row for a few days, but then they belong to us. We dare not make any allowances. We are only doing the worker a favor by freeing him from a parasitic leadership which has only made his life hard. Once the unions are in our hands, then the other parties and organizations cannot hold out for long. In any case, the decision was made yesterday on the Obersalzburg. There is no turning back. We must let events take their course. In one year all of Germany will be in our hands.[36]

35. See BDC: File Schmeer.
36. Goebbels, *Vom Kaiserhof*, p. 299.

On April 21, Ley sent orders out to the provincial chieftains, the Gauleiters, who would coordinate NSBO, SS, SA, and other party entities in the action.[37] Although the NSBO was officially responsible as "bearer" of the project, the Gauleiter really had the authority, although they were to cooperate closely with the local NSBO men, who in most cases were to be the commissars who stepped in in place of local union leaders. The major target was to be, of course, the unions under the aegis of the ADGB and the AFA-Bund. The Nazis tooks pains to ensure that the Christian unions and the conservative white-collar union, the Deutschnationaler Handlungsgehilfenverband (German National Association of Retail Clerks), were not involved. They were expected to "synchronize" themselves voluntarily.[38] To involve any other organizations related to these two umbrella unions was to be left up to the discretion of the Gauleiter. In Berlin the "action committee" itself was in charge of the operation. Union buildings were to be seized and union leaders taken into protective custody, but this order stopped short of the local level. Local committee chairmen and employees were to be left alone. This was done in part in order not to create too much consternation on the part of workers on the local level and, one suspects, in part in order to deprive the NSBO of total control of the soon-to-be defunct trade-union organization.

The orders made it clear that the operation was not to interfere with payments being made to union members. Workers were to get the impression that business was being carried out as usual with little disruption. As soon as possible, rallies with free admission were to be held to reassure the workers, and in the meantime, the action was to proceed under the strictest discipline.

Inevitably, there were leaks and confusion. As a result, in some

37. See Rundschreiben 6/1933 of April 24 in BAK, Schumacher Sammlung, 235. He chose the Gauleiter not only because they were in a position to keep an eye out on the behavior of the overeager local NSBO people but also because giving orders to them enhanced his command position as ROL of the party.

38. Which, in fact, they did, although the Christian unions apparently did not cooperate successfully enough. On June 24 Ley ordered their property confiscated and their leaders expelled from the DAF because of "ingratitude and disloyalty" as well as corruption. *Der Deutsche*, no. 145, June 24, 1933. In reality, Ley had spared the Christian unions in the first place, so that he could use one of their leaders, Bernard Otte, to try to secure official recognition of the DAF as the German representative at the International Trades Union Congress in Geneva. When Otte, who accompanied Ley to the meeting, failed in his task, there was no longer any use for him or his organization, so Ley ordered it disbanded. See Krohn (Labor Ministry) Denkschrift, "Zur Situation in der früheren deutschen Arbeiterbewegung," November 1933 in BAK, R41(Krohn)/5008.

areas, such as Dresden and Lübeck, the operation was begun prematurely.[39] In others, jurisdictional confusion arose. In Hamburg, the local SA hesitated to take orders from the political wing of the party and requested confirmation from their superiors.[40]. In Berlin, some Nazis interpreted the instructions much too broadly. One NSBO local proposed taking over and reorganizing the whole city mass transit system, while another party comrade interpreted his instructions as allowing him to take over the huge Tietz department store chain.[41] But all this was to be expected in the euphoria of another prospective large-scale action against the enemies of the regime.

On May 1, now a paid national holiday, mass celebrations went on. In Berlin, Hitler himself spoke before hundreds of thousands of workers at the Tempelhof airport. His speech closed with the singing of the national anthem and the Horst Wessel song, followed by a gigantic fireworks display. The whole affair was a psychological masterstroke and left labor leaders in a state of powerlessness and despondency. The next morning the other shoe fell. In coordinated action all over Germany the union buildings were seized, functionaries from Leipart on down arrested and incarcerated (Leipart himself was ill and had to be taken to a hospital), bank accounts were frozen and confiscated, union presses and papers closed down. From a Nazi point of view the operation was a roaring success.[42] Ley issued a patronizing but from his perspective undoubtedly sincere, proclamation to the workers: "Workers, your institutions

39. See Shumann, *NS und Gewerkschaften*, p. 67.
40. See SA-Untergruppe Hamburg to SA-Gruppe Nordsee of April 26, 1933, in BAK, Schumacher Sammlung, 235.
41. See Landkamm (NSBO Fachgruppe BVG, Berlin) to Erich Kube (Oberpräsident of Berlin and Brandenburg) of March 29; also Johannes Engel (Berlin Stadtsrat and founder of the NSBO) to Kurt Daluege (Prussian Interior Ministry) of April 11, both in BDC: File Engel.
42. For Ley's use of violence on May 2, see BAK NS5/3940; also *Braunbuch über Reichstagbrand und Hitler-Terror* (Basel, 1933). The translated text of Hitler's speech is in the official publication of the DNB, *The New Germany Desires Work and Peace* (Berlin, 1933), pp. 31–7; the seizure was clearly a revolutionary act. Only on May 12 did the Berlin *Oberstaatsanwalt*, Dr Burchardi, officially order the property of the unions seized, with Ley as trustee. The DAF officially received the property by law in December 1937. See report by Claus Thormählen, "Die Vermögenswerte, die DAF im Zuge der Auflösung der Gewerkschaften übernommen hat," November 5, 1947, in BAK, NS5II/3490. For documentation on the disposition of former union property, see US National Archives Microcopy T-580, 549. Ordner 692. Ley authorized the release of arrested union functionaries from protective custody to the extent that they were not involved in corruption. Circular 15/33 in BAK, NS25/489.

are sacred and unassailable to us National Socialists. I myself am a poor son of peasants and have known poverty. Worker, I swear to you that we shall not only preserve everything you have; we shall extend the protective laws and rights of the worker, in order that he might enter the new National Socialist state as an equal and respected member of the nation."[43] Within several days Ley could report his success to Hitler. Nor did he waste any time filling the huge vacuum by the demise of the unions. On May 6 in a proclamation of gratitude to SA, SS, NSBO, and party people, he signed himself as "Leiter der DAF" (Director of the German Labor Front).[44] He also lost no time in taking back his provisionally bestowed authority to the Gauleiter, who were now obliged to vacate the union buildings and to refrain from interfering in the inner affairs of the trade unions and in the coming formation of the DAF.[45] In the ensuing weeks, as a kind of justification for their actions, the Nazis published reports on the incredible waste and corruption they purported to discover in the files of the unions, thus discrediting the entire union leadership in the eyes of many middle-class Germans.[46] More rallies were held in the weeks after the action to reassure the workers. On May 10, with great fanfare the "First Congress of the DAF" was held in Berlin with 500 representatives of the "coordinated" organizations invited. Also in attendance was a distinguished group including the Cabinet, the minister presidents, the Reichsstatthalter, the Gauleiter, and representatives from the Army, diplomatic corps, SA, and the SS. Hitler himself spoke and concluded by saying: "Nothing in life could make me prouder than, at the end, to be able to say: 'I have won over the German worker for the German Reich.' "[47] While the rally was going on, SS and SA, acting on Göring's orders, confiscated the property of the Social Democratic Party all over Germany. On May 19 Ley staged a similar congress for the white-collar employees, in which, with his characteristic

43. See Konrad Heiden, *Der Fuehrer: Hitler's Rise to Power* (Boston, Beacon, 1969), p. 600.
44. See *Arbeitertum* no. 6, 1933, p. 22; also Lölhöffel, "Umwandlung," in Esenwein-Rothe, *Wirtschaftsverbände*, p. 158.
45. See Ley Anordnung no. 23/33, May 13, and circular letter no. 14/33, May 15, in BAK, NS22, vorl. 659.
46. See *Der Deutsche*, no. 103, May 4, for the initial announcement of scandals uncovered; also Starcke, *NSBO zur DAF*, pp. 66–8; Schumann, *NS und Gewerkschaftsbewegung*, pp. 72–3. *Arbeitertum*, no. 11, August 1, 1933, published a long account of corruption in the Christian trade unions.
47. For Hitler's remarks, see DNB, *New Germany*, p. 52; also Schumann, *NS und Gewerkschaftsbewegung*, p. 76.

frankness and hyperbole, he betrayed the nervousness which came from skating near the edge of the social precipice: "Today we achieve things in an hour which are mightier and larger than those achieved in decades earlier. Sometimes it's almost enough to make you afraid."[48]

The German Labor Front took organizational shape and ideological direction, then, in the forcefield of competing power interests in the early days of the Third Reich. On the one hand, the radical Nazis — and in his heart Hitler was one of them — were convinced that the National Socialist revolution was far from over. Rather that the *Machtergreifung* represented only the first stage of that revolution and that a second, and more thoroughgoing one, was to follow. For some, particularly the unemployed in the SA, this meant a radical restructuring of property relationships which would inaugurate a real German "socialism." For others, particularly the thousands of NSBO commissars, many of them former students, bankrupt businessmen, long-time party activists, and ambitious workers, the revolution meant creating for themselves sinecures in the coming Labor Front as officials of a huge NS union. For others it meant interfering in economic enterprises at all levels in order to make a place at the trough for themselves in the New Order. For still others it meant the opportunity to give concrete shape to that part of Nazi ideology which intended to abolish traditional class and caste differences by inaugurating the pseudo-medieval society of estates. For Ley, it meant achieving his task of integrating the worker into the *Volksgemeinschaft* as a step toward building that conflict-free society. Indeed, in his proclamation to the workers on May 2, he said: "Today we are entering the second stage of the National Socialist revolution. . . . Certainly, we have power, but we do not as yet have the whole people. You, German worker, we do not have 100 percent. And it's precisely you that we want; we won't let you go until you have committed yourself to us unreservedly."[49]

There were powerful radical forces on the loose in Germany in the confusing early months of 1933 and their dynamic should not be underestimated.[50] For a while Ley himself was caught up in them.

48. Ley's remarks in Wolff's *Telegraphisches Büro*, no. 1202, May 19, 1933, in BAK, R43II/527b.
49. See Wolff's *Telegraphisches Büro*, no. 1039, May 2, 1933, in BAK, R43II/528.
50. For an excellent insight into the work of the NSBO commissars on a regional level, see, for example, the "Tätigkeitsbericht für Mai 1933" of the NSBO comissioner for former ADGB property in Bavaria, Karl Weygold in BAK, NS26/280.

On the other hand, the traditional forces in Germany — powerful big business interests and the government ministries in particular — looked with a jaundiced eye on what many regarded as Nazi crackpot schemes which would only get in the way of economic recovery. These interests made themselves felt strongly in May not the least at the cabinet level, when the question of unions and workers came up. So, in a sense, the very class struggle which the Nazis were determined to abolish went on during the early months of 1933 within the context of the shaping of the new DAF and its authority. Would it become the massive Nazi trade union which many NSBO functionaries wanted it to be, that is a strong economic and political factor representing worker interests in the new Third Reich? Or would it evolve into something far different?

For Muchow and his associates there was little question but that the DAF represented the workers' advocate in Nazi society and that the NSBO was to be the chief recruiting ground for its leadership personnel. He had written, "But one thing is for certain, that under National Socialist leadership the unions will experience their greatest flowering." And he included under the jurisdiction of the Nazi union "salary and wage scales, labor protection, sanitation in the workplace, occupational training, in short, the whole social-political realm." His friend, Walter Schumann, agreed and asserted only that new organizational forms were necessary so that the "youthful forces in the unions which yearn for the new, can construct something better."

It is some indication of the momentum that the NSBO people had built, that the way in which the ADGB was taken over, the organizational structure of the new DAF as well as its main leadership personnel, reflected their ideas. The events of May 2 seemed to indicate that the old unions were simply being transformed into part of the body of the NSBO. The ADGB press bureau became the NSBO press office; the NSBO paper, *Arbeitertum*, now became the official organ of all former members of the captured unions, while NSBO *Pressewarte* replaced all former union editors.[51]

Moreover, the organizational schema of the new DAF was a perfect representation of the impending corporate state (*Ständestaat*) in which the former blue- and white-collar unions would represent

51. See *Der Deutsche*, no. 102, May 2, 1933; also Otto Marrenbach, *Fundamente des Sieges, Die Gesamtarbeit der deutschen Arbeitsfront 1933-1940*. 2nd edn (Berlin Verlag der DAF, 1940), p. 94.

two of five pillars holding up the DAF edifice. The former ADGB, with its twenty-seven affiliate unions became one organizational pillar under the "commissar" Schumann. The former AFA-Bund with its ten union affiliates became another pillar under its "commissar" Peppler. To follow at a later date were the other pillars representing the other prime corporate segments of German economic life: the free professions, small retail trade and commerce, and big business. The roof supported by these corporate pillars would be the DAF central bureau with offices for such far-reaching purposes as organization, leadership, press and propaganda, education and schooling, youth, economic organizations, and so on. Moreover, this already mammoth organizational scheme was designed to metastasize over the entire length and breadth of the country. Each of the pillars was to have a horizontal as well as vertical organization with regional, state, and local suboffices corresponding to the 13 state labor office districts and 361 regional and local labor offices. It represented the potential for a bureaucratic leviathan which Ley would accept fully once he faced the necessity of changing the Labor Front from Nazi super-union to a totalitarian mass organization.

To preserve the illusion of participation from below, Muchow had even built into the bureaucratic structure two ostensible consultative organs called the "kleine" and "grosse Konvente". These never had, however, more than an advisory function and their members were appointed by the very people whom they had the task of advising. Both soon became moribund bodies.

Indeed, the pillars themselves never got off the ground in any representative sense. Ley saw to it from the outset that the central bureau with its many offices, reflecting the *Führerprinzip*, functioned as a command agency which transmitted orders down to the pillars, a task which was facilitated by the fact that each pillar had a representative in the central bureau. Moreover, only three of the five pillars ever really took shape at all. Small retail trade took its place alongside the blue- and white-collar unions as a modified form of the Nazi organization Militant Association of Commercial Small Business (Kampfbund für den gewerblichen Mittelstand). The other two pillars, the free professions and big business, never really came into existence at all. Indeed, the whole idea of a radical restructuring of the economy along fascist corporate lines, which was reflected in Muchow's organizational schema, never got off the ground. Although it had important spokesmen in the party in the persons of Otto Wagener, head of the party's Economic Policy Office and commissar for the economy, and Gottfried Feder, one of the party's original founders and a self-styled economic specialist, the power of big business soon thwarted the schemes of those who dreamed of a corporativist society.[52]

Not only the organizational format but also the personnel of the new Labor Front was drawn largely from NSBO people, even though the NSBO was organizationally kept separate from the DAF. Demonstrating his need for these older Nazi veterans of the war in the factories, Ley issued a proclamation on June 2 to the effect that the NSBO "alone provides the functionaries of the Labor Front and thereby oversees the tasks of the Labor Front."[53] So old NSBO stalwarts like Biallas (press office), Peppler (social office), as well as Muchow and Schumann, played a major role in the newly created DAF.

More importantly, for a time during the heady days of May and June 1933 Ley himself, apparently caught up in the momentum of events, publicly embraced the ideological position of the NSBO radicals. He warned "irresponsible elements in the employers' camp" not to use the dissolution of the trade unions "to curtail wages and thus to satisfy their lust for profits." He also warned against violating any negotiated wage agreements and asked NSBO people to be watchful in the factories and report any violations to him. He also accepted the role of DAF as worker advocate when he proclaimed that wage negotiations "will from now on only be conducted by the Action Committee for the Protection of German Labor."[54] Even more provocatively, he came out strongly against "yellow" company unions and for a minimum wage. "The working person," he asserted, "should receive a compensation which he needs for a secure existence."[55]

Nor did Ley hesitate to announce a fulsome role for the DAF in determining social policy. On May 15 he issued a joint decree with Otto Wagener, commissar for the economy and spokesman for a corporativist society, calling for an eight-week truce in the factories during which time representatives of the DAF and industry would "order wage relationships, watch over labor protection, labor law, and social measures and prevent by all means economic

52. On the original organization of the DAF, see Lolhöffel, "Umwandlung," pp. 157-69; Reichhardt, "Deutsche Arbeitsfront," pp. 33–4.
53. See Ley circular letter no. 18/33 in BAK, NS22, vorl. 838.
54. See *Arbeitertum*, no. 6, May 15, 1933; Broszat, *The Hitler State*, pp. 142, 184.
55. See *Der Deutsche*, no. 121, May 25, 1933; Mason, *Sozialpolitik*, p. 110.

sabotage."[56]

Thus encouraged by their leader, DAF functionaries began to issue a torrent of orders and directives designed to influence economic policy in a variety of areas. The Office for Social Questions proclaimed its desire that female workers receive equal pay for equal work (a position that Ley would later embrace even in the last years of the war) and urged that pressure be put on firms to hire new workers rather than imposing overtime on existing personnel. The head of the Wage Office issued orders that vacation time granted to workers in 1933 could not be less than that of the year before and that during vacations workers had to be paid their wages in full, based on the 48-hour week.[57] Such official proclamations from the top of the new DAF were but the tip of a very large iceberg. At the bottom of the structure the orgy of wildcat activities continued to the point where even Muchow recognized the need to bring the masses to heel. He complained in a special bulletin that many of the rank and file had "demonstrated a regular caesar complex and in doing so have made the NSBO appear ridiculous." Vis-à-vis the authorities, heads of firms and even party offices, he continued cynically, NSBO functionaries had "displayed an arrogant demeaner undiluted by any professional expertise." In many middle-sized firms, "adolescent NSBO members" were extorting higher wages for themselves in "good bandit fashion."[58] Moreover, it was also becoming clear that large numbers of Socialists and Communists had been infiltrating the lower ranks of the NSBO and DAF in order to camouflage their activities. Muchow saw no alternative but to inaugurate a general purge. A hundred thousand members would have to be thrown out. All new functionaries would hold offices only provisionally until they could be properly schooled. They were also to stay out of the business of the unions and stop the "nonsense" of giving themselves special titles like "commissar." At the same time, Muchow inaugurated a number of steps to counter Marxist infiltration. The DAF Organization Office was to draw up a "list of outlaws" so that former Socialists and Communists could be combed out of the DAF and NSBO. Members were also forbidden to frequent former haunts of left-wingers. Any NSBO members or functionaries, moreover, whose membership number was higher

56. See *Der Deutsche*, no. 115, May 18, 1933.
57. See *Der Deutsche*, nos. 131 and 132, June 8 and 9, 1933, respectively.
58. See Muchow, special bulletin of July 10, 1933, in BAK, NS26/283.

than 450,000 were forbidden to occupy any DAF offices.[59]

Muchow's prophylactic measures were coming rather late, however. For a powerful backlash against radical Nazi grass-roots wildcat activities was already making itself felt from the government ministries, big business quarters, and even the party itself.

The initial reaction on the part of business and government to Nazi activities directed at the trade unions and the economy was one of wariness combined with confusion. A law of April 8 giving the NSBO equal status with unions in plant elections and representation before labor courts was designed to divert the NSBO from its social-revolutionary goals by giving it time-consuming chores to do. All the law did, however, was to further encourage the NSBO leaders in their goal to fashion a Nazi union.[60] On May 4, just two days after the smashing of the trade unions, the Cabinet puzzled over what to do next. Hitler himself only knew that "the former form of worker representation could not be maintained in the future," but otherwise could only think of forming a committee of three or four men to study the question. The idea of assigning commissars for the unions was also discussed, with the representatives of the ministries, clearly wary of wildcat activities, suggesting that any commissars appointed be attached to some government agency.[61] Throughout May and June, in fact, the idea of a Reichskommissar for the trade unions floated around in top state and party circles.[62] In the meantime, as we have seen, events took their own course with the wildcat, grass-roots activities. In Hamburg, NSBO pressure kept a mine open that was supposed to close down. In the Ruhr at a number of locations local NSBO functionaries threatened owners with the Gestapo and concentration camps. The NSBO also tried frequently to enter into collective bargaining on behalf of the workers, although this was no longer legal.[63] By early June, the various ministries

59. See Muchow, special circular of June 27, 1933, in BAK, NSD50/127; also Schmeer, circular letter no. 23/33 of June 26, 1933, in US National Archives microcopy T-580, roll 549, Ordner 692.
60. See Schumann, *NS und Gewerkschaftsbewegung*, p. 66; the law also postponed elections of worker representatives in the factories until September "in the interest of public security and order." In September the elections were once again postponed. See *Gesetz zur Änderung des Gesetzes über Betriebsvertretungen* in R43II/550; see also Martin Broszat, *The Hitler State*, trans. John Hider (New York, Longman, 1981).
61. See protocol of *Chefbesprechung* in BAK, R43II/527b.
62. See documentation in NS22, vorl. 659.
63. Various examples appear in Mason, *Sozialpolitik*, pp.102–3; for warnings against this kind of activity, see Anweisung 6/33 of the DAF Organization Office,

began to show a heightened concern in the face of these activities. The Labor Minister, Seldte, complained that the DAF had been arbitrarily passing regulations in the area of vacation and wage policy. Interior Minister Frick complained that all the grass-root activities which were ongoing under the rubric of corporativism (ständischer Aufbau) were undermining the whole municipal structure of Germany and eating away at his authority as minister. The Traffic Minister complained that NSBO interference in the command structure of the national railroad was threatening the whole basis of authority and discipline on which the agency functioned.[64] Even the Gauleiter expressed concern. Fritz Sauckel, party leader in Thuringia, wrote to Hitler complaining about the excesses of the NSBO, even though he was careful to assure the Führer that he had everything under control.[65]

After an initial period of confusion, however, the men of the ministries and big business caught their collective breaths and began to take concrete action. Some legislation had already been passed to head off radical interference in the economy. Most importantly, the law establishing Trustees for Labor (Treuhänder der Arbeit) of May 19, 1933, aimed at heading off radical interference in the economy by introducing a state authority with sufficient power to stave off interference by unwelcome party agencies. The thirteen Trustees were men, who, with perhaps one or two exceptions, were scarcely likely to sympathize with the radical populists in the NSBO. Five were corporate lawyers, four were high officials from several states, one a private attorney, and as a sop to the party, Johannes Engel, founder of the NSBO in Berlin, and Wilhelm Börger, a NSBO spokesman, were also named as Trustees (of Brandenburg and Rhineland, respectively). The job of the Trustees was basically to keep an eye on the business practices of industry, particularly in the area of wages, mass firings, and working conditions, to control the formation of the Nazi "trust councils" in the factories, as well as to function as the government's eyes and ears

---

July 12, 1933, in BAK, NS51/255. As late as October Schumann still had to warn that the individual unions within the "Gesamtverband der Deutschen Arbeiter" were under no circumstances to undertake negotiations with any agency on any subject, especially wages. Directive of October 20, 1933, in ibid,. NS51/256.

64. Seldte's complaint expressed in Cabinet meeting of June 8, see BAK, R431/1463. Frick's appears in a letter of June 12 to Hitler and the Cabinet in BAK, R43II/348. See Eltz-Rübenach Vermerk, undated but probably June 28 in BAK R431/1053, p. 82.

65. Sauckel to Hitler, June 10, 1933, in BAK, R43II/1382.

within the corporate world. The power of the Trustees was determined by law. As the DAF emerged, it would try to carve out for itself a position as rival to the Trustees; this would be a difficult task, for the law which created the Trustees foresaw little or no function for the Labor Front.[66]

As spring turned to summer, the conservatives consolidated their position as more and more complaints came in about unauthorized behavior in the lower formations of the Nazi Party. Big business closed ranks by incorporating its hitherto two largest associations (the Reichsverband der deutschen Industrie and the Vereinigung der deutschen Arbeitgeberverbände — the Reich Association for German Industry and the Alliance of German Employers Associations) into one large representative organization, the Reichsstand der deutschen Industrie (Reich Estate of German Industry). Its goals were (despite its *ständisch*-sounding name) to defeat both corporativist and nationalization schemes then circulating widely in radical Nazi circles and to defend the rights and prerogatives of private industry. Only then could its leaders achieve the quiet and stability needed to rebuild the economy.[67] Hitler shared this interest with them. His top priorities were job creation and rearmament, two goals which complemented each other nicely. As a result, Hitler brought a number of these men into his government. Most important were Franz Seldte, a prosperous chemical manufacturer and head of the largest veterans' organization in Germany, the Stahlhelm, who became Minister for Labor and one of Ley's main opponents; and Economics Minister Kurt Schmitt, Generaldirektor of the large Allianz insurance company. Schmitt, who was already ill with heart disease, would not be so effective an opponent of Ley; but his successor a year later, Hjalmar Schacht, would more than make up for that. Lending their expertise to these ministers were bright civil servants like Ludwig Grauert, State Secretary in the Interior Ministry, and Werner Mansfeld, Ministerialrat in the Labor Ministry and soon to be author of the comprehensive Nazi labor legislation. These men, joined by the Trustees of Labor, lost no time in discrediting corporativist ideas and in thrusting aside the prime Nazi exponents of these views, Wagener and Feder. Trustee Klein of

66. For brief biographical sketches of the Trustees, see Wolff's *Telegraphisches Büro*, no. 1447, June 15, 1933, in BAK, R43II/532. On the functions of the Trustees, see Mason, *Sozialpolitik*, p. 118. Broszat in *The Hitler State*, p. 185, n. 32, suggests that Trustee Börger tried to keep the NSBO out of Ley's hands.

67. See Boelcke, *deutsche Wirtschaft*, p. 95.

Westphalia wrote Hitler that corporativism was nothing more than "disguised liberalism and a half-measure," while Nagel of Silesia insisted that the NSBO had been thoroughly infiltrated by communists and socialists who were renewing the class struggle.[68] In doing so the newly appointed men were sure of Hitler's support. However radical Hitler might have been in his intentions to reorder Europe and the world, he was rational enough to know the only source of his means: modern industrial society resting on the foundation of private enterprise and backed by the bureaucratic state. Indeed, he revealed his general support for the private sector at a meeting of several dozen important industrialists, including Krupp, Bosch, Siemens, Stinnes, Thyssen, on May 29:

> It appears to me not to be correct to believe that this solution can be achieved by the state alone. . . . I am convinced that we can only solve the problem on the part of the state through offering stimulation in many areas, clearing aside difficulties and in many areas advance things, for example through the way the tax law is handled. In the last analysis, however, I believe that naturally the final solution to the question will have to be taken in hand by our general economy.[69]

Elements of the party did their share as well, as the always business-friendly Hermann Göring issued instructions to Prussian police authorities to aid the Trustees in enforcing their orders and directives, since the Trustees did not as yet have staffs of their own.[70]

This enormous backlash against Nazi populism culminated in Hitler's announcement in early July, 1933, that the National Socialist revolution was over. In two important speeches, one at a meeting of higher SS and SA leaders at Bad Reichenhall on July 2 and one at a meeting of Reichsstatthalter on July 6 he proclaimed that the fusing of party and state was complete and that the revolution had met its goals. "Revolution is no permanent condition," he said, "it must not

68. On the mixing of rearmament and job creation, see Hitler's remarks at a meeting of the government committee on work creation of February 9, 1933, in BAK, R43II/536, pp. 27–8; on the appointment of men from the world of big business, see Schweitzer, *Big Business*, p. 360; Mason, *Sozialpolitik*, p. 117; Boelcke, *deutsche Wirtschaft*, pp. 66–7; see also Klein to Hitler of September 9, 1933, in BAK, R43II/527b; Nagel to Labor Minister of August 7, 1933, in BAK, R43II/532; Heiden, *Fuehrer*, p. 651, talks about the "successful bandits locking up those who had been less successful."
69. See "Besprechung mit Industriellen über Arbeitsbeschaffung," in R43II/536, pp. 341–9. Ley was present at this meeting.
70. See *Der Deutsche*, no. 161, July 13, 1933, in BAK, NS26/282.

be allowed to develop into a lasting phenomenon. One must direct the released stream of revolution over into the riverbed of evolution."[71]

Nazi radicals did not take this message well. In city after city, like Berlin, Frankfurt, Dresden, Essen, Dortmund, Kassel, Königsberg, and Freiburg, SA and NSBO people created tumults, with the Hitler-loyalists fighting the others. Hitler struck back hard, particularly against the SA. At the beginning of August a wave of arrests set in. In Frankfurt all SA units were disbanded; in Berlin alone 3,870 men were expelled from the organization. These arrests also provided an opportunity to purge the NSBO. It was within the context of this purge that on September 12 Muchow was accidently shot under rather suspicious circumstances. Goebbels expressed his profound sympathy to Ley at the loss of Muchow, but everyone realized that with his death the main animating force behind the NSBO dream of a Nazi union ensconced in a corporativist society had been dealt a lethal blow.[72] The Nazi radicals would remain a force to contend with until the bloody purge of the SA in June 1934, and could not be taken lightly, as Ley found out. But with Hitler's decision to take the evolutionary road, which led to economic recovery and rearmament, the dreams of the radicals were no longer on the cards for Nazi Germany.

During the months between the smashing of the unions in May and the end of the year, then, Ley often found himself between a rock and a hard place. Even as he began to expand the jurisdictional scope of the new DAF, he had to keep a watchful eye out to left and right, always testing the political wind, gauging the relative strength of his allies and opponents while, at the same time, trying to give organizational reality to his dream of creating the conflict-free society through education and *Betreuung*.[73] At times he took actions or made verbal gestures which seemed to curry favor with the

71. See Schumann, *NS und Gewerkschaftsbewegung*, p. 99; for Hitler's remarks to the Reichsstatthalter, see the *Akten der Reichskanzlei. Regierung Hitler 1933–1938*, published jointly by the Historische Kommission bei der Bayerischen Akademie der Wissenschaften and the Bundesarchiv, Teil I: 1933/34. Vol. I (Boppard, Harald Boldt Verlag, 1983), Document no. 180, pp. 629–36.
72. See Starcke, *NSBO und DAF*, pp. 198–9; also Internationale Transportarbeiterföderation, *Fascismus-Berichte*, Amsterdam, May 4, 1935, p. 6, in which is reported that Muchow was killed by one Willi Mähling in a wine tavern at Bacharach in a fight over a woman. Mähling then reportedly killed himself with two (!) shots to the head. Cf. *Arbeitertum*, October 1, 1933, pp. 9f.
73. A July directive from the DAF Organization Office demonstrated how much the situation was still in flux with respect to the final organizational form the DAF would take. "The transition to the really perfect and ideal form can only come

radicals; at other times he seemed to accommodate business or state interests. But increasingly as the year drew to a close, he seemed ready to abandon the radicals and make an arrangement with the powers that be within the framework of which he could begin to fashion his DAF. That process, however, more often than not would put him on a collision course with the institutions of party, state, and the economy.

As the bureaucratic jousting went on between Ley and both radicals and conservatives over what the DAF would become, the Reich Organization Leader did not neglect to expand its jurisdictional horizons. He swallowed other organizations whenever he could. In July he took over the self-help organization of the largest veterans' organization, the Stahlhelm-Selbsthilfe. In August the Nazi women's organization, the NS-Frauenschaft, became part of his empire.[74] At the same time, despite financial difficulties (income was falling rapidly at this stage, as disgruntled workers withheld their dues in droves), Ley began to spread money around to enhance the DAF image. The city of Berlin received 200,000 marks to provide interest-free credit to impoverished master craftsmen.[75] The DAF also staged a series of public events, parades, rallies, and so on, and tried to coerce employers to take part, thus giving testimony to the existence of the new Nazi *Volksgemeinschaft*. Coercion also took a more ominous form as the NSBO paper wrote gleeful accounts of factory owners thrown into concentration camps for violating wage agreements.[76] In October, at Hitler's behest, Ley himself undertook a major six-week factory inspection tour to drum up support for a workers' referendum in November. Such tours would become one of Ley's favorite activities.

During the final quarter of 1933 Ley demonstrated in both words and actions that he was turning his back on the NSBO radicals and edging toward a necessary accommodation with business and government — but had not given up at all on his intent to fashion the DAF, as part of his party empire, into a significant integrating force for the Nazi regime.

---

organically in good time; one must think in extended time periods." Anweisung 6/33, July 12, p. 2, in BAK, NS51/255.

74. On the Stahlhelm-Selbsthilfe, see Ley Anordnung, July 3, in BA NS51, vorl, 256; on the NS-Frauenschaft, see *Der Deutsche*, no. 196, August 22, in NS26/282.

75. See *Der Deutsche*, no. 224, September 24, in NS26/282.

76. See *Der Deutsche*, no. 155, July 6, for story on rallies in ibid. For an example of punitive treatment of businessmen, see *Arbeitertum*, October 15, quoted in Broszat, *The Hitler State*, pp. 190–1, n. 91.

As recently as August, Ley was still struggling to fit corporativist language into his public conceptualization of the DAF. Typically, he resorted to pseudo-religious terminology, invoking the image of the trinity. *Ständischer Aufbau*, he said, was the body, providing material nourishment, while the DAF represented the soul and spirit, the former expressed in the ideological training function of the DAF, the latter in professional advancement. It was all nonsense, but no more so than many other corporative ideas. Glimmering through, though, remained the core ideas of education and *Betreuung*. Ley was well aware of the confusion which surrounded corporativism. He later admitted that he had "never met two National Socialists who were of one mind about *ständischer Aufbau*. It was simply a catastrophe in June and July of 1933. I can admit to you there were nights I couldn't sleep over *ständischer Aufbau*." It was "an absolute chaos of thought, a complete confusion."[77]

Also during the summer, Ley was still taking on the ministries with impunity. He viciously attacked the State Secretary in the Labor Ministry, Johannes Krohn, and his Ministerial Director, Engel, for supposedly sabotaging Ley's efforts to gain recognition for the German labor delegation at an international labor conference in Geneva the previous spring.[78] His attacks suffered somewhat in their credibility, however, when it became known that he had infuriated the Latin American delegations, when he suggested at a news conference that their representatives looked like someone "had lured them out of the jungle with bananas."[79] In part, because of Ley's indiscretions, the German delegation had left the conference on June 19.

As autumn approached, however, Ley began to observe more caution. On September 20 he sat in on a meeting of the General Council on the Economy, a one-time gathering of luminaries from big business and the ministries which included Schacht, Thyssen, Krupp, Bosch, Siemens, and others. After a long period of silence, while the others were discussing ways in which to get the economy rolling again, Ley finally interrupted with an appeal on his own

77. On Ley's definition of *ständischer Aufbau*, see Wolff's *Telegraphisches Büro*, August 12, in BA R43II/527b; his later remarks were made in a speech at the 1937 Party Day of Labor. See Mason, *Sozialpolitik*, p. 101.
78. See Ley to Seldte of August 9 in BA R41(Krohn)/5007.
79. See Joachim G. Leithäuser, *Wilhelm Leuschner. Ein Leben für die Republik* (Cologne, Bund Verlag, n.d.), p. 122; a protocol, undated but close to August 12, 1933, generated within the Labor Ministry details events at the conference in Geneva. See *Akten der Reichskanzlei*, Vol. I, Document no. 203, pp. 713–15.

behalf – one which was completely out of context. He tried to allay suspicion about the DAF by underscoring its educational function to build faith and trust among the workers. He also emphasized the necessity of having the workers in some kind of organization, in the process revealing again his deep-seated fear of another November 1918: "I tell you, gentlemen, nothing is more dangerous to the state than people without a home . . . when one is rejected by the state, then that is a dangerous situation . . . Now, if the state had said: "No, you don't matter, we don't want you, perhaps one day your children, but not you. You're rejected' — believe me that would have been fateful." He concluded by claiming that the DAF had played an important role in regaining the trust of the working man and that those present should change their minds if they still thought that the organization was breeding Marxism and class hatred. There was a (presumably) awkward silence as Ley stopped, then Thyssen. the industrialist, changed the subject back to the theme of work creation. But Ley had made his point, and that night Hitler seemed to support that point in a speech to the same group in which he emphasized in very non-technical terms the crucial necessity of "educating" the workers.[80] Later in the month, Ley also demonstrated conciliation towards the Labor Ministry by taking back all the things he had said about Krohn (although relations between Krohn and the DAF functionaries would remain a sore spot for years to come). His prudence at this point was no doubt increased by Hitler's sharp admonitions against continued "revolutionary" activities delivered on the occasion of the Reichsstatthalter conference on September 28.[81]

It was November, however, which witnessed a real turning point in Ley's attitude toward the radical position. On November 17 he issued a set of directives which abolished both corporativist and trade-unionist organizational concepts as formats for the DAF and marked the beginning of the DAF as a totalitarian mass organization. Members would no longer join one of Muchow's original pillars but rather would become individual members of the DAF and be dealt with as such. At the same time, as a kind of sop to the still numerous NSBO people, Ley ordered that all DAF offices would be run by the heads of parallel NSBO offices in personal union.[82]

80. Minutes of this discussion are in BA R43II/321, pp. 2–207.
81. See BA R43II/1392, pp. 43–52.
82. See Ley Anordnungen 13/33, 14/33, and 16/33, respectively, in BA NS51, vorl. 256.

Three days later, Ley tried to explain his position and what he had been doing to the Reichstagung of the NSBO in Munich. In a long, tortuous, often confusing speech, in which he came across as disorganized and moody, Ley revealed that he was rejecting corporativist and trade-union thinking. "Abandon all the old union thinking," he shouted, "educate yourselves! We cannot heal ourselves with the methods which brought the Marxists and Christian Socialist's to their doom. We have to recognize that. If we do not find new methods, and quite basic ones, then we will go under just like they did." Speaking of corporativist ideas, Ley admonished, "These concepts must be gone from our people, all of it gone. Party comrades, corporativist thinking is gradually beginning to get me down; it's gradually becoming a nightmare for me. . . . We don't have a precedent, nowhere, no. Fascism with its corporations is no example for us, that we want to say quite clearly." Then, as if to suggest that the radicals had been the main thorn in his side, Ley admitted that his biggest problem had been to convince business circles that the DAF was not "a bunch of 12 to 15 million Marxists and Bolsheviks." In an apparent effort to curb the lingering radicalism, Ley announced that the NSBO will be ever more closely bound to the DAF and the DAF, in turn, to the Political Organization of the Party. In fact, he even seemed to try optically to virtually erase the differences among these party organizations. New uniforms for functionaries would not even reveal what organization they were serving in. Moreover, he emphasized that party functionaries of whatever organization were part of a larger endeavor and just happened to have a specialized task. "I don't feel myself to be the leader of the Labor Front, as representative of the workers. . . . I feel myself to be the political agent of the Führer, as staff leader of the Political Organization, who happened to be commissioned with the special task of cleaning up the filth and dirt and chaos in the factories left there by the Liberal and Marxist parties, and to bring the people together again and have them march!" The strong implication was that the NSBO was not to stand out with its own program and agenda, but to blend into the Political Organization of the party and do what it was told. It was the party which would come to the forefront of events.

Ley also advocated, somewhat defensively, his central concept of education and *Betreuung*. "The social question is not a matter of wage agreements," he thundered, "but a matter of training and education." He went on to say that education is not simply a pale replacement for union activity but crucial in its own right: "You know yourselves that even in our own ranks one runs up against blockages and resistance, so that one might believe that education and training are perhaps nothing, a trifle, an embarrassing phrase used because one does not want to undertake union work as it has been in the past."

But Ley, still obviously haunted by 1918, did not neglect to mention as well the material benefits which unions used to provide and which the DAF would now bestow in much greater largesse. Wages would have to go up; prices would have to come down. And the DAF would provide only the best for the workers' free time. He added revealingly that it was not important for the worker to be a National Socialist as long as "he respects us."

At the end of his long, repetitive, and ill-organized speech, Ley, as if realizing that he had been waffling, announced to any journalists in the hall that it was strictly forbidden to write anything about his speech. He would bring out a communiqué himself.[83]

At the same time that Ley was gingerly putting distance between himself and the radicals, he was edging closer to industry and the ministries. On November 27, after what Ley would later call "long, difficult negotiations," he, Seldte, Schmitt, and Keppler (Hitler's specialist for economic questions) signed a "treaty" which essentially recognized that the Labor Front was not to be a super trade union or the representative of labor in the Third Reich, but rather a mass organizaton composed of both business and workers, which would devote itself to education and *Betreuung*, that is to integrating the workers into the regime on terms largely congenial to business. Now that the DAF seemed "harmless," the Reich Estate of German Industry was willing to encourage businessmen to join as individuals.[84]

The fall of 1933, then, witnessed an important milestone in the development of the DAF. But the months leading up to it had been hectic ones for Ley, as he struggled both against government agencies and party fanatics; but once he had sniffed the political winds, he had dealt ruthlessly with those who seemed to take the DAF in too risky a direction. He later admitted that this period had been "an eternal struggle. I can assure you that I wouldn't want to live

83. The entire text of the speech is in BA NS51; vorl. 256. See also Broszat, *The Hitler State*, p. 145.

84. The text of the agreement is in BA R43II/557; see also Broszat, *The Hitler State*, p. 146.

through this period again. God only knows that many failed then. No one has regretted that more than I myself; but I had to act. . . . I had to remove the men who got in my way. There was no turning back. Either I succeeded or everything was destroyed."[85]

But the struggle was far from over. In a sense, it was just beginning. The radicals were still in the DAF in large numbers, and they would by and large determine its activities at grassroots level. Nor were they willing to accept without resistance the transformation of the DAF from trade union to something very different. Ley still had ambitions which extended beyond what even suspicious corporate executives and government ministers imagined, and the dynamic of the regime lent impetus to Ley's dreams. Nor were those same businessmen and ministers being passive. In the halls of the ministries, busy officials were hastily drafting a major labor law which foresaw little future role for the DAF: 1934 would witness renewed jurisdictional warfare.

85. See Ley, *Deutschland ist schöner geworden*, p. 264.

CHAPTER 6

The Organizational Dream

The multifaceted DAF organization must be seen as partly the result of the constant pursuit of jurisdictions, which was one of the hallmarks of the Third Reich, and partly the result of Robert Ley's fertile imagination, as he thought of more and ever more grandiose ways to educate and "take care of" the German people. It is then perhaps more rewarding to view the DAF not so much in the form of an institutional study — it is too much of a metastasizing cancer for that — but rather as the creature of Ley's dreams as those dreams were mitigated, circumscribed, and encouraged by the Nazi polycratic system.[1] Just as the utopian dreams and destructive nihilism of National Socialism met in Ley, so the DAF itself had a constructive and destructive side. In the broadest sense it did in many ways function as a workers' advocate and demonstrably helped to "humanize" the workplace in Germany.[2] On the other hand, in its refusal to accord the workers the autonomy of responsible citizens, in its constant surveillance of their activities, and in its role, in cooperation with the Gestapo, in keeping the labor force under control in its use of racial criteria in bestowing the often considerable benefits of the system, and in its instrumental use of those benefits to raise productivity to sustain a destructive war of cônquest, the DAF demonstrated the destructive nature of National Socialism.

By the end of 1933 Ley was rapidly taking the DAF organization away from its original structure and ideology. The union structure, with relatively autonomous pillars composed of the various craft

1. On the polycratic nature of the Nazi system, see Peter Hüttenberger, "Nationalsozialistische Polykratie", *Geschichte und Gesellschaft*, vol. 2 (1976), pp. 417–42.
2. Timothy Mason, *Sozialpolitik im Dritten Reich*, 2nd edn (Opladen, Westdeutscher Verlag, 1977), p. 190, points particularly at "Strength through Joy" and "Beauty of Work" as important sociopolitical efforts to "humanize" their workplace.

unions, and the corporative spirit which animated it, gave way to a totalitarian mass organization based on the Führer-principle of "Verantwortung nach oben" and "Authorität nach unten" (responsibility upwards and authority downwards). The corporate sense of craft or occupation as foundation succumbed to the idea of plant or factory as the basic building blocks of the Nazi community. This was in line with the new Law for the Regulation of National Labor (Gesetz zur Ordnung der nationalen Arbeit, hereafter AOG) and was expressed in Ley's order of January 25, 1934, on the "Reorganization of the German Labor Front."[3] Since members now joined as individuals and not by craft union, they were deprived of a mechanism by which they could represent their craft interests. Instead, the new command structure put them under the control of the central offices of the DAF. The workers, recognized only as individuals or members of a Nazi "factory community," could thus be atomized and lost any autonomous organization of their own.

It was some indication, however, of the resistance which the NSBO people developed against this "betrayal" that while dissolution of the craft-union organizations came immediately, that of the white-collar employees, where many of the NSBO people had offices, was postponed and implemented gradually. More importantly, Ley gave the NSBO people a considerable sop: he indirectly restored part of the *ständisch* component by creating eighteen so-called Reichsbetriebsgemeinschaften (Reich Plant Communities), each of them reflecting a sector of the economy, as sinecures for the old NSBO reliables. These had little independence, as they were under the control of the central office of the DAF, and little function, beyond being part of the DAF effort to infiltrate vocational education, and by 1938 they had lost their organizational integrity entirely and simply became specialty offices (*Fachämter*) in the DAF bureaucracy. But in the meantime, they represented a compromise with the radicals which afforded Ley the necessary time to build his strength and await the outcome of the "second revolution," which peaked in the Röhm purge of June 1934.[4]

It is difficult to sketch the central administrative structure of the

3. For Ley's order, see Anordnungen 1, 2, 3/1934 of January 24 and 25, 1934, in BAK, NS51, vorl. 256; see also Gerd Rühle, *Das Dritte Reich. Dokumentarische Darstellung des Aufbaues der Nation* (Berlin, 1934), vol. 2, pp. 155f.; Otto Marrenbach, *Fundamente des Sieges*, 2nd edn (Berlin, Verlag der DAF, 1940).
4. See Hans Joachim Reichhardt, "Die Deutsche Arbeitsfront" (FU Berlin, 1956), pp. 46–48; also Peppler (Sozialamt) directive of December 4, 1934, on the duties of the local Reichsbetriebsgemeinschaftsleiters, in BAK, NS51, vorl. 256.

DAF, except as snapshots valid only at one time or another.[5] The structure was almost constantly in flux, with one reorganization following upon another. Offices were divided, then redivided, then recombined in different fashion. No wonder that the author of a book on the DAF published in 1934 felt constrained to say, "In consideration of the initiated reorganization, made necessary in the wake of the National Socialist revolution, it is not possible to foresee the final organizational form of the Deutsche Arbeitsfront as this book goes into print."[6] It was also continually expanding and growing more complex — from nine main offices in 1934 to sixty in 1939 — which reflected the jurisdictional imperialism and dynamic of Ley and his people. It was quite apparent that Ley had not listened to the advice of one of his main associates Claus Selzner, who had warned: "Do not organize what you can, but what you must. Above all heed the maxim: to organize means to simplify."[7] In the immense, growing and kaleidoscopic empire that was the DAF, however, some constants remained. For one thing, the constant reorganizations led generally in the direction of tightening the lines of authority. Each reorganization restricted the ability of various offices to communicate in parallel with one another or with agencies outside the DAF.[8] And the most important offices — those at the top — generally remained to a fairly consistent degree in the hands of the old-timers, whom Ley had recruited at the outset, many of whom were his old cronies from the early days of the movement. As the bureaucracy grew, so did the authority and jurisdiction of these men. Nor was their collaboration without often serious rivalries. In this sense the DAF bore a close resemblance to the Nazi regime as a whole. Indeed, in popular parlance the symbol of the DAF, a gear with teeth, was often called "the saw with which people within the DAF

5. The best brief overview remains Dieter von Lölhöffel, "Die Umwandlung der Gerwerkschaften in eine nationalsozialistische Zwangsorganisation," in Ingeborg Essenwein-Rothe, *Die Wirtschaftsverbände von 1933 bis 1945* (Berlin, Duncker & Humbolt, 1965), pp. 1–184; also good, though somewhat dated, is Reichhardt, "DAF," pp. 46–57.
6. See Gerhard Starcke, *NSBO und Deutsche Arbeitsfront* (Berlin, Verlag des Reimar Hobbing, 1934), p. 70.
7. Ibid., p. 70; for a *circa* pre-June 1935 directory of the DAF offices and their occupants as well as a Gau directory, see BAK, NS26/281.
8. See, for example, Ley order of September 24, 1935, enjoining DAF officials not to go to the Gestapo on their own but through the Information Office of the Central Offices in BAK, Schumacher Sammlung, 223; also Ley order 14/38, n.d., but in 1938, directing that, with several exceptions all communication between the DAF and State and party offices must go through Marrenbach, in BAK, NS8/192.

saw each other off."[9] (See Plate 7.)

At the pinnacle of the organization was Ley himself, who ruled as Leader of the Deutsche Arbeitsfront, one of a number of positions which he held in his capacity as Reichsorganisationsleiter of the NSDAP. Indeed, as time went on it was often difficult to distinguish one capacity from another. This was not only true at the top but below as well, for a number of his subordinates held dual positions in ROL and DAF, a phenomenon which led a number of Nazis to refer caustically to the "tail wagging the dog."[10]

Under Ley's command was the DAF Central Bureau, the bureaucratic head of the vast DAF empire. It was divided up into a number of jurisdictions (called *Hauptarbeitsgebiete*, or main work areas). The most important of these were as follows.[11]

The Adjutants' Office handled Ley's personal affairs. The Personnel Office carried out much of the day-to-day business of the DAF, particularly negotiations with government ministries. Because of Ley's frequent and lengthy absences, both were particularly crucial. Both were headed by Otto Marrenbach, an old crony of Ley's from the *Kampfzeit*, who had joined Ley in his own home town of Waldbröl in 1927 and helped him to "conquer the Bergisch Land" in subsequent years.[12] Marrenbach was known as a good administrator, "precise and simple in his orders, liked by all co-workers and employees." He also had a reputation for sober objectivity which made him the preferred negotiating partner for the government ministries. As Ley's own personal secretary, Fräulein Brueninghoff, noted years later: "Often [Marrenbach] made good the injustices committed by Ley and prevented hasty decisions by Ley, who was very impulsive."[13] As head of both offices, Marrenbach wielded enormous power and might well be called the "general manager" of the DAF.

9. See Saupert (aide to the party treasurer, Schwarz) visitor's memo of February 9, 1938, in US National Archives, T-580, Roll 81, Frame 393. Saupert refers, in particular, to rivalries and shifting alliances among Marrenbach, Schmeer, and Simon.
10. Ley had occasion from time to time to remind his people of the parallel organization of party and DAF, as in his circular letter of October 12, 1935, in BAK, NS51, vorl. 256.
11. According to the reorganization at the turn of the year 1936–7 following the proclamation of the second Four-Year Plan.
12. See Walter Kiehl, *Mann an der Fahne* (Munich, Zentralverlag der NSDAP, 1938), p. 45.
13. See Brueninghoff Interrogation, in US National Archives, RG238, Justice Jackson file, p. 3.

The Staff Office was largely responsible for liaison with the party and charged with the particular task of assuring ideological *Gleichschaltung* between DAF and party. To assure this coordination the head of the staff office was simultaneously in personal union head of the Main Staff Office of the ROL. This task was carried out by Heinrich Simon, who along with his father, was an "old fighter" from the Gau Cologne-Aachen in the 1920s.[14]

As always in a bureaucratic entity, the Organization Office was of great importance, made even more so in the case of the DAF by the fact that for all intents and purposes it was combined with two other "working areas" all under one man, another of Ley's most effective managers: Claus Selzner. Selzner, a war veteran and early activist in *völkisch* affairs, had been a party member since 1925 and very active in a number of capacities, including newspaper editor and Kreisleiter in Ludwigshafen, where he founded the first NSBO cell at IG Farben. He was also a notorious Parteiredner. Scarcely less radical than Ley in his public appearances, he had been forbidden to speak in Upper Bavaria in 1932 after uttering such remarks as, "In the Bartholomew Night of the German people throats will be cut" and "Mussolini represents German interests better than former Foreign Minister Stresemann."[15]

Besides the Organization Office, which had the responsibility of coordinating most other offices of the DAF to the extent that they were not themselves independent, Selzner also controlled the working area "Sicherung des sozialen Friedens" (Securing Social Peace), which among other things administered the eighteen Reich Plant Communities as well as all the offices which dealt with people in their capacity as workers. These included offices for legal consultation, youth, women, and social affairs. In addition, Selzner also controlled the area called "Hebung des Lebensstandarts" (Raising the Living Standard), which included those DAF offices which addressed the general needs of people as members of the national community. These included offices for health, homesteads, sports, vocational education as well as the immensely successful "Strength through Joy" leisure and travel organization. All of these functions gave Selzer an important role in the DAF attempts to become a

14. See Kiehl, *Mann an der Fahne*, pp. 41–4.
15. On Selzner's background see material in Berlin Document Center: File Selzner, including handwritten *Lebenslauf*. For above remarks attributed to him, see Präsidium der Regierung Oberbayern to Bezirksämter, no. 422 of February 24, 1932.

social "super agency." Like several other top DAF officials, Selzner also occupied an analogous position in the ROL as head of its Main Organization Office. Ley's faith in Selzner was such that he gave him full powers to establish the DAF in Austria after the Anschluss in 1938.[16]

When it came time to appoint a liaison to the newly proclaimed Second Four-Year Plan in 1936, Ley chose another old comrade, Rudolf Schmeer, who had served the party as Redner in Ley's Gau in the 1920s and later became Reichsinspekteur when Ley took over the ROL after the Strasser crisis.[17]

But Ley also looked for talent as well as political reliability. It was some indication of Ley's ability to pick good administrators as well as loyal old comrades that several men who were to become leading lights in the Third Reich served the DAF. These included Fritz Todt, head of the Office for Technical Sciences, who later lent his administrative and engineering experience to building the West Wall as well as the autobahns and who became Hitler's first Minister for Armaments and Munitions; Albert Speer, who was Todt's successor as Minister for Armaments, served as head of the DAF "Amt Schönheit der Arbeit" (Beauty of Work) and was responsible for the campaign to beautify the German workplace; and Bodo Lafferentz, head of the "Amt Reisen-Wandern und Urlaub" (Office for Travel, Hiking, and Vacation) who would later take over the large Volkswagen works for the DAF.

The DAF was not just a giant bureaucratic complex in Berlin. Its organizational network stretched nationwide. Given the close connection between DAF and ROL, it is not surprising that the geographic organization of the DAF was nearly a mirror image of that of the NSDAP; indeed, often the Ort, Kreis or Gau functionary of the party was simultaneously the DAF functionary in personal union, which reflected Ley's dual position at the top, as Reichsorganisationsleiter of the party and head of the DAF. The DAF functionaries were distinguished from the party ones by the designation *-Walter* (party tended to be *-Leiter*). Hence, the party county functionary was the Kreisleiter, while his DAF counterpart was the

16. See Selzner circular letter of April 13, 1938, quoting Ley's grant of authority for Austria, in BDC: File Selzner.
17. See Kiehl, *Mann an der Fahne*, pp. 60–2. Kiehl mentions a number of lesser lights in the DAF who had been Ley's cronies in the early days, including Richard Schaller (p. 98), Karl Maletz (pp. 75–9), Alfons Balette (p. 63), and Joseph Bosbach (pp. 52–9).

Kreiswalter. (In the KdF the term *Warte* was used.) This dense parallel network extended all the way down to the cell and block level, including both the factory and the dwelling, so that scarcely any *Volksgenossen* escaped the encompassing grasp of the DAF, whose local people were to be "knowledgeable about everything," in order, as Ley put it, to distinguish the "decent" people from the "indecent" ones.[18] Much of the DAF activity went on at the local level and the variety of this work is reflected in the fact that local DAF offices frequently had as many as seventeen functionaries acting in various capacities in the factories, either gathering information, organizing a multitude of activities, or just plain interfering in local plant operations.[19] These ambitious local people often went far beyond their orders — or even countermanded them — and created much of the dynamic which made Ley's empire expand inexorably.

Ultimately, the DAF maintained a full-time paid corps of 44,500 functionaries (apart from hundreds of thousands of part-timers) and controlled a revenue three times that of the party itself.[20] The DAF also maintained generous pay scales that shocked even people in other party organizations, especially in the SA. This led to the revival of an old accusation which had been leveled at the NSBO in the form of the acronym "*N*och *S*ind die *B*onzen *O*ben" (The party hacks are still on top).[21] The organization came to be staffed with young careerists who were motivated both by the Nazi dream and by the generous emoluments that rank and office promised. At the top Ley's cronies were overrepresented — and their corruption would become notorious.

Nothing better illustrates the essential normlessness of the Nazi regime and the near "sovereignty" of its competing bureaucratic

18. For the DAF geographic organization, see *Organisationsbuch der NSDAP*, 7th. edn, 1943, pp. 218–22; Reichhardt, "DAF," pp. 52–3; Robert Ley, remarks in *Durchbruch der sozialen Ehre*, 7th edn (Berlin, Zentralverlag der NSDAP, 1939), pp. 90f.; also see *Dienstrichtlinien für den DAF-Blockwalter*, Gau Württemberg-Hohenzollern of July 15, 1936, in BAK, NSD 50/6.
19. For the full panoply of local DAF offices, see Marrenbach, *Fundamente*, p. 26; even more extensive is Ley order 24/39 of July 25, 1939, published in *Amtliches Nachrichtenblatt der DAF*, no. 3, in US National Archives, T-580, Ordner 694, which discusses the duties of the *Betriebsobmann* in factories of different sizes.
20. See Reichhardt, "DAF," p. 56, on staff. He accepts the 1939 Jahresbericht of the Finanzwirtschaft der DAF for this figure and for the incredible 1,385,475 volunteers working part-time for the DAF; on DAF finances vis-à-vis the party, see Timothy Mason, "Labour in the Third Reich 1933–1939," *Past and Present*, no. 33 (April 1966), p. 120.
21. See Gestapo to Finance Ministry of October 31, 1933, pointing to discontent in the party over DAF salaries in BAK, R43II/531.

empires than the debate over the legal status of the DAF. It was an unprecedented type of organization, which, encompassing both workers and managers, seemed to be neither fish nor fowl. But it did need to be somehow defined both within the framework of the multijurisdictional Nazi system, which defied norms, and the German legal system, which tried to establish them. Ley did not always see it that way. Just as Hitler was not really interested in clarifying the relationship between party and state, for to keep the relationship vague only enhanced his power, so Ley was content to keep the legal status of the DAF foggy for the same reason. He was trying, as Reichsorganisationsleiter, to built his own *Hausmacht* in the DAF and did not want the organization, with its vast wealth, to come under the scrutiny of party treasurer Schwarz. Hence the debate over whether the DAF was to be a "division" of the party (*Gliederung* like the SA, SS, and HJ) or an "affiliate" (*angeschlossener Verband*, which consisted of professional and interest groups). The former were an integral part of the NSDAP and had no separate legal identity or treasury. The latter were separate organizations which had their own resources and were legal personae. They were "*betreut*" by the party.[22] Nor did he want the DAF to be seen, in a juridical sense, as the legal successor to the defunct trade unions, for that might expose him to legal action bearing on claims to former union property and wealth. Hence, he resisted attempts on the part of government ministries to draft laws concerning the nature of the DAF, which would either establish its financial liability or expose it to the scrutiny of the state Auditing Office (the Rechnungshof).

It is almost amusing to follow the various terms used in the tug-of-war between those who wanted to clarify and those who desired to obfuscate the true nature of the DAF. Was it a "division" of the party (it was until March 1935)? Or was it an "affiliate" (it was after March 1935)? Was it a legal persona or not? The debate went on for years, often dissolving into convoluted terminology which represented abortive attempts to combine legal norms with NS normlessness. "It is neither a legal entity under private law nor a corporate body under public law but rather a legal persona under public law in its own right" ran one definition. "As a National Socialist community it is a bearer of rights and duties. It has legal capacity and is subordinate to the Führer", went another.[23] In the

22. See Orlow, *Nazi Party 1933–1945*, pp. 6f; and Reichhardt, "DAF," pp. 72ff.
23. These debates with their proposals, refutations, and counterproposals fill the

end, nothing was settled, and all the participants understood why. An early DAF publication noted in a wonderfully revealing sentence, "The division of responsibilities between the DAF as an organ of the NSDAP and the authorities of the state social administration can frankly only be understood in its complete significance when one considers the peculiarity of the total relationship between party and state in the National Socialist Reich".[24] Several years later, the State Secretary in the Justice Ministry admitted, in exasperation and not with glee, that: "Difficulties have their origin in the unsatisfactory solution of the problem party-state."[25] Years later during the war the DAF itself foresaw a future great reform which would introduce a truly National Socialist legal system, but that for the immediate future the DAF would remain what it had been: a "National Socialist community" and a "legal entity of a special sort."[26]

That was fine with Ley, who, in his internecine party struggles with Schwarz, Hess, and Bormann, preferred that confusion reign. It agreed with his gradually developing plans to make the DAF independent, even from the party itself — plans which he would reveal in 1938 at the height of his prewar aspirations. In the meantime, Ley was well aware that he was skirting the edges of the law in his appropriation and expenditure of former union funds, but those fears were allayed by Hitler's backing. In a revealing remark reminiscent of the *Kampfjahre*, when Ley's childhood fears of repeating his father's disgraceful incarceration were cancelled out by Hitler's assurances that his activities were of great social and political utility, Ley said:

> Once I said to the Führer: 'Mein Führer, every day I'm really standing with one foot in jail, for I am still trustee for comrades Leipart and Imbusch [former trade-union leaders]. And if they should demand their property back one day, I shall have spent it all in building or spent it in some fashion. But they won't find it in the same condition as when they turned it over to me. Therefore I would have to be condemned!' Thereupon the Führer laughed and said that I appeared to find this situation to my satisfaction. It was difficult for all of us. Today we laugh about it.[27]

---

pages of the Reich Chancellory correspondence. See especially, BAK, R43II/529–31; For a useful summary, see *Akten der Reichskanzlei*, vol. I. p. 993, n. 27.

24. See *DAF Wesen-Ziel-Wege*, in BAK, NSD50/567, p. 10.
25. See ministerial discussion of April 16, 1936, in BAK, R43II/530.
26. Marrenbach, *Fundamente*, p. 21.
27. Quoted in Reichhardt, "DAF," p. 75.

The confusion over the legal identity of the DAF revealed something else about the role of Ley's affiliate in the Führer state, something which did not favor Ley's ambitions and which had to be overcome — the fact that the DAF really did not have jurisdictional authority clearly recognized by anyone (unlike the SS, for example, which was gathering police powers in its hands). The DAF had no independent command authority or power to issue decrees and ordinances (except internally). It was also forbidden by law to do things that trade unions normally do: bargain for wages and benefits, order improvements in working conditions, administer pension and social insurance funds, or run apprenticeship programs. As a result, Ley had to discover other ways to wield power or to craftily arrogate these functions unto himself. He tried gradually to do so, in part by transforming the DAF into a social "super agency," in part by implementing his wider vision of "schooling and *Betreuung*." In the meantime, the lack of jurisdictional authority on the part of the DAF was initially balanced out by other advantages.

The Labor Front possessed a certain legitimacy by being a Nazi organization and, indeed, with the exception of R. Walther Darré's Reichsnährstand, which pretty much limited itself to the agricultural sector, was virtually unrivaled in the general area of social policy. Its close relationship with the party proper, through Ley's position as ROL, gave it additional backing and authority. In addition, the DAF enjoyed a close working relationship with Goebbels and the Propaganda Ministry as well as with several Gauleiter.[28]

The DAF also represented a very lage upward mobility ladder for tens of thousands of Germans, especially at lower levels, who could nurse their career ambitions as well as find outlets for social idealism or social resentments, depending on their inclinations. These people, most of whom were not party members and therefore were not directly under the control of the local party leader, provided much of the grass-roots dynamic of the organization and often used the latitude they possessed in full measure.[29]

Last but not least, the DAF enjoyed an incredibly large member-

28. See undated mutual order for cooperation signed by Ley and Goebbels in the wake of Hess's order of October 20, 1934, in BAK, NS25/455.

29. Local party leaders pleaded with Schwarz to loosen his ban on new party memberships in order to bring DAF people into the NSDAP and under their disciplinary control, but, to their frustration, he did so only rarely. See Peter Hüttenberger, *Die Gauleiter, Studie zum Wandel des Machtgefüges in der NSDAP* (Stuttgart, Deutsche Verlagsanstalt, 1969), p. 132.

ship of (Ley hoped) virtually all gainfully employed Germans and their employers as well as the immense financial resources acquired from the trade unions and constantly augmented by the dues of that membership. These two last factors — membership and finances — deserve a closer look.[30]

As the DAF evolved from an edifice supported by quasi-independent pillars formed by occupational groups to a totalitarian mass organization, the basis for membership changed. Membership based on what union one had belonged to (the *Verbände*) disappeared, and individual membership of both employer and employee took its place. This was a membership in a large national organization and not in the local, trade, or professionally oriented affiliate of a national organization. People joined then as isolated individuals.[31] Institutional membership was also permitted, and several large organizations including the Reichskulturkammer, the Deutsche Rechtsfront, the NS-Lehrerbund as well as Schachst's Organisation der Gewerblichen Wirtschaft, did so, which meant that their members also became part of the DAF, though not as individuals.[32] What Ley really had in mind was a transmogrification of Strasser's old scheme of taking NS organizations and letting them grow until they became, in a sense, coterminous with the nation itself. If Ley could expand his DAF to include all Germans who worked in whatever capacity, then he would be able, through education and *Betreuung*, to recast them in his "brown collectivist" image and, at last, achieve the harmonious, conflict-free society. Thus although membership in the DAF was theoretically entirely voluntary, Ley and the DAF put enormous pressure on people in a variety of ways to join.[33]

Ley's own public remarks left little doubt as to his intent. "Whoever doesn't want to march in our midst," he once said, "we'll tread on his heels until he does. Either he marches along or he remains by the wayside. Among our people we can only use men and women who march forward and not backward."[34] Or, as he spoke to a group of Ruhr industrialists in April 1934: "When someone comes to

30. Mason, *Sozialpolitik*, pp. 176–77 also points to the advantages of financial security and political legitimacy.
31. See "Richtlinien über die Mitgliedschaft zur Deutschen Arbeitsfront," issued by the DAF Schatzmeister on July 9, 1934, in BAK, NS51, vorl. 256.
32. See Lölhöffel, "Umwandlung," p. 174.
33. Forbidden to join of course were Jews; and after October 1937 Mischlinge and anyone married to a Jew (*jüdisch versippt*) as well. See Ley order 52/37 of October 20, 1937, in BAK, NS22, vorl. 649.
34. From *Soldaten der Arbeit*, p. 33.

me and says: 'I don't want to join your DAF' then I answer him: 'My dear friend, that's not your decision!. . . . The DAF has unwritten laws and no one will be able to extricate himself from these unwritten laws."[35]

The stiffest pressures came at the grass-roots level, however, where local DAF functionaries were always putting on propaganda displays to get one shop or another to collectively join the organization. Often owners and managers, sometimes under local DAF pressure, would actually include obligatory membership as a precondition for employment, something which caused controversy and provoked protests from the Labor Ministry.[36]

Apart from these direct pressures, indirect ones also existed. In the absence of a satisfactory rise in living standard, the only way workers could avail themselves of the undeniably attractive amenities which the regime offered — such as KdF voyages — was to join the Labor Front. As a result, many workers quite justifiably felt that, official pronouncements to the contrary, membership was really obligatory.[37]

In two categories, however, Ley was thwarted in his overreaching membership ambitions — by Hitler himself. The dictator exempted peasants and civil servants, responding to pressures both from his peasant leader, Darré, and from government ministries. In public, Ley accepted these limitations and even justified them in his own clumsy way. These groups do not have to be educated to the idea of *Volksgemeinschaft*, he observed; the peasant because he is already a member of the *Volk* community by virtue of his "love of the soil and through the mystical relationship of race and blood to the soil"; the official, because "whoever as civil servant has not yet recognized the value of his people, won't be capable of learning so by means of the best schooling".[38] In private, Ley tried to recruit these people anyway, as is attested to by his rivalry with Darré over the rural landless laborers. Ley also occasionally tried to force DAF people

35. Quoted in Reichhardt, "DAF," p. 90.
36. See circular letter no. 8 of October 8, 1935, from Mende (DAF Central Office) to all Gauwalter noting complaints about forcing membership as a condition of employment.
37. This was certainly the impression gained by the Sopade reports. See, for example, a May 1935 report which, after quoting Ley, noted, "Everyone familiar with national socialist propaganda knows that in the national socialist lingo these words mean 'You must join,' " Sopade, 1935, p. 578.
38. See Robert Ley, *Der ständische Aufbau und die Deutsche Arbeitsfront* (Berlin, Verlag der DAF, 1933), p. 6.

1. Ley in uniform during World War One.

2. Ley during the roll call of Amtsleiter of the NSDAP, Nuremberg 1934.

(*above*) 3. Ley meeting the action group charged with destroying the independent trade unions, April 1933. Left to right: Brinckmann, Biallas, Peppler, Schmeer, Müller, Ley, Schumann, Muchow.
(*below*) 4. Ley and his SS hosts at Dachau. To Ley's left "Papa" Eiche.

5. Rally in the Berlin Lustgarten to proclaim the Law for the Regulation of National Labor, January 14, 1934. The speaker is Johannes Engel, Trustee of Labor for Brandenburg.

6. DAF fair in Berlin, *c.* 1937. The slogan reads "In the future there will be only one aristocracy — the aristocracy of labor!".

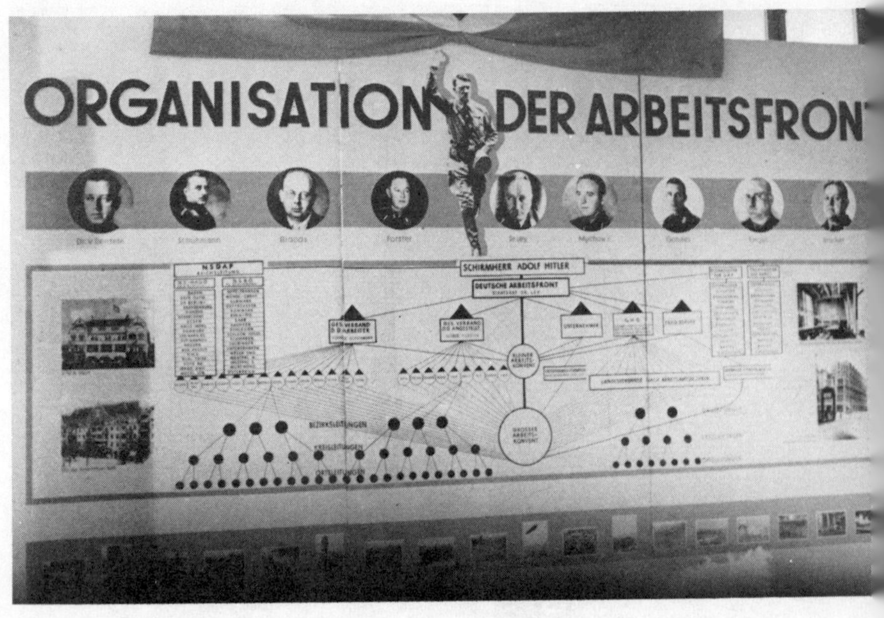

7. DAF organization chart. An exhibit at the DAF fair in Berlin.

8. The "Strength through Joy" (KdF) office "Feierabend" in Worms, *c.* 1939. These storefront rooms presented a variety of after-work activities.

9. The KdF ship *Wilhelm Gustloff*. Ocean cruises ostensibly brought upper-class vacations to working-class people.

10. Hitler launching the KdF ship *Robert Ley* in 1938.

11. Robert Ley on the *Robert Ley*.

12. A KdF tour group leaving for Upper Bavaria. Millions of workers took part in these relatively inexpensive trips.

13. Propaganda for the Volkswagen "Beetle", known officially as the "KdF-Wagen". Germans paid premiums for a car they did not come to drive until after the war.

(*above*) 14. KdF gymnastics lessons at Berlin-Wannsee, 1937.
(*below*) 15. Reichsberufswettkampf, 1936. Bricklayers performing.

16. Model settlement for workers. The one-family cottage capacious enough for a large family was an important DAF goal. It combined population policy with a major attempt to integrate the working class into Nazi society.

out of other kinds of organizations by forbidding dual membership. This was particularly true with regard to confessional organizations, a policy which greatly discomforted DAF leaders in Catholic areas, who foresaw a great diminution of DAF membership when people were confronted with the choice between their traditional affiliation and the Labor Front.[39]

In the end, though, the various pressures worked. In May 1933 the DAF had about 4.7 million members. Membership grew to 14 million in 1934; 16 million in 1935; 20 million in 1938, and 22 million by outbreak of war. In 1939 Ley came close to reaching his goal, when out of a total of 25. 3 million workers and employees, 22 million were DAF members.[40]

DAF membership was closely tied to DAF finances: the more members, the more money for Ley's coffers. But Ley had some serious financial problems for the first year or so. Many workers quite understandably refused to see the violently imposed DAF as "their" organization and withheld their dues initially. Between May and October monthly dues allegedly fell from 17 million to 8 million marks.[41] Moreover, the transformation during the subsequent year from union-based to mass-based organization cost, by Ley's own admission, 47.5 million marks in dues.[42] Only after April 1935, when the transformation of the DAF was largely completed and dues were being collected through payroll withholding, did the situation become "normal" and Ley could count on steadily increasing wealth.[43] By 1939 70 percent of all firms were withholding, and as a consequence the DAF collected 539 million marks in dues alone that year.[44]

The dues were collected on a weekly or monthly basis depending on how often one were paid and were calibrated by income.[45] In twenty categories dues went from 20 pfennigs for those at the bottom to 12 marks for those earning 740 marks or more. The DAF claimed

39. See circular letter from DAF Gauwalter, Gau Bayerischer-Ostmark of August 22, 1935, to all Kreiswalter. US National Archives, T-81, Roll 66, Frame 75289–290.
40. See Lölhöffel, "Umwandlung," p. 173, n. 138; see also comparable figures from Ley, *Durchbruch der sozialen Ehre*, p. 128.
41. See Mason, *Sozialpolitik*, p. 111.
42. See Robert Ley, *Deutschland ist glücklicher geworden. Zwei Reden auf dem Reichsparteitag 1935* (Berlin, Verlag der DAF, 1935), p. 6.
43. Krosigk, the Finance Minister, resisted payroll deduction initially, but gave in after the DAF agreed to take over administrative costs. BAK, R43II/529.
44. See Mason, *Sozialpolitik*, pp. 182; Reichhardt, "DAF," pp. 56, 64.
45. Chart on dues schedules taken from Richtlinien über die Mitgliedschaft zur [DAF], July 9, 1934, in BAK, NS51, vorl. 256, pp. 6ff.

that it took on average 1.5 percent of gross income as dues with an average monthly due of 1.51 marks.[46]

As for the disposition of these eventually vast funds, there existed a basic division of opinion between the official pronouncements of the DAF and much grass-roots worker opinion. According to the DAF, the workers were getting more for their money than they ever had before. Most of the funds were going ostensibly for individual aid to the unemployed, accident victims, the indigent, and so on, as well as to health care, schooling, and the popular "Strength through Joy," although the DAF admitted to extraordinarily high administrative overheads (one source admitted 27 percent; Ley spoke of 22 percent; the old unions admitted to between 2.5 and 4 percent.)[47]

Many workers saw the money going elsewhere. There were constant complaints contrasting the ruthlessness with which the DAF collected dues with the niggardliness with which it dispensed services.[48] Many saw the cesspool of corruption as a black hole swallowing up their dues. Indeed, the Sopade reports noted on one occasion that "in the list of corruption cases which we have put together in our last reports, the Labor Front takes first place."[49] And if it was not corruption, then it was party affairs or rearmament for which the dues money was appropriated. It was common, for example, when a squadron of warplanes flew over, for the workers to point and say, "There fly our dues."[50]

What the workers did not completely realize, however, and the DAF only cautiously admitted, was that a great deal of the money under DAF control went to finance its huge business operations. It is important to examine this part of the DAF empire, for it represents an important element in the DAF rivalry with business and government, a springboard for Ley's claim on more and more quasi-governmental jurisdictions and part of the expression of his ideological dream.

46. See DAF *Schatzmeister* Brinckmann, "Was geschieht mit den Beiträgen?" in Hans Bialles and Gerhard Starcke (eds.), *Leipzig; das Nürnberg der DAF, 1935*, in BAK, NSD50/8, p. 128.
47. See Brinckmann, "Beiträge", pp. 128–9, where the month February 1935 is given as an example; Ley's figure and that on the trade unions is from Sopade, 1936, p. 866.
48. For example, Sopade, 1935, pp. 38, 588–9; 1936, pp. 868ff.
49. Ibid., 1934, p. 447; for other examples of reports on extensive corruption, see 1934, pp. 54–60, 235–46 319–21; 1935, pp. 87–106, 484–503; 1936, 217–50, 1139–60. As the years went by the number of cases reported increased steadily.
50. Ibid., 1935, p. 578.

Perhaps in keeping with its somewhat schizophrenic identity as an organization housing both workers and bosses, the DAF was not just a major party agency aspiring to create social policy vis-à-vis German workers; it was also a giant business conglomerate. Robert Ley presided over an empire which included construction, insurance, publishing, automobiles, consumer retailing, banking, and various holding companies.

In part, the business holdings — housing firms like Neue Heimat for example — had been inherited from the former trade unions. In part, they were acquired as part of Ley's ideological fervor to educate and "take care of" the German people. In part, they represented leverage by which Ley could increase the power and jurisdiction of the DAF, particularly in competition with the government and the business world. Indeed, parts of Ley's empire reflected his specific ambitions in the larger realm of social policy. He had always dreamed of providing decent housing for the poorly paid German worker; of a financially secure retirement for the elderly *Volksgenosse*; of an educational-propaganda structure to turn Germans into believing National Socialists. After the war broke out he would add several important jurisdictions to his collection of titles, which, had Germany won the war, would have permitted him to be virtually a "social policy czar." They included responsibility for planning a comprehensive social security system (his *Volksversorgungswerk*) as well as for residential housing (in his capacity as Reichswohnungskommissar). The business empire represented, in a sense, the chance to get a leg up on these activities.[51] Even Ley's involvement in consumer products had an ideological and propagandistic basis. Ley came up with ideas for a whole variety of "people's" products in the attempt to demonstrate that National Socialism could provide ordinary Germans at reasonable prices with those amenities which had traditionally been reserved for the "better off" (*besserbemittelte*) classes. The best known, and most representative, of these "*Volks*-" products was the Volkswagen; but many others were also envisioned, including the "people's radio receiver" (*Volksempfänger*) the "people's refrigerator" (*Volkskühlschrank*), and the "people's dwelling" (*Volkswohnung*). The value of the "people's radio" was clear; it provided a mechanism with which Hitler could reach all the people,

51. See Chapter 9 below for Ley's wartime activities. Most of the data on DAF business enterprises comes from "Die wirtschaftlichen Unternehmungen der Deutschen Arbeitsfront" [hereafter "Unternehmungen"], n.d., but after 1939, published by the DAF, in BAK, NSD50/24.

at home and at the plant. Accordingly, Ley distributed 50,000 special radios (named the DAF 1011) at a cost of 295 marks each to be installed in factories for the political edification of the workers.[52]

Since the DAF did aspire in a sense to be the worker's advocate, Ley was a little sensitive about presiding over a set of capitalistic enterprises, and from time to time felt compelled to justify them. He emphasized that although their form was capitalistic, their guiding spirit derived from National Socialism; indeed, to the extent that they were *gemeinnützig* (served the public good), they were to be models for the German future. Many of them bore the designation *gemeinnützig* in their titles. Ley was also at pains to acquire firms which had a reputation for representing the *völkisch* cause in the past, as was the case with one insurance company and a publishing house. In a DAF report on its business enterprises, Ley's associate, Otto Marrenbach, took pains at the outset to say:

> The *Betreuung* of the German people at the workplace, after hours, in their free time, at home and in the family is the highest goal of the DAF; for that reason this community [the DAF] which encompasses the entire German people cannot come under the suspicion of fostering and advancing private-capitalist ideas in its enterprises. Precisely the opposite is the case. Despite the formal legalistic capitalist form, the DAF enterprises are active in a completely different sense, namely in the formation and realization of a new economic and social work ethos.[53]

But even if the DAF corporate empire did consider itself outside the traditional framework of capitalism, it often behaved as if it were not. Spearheaded by its very liquid banking operation, the DAF elbowed its way into many sectors of the economy, often competing outright with various firms, often granting credits or contracts "selectively," both to improve its own financial position as well as to further the larger social goals of the DAF.

The DAF financed its activities largely from the coffers of the Bank der deutschen Arbeit (Bank of German Labor, the BdA), which it had seized from the trade unions in May 1933. Not long after its confiscation, Ley proclaimed the BdA to be the official National Socialist full service bank with, ultimately, thirty-five

52. See *Der Angriff*, August 6, 1935, p. 3; also Laurence van Zandt Moyer, "The Kraft durch Freude Movement in Nazi Germany 1933–1939," unpublished dissertation, Northwestern University, Chicago, Illinois, 1967, p. 112.
53. Marrenbach, *Fundamente*, p. 373.

branches in Germany, Austria, and the Sudetenland.[54] The bank had enormous sums at its disposal. The millions in DAF monthly membership dues were kept there, as were profits from DAF business enterprises. Money from various party collections and public subscriptions, including the *Winterhilfswerk*, found their way there. Ley put pressure on a wide variety of party agencies to avail themselves of the bank. Nor were DAF functionaries loath to "encourage" private businesses to open accounts. If this were not enough, Ley had special, innovative savings plans set up to enhance the bank's cash reserves. Already in 1934 the "Strength through Joy" organization set up travel-fund accounts as vehicles for workers to save up for vacations. At 50 pfennigs per week, the average worker could save enough in eighty weeks to finance an eight day vacation. This account started with a modest balance of 12,000 marks in November 1934; by April 1937 the balance has risen to 6 million marks. Similarly, the famous subscription savings plan for the Volkswagen brought large sums into the coffers of the BdA (ultimately 280 million marks) as did the "Iron Savings" (*Eisernes Sparen*) plan to soak up purchasing power during the war.[55] Deposits grew so fast from the outset that by mid-1934 the Reichsbank President, Hjalmar Schacht, was moved to complain to Hitler about it. While total deposits at the Deutsche Bank had scarcely increased at all during the first half of the year, BdA deposits had gone up by 100 million marks, in part, hinted Schacht, owing to its relations with party organizations.[56] By 1938 the BdA had over 20 million marks in cash reserves, current deposits of over 512 million and a turnover of over 15 billion marks.[57]

Ley made a number of uses of the funds deposited at the bank. During the first year especially, the bank aided in the regime's job-creation program by granting credits at favorable rates of interest to small- and medium-sized enterprises. During the first half of 1934 alone, the bank provided 45 million marks in credits.[58] As time went

54. See Ley circular letter 11/33, n.d., in BAK NS25/489; Marrenbach, *Fundamente*, pp. 373–88.
55. On the KdF savings plan, see *Wirtschafts- und sozialpolitische Rundschau*, March 8, 1938, p. 1. For complaints about pressures put on private businesses, see exchange between the *Kommissar für das Kreditwesen* and the DAF *Leiter der Zentrale für die Finanzwirtschaft*, May 20 and 21. August 1939 in BAK R32II/529, pp. 229–32; generally also *BdA Geschäftsbericht: 1938*, in BAK NS22, vorl. 670, 1938.
56. Schacht to Hitler, June 25, 1934 in BAK R43II/531.
57. See *BdA Geschäftsbericht: 1938*, in BAK NS22, vorl. 670; also "Entwicklung der Bank der deutschen Arbeit von 1935 bis 1941," in BAK R43II/529, p. 242.
58. Ley boasted in 1934 that the very high liquidity of the bank put it in an especially

on, the bank helped to support a wide range of ongoing DAF activities ranging from direct supports of disadvantaged individuals to public health to vocational education to legal counselling. Ley also drew on its funds for special projects, like the KdF and the original Volkswagen capital.[59] As its credit-granting activities expanded, the BdA also became for Ley a tool to foster DAF activities in local plants. If the factory owner wanted to buy new machinery on credit, the BdA was ready — if he provided clean washroom facilities and well-lighted cafeteria the local DAF Obmann had been demanding.[60]

Unfortunately, as Hitler's adjutant Fritz Wiedemann, once put it, "When it came to money Ley operated very liberally." The enormous sums of money were simply too tempting to avoid corruption. When it came to party members, or friends of party members, the BdA was not always too careful about orthodox banking procedures. On one occasion Sepp Dietrich, commander of Hitler's SS bodyguard, borrowed 40,000 marks from the bank to purchase a villa which he coveted in Berlin. After two years he grew tired of the villa and decided to sell it and build one near Munich. An obliging Ley ordered, "The man must not suffer any loss from the sale. Therefore the BdA will take the villa off his hands for 80,000 RM cash" On another occasion a young woman approached Wiedemann for intercession; she wanted to take out a loan to repay a 2000-mark debt. Once again the BdA was ready. One bank official offered to lend Wiedemann 20,000 marks. He would then give the young lady her 2,000 marks and keep the remaining 18,000 for his own purposes. Each year at Christmas the bank would write off 10,000 marks, and in two years the debt would be cleared and the adjutant could borrow more. As the astonished Wiedemann protested at such unorthodox procedures, the bank officer assured him that such procedures were quite common at the bank.[61]

Such corruption with regard to favored customers had its parallel in those who managed the operation. Ley allowed them to pay themselves salaries that bordered on the obscene. So much so that

---

favorable position to grant credits. See Robert Ley, *Rede zum Reichsparteitag* (Berlin, Verlag der DAF, 1934), p. 11.

59. See *DAF Rechenschaftsbericht: 1936* for a percentage breakdown. BAK NSD 50/20.

60. For suggestions along precisely these lines, see, for example, DAF-Gauobmann München-Oberbayen to Heinrich Simon, *Zentralstelle für die Finanzwirtschaft der DAF*, January 17, 1939, in BAK NS22, vorl. 670.

61. The source for these anecdotes is Fritz Wiedemann, *Der Mann der Feldherr werden wollte* (Velbert, Blick & Bild Verlag für politische Bildung, 1964), pp. 194ff.

outraged Nazis in Frankfurt lanced articles in the local papers revealing the actual amounts. So scandalous were the salaries that they became a major factor in party treasurer Schwarz's attempts to gain the power of oversight over DAF finances. In July 1935 Martin Bormann wrote to Schwarz complaining that in a situation where rising prices were confronting frozen wages for workers it was outrageous that the BdA board of directors were drawing salaries well in excess of that of government ministers. (Two of them earned 84,000 marks per year).[62] Immediately thereafter, Schwarz wrote the first of a series of letters to Ley demanding a list of all BdA employees and their salaries so that he could take steps to bring them more in line with other party salaries and thus assuage the dissatisfaction being exhibited in the various Gaus. Ley demurred.[63] Even in the highest councils of the BdA, charges and countercharges of corruption abounded. The president of the bank, Karl Müller, accused one of the directors, Rosenhauer, of being far too lax in granting terms of credit. He also accused the DAF treasurer, Brinckmann, of losing 40 million marks in membership dues between October 1934 and April 1935![64] The result was that Ley forced Müller to go on leave.

Ley's insurance empire consisted of ten insurance companies involved in life, health, and casualty insurance with a total working capital of 3 billion marks. The policies which they collectively issued amounted to 10.2 percent of the amount of *all* insurance funds in Germany and 12 percent of all *private* insurance funds. Ley boasted that the DAF was the second-largest insurance carrier in Germany.[65] Here again Ley was mindful of ideology, especially lest people criticize his business empire for being just another capitalist conglomerate. As the DAF proudly pointed out, one of the insurance companies, the Deutscher Ring, had been founded in 1913 based on three principles: that Jews and anti-*völkish* people be excluded from purchasing policies; that the firm be consciously a counterweight to the fast growing Marxist insurance plans (presumably those of the unions); and that the firm should carry out its task "not according to

62. See Bormann to Schwarz, July 25, 1935, in BAK NS22, vorl. 670.
63. See Schwarz to Ley July 26 and August 7, 1935, respectively, in BAK NS22, vorl. 670, and Schumacher Sammlung, 223.
64. See Müller to Ley, July 16, 1935, in BAK NS10/134, pp. 96–100; before his removal Müller frustrated Ley in a number of financial transactions. See Sopade, 1936, p. 235.
65. See Marrenbach, *Fundamente*, p. 376–7; for Ley's boast, see *Arbeitertum*, no. 24, March 15, 1936, p. 7.

capitalist principles, but by the overriding principle of social responsibility."[66] In the end Ley's experience with the insurance empire helped inform a number of ideas which appeared in his wartime *Volksversorgungswerk*.

Ley had proclaimed that "the most important of the problems in the life of the *Volk* which the party had tackled was housing."[67] He firmly believed that one of the most important elements in *Betreuung* was decent housing. As a result he involved the DAF in many different ways in residential housing and claimed as one of his most important future bailiwicks during the war that of Commissar for Residential Housing. Accordingly, another important component of the DAF empire was represented by housing and settlement companies. Concentrated in the "Gruppe Wohnungsbau" of the DAF Office for Economic Enterprises, there were forty such companies with a total capital of 41 million marks. Again Ley emphasized the aspect of "social responsibility," and consequently these companies concentrated their activities in areas where housing shortages were quite acute, as was the case in the industrial Ruhr and Silesia. Often the DAF built housing on its own — it had 46,331 dwellings by the end of 1939 — often it constructed the shells and let local firms do the finishing work by subcontract. Much of the building was done through the DAF-owned Deutsche Bau-Aktiengesellschaft, with sixteen branch offices nationwide. Via a variety of holding companies, the DAF participated in the construction of a further 40,000 buildings (including barracks) to the tune of 300 million marks. Here again the DAF did not hesitate to use its political muscle in competing with other private firms. In 1939 Ley got his former employee, Fritz Todt, now in charge of regulating construction for the government as Generalbevollmächtigte für die Regelung der Bauwirtschaft, to allocate to the DAF vital building materials for 20,000 more dwellings.[68]

DAF construction, in turn, linked up with Ley's efforts to use the "Schönheit der Arbeit" (Beauty of Work) program to make the home and the workplace "pleasant, dignified and healthy."[69] Under the direction of Baurat Schulte-Frohlinde, director of the Architecture Office of the DAF, the DAF used its local patronage to engage "Gau-

66. See "Unternehmungen," p. 38.
67. Ibid., p. 157.
68. Details on this aspect of DAF operations are in ibid., pp. 56–9, 101–3 and 115–23.
69. See Marrenbach, *Fundamente*, p. 320.

architects" to design or oversee the designing of future dwellings and factory installations such as cafeterias and recreation rooms. To this end the DAF formed two more companies in 1938, the Feinmechanische Werkstätte Mikronwerk near Aschaffenburg and the Gemeinschaftshaus der DAF-Siedlung Mascherode near Braunschweig.

Ultimately, Ley would use this part of his empire as a springboard to demand authority — as Wohnungskommissar — over the entire residential construction industry. He determined to unify all aspects of that industry — including materials, labor, and capital — and standardize it as a crucial element of postwar social policy.[70]

As we have seen, the concept which went arm in arm with *Betreuung* was education — or more accurately propaganda. Although Ley had a good working relationship with Goebbels and the massive Ministry of Propaganda apparatus, he could not resist setting up a press and publishing apparatus of his own totalling sixteen different houses within the DAF.[71] The flagship of this apparatus was the Verlag der deutschen Arbeitsfront, the main publishing house of the DAF. This operation mushroomed from a modest sixteen employees and 20,000 marks in capital in 1933 to 876 employees and 800,000 marks in 1938. It published a variety of DAF newspapers, including the old NSBO *Arbeitertum*, at least twenty regular serialized information sheets from various DAF offices; the DAF ideological paper, the *Deutsche Arbeits-Korrespondenz*, and eighty-three different *Schulungsblätter* (educational newsletters) to name only a few. In all, the journals alone taken together reached a circulation of over 256 million copies in 1938. Some 389 different printing and paper companies were awarded contracts totalling 9.5 million marks by 1937. Ley loved to collect data, and to disseminate it in the right ideological context, and in doing so unleashed a printing orgy which must have represented the greatest threat to the Bavarian forest until the advent of acid rain. And we are only discussing the flagship operation.

In addition, the DAF controlled the Hanseatische Verlagsanstalt. Founded in 1893 by prominent *völkisch* and anti-semitic theorists Johann Hinrich Wichen and Friedrich Raab, and later taken over by the right-wing German Nationalist Association of Retail Clerks, this institution had long published a multitude of anti-liberal, anti-

70. Ibid., p. 379.
71. Information on the DAF publishing operations comes from "Unternehmungen", pp. 101–23.

semitic and *völkisch* works dressed up in scholarly garb. It had always seen as its task overcoming such "nineteenth century slogans as freedom of inquiry and objectivity." Ley updated its purpose to "offering publishing possibilities to ideas born of the National Socialist revolution."[72]

Under DAF auspices the press opened its pages to such authors as Walter Frank and Carl Schmitt and published "scholarly" books on history, political science, military science, and *Kulturpolitik*. It even published a series of legal commentaries written by such eminent jurists as SS-Gruppenführer Reinhard Heydrich and Reichsärzteführer Wagner.

Like other DAF business operations, this publishing house also served to advanced Ley's social goals, most dramatically by publishing mass literature in areas into which Ley was trying to extend DAF jurisdiction, most dramatically leisure time and vocational training. Finally, the DAF also controlled the "Bücherborn" Deutsches Buchhaus, which was both a peripatetic retail outlet and the second largest mail order book club in Germany.

These were among the more important parts of the DAF business empire, but they by no means exhaust the list. One could also mention the Dianabad, a health spa; the Deutsches Nationaltheater in Berlin as well as "Sevag," one of the first modern supermarkets with thirty-one branch operations. Nor may one forget the network of consumer cooperatives which Ley had seized in 1933. Important also was the so-called Arbeitswissenschaftliche Institut (Institute for Labor Scholarship), a kind of DAF think tank, which, with its huge library and data-gathering capability, produced an endless series of think pieces which gave the ideological rationale and organizational detail to many of Ley's schemes.

But this list would not be complete without the best-known and most illustrative enterprise of all – in terms of concept, scope, and execution – the *Volkswagenwerk*. Hitler had long wanted the German auto industry to build a car which ordinary working Germans could afford. Nothing underscored quite so dramatically the class society which the Nazis were trying to overcome as the difference between the few who could afford a car and the many who could not. Hitler dreamed of a "people's car" for under 1,000 marks; it was a dream which dovetailed nicely with Ley's own schemes.[73]

72. Ibid., p. 117.
73. A good source on the Volkswagen story, from which much of the following is derived, is Walter Henry Nelson, *Small Wonder: The Amazing Story of the Volkswagen*

After the automobile industry dragged its heels on the project and asked for government subsidies, Hitler decided that the regime should take on the task itself. Ley was immediately at hand. The result was that in May 1937 the company for Preparation of the Volkswagen (Gesellschaft zur Vorbereitung des Volkswagens, soon dubbed "Gezuvor" or "Go ahead!") was created with 480,000 marks initial capital provided by the DAF. Management consisted of Ferdinand Porsche, the auto magnate, Jacob Werlin, a Munich Mercedes salesman who advised Hitler on cars, and Bodo Lafferentz, Ley's aide. By early summer 1938 Hitler had his prototype.

Ley addressed the funding problems by introducing his famous subscription savings scheme under the aegis of the Nazi leisure time organization "Strength through Joy," or "Kraft durch Freude" – indeed, technically the VW was known as the "KdF-Wagen." Ley announced the scheme himself to a workers' rally in Cologne on August 1, 1938. He heralded the Volkswagen as "The greatest social work of all time and all countries. The people's car is the Führer's very own work. The Führer lives and works with this as his pet idea." The factory for building the VW, Ley announced, would become "the materialization in stone and iron of the idea of classless education, settlement work, national health, and the beauty of work." He continued, "It is the Führer's will that within a few years no less than 6,000,000 Volkswagens will be on German roads. In ten years' time there will be no working person in Germany who does not own a 'people's car.' "[74]

Eventually, 336,668 Germans at 5 marks per week put aside 280 million marks for their car. When they had their savings book full of stamps, they could turn it in exchange for the title — providing that the car had been produced. Meanwhile, the money saved reposed in the vaults of the BdA — and no interest was paid on it.[75]

Ley's aide, Lafferentz, was charged with the task of finding a site for the proposed factory. He found it on the Lüneburger Heath near the village of Fallersleben. Much of the proposed site belonged to Count Werner von der Schulenburg, who resisted forfeiting his land.

(Boston, Toronto, 1965), pp. 51, 58–70, 73–5, 77–84, 95–6; also P. Kluke, "Hitler und das Volkswagenprojekt," *Vierteljahrshefte für Zeitgeschichte*, vol. 8 (1960), p. 360. The plans for a Volkswagen were discussed in the Reich Chancellory in April 1934. See Aktenvermerk, 11, April 1934, in BAK R43II/753, pp. 8–10.

74. See Nelson, *Small Wonder*, pp. 59–60.

75. See "Vermerk über den Volkswagen," 13 March 1940, in BAK R43II/751, p. 15.

He fought the edict and secured the cooperation of a number of agencies, including the Oberpräsident of Hannover. But his resistance was in vain; Ley won and the property became the site of an immense VW plant with a proposed town which was to house 24,000 workers and their families.[76]

On May 26, 1938, Hitler laid the cornerstone of the new factory. Ley opened the ceremonies with the words:

> My Führer! What has been started here — this factory and everything which will come of it — is basically and singularly your work, my Führer. Your great idea and your great faith taught us that man develops himself only through work and that deeds, rather than words and phrases, represent socialism, and that man benefits only from that which he has gained through work . . . . This Volkswagen factory is one of your own favorite creations. We know how you thought of giving the German people a good but inexpensive motor vehicle even before you came to power and how you have even since imbued with new strength all the designers and others who labored on this car!

Then Hitler spoke: "This car shall carry the name of the organization which works hardest to provide the broadest masses of our people with joy and, therefore, strength. It shall be called the KdF-Wagen! I undertake the laying of the cornerstone in the name of the German people! This factory shall rise out of the strength of the entire German people and it shall serve the happiness of the German people!"[77] (See Plate 13.)

Construction proceeded over the ensuing months. Four great buildings totalling 200,000 square meters comprised its core. The costs for 1939 alone ran to 78 million marks and the project consumed 12 million bricks and 80,000 tons of cement in the first year. DAF architects busied themselves with every detail and planned a town with all the greenery and amenities which Ley thought appropriate for the utopian Nazi community; responsibility for the dwellings was turned over to a DAF holding company, Neuland, which was capitalized with 22 million marks.[78] Then the war came

76. For resistance to the project, see letters from Viktor Lutze, Oberpräsident of Hannover, to Reich Chancellory, December 21, 1937, and from the Deutsche Adelgenossenschaft to the same office of March 1, 1938, in BAK, R43II/753, pp. 110 and 126 respectively.
77. Speeches are in the *Deutsches Nachrichtenbüro*, no. 869, 27 May, 1938, in BAK R43II/751, pp. 2–4.
78. See Marrenbach, *Fundamente*, pp. 381–6; on the larger project at Fallersleben, see

and work stopped on the partially constructed project. In the end only 250 Volkswagens were built — elsewhere — and none ever reached a German consumer. It was all propaganda and flim-flam, one is tempted to conclude. Just a front for military production from the outset. That is a comfortable assessment and yet does not get at the truth. There is every indication that the Nazis were entirely serious about the "people's car" concept and intended to renew work on the project after the war. Certainly Ley was serious about it, not only because it was part of his *Betreuung* schemes but also because widespread ownership of cars contributed to precisely the suburbanization process which the Nazis hoped would break up the inner-city working-class subcultures. Ley's vision of little family row houses with picket fences amidst greenery had the very practical ideological purpose of creating a brand new, national basis for Nazi culture which would replace the older subcultures in Germany.[79] What the VW episode really illustrates is the fatal flaw in Nazi ideology and practice, that the benefits of the national economy were not to be distributed to create just an early version of the modern Western mass consumer society, but that they would serve to legitimize a regime which had usurped the sovereignty of the German people and would be the carrot which (along with the stick) the regime would use to exact a heavy sacrifice in its violent pursuit of a European new order. The war stopped the VW not because the Nazis had not been serious about the project all along but rather because of the contradictions in Nazi ideology which the war laid bare. The fruits of the German economy were not an end in themselves but the means to an end which swallowed up and destroyed those very fruits.

This mighty empire allowed Ley to approach his task both macrocosmically and microcosmically: macrocosmically in terms of using the DAF to try directly to influence the economy and society as a giant super-agency on a par with and rivaling government and industry; microcosmically, in terms of developing a host of affiliated sub-organizations which touched the employed directly as people — inside and outside the plant. The two tended to reinforce one another, and to get tangled in the coils of their mutual contradictions.

Marie-Luise Recker, *Die Großstadt als Wohn-und Lebensbereich im Nationalsozialismus. Zur Gründung der "Stadt des KdF-Wagens* (Frankfurt, Campus Verlag, 1981).

79. See James Shand, "The Reichsautobahn: Symbol for the Third Reich," *Journal of Contemporary History*, vol. 19 (1984), especially pp. 191–2.

In the meantime, two documents, both produced in 1934, reflected the tension between Ley's aims and the restrictions which government and industry attempted to put on his activities. The first, the Law for the Regulation of National Labor, appeared early in the year and represented a comprehensive piece of Nazi labor legislation. It would also represent a stumbling block which Ley would have to circumnavigate. The second, the Führer Decree of October 24 of that same year, gave full expression to Ley's claim of totality for his DAF.

The smashing of the trade unions and the end of collective bargaining left a huge vacuum which had to be filled by major labor legislation. The Trustees of Labor, who were the government's watchdogs over management–labor relations had been a provisional measure and not anchored in any broadly conceived juridical concept. The swift emergence of the DAF lent some urgency to the task of formulating labor legislation; the agreement between Ley and the industrialists in November 1933, which brought the Reichsstand der Industrie, the representative organization of big business, into the DAF as an institutional member set the stage for the government to move quickly at the turn of the year to promulgate the legislation. Drafted largely in the Labor Ministry, the Law for the Regulation of National Labor (hereafter AOG) was proclaimed on January 20, 1934.[80] (See Plate 5.)

The thrust of the law was to give management decisive authority over emasculated labor under vague government oversight, but within the context of neo-feudal National Socialist concepts of a national racial community.

Gone were traditional terms for owner and worker (*Arbeitgeber* and *Arbeitnehmer*) for these smacked too much of old-fashioned capitalism and class conflict. Instead, the boss was now designated the plant leader (*Betriebsführer*) while his workers were transformed into his retinue (*Gefolgschaft*). In this application of the *Führerprinzip* to the factory the boss had now very extensive authority over his employees and a nearly unrestrained right to determine factory regulations (*Betriebsordnung*) in such vital matters as working conditions, hours, and method of payment. The workers, for their part, were to

80. For Cabinet-level discussions on the draft of the law, see Ministerbesprechung, January 12, 1934, in *Akten der Reichskanzlei*, vol. I, no. 284, pp. 1070ff. For the text of the law, see *Reichsgesetzblatt*, no. 7, January 23, 1934, part I, p. 45ff. See also Reichhardt, "DAF," pp. 98–104; Martin Broszat, *The Hitler State*, trans. John Hiden (New York, Longman, 1981), p. 147; Mason, *Sozialpolitik*, p. 117–20.

obey. But, in true neo-feudal fashion, the boss also had obligations to his employees; he was at all times to be solicitous of their general welfare, a social reponsibility which Nazi propaganda frequently trumpeted and which many employers came to resent, especially when DAF Obmänner reminded them of it too pointedly. It was thus the factory itself which under the AOG was supposed to be the basic unit of the National Socialist people's community, a *Volksgemeinschaft* which the Nazi regime hoped would emerge out of the new relationship between employer and employee (see Plate 6).

All the talk of ending class conflict and establishing social harmony could not disguise the fact, however, that the workers had suffered an enormous loss with the destruction of their unions. Accordingly, the AOG threw them several sops. The regime did not dare to abolish entirely some sort of institutionalized worker organization within the factory. Traditionally, that organization had been the factory council (*Beitriebsrat*). These councils had played a major role in protecting workers' rights in the plants and, even after the events of May 2, 1933, the Nazi regime had hesitated to dismantle them. Now, however, they were replaced by the so-called "trust council" (*Vertrauensrat*), which, as the name suggested, was supposed to express the good will and harmony which the Nazis hoped to engender in the place of class conflict and adversarial plant politics.[81] A shadow of their predecessors, the trust councils had only an advisory capacity and could not function at all independently of the plant leader. Although initially designed to be an elected body, worker participation in elections in which their own candidates had to be approved by the boss was so embarassingly slight, that finally after 1935 further elections were postponed indefinitely.[82]

The other sop for the workers lay in the concept of *Ehrengerichtsbarkeit* (courts of honor). This concept combined a method of elevating the status of workers while at the same time providing an indoctrination device. The Nazis were keen about integrating the worker into society, in part by raising his self-esteem (which was to have the corresponding effect of lowering his class consciousness). The Nazi honor concept insisted that all work, whether performed by the managers or workers, was of equal moral value and that it

81. The *Betriebsräte* had responsibility for complaints to the management, supervising wage scales and other items arrived at through collective bargaining, cooperation in determining factory regulations, passing on grievances for appeal, and so on.
82. See Hans-Gerd Schumann, *Nationalsozialismus und Gewerkschaftsbewegung* (Hannover, Frankfurt, Norddeutsche Verlagsanstalt, 1958) pp. 128–9.

was incumbent upon all members of the "plant community" to recognize this fact in daily intercourse. To besmirch the honor of one's boss or employee was considered to be a blow to the plant community. Correspondingly, "courts of honor" were provided for by the AOG, before which both worker and manager could be hailed for any of a number of infringements. The result might be warnings, fines, or in extreme cases, discharge or loss of control of a business, although penalties were usually light, since the courts were viewed primarily as an educational device.[83]

To make the factory the key unit in labor relations, to say nothing of the future *Volk* community, was a risky enterprise. After all, the *Volksgemeinschaft* would take a while to develop. In the meantime, the state still had a role to play, and the framers of the law envisioned using the extant Trustees of Labor to play that role. The duties of the Trustees, however, were not completely clearly spelled out.[84] They could oversee the extent to which employers were observing, minimally, the wage scales which the regime had inherited from the pre-May time and, by and large, retained. They were alert to mass discharges (no owner could fire more than 10 percent of his workforce without the Trustee's permission); they also played a role in the formation of the trust councils (when managers and workers could not agree on candidates). In addition, they had a vaguely -worded authority to work out and revise wage scales. And, of course, they reported back to the Labor Ministry on conditions generally. But beyond that, the Trustees had no clear-cut authority or vested power. They were a watchdog and, in some cases, court of appeal.

Thus the relationship between the trustees and the DAF would always be problematic. They might work together on occasion. The Trustees could also represent a stumbling block to DAF activities. However, because their authority was vague and their budgets — and hence their staffs — were small, the Trustees were vulnerable to the depredations of the DAF, especially at the local level, where the Labor Front had the advantage of numbers and funds.[85]

83. Ibid., p. 124; also Arthur Schweitzer, *Die Nazifizierung des Mittelstandes Bonner Beiträge zur Soziologie*, vol. 9 (Stuttgart, Ferdinand Enke Verlag, 1970), pp. 140–1; Mason, Sozialpolitik, p. 119.
84. On the Trustees and their role, see Schumann, *Nationalsozialismus*, pp. 122–3; Volker Hentschel, *Geschichte der deutschen Sozialpolitik* (Frankfurt, Suhrkamp, 1983), p. 101; C.W. Guillebaud, *The Social Policy of Nazi Germany* (1940; New York, Howard Fertig, 1971), pp. 24–8, 32–5, 70–1.
85. Mason, *Sozialpolitik*, p. 202.

On the whole, government and business could look with some satisfaction on the new law. Not since the late nineteenth century, when the watchword was "Herr im Hause" (master in his own house), was the businessman so firmly in the saddle (despite the annoyances of Nazi ideology). Never had labor been so completely emasculated. The state stood poised in its watchdog role — and the law provided virtually no sociopolitical role for Ley's DAF.

For Ley, then, the AOG was a hindrance to be circumverted, even if he agreed with its ultimate goal of social harmony and with the Nazi terminology with which it was infused. With remarkable candor he said in public: "As they [the enemies of the DAF] noted, however, that we might be succeeding in completing our structure, they quickly wanted to shove a barrier in our way: the Law for the Regulation of National Labor. But I wasn't lazy; I immediately took things in hand. I was off like a shot. It was a difficult struggle."[86]

And certainly the other DAF leaders, as they tried to fashion their "super-agency," could only agree. As DAF Amtsleiter Theo Hupfauer said in a 1937 speech, commenting on a proposed solution to problems between Trustees and the DAF: one should not reject this solution out of hand "by referring to a law which in many respects is already outdated."[87]

If the AOG was the state's attempt to put labor relations within a normative, juridical framework, the Führer decree of October 24, 1934 was Ley's response. By asserting a totalitarian claim to virtually open-ended jurisdiction over labor (and, indeed, sociopolitical) affairs, it represented a counterassertion reflecting the normlessness of the Nazi regime. Between the two events lay nine months and some dramatic developments which strengthened Ley's position and, undoubtedly, encouraged him to make his "totality" claim. During that time the DAF grew rapidly in strength, numbers, and funds. Perhaps more importantly, the summer of 1934 witnessed the eclipse of the radicals in the Nazi Party in the form of the Night of the Long Knives, when Ernst Röhm and the SA leadership were murdered. That event fatally weakened the radical NSBO in the DAF as well, and Ley took the opportunity to purge his organization of many of them. Thus emboldened, he went on.[88]

86. Robert Ley, *Wir alle helfen dem Führer*, ed. Heinrich Simon (Berlin, Zentralverlag der NSDAP, 1937), p. 101.
87. Quoted in Reichardt, "DAF," p. 87.
88. Among those who were purged from the DAF in the wake of the Röhm affair were Schumann, Klapper, Krüger (NSBO Propagandaleiter), Hauenstein (publisher

The Führer Decree of October 24 is typical of the power-plays which dot the history of the Third Reich. In the jurisdictional thicket of that regime, power was often not institutionalized but rather was bestowed in a very personal way by Hitler on one or another of his henchmen. Thus the ultimate weapon in jurisdictional conflicts with one's rivals was the *Führerorder*. It bestowed instant authority on its recipient in whatever area stipulated in the decree, and the dictator's subordinates constantly gravitated around him like electrons around a nucleus, anxious to solicit whatever specific bit of authority they might talk Hitler into awarding them. Thus it was, in October 1934, while conversations were being conducted in both ministry and party circles with regard to a DAF law, that Ley acted.[89] A draft of a DAF law was being worked upon in Hess's office, and Hess sent it as a matter of routine to Ley for consultation. The next day Ley took the draft to Hitler and got him to sign it as a decree, allowing Hitler to believe that Hess was in full agreement. The decree was not countersigned by any government minister; nor was it published in the *Reichsgesetzbuch*. Several days later, when the truth came out, Hess requested Ley not to issue any specific orders based on the decree until the situation could be clarified. He also requested that Ley not discuss the decree in the press. Instead, Ley trumpeted the decree as the foundation of the DAF's role in National Socialist Germany.[90] Typically, Hitler neither revoked the decree (which would have been to admit to a mistake) nor would he entertain any other drafts of a "DAF law." As a result, the fraudulently obtained decree became the basis from that day on to Ley's claims of totality for the DAF.

The decree proclaimed the DAF as "the organization of gainfully employed Germans of head and hand"; its goal was "the formation of a genuine people's and achievement community of all Germans" (*Volks- und Leistungsgemeinschaft*).[91] The key passage, however, was in

---

of the DAF-Calendar) and Brucker (leader of the Reichsverband der Ortskrankenkassen). *Sopade*, 1934, pp. 450–2.

89. See letter from Bormann to Goering of March 4, 1938, which is a response to Ley's 1938 draft of a DAF law, but which contains for reference purposes a letter from Hess to Ley of October 31, 1934, referring to the background of the 1934 decree, in BAK, R43II/529, vorl. 126.

90. The decree appeared the next day in all major papers. See, for example, *Berliner Börsen-Zeitung* of October 25, 1934. This was neither the first nor last time that high officials would find out through the press about important developments affecting them.

91. Text of the decree in BAK, NS25/1395, pp. 72–4.

paragraph 7 of the decree and read as follows:

> The DAF is to ensure labor peace by creating an understanding among factory leaders for the legitimate claims of their retinue and among the retinue for the situation and the possibilities of their plant.
>
> The DAF has the task of finding that compromise between the legitimate interests of all concerned which correspond to National Socialist principles and which limits the number of cases which are to be referred to the state agencies solely responsible according to the law of January 20, 1934.
>
> The representation of all parties which is necessary for this compromise is exclusively the concern of the DAF. The formation of other organizations or their activity in this area is forbidden.

This decree, as Ley defined it, gave the DAF exclusively the role of being the "honest broker" in the German factories, of balancing out the interests of management and labor, while at the same time "schooling" both in National Socialist principles. It was the charter of the DAF as totalitarian "super-agency," which arrogated unto itself "the shaping of social life" in the factories, including matters of wages, vacations, and firings. Moreover, the decree also vested in the DAF the authority for supervising vocational education in Germany.[92] No wonder von der Goltz, speaking for employers, said that if the decree remained in force it must "frankly be said that this development presages the threat of a union of massive force."[93]

Ley did not intend to make the DAF into a union — his plans were much broader than that — and in implementing them he stepped on many toes in government, industry, and in the party itself. Before turning to the ensuing competitive struggles, however, it is necessary to examine the general thrust of DAF activities between 1934 and the outbreak of the war and the challenge they posed to other power centers in the Third Reich.

92. For Ley's commentary on the decree of January 2, 1935, see BAK, NS22, vorl. 216.

93. Goltz was one of many who complained to the Reich Chancellory about the decree. See BAK, R43II/530.

CHAPTER 7

The Jurisdictional Grasp

Vested with the all-encompassing, though vaguely stated, mandate expressed in Hitler's decree of October 1934, Ley and his people proceeded to challenge government and industry. Though the DAF did not possess any specifically stated executive power — it could not issue legally binding decrees, for example — it did, basing its claim on Hitler's decree, use a broad range of techniques, including "schooling" and *Betreuung*, to acquire the bits and pieces of power which Ley hoped would enable it to become the "super-agency" of social and economic life in Germany.[1] These techniques can very broadly be arrayed under the rubrics of macrocosmic and microcosmic. The first implies activities on the national level by which the DAF tried to exert a decisive influence in such critical areas as wages and prices, thus invading the turf of both the corporate world as well as that of several government ministries. The second implies a grass-roots effort to make the DAF a "presence" in the life of every gainfully employed German, both at the place of work and outside the workplace. These included efforts ranging from beautification of the workplace to improvement of working conditions and terms of dismissal, to providing a myriad of entertainment and vacation possibilities, to establishing new apprenticeship programs. The rationale given in all cases was twofold: to break down class conflict and to prepare Germans to be members of a *Volksgemeinschaft* on the one hand, as well as to raise the productivity of the German worker on the other, so that the Third Reich might successfully face all the difficult challenges which Hitler had in store for it. These were not,

1. See, for example, an announcement in the official news bulletin of the DAF on November 20, 1937, which reads, in part, "According to the Führer order of October 24, 1934, the DAF is charged with the task of efficiently steering social policy for the whole German people." In BAK, NS22, vorl. 649.

however, always mutually compatible goals.

Despite setbacks and temporary compromises with his opponents, Ley and his people never ceased to stake out openly a very large claim for the DAF in the realm of social and economic policy. Already in 1933, soon after the formation of the Labor Front, Ley specifically mentioned the areas of old-age pensions, credit granting, and consumer co-ops as legitimate concerns of the new party organization.[2] Less than two years later, in March 1935, just after signing a far-reaching compromise with business and industry, Ley could not resist restating his broad jurisdictional claim:

> It is a question of whether the social order will be as we want it to be. Up to now we have only swept away the dirt and trash which we encountered; we have formed a new edifice, the Labor Front. We have preached, acted, and practiced community. But that's not enough. . . . Unless we in practice shape the fate of the individual German — and that means to be able to intervene in social policy and thereby in economic policy — all our efforts would have no purpose.[3]

The following year, Franz Mende, head of the DAF Social Office, went even further and proclaimed the actual primacy of the DAF: "Labor Front, economic associations and trustees are the three pillars of economic policy. The leadership, however, lies with the Labor Front, because the sociopolitical apparatus can only be directed by the community of all who labor."[4]

One critical area in which the DAF staked jurisdictional claims to influences on social and economic policy was wages. This area was especially important because it represented the dilemma which the regime faced in trying simultaneously to rearm the country and to integrate the worker into the system.[5] Hitler's number-one priority from the outset was to restore Germany's military sovereignty and power (*Wiederwehrhaftmachung*, as it was called). Rearmament was an expensive proposition, however, one which called for enormous

2. See Robert Ley, *Der ständische Aufbau und die Deutsche Arbeitsfront*, (Berlin, Verlag der DAF, 1933), pp. 9–10.
3. Robert Ley, *Deutschland ist schöner geworden* (Berlin, Mehden-Verlag, 1936), p. 136.
4. Quoted in Arthur Schweitzer, *Nazifizierung des Mittelstandes Bonner Beiträge zur Soziologie* (Stuttgart, Ferdinand Enke Verlag, 1970), vol. 9, p. 146.
5. For an excellent discussion of the wage question in Nazi Germany see Tilla Siegel, "Lohnpolitik im nationalsozialistischen Deutschland," in Carola Sachse et al., *Angst, Belohnung, Zucht und Ordnung. Herrschaftsmechanismen im Nationalsozialismus* (Opladen, Westdeutscher Verlag, 1982), pp. 54–132. Still useful as well is Gerhard Bry, *Wages in Germany* (Princeton, Princeton University Press, 1960).

amounts of public investment and spending. One way to keep costs down was to keep wages down, and the government consciously embarked on such an expedient, actually freezing wage scales in 1933 at the minimum levels inherited from the pre-Nazi wage agreements. Keeping wages low had the additional advantage, it was hoped, of reining inflation, which would have been generated by rising wages confronting fewer goods, as armaments quickly took priority over consumer goods.[6]

These steps to keep wages down conflicted, however, with the regime's other urgent priority — to integrate the worker into the *Volksgemeinschaft*. Hitler feared (as did Ley) that a working class not solidly imbued with National Socialist principles and relatively satisfied materially might repeat the uprising of 1918 if the pressures of rearmament (or subsequent war) became too great. In light of this, the party, although it fully supported the rearmament priority, also felt compelled to make a range of concessions to the workers, not the least of which was higher wages (or their equivalent). And the party's wing in dealing with the workers, was, of course, the DAF. Ley thus found himself caught in the dilemma of having, on the one hand, to improve the productivity of the workers so that Germany could undertake the task of violently reordering Europe. This meant placing burdensome demands on them. At the same time, Ley also had to legitimize his "Labor" Front in the eyes of its constituents by representing to the greatest extent possible their interests. Attempts to get off the horns of this dilemma were not always successful.

One was to draw attention away from wages by emphasizing instead the less costly method of enhancing the social status of the worker. The DAF did a great deal of "educating" to this end. The assumption was that if the worker could be cured of his inferiority complex, instilled in him by Marxists and Jews, and then given a sense of honor and self-worth, then he would be psychologically ready to join the *Volksgemeinschaft*. As Claus Selzer put it, "The dirty factory led to talk of the dirty worker." This attitude, he continued, "engendered of necessity an inferiority complex and thereby the proletariat. The proletariat experiences work as a weight and a burden instead of as joy and dignity."[7] Ley himself often announced

6. For example, during the period 1932–8 heavy industry expanded by 200 percent while consumer industry did so by only 38 percent. See R.J. Overy, *The Nazi Economic Recovery 1932–1938* (London, Macmillan, 1982), p. 54.
7. In *Freude und Arbeit*, vol. V (1937), pp. 32–4, quoted in Annegret Walesch, "Das

publicly that this task took precedence over higher wages. As he said at Nuremberg in 1935, "It is not raising wage levels that is our goal, rather lifting the standard of life of the individual must be achieved."[8] But he could not escape the need to act on wages as well, so that some of the DAF claim to primacy in *Sozialpolitik* took the form of pushing for higher wages in a variety of forms.

In mounting this challenge, Ley had several advantages. For one thing, the economic boom which rearmament unleashed in 1936 and thereafter put tremendous upward pressure on wages anyway, as various industries competed with one another for scarce skilled labor. Many of them offered "inducement wages" (*Locklöhne*) far above the going rate, and one firm even offered its "retinue" VW automobiles![9] Government agencies were constantly complaining about "unrestrained wage bidding"[10] and deplored the fact that "no worker can be induced to take a job at the official wage rates."[11] If wages in some industries (mainly armament and construction) were going up at that tempo, then the DAF was in a position to push for others as well. For another, despite government efforts generally to keep prices down, prices of a number of items crept up anyway, particularly after the spring of 1935. This was particularly the case with the prices of agricultural products, which, thanks to the efforts of Darré and the *Reichsnährstand*, had been exempted from the outset from any price freeze. As prices crept up, real wages in many areas automatically went down. In this situation the DAF often took action to restore the real buying power of workers.[12]

Amt 'Schönheit der Arbeit' in der NS-Organisation 'Kraft durch Freude'," unpublished manuscript at Institut für Sozialgeschichte, Bonn.

8. In his speech on September 14 at the party day celebration, in Ley, *Deutschland ist glücklicher geworden Zwei Reden auf dem Reichsparteitag 1935* (Berlin, Verlag der DAF, 1935), p. 16.
9. Excerpt from the *Sozialberichten der Reichstreuhänder der Arbeit* for the 4th quarter of 1938, quoted in Timothy Mason, *Arbeiterklasse und Volksgemeinschaft* (Opladen, Westdeutscher Verlag, 1975), Document 150, p. 862.
10. See letter from the president of the Brandenburg Landesarbeitsamt to the president of the Reichsanstalt für Arbeitsvermittlung und Arbeitslosenversicherung, January 8, 1938, in BAK, R41/151, p. 11.
11. See letter from Oberpräsident of Sachsen to Economics Minister et al., April 25, 1938, in BAK, R41/151, p. 23.
12. The government was also very concerned about prices. Krohn (Labor Ministry) wrote to Darré (Agriculture Ministry) on September 1, 1935, expressing his concern that higher food prices would "lower the purchasing power of wages and salaries in many places in Germany to such an extent that the living standard of the workers and low-paid white-collar employees would be sorely threatened." In BAK, R43II/378.

Finally, the government never really developed a thoroughgoing, well-thought-out wage policy which would fit rationally into other aspects of economic policy. To do so was extremely difficult for two reasons. For one thing, the AOG had put wage determination at the factory level in the hands of the "plant leader," thus radically decentralizing the process. A real government wage policy would have demanded more centralization. For another, as Tilla Siegel recently suggested, in the polycratic Nazi system of competing power formations, to have attempted a comprehensive settlement of the wage question would have meant settling the basic power question within the regime — and none of the power structures dared to risk that kind of confrontation.[13] As a result, everyone postponed developing a true *Lohnordnung* into the indefinite future and, in the meantime, the government contented itself with an array of largely *ad hoc* measures, such as price controls, limitations on freedom of movement, issuance of labor pass books, the setting of minimum and maximum wages, and so on, in order to deal piecemeal with the whole issue of wage policy.[14] This lack of coherence in wage policy created just the kind of opening which Ley and the DAF needed to interfere in social and economic policy.

One means of using the DAF to put upward pressures on wages was to use its formidable propaganda apparatus simply to proclaim the need for higher wages and to promise that the DAF would act to achieve them. This was particularly true during the first several years of the regime, when Nazi agrarian policy started pushing the price of food up. Already in 1933, Ley took the initiative in proposing an overall centralized structure which would incorporate both a minimum wage as well as the principle of productivity in determining wages.[15]

The following year, in his speech before the assembled notables at the Nuremberg party day, Ley hinted that the DAF would play a role in wage policy and that wages would go up. Given the wage

13. See Siegel, "Lohnpolitik," p. 100. Ley himself, quoting the Führer, said that "it must be our theory . . . to be bound by no doctrine. It is advisable to introduce this sentence, minted for the discussion of economic policy, into the wage policy discussions as well." Quoted in ibid., p. 65.
14. See Hans-Erich Volkmann, "Die NS-Wirtschaft in Vorbereitung des Krieges" in Wilhelm Diest et al. (eds.) *Das Deutsche Reich und der Zweite Weltkrieg, Vol. I: Ursachen und Voraussetzungen der deutscher Kriegspolitik* (Stuttgart, Deutsche Verlagsanstalt, 1979), pp. 290ff.
15. Robert Ley, "Gestaltung des kommenden Tarifwesens," undated but for year (1933). In BAK, NS22, vorl. 649.

freeze which Hitler had proclaimed, Ley had to be careful in his use of words, but when he noted that the Sozialamt, the very DAF office which was in charge of efforts to carry out the terms of the AOG, would also have as its main task the "observation" of wages and that "in a short time happy results would be obtained," the signal was unmistakable.[16]

On May 1, 1935, on the occasion of his Labor Day proclamation Ley promised the German worker a "just wage." Picking up on the theme, he composed a think piece by that same title in August to submit to Hitler. Again, he was careful in his language, defining the just wage "not as a sum of money in itself for work performed, rather we understand by it that the individual had sufficient means to afford him a cultivated lifestyle."[17] In any other words, this meant, if not wage increases *per se*, at least the prevention of price rises which would undercut the workers' means. Indeed, in his letter to the dictator, Ley emphasized the havoc which the increase in food prices was playing with workers' real incomes.[18]

Nor did Ley stop with words. On any number of occasions his presence in a given area would lead to direct (and forbidden) negotiations between local DAF functionaries and businessmen. Early on these were actually publicized, as with a case in Bielefeld in December 1933 which the DAF paper *Arbeitertum* carried under the headline "The Labor Front brings wage increases." Here Ley's visit "was not limited to a demonstrative effect but rather led to highly practical results for the workers of the Bielefeld metal industry."[19]

At the grass-roots level, local DAF people and many workers believed Ley's promise of higher wages and acted accordingly. As the Trustee of Labor in Saxony remarked bitterly: "In DAF meetings wage questions are the dominant theme. In many cases the meetings take a violent turn. Several had to be broken up because of unrest. . . . The workers think the time has come when the DAF will finally honor its promise of wage increases."[20]

Government records were full of specific cases of DAF direct intervention at the regional and local level. In Brandenburg the

16. See Robert Ley, *Rede zum Reichsparteitag 1934* (Berlin, Verlag der DAF, 1934), p. 9.
17. See Ley's Denkschrift, "Der gerechte Lohn und der gerechte Preis," undated but from August 1935 in BAK, NS10/60, pp. 104–8.
18. Ley to Hitler, August 15, 1935, in BAK, NS10/59, pp. 8-9; already in November 1933 Ley had proclaimed a great campaign under the motto "Down with Prices!" Speech to NSBO functionaries in BAK, 5I, vorl. 256, p. 33.
19. See *Arbeitertum*, no. 119, December 1, 1933, p. 1.
20. Quoted in Schweitzer, *Nazifizierung*, p. 149.

DAF published new wage scales for long-distance truckers without the concurrence of the Trustee.[21] In Silesia, where kitchen workers on Wehrmacht construction projects were getting the lowest possible wages, the DAF intervened with a direct subsidy to bring the wages up to par with autobahn construction workers.[22] In Saxony the DAF was making propaganda out of low agricultural wages in order, the Trustee complained, to sow discontent among the already dissatisfied workers.[23] From the Nordmark, the complaint was voiced that "The DAF functionaries frequently try to achieve something by direct negotiations with the plant leaders."[24] After commissioning a study of the wage structure in Halle-Merseburg, high DAF functionary Schmeer put pressure on the Reichskommissar für Preisbildung (Commissar for Price Formation) to reform a wage system which caused such wage discrepancies at the local level as to distort the entire labor market.[25]

This activity reached its peak during late 1937 and early 1938, when the DAF pushed for wage increases for specific categories of workers, including employees of consumer co-ops and dairy workers. In August 1937 a conversation between Hitler's main economic adviser, Wilhelm Keppler, and officials in the Labor Ministry, revealed the consensus among those present that "the Labor Front, contrary to original intent, was developing more and more into a union and in its opposition to the Economics Ministry . . . had been pushing for sweeping increases in wages."[26]

This constant pressure from the DAF, anxious to gain acceptance from the workers, ran into the contrary goal of the regime — to keep costs low, including wage costs — so as not to threaten rearmament. More and more one heard complaints from government officials and from party circles as well about the DAF propaganda with regard to wages. In October 1937, Hess actually issued instructions to the party — but pointedly aimed at the DAF — to end open demands for wage increases and cease the endless fishing for popularity (*Popularitätsacherei*).[27]

21. Report of the Trustee of Labor of May, 1937, quoted in Mason, *Arbeiterklasse*, Document 36, p. 339.
22. Report of the Trustee of Labor for March, 1937, in *ibid.*, Document 30, p. 305.
23. Report of the Trustee of Labor for May, 1937, in ibid., Document 36, p. 338.
24. Report of the Trustee of Labor of May 1937, in ibid., Document 36, p. 339.
25. See Schmeer letter of August 20, 1937, in ibid., Document 62, pp. 466–9.
26. See Krohn Vermerk of August 28, 1937, in BAK, R41 (Krohn), 5009.
27. See Anordnung, October 1, quoted in Mason, *Arbeiterklasse*, Document 60, p. 463.

But, as Ley and his people had already discovered, there was more than one way to skin a cat. Though it was increasingly difficult to argue for formal hourly wage increases, actual increases could be obtained indirectly by forcing employers to grant a series of benefits to their workers. These included extra allowances, such as Christmas bonuses, full compensation for holidays which fell during the work week, compensation to workers for wages lost during weeks at military service and extra bonuses for workers with more than three children.[28] The DAF also pushed for reduced taxes and social service fees in special cases, for profit sharing, and for better terms in piece-work.[29] In addition, the Labor Front put pressure on government to change the terms of discharge in favor of the workers, in part by granting lengthier notice before termination, in part by extending the protection of the law to workers in plants with a minimum of ten workers to all plants.[30] The many social services which the DAF and the regime imposed on businesses, including free meals, Christmas parties, vacation pay, and so on, also amounted to an indirect wage increase, at least in the eyes of the government. One estimate concluded that for a plant employing 2,300 workers, ten months' worth of extras amounted to 235,000 marks — roughly 10 marks per man per month in costs.[31] Nor was the DAF in its propaganda gentle on the "plant leader" who did not recognize his social obligations vis-à-vis his "retinue." As Ley said in a speech before NSBO functionaries on November 20, 1933: "Show me your workers! If they're all right, then you're all right. If they're dissatisfied, poorly nourished, if they're dirty and down at the heels, then you are guilty and no one else. That must be the maxim."[32]

On rare occasions, horror of horrors, the local functionaries would even support strike action. In one case 280 workers in a glass factory in Altenfeld went out on strike. Instead of trying to intervene, the men on the "trust council," among them SS and DAF men, actually joined the walkout.[33]

28. See Schweitzer, *Nazifizierung*, pp. 143–4, who lists the most common demands which the DAF made on owners.
29. See Timothy Mason, *Sozialpolitik im Dritten Reich*, 2nd edn (Opladen, Westdeutscher Verlag, 1977), p. 257.
30. See Seldte to other ministries, November 23, 1935, in BAK, R41/24.
31. See Knoff (Arbeitsamt Berlin) to Gassner (president of the Brandeburg Landesarbeitsamt), December 20, 1937, in BAK, R41/151, p. 13.
32. In BAK, NS52, vorl. 256, p. 13.
33. Excerpt from the monthly report of the Trustees of Labor for February 1937 in Mason, *Arbeiterklasse*, Document 27, p. 292.

Eventually, as we shall see, Ley himself had to make major concessions on the wage front. After June 1938 he was forced to support the officially proclaimed wage ceilings and, generally, to order his people to support a policy of keeping wages and prices stable. In one directive he said, "I must demand from every functionary of the German Labor Front all-out action." But then added, as if aware of the tremendous pressures from below, "It will take great insight and strong character perhaps to have to say No for once."[34] And, indeed, the reports of the Trustees for the first quarter of 1939 reveal continuing grass-roots DAF pressures for direct and indirect wage increases, including a particularly egregious case in Nuremberg, where a DAF legal advice office actually went to court disputing the power of the Trustee to change the length of notice of termination.[35]

Thus during the first five years of the regime, and in many cases beyond, the DAF tried through interference in the economic question of wages and prices both to ingratiate itself with the German workers and to carve out one area of jurisdiction which might lead to it becoming a "super-agency." Certainly, if Hitler had won the war, Ley would have been in a strong position to influence and shape any future Nazi *Lohnordnung*.

A second socioeconomic area into which the DAF made significant encroachments after 1933 was that of vocational training.[36] Once again, Ley could fall back on the Führer order of October 1934 which explicitly put the DAF in charge of vocational education. Vocational training had always been important in Germany, where a virtually unique system of instruction on the job had evolved, with masters teaching apprentices. In trades and handicrafts the training was supervised by chambers of commerce through participating firms. By the 1920s the system had moved to industry as well, where large companies themselves supervised the training. The area was a tempting one for Ley and the DAF. For one thing, ideological "education" was one of Ley's main thrusts anyway, and it was tempting to combine professional with ideological training. For another, the area of vocational training provided Ley with yet

34. See Ley's Rundschreiben of December 19, 1938, in BAK, R41 (Krohn), 5011.
35. Excerpt quoted in Mason, *Arbeiterklasse*, Document 156, pp. 950–1.
36. Two excellent studies of vocational education are Rolf Seubert, *Berufserziehung und Nationalsozialismus* (Weinheim and Basel, Beltz Verlag, 1977) and Theo Wolsing, *Untersuchungen zur Berufsausbildung im Dritten Reich* (Kastelbaum, Aloys Henn Verlag, 1977).

another entrée into socioeconomic policy, for control of education meant among other things the right to set standards and determine curricula.

Vocational education also presented a tempting vacuum. Both government and industry had relatively neglected this area, first, because of the First World War and then, later, because economic hard times and high unemployment levels did not create much demand to supplement the ranks of skilled labor. This trend continued even during the initial period of the Third Reich. Continuing high unemployment left business uninterested, while the new regime, not yet willing to interfere in business matters and more interested in basic job creation, did little to affect vocational education.[37]

Ley and the DAF, however, were very interested. Lacking specific executive authority, Ley found in vocational education another one of those areas into which he could insinuate himself. He was also responding shrewdly to what would soon become an urgent need. The massive rearmament program which Hitler was planning would demand highly skilled labor in unprecedented numbers. An expanded vocational education program under DAF control could fill this need and give Ley an important role in the recovery of Germany's military sovereignty and power.

Ley's tactic was to take over the chambers of commerce which had been administering vocational training in trades and handicrafts and to send his people to the individual large firms which handled the job in industry.[38] With respect to industry he had just the man, the organization, and the ideology to take on the challenge. The man was Karl Arnhold. The organization was Dinta (Deutsches Institut für Technische Arbeitsschulung, or German Institute for Technical Labor Training). The ideology was totalitarian, and Arnhold had developed much of it himself.[39]

Born in Wuppertal, not far from Ley's old stomping grounds, Arnhold trained as a mechanical engineer and served as a lieutenant during the war. After the war he joined various right-wing organizations, fought against the French during the occupation of the Ruhr, and served several months for sabotage during that struggle. In

37. Wolsing, *Untersuchungen*, p. 496.
38. Ley's attempts to control trades and handicrafts is best told within the context of the rivalry between him and Schacht in the next chapter.
39. On Arnhold's background and his ideas, see Seubert, *Berufserziehung*, pp. 64–5; also Wolsing, *Untersuchungen*, pp. 35–63.

1925, Albert Vögler, leading member of the Stinnes concern and general director of the Steel Trust, asked Arnhold to head the newly founded Dinta.

Arnhold's concept was to apply the methods and principles of the Prussian military tradition to the factory. His analogies always smacked of soldierly leadership, of war in the trenches, of the comradeship inherent in the community of all Germans. "We should finally recognize," he said once, "that we in Germany *are still living in the trenches today* even if the real war has been over for a long time."[40] If he could get the workers to define themselves in terms of a military brotherhood subject to strict discipline, then he could wean them away from class consciousness, socialism and the trade unions.

Accordingly, Dinta attempted to get at the workers, particularly young workers, at precisely the spot where the unions had their focus and stronghold — the factory. The idea was to combine vocational and ideological training in such a way as to promise the worker advancement while simultaneously, by approaching him as a "whole" person, to lure him away from his working-class subculture and integrate him into the business community. The final goal: a worker who was both more productive and more compliant and whose "soul" would be won. Years before the Nazis came to power, the Dinta idea represented a totalitarian claim on the part of business vis-à-vis labor. As Arnhold put it, it would be a struggle "for the soul of the German individual" which would "be fought out on the field of education and with educational means."[41] And, like the Nazis later, Dinta was careful to couch its efforts not in terms of class conflict but in the language of community, upward mobility, and heightened productivity. Indeed, Arnhold provided much of the terminology and conceptualization which Ley would appropriate for his DAF. Long before the Nazis were in power and the AOG on the books, Arnhold was talking about the "plant leader" and his "retinue" both forming the "plant community" (*Werkgemeinschaft*), where through discipline and obedience the "new whole man" would rise to new heights of performance and productivity. Ley bought it all — he was particularly fond of the military analogy and used it frequently in his speeches.[42]

40. Seubert, *Berufserziehung*, p. 97. Emphasis added.
41. Ibid., p. 77.
42. Ley especially liked to compare the roles of the "plant leader" and the DAF *Obmann*, respectively, with those of the company commander and the company "Spiess," the "mother of the company" in Frederick the Great's army. See DAF

There is some indication that Ley already had become familiar with Arnhold and his ideas while still at IG Farben in the mid-1920s.[43] It would be surprising if he had not, since Arnhold was amazingly prolific in propounding his concepts. At any rate, Ley introduced Arnhold to Hitler in 1931. Arnhold fashioned close connections with the NSDAP. He was close to Konstantin Hierl, future boss of the Nazi Labor Service, for example, and viewed Hierl's organization as a kind of permanent labor army. In April 1933, Ley once again made contact with Arnhold with the intent of co-opting him and Dinta into the DAF. On May 1 — one day before the smashing of the unions — Arnhold joined the Nazi Party.[44] On July 26, Ley issued an order absorbing Dinta, which now became the DAF Office for Vocational Training and Plant Leadership. Arnhold was brought along and actually took over the office in 1935. Ley, in his order, gave the Dinta a clear mandate.

"It is of decisive importance that the new generation in industry and artisanry receive a systematic on-the-job training and schooling in the National Socialist spirit. I commission Dinta with the task of taking all steps necessary for a general introduction of these schooling methods."[45]

Less than a year later, at the second congress of the DAF and in Hitler's presence, Ley reiterated his claim to jurisdiction over vocational education and linked it to Germany's industrial recovery: "Germany will once again achieve its world prestige from an economic perspective when it succeeds in producing work of high quality. This entails, however, training the German to be the best skilled laborer. The German Labor Front will achieve this great task by putting vocational education for young workers on a new footing."[46]

As we have seen, authority over vocational education found ultimate expression in Hitler's decree of October 24, 1934. Soon Ley's gigantomania set in. Dinta was vested with a formidable organizational network which mirrored that of the DAF itself. By the end of 1936 Dinta had 400 apprenticeship schools with a further 150 under construction. It hired 25,000 vocational teachers. Already

Sozialamt, *Deutsche Sozialpolitik* (Berlin, Verlag der DAF, 1937), pp. 7–8.

43. John Gillingham makes this assertion in his article "The 'Deproletarianization' of German Society: Vocational Training in the Third Reich," *Journal of Social History*, vol. 19 (spring 1986), p. 426.
44. See Seubert, *Berufserziehung*, pp. 98–9.
45. From *Der Deutsche*, no. 173, July 27, 1933, p. 13.
46. In *Westdeutscher Beobachter*, May 5, 1934.

2.5 million workers had taken courses. Its funds seemed unlimited. In 1937 alone Dinta spent 11 million marks.[47]

This represented a formidable challenge. On one level it was a provocation to business, for it challenged the authority of the older, more traditional organization which developed vocational education programs for business — the Datsch (Deutscher Ausschuss für Technisches Schulwesen, or German Committee for the Technical School System). On a higher level, it represented a challenge to the Ministries of Economics and Labor. Both these ministries knew that if Ley got control of vocational training and apprenticeship programs, he would have an entrée into vital areas of social policy the authority for which lay with the ministries — not the least of them wage policy. Government determined to resist this encroachment.

It would be a long, drawn-out struggle, fought behind the scenes, just as the gradual takeover of vocational education was a quiet, day-to-day affair. But Ley never liked quiet, day-to-day endeavors. Like his master, he liked public drama and widely publicized campaigns. Accordingly, he mounted a more public challenge to business and government; part of it focused on the factories, part on the individual worker. In both cases, the concept was Arnhold's. The first approach, involving the individual, was called the *Reichsberufswettkampf*, or Reich Skills Competition. This approach, inaugurated in 1934, was augmented two years later by another approach on the factory level, the *Leistungskampf der deutschen Betriebe* or Performance Competition of German Factories. Both promised still greater access for the DAF both into individual workers' lives and into their plants.

The Skills Competition had begun as a kind of "skills olympics" in the Hitler Youth organization in 1933. Ley quickly saw its potential and joined Hitler Youth leader Baldur von Schirach in sponsoring a greatly expanded competition. In 1938 the competition was broadened to adults. Now any German — provided he or she was Aryan — could participate.[48] Supervised by the DAF *Fachämter*, the competitions ensued in nineteen categories reflecting most areas of economic endeavor in society, including mining, banking, agriculture, textiles, construction, and so on. They began typically in

47. See Otto Marrenbach, *Fundamente des Sieges*, 2nd edn (Berlin, 1940), pp. 278–92; also Mason, *Sozialpolitik*, pp. 197–8.

48. See Marrenbach, *Fundamente*, pp. 278ff.

February on the local level. The winners then proceeded to the Gau competitions in March and to the national finals in April. At each level dramatic publicity ensured widespread participation.[49]

Participants were tested in three areas: in vocational performance, both practical and theoretical; in ideological reliability; and in sports. There were ten levels of competition (*Leistungsklassen*), based on skilled and unskilled jobs and on the number of years one had been in an apprenticeship program.

The response was enormous and, for the regime, gratifying. From 1934 to 1937, when competition was limited to youth, the number of participants leaped from 500,000 to 1.8 million. By 1939, when adults were also taking part, the total number of competitors was over 3.5 million (see Plate 15).

For the DAF, these "olympics" had a number of advantages. They provided firm linkage between the goals of higher performance and ideological training. Each winner set the standards to be excelled. This aided performance. Each winner also received substantial material benefits from the regime, including shortened apprenticeship time, scholarships, support in moving up or laterally in his craft, free books and tools, and so on. Since many of the victors were from very modest social circumstances, such material "aid to the gifted" on the part of the regime went a long way to fostering the impression both of *Volksgemeinschaft* and of upward mobility. The tremendous response of youth to these competitions also created the impression that young people strongly supported the regime and its tenets.

More specifically, the DAF gained in three practical ways. First, it got another foot in the factory door. If apprentices from certain firms performed below par in the competition, then the DAF could — and did — withdraw the right of those firms to train apprentices. In 1937 alone, 110 firms lost that right. And the DAF was ready to fill the resulting vacuum with its own apprenticeship training. Secondly, being in charge of determining the winners and their resulting emoluments gave the DAF leverage in the important area of *Berufslenkung*, that is steering people into certain specific careers or job categories according to perceived need. In many cases, for example, to make sure that the winners were given a boost in their job situation, the DAF would put pressure on firms to promote them or

49. Much of the material here on the Skills Competition is from Wolsing, *Untersuchungen*, pp. 496–545.

to shift them to other positions where their qualifications could better be used and rewarded. This often involved the DAF paying moving expenses or salary differentials.

Finally, the success of the competition both reflected well on Ley and his organization and demonstrated how far one could get in jurisdictional struggles despite the lack of formal executive authority. Ley himself was well aware of this fact. As he admitted much later, in 1944, looking back: "Since we didn't have any governmental decrees or other laws we had to procure for ourselves other levers of power and possibilities for influence. So I happened on the competition idea. I might well never have stumbled on the competition idea. In that case I would have ordered everything with paragraphs; would have churned out one decree after another."[50]

If Ley foresaw the Skills Competition as a device to unleash a competitive struggle for higher productivity on an individual basis, then the *Leistungskampf* was to represent a similar competition on a factory-wide basis. And just as the Skills Competition offered Ley the opportunity to interfere in vocational education and apprenticeship programs, the Performance Competition opened still greater opportunities to interfere in virtually every element of the production process. In fact, the competition gave Ley the "most important lever" in revising the content of the AOG, infringing on the independent power of the entrepreneur in his factory and in seizing whole areas of economic and social responsibility from the Ministries of Economics and Labor.[51]

The *Leistungskampf* can best be seen in connection with the Second Four-Year Plan, which Hitler announced at Nuremberg on September 9, 1936, and which was to prepare the German economy and people for war. Ley already was aware of Hitler's dissatisfaction with the leadership of the Economics Minister, Schacht, in retooling the German economy, and saw another opportunity.[52] Once again, as in October 1934, Ley got his master to sign a decree on August 29, 1936, proclaiming a universal competition among firms to be awarded the distinction of "National Socialist Model Factory" (*Musterbetrieb*).

50. Quoted in Hans Joachim Reichhardt, "Die Deutsche Arbeitsfront" (FU Berlin, 1956), p. 145.
51. See Jürgen Reulecke, "Die Fahne mit dem goldenen Zahnrad: der 'Leistungskampf der deutschen Betriebe' 1937–1939," in Detlef Peukert and Jürgen Reulecke (eds.), *Die Reihen fast geschlossen* (Wuppertal, Peter Hammer Verlag, 1981), p. 255.
52. See Mason, *Sozialpolitik*, pp. 249ff.

Companies which best realized "the idea of National Socialist factory community in the sense of the Law for National Labor and in the spirit of the German Labor Front" would be proclaimed "Model Factories" and were awarded the privilege of flying the DAF pennant. Ley had the power to determine the criteria for the competition and to choose the winners.[53]

This decree was published by Ley on September 2 along with a renewed version of the October 1934 decree asserting again the exclusive right of the DAF for the "Formation of a general people's and performance community of all Germans." As usual, government officials learned about this startling new development from the papers. Five days later, on September 5, the ministers were able to read something else in the paper — lest the proportions of Ley's challenge had not yet dawned on them. Ley proclaimed in his paper, *Angriff*: "With that we are placing the factories under our requirements, are creating a new and effective means to realize the totality claim of the German Labor Front and to fill every plant with National Socialist conviction."[54]

The next day, September 8, Hitler proclaimed his Four-Year Plan (also without informing his ministers in advance) and called for "the unified direction of all strengths of the German people and the strict combining of all relevant jurisdictions in party and state."[55] Hitler put Hermann Göring in charge of the Four-Year Plan, but obviously the announcement of "combining jurisdictions" was too great a temptation for Ley to ignore. Ley sought — and received — Göring's blessing for the competition, a step which Göring would soon regret. Getting right down to work, Ley assigned one of his best men, Theo Hupfauer, head of the DAF Office of Social Responsibility, to run the competition.

Basically, if an owner wanted his plant to qualify as an "NS Model Factory," he had to fulfill some basic requirements in five general areas: (1) preserving and guaranteeing social peace; (2) preserving and heightening *Volkskraft*, that is following National Socialist social policy with regard to marriage and family life; (3) preserving and heightening labor productivity; (4) raising living standards; and (5) fulfilling the economic goals of the Four-Year

53. See Marrenbach, *Fundamente*, p. 326.

54. Article of September 7, 1936, quoted in Mason, *Sozialpolitik*, p. 249.

55. Quoted in Dietmar Petzina, *Autarkiepolitik im Dritten Reich. Der nationalsozialistische Vierjahresplan* (Stuttgart, 1968), p. 57.

Plan.[56] There was practically no aspect of factory life that did not fall under these five areas. Thus the contestant had to expose himself to the scrutiny of DAF functionaries in a variety of ways. Under category 1: was he looking out in a fatherly way for the well being of his "retinue"? Was he fostering comradeliness? Did he join them for free beers at regular intervals after work? Had he replaced the time clock with the *Betriebsappell* (morning roll call)? Did he join the workers in uniform to march with the DAF *Werkschar* (ideological militia)? Under category 2: did he promote marriages, educate his female employees to be wives and mothers, provide bonuses for heads of large families? Under category 3: did he provide a clean, well-lit factory environment; toilet facilities, cafeterias, swimming pools? Did he take necessary safety precautions? Under category 4: had he lengthened the time of notice of termination? Raised piece-work rates to reward higher productivity? Provided profit sharing? Given Christmas bonuses? Under category 5: had he raised productivity? Had he been efficient in procurement of raw materials; eliminated waste; reused old materials where possible; tested new tools or techniques? This represents only a partial list. Actually, the areas of interference were limited only by the imaginations of DAF activists.

Participation was ostensibly voluntary, but then, so was membership in the DAF. Like so many "voluntary" activities in the Third Reich, participation in the *Leistungskampf* was often "encouraged" by local DAF people in great advertising campaigns. As a result, Ley registered another stunning success. In 1937 the first full year of competition, 84,000 firms took part. The following year it was 164,000 and in 1939, 272,000. In the first year of competition 1,683 firms were awarded the first level of prize: the Gau Diploma. Another 266 received the second prize of DAF Golden Pennant, while 103 received the designation NS Model Factory.[57] Nor was Ley loathe to combine jurisdictional imperialism with economic gain. In many cases this meant inducements to work with one or another part of the DAF business empire. As one local directive stated it, "I insist that the factories to be tested be approached without exception by the local Obmänner [to establish] as close a cooperation with the Bank of German Labor as possible." He added that such a connection

56. These are detailed in *Angriff* of December 10, 1937, quoted in a resistance report entitled "Zum Reichsbetriebswettkampf," in BAK, R-58/447, p. 145. This report also details the various social criteria for judging the plants.
57. See DAF report "Deutsche Musterbetriebe," in BAK, NSD50/570.

should be one of the factors taken into account in judging a factory's qualifications in the *Leistungskampf*.[58]

The Performance Competition thus opened an enormous competitive front between the DAF, on the one hand, and business and the ministries on the other. And Ley's enemies were scarcely comforted to hear Hupfauer, administrator of the competition, say, "The Performance Competition will be an instrument to facilitate the revolutionary advance of the German Labor Front in the sector of German labor policy."[59] Nor would they hear with equanimity Ley proclaim his goal to make "the whole German economy one National Socialist Model Factory."[60]

Two other areas, briefly, in which Ley sought to involve the DAF as putative "super-agency" were those of social insurance and national housing. Both reflected important parts of the DAF business empire and both would eventually come to represent Ley's pyrrhic "paper" victories in the early years of the war.

To provide an extension of Bismarck's pioneering social insurance within the framework of Nazi ideological tenets had long been part of the NSDAP dream, reflected in point 15 of the original party program.[61] This area was especially attractive to Ley for several reasons. It offered an important field for social integration through *Betreuung* — and this was Ley's specialty. The DAF, as part of the legacy of the destroyed unions, was already granting benefits on a large scale to the sick and unemployed. It was a natural step to broaden that base by encroaching on what had been a governmental function. Moreover, the tremendous amounts of money involved in insurance and pension funds could not but have attracted Ley's eye. Added to that was the fact, as we have noted, that insurance *per se* was an important component of the DAF business empire. And finally, the legacy of social insurance from the last years of Weimar offered another one of those tempting vacuums which Ley could never resist. The painful emergency measures of Chancellors Brüning and Papen in the closing years of the Republic had had the effect of reversing much of the progress made in social insurance during the

58. See Knaden (Kreisobmann Essen), circular letter no. 66/38 of September 9, 1938, in BAK, R43II/529, p. 226.
59. See Mason, *Arbeiterklasse*, no. 65, pp. 484.
60. See Ley Announcement of December 30, 1938, in *Amtliches Nachrichtenblatt der DAF*, in BAK, NS22, vorl. 649.
61. See letter Seldte (RAM) to Ley of June 12, 1939, in which Seldte argues his intent to fulfill this point in the party program. BAK, R41 (Krohn), 5012.

earlier years. What had been social insurance gave way to the dole, as the regime cut benefits, limited many of them to those below poverty level, and introduced humiliating means tests.[62] The resulting mass despair and loss of confidence in the system gave the Nazis one of their most important propaganda opportunities. They proclaimed a broad system of coverage as the *right* of all Germans and promised a thoroughgoing reform after they came to power.

Once the Nazis were in power, however, they typically hesitated, as they did in most areas where they had proclaimed the necessity for far-reaching reform. The Labor Ministry, in whose bailiwick social insurance for the most part belonged, temporized. Instead of embarking upon a thoroughgoing reform, Seldte and his people combined ideological appeals with *ad hoc* measures, as the endless debates over items like health insurance fees illustrated.[63]

In the meantime, plans were being hatched in circles around and within the DAF as well. Throughout much of 1933 these were couched in the language of "corporativism," but, as Ley and the DAF backed away from that ideological position toward the end of the year, the ROL began to see the DAF as a giant social insurance "carrier" for an all-encompassing "unity" insurance scheme which would protect the *Volksgenossen* from cradle to grave. Dr Fischer of the DAF Office for Social Policy formulated the goal clearly: "A unity insurance with the simplest possible premium collection, with clearly delineated services, with the most parsimonious administration, with an easy-to-survey structure, with expedient appeal mechanism is the goal for which we are striving."[64] His associate, Mende, already had plans to incorporate social insurance into the DAF Social Office.[65]

In February 1934 Seldte did initiate some action toward preparing a social security law "in the spirit of the National Socialist state," by creating a packed committee. His man Krohn chaired it. Ley and the DAF were represented, but outnumbered. In the end, the so-called *Aufbaugesetz* of July 1934 was passed, bringing some reforms into the areas of sickness, accident, and old-age insurance.

62. For a detailed discussion of this dismantling, see Ludwig Preller, *Sozialpolitik in der Weimarer Republik* (Düsseldorf, Droste Verlag, 1978), pp. 399–495.
63. For an excellent study on social insurance, upon which I have relied heavily, see Karl Teppe, "Zur Sozialpolitik des Dritten Reiches am Beispiel der Sozialversicherung," in *Archiv für Sozialgeschichte*, vol. XVIII (1977), pp. 195–250.
64. In *Soziale Zukunft* (1933), p. 80, quoted in Teppe, "Sozialpolitik," p. 218.
65. See ibid., pp. 208, 217; also Mason, *Sozialpolitik*, p. 37f.

But although the law used some of Ley's language, basically it kept the old system intact.[66]

Ley had suffered an initial defeat. But the battlelines were drawn. Hereafter, his strategy would be twofold. His Institute for Labor Science would draw up ever more comprehensive plans for a national unity social insurance plan (soon to be dubbed *Deutscher Volksschutz* (German People's Protection), while at the same time taking pot shots at the existing system and the ministries supervising it. At the DAF meeting at Leipzig in December, 1935, he proclaimed the need to totally revamp the system. "Reforms will serve no purpose," he said, "since what is in place today is totally bankrupt and broke. It has no more value. We won't back off our demand that the current social insurance system is completely out of date and will have to be restructured in a revolutionary way into a social obligation."[67] To give institutional shape to his demand, he ordered in June that the DAF Social Office be divided into the Office for Social Insurance under Peppler and the Office for Labor Policy under Mende.[68]

The fourth important area into which Ley ventured was that of housing, or, as the Nazis put it, "homesteads and settlement." Here again, a combination of ideological, economic, and jurisdictional factors prevailed. How and where people were to be housed was all wrapped up in Nazi ideological predilections. The Nazi petit bourgeois dream — which Ley fully shared — was a nation of family homes, preferably with a garden plot and the proverbial picket fence, where happy Germans could have large families in a healthy environment. The goals were to end the old difference between city and countryside by combining the best of both and to enable even the German workers to come into contact with the racially invigorating soil. As Ley's ideologist put it, "The DAF has . . . from the very beginning viewed in settlement a means to bind the most valuable workers to the soil and give them the opportunity to live decently, to earn extra income by tending garden and stall and, in the course of their lifetimes, to acquire a bit of property, however small."[69] (See Plate 16.)

66. See Volker Hentschel, *Geschichte der deutschen Sozialpolitik 1880–1980. Soziale Sicherheit und kollektives Arbeitsrecht* (Frankfurt, Suhrkamp, 1983), pp. 103, 136ff.; also Teppe, "Sozialpolitik," p. 212ff.
67. Quoted in Teppe, "Sozialpolitik," p. 238.
68. See *Amtliches Nachrichtenblatt der DAF* (1935), p. 169, in BAK, NSD 50/53.
69. See Marrenbach, *Fundamente*, p. 214.

This settlement could take one of several approved forms: a house with a small attached farm (*Landwirtschaftliche Nebensiedlung*), a family home with a bit of land for cultivation (*Kleinsiedlung*), or a home in a small community or on the edge of a town with a garden (*Heimstätte*). What was not acceptable was what had been termed *Stadtrandsiedlung*, that is temporary living quarters for the unemployed on the fringes of cities subsidized by the government.[70] These had been common during the Depression, and the Nazis had fulminated against them. Clear in the pattern of acceptable and unacceptable settlements was another major goal of the regime: to break up the working class subcultures of the cities and create the basis for a "rurban" Nazi social culture. Added to this, by the way of Ley's own motivation, was the fact that the DAF possessed a large construction empire, the expansion of which would dovetail nicely with large-scale plans for adding to existing German housing stock. And finally, responsibility for housing would also create an additional lever to interfere in the private lives of the people. Indeed, the DAF did not hesitate, for example, to interfere in conflicts between landlords and tenants. This and other activity was perceived by the ministries as an encroachment on their turf.[71]

Once again, as in other areas, a convenient vacuum appeared invitingly to Ley and his people. In July 1933 the government had incorporated the jurisdiction of housing and settlement into the Economics Ministry and entrusted authority to old party veteran and economic crank Gottfried Feder, who was advanced to Reichskommissar für das deutsche Siedlungswesen (Commissar for the German Settlement Organization) in March 1934. In December 1934, however, in the wake of the reaction against radical economic ideas which followed the Roehm putsch on June 30, Feder was fired from his job and responsibility for settlement went back to the ministries. But Feder's appointment in the first place had established the party's claim in the settlement and housing area, and now Ley moved to pick up the torch.[72]

70. See Schweitzer, *Big Business and the Third Reich* (Bloomington, Indiana University Press, 1964), p. 211.
71. For reference to interference in tenant strife, see Schneider (DAF Reichsbetriebsgemeinschaft Handel) to DAF Sozialamt of November 6, 1935, in BAK, NS51/14. For a report on local DAF settlement activities, see *Tätigkeitsbericht*, 1935, of the DAF Kreisheimstaettenamt Regensburg in National Archives of the US, Microcopy T81, Roll 70, Frames 802253–7.
72. For a brief background, see Marie-Louise Recker, *Nationalsozialistische Sozialpolitik im Zweiten Weltkrieg* (Munich, Oldenbourg, 1985), pp. 13–14.

Already in January 1934 the DAF put its foot in the door by calling for plans to create homes for veterans of the SA and SS all over Germany: "The plan consists of creating individual homes for tested fighters of National Socialism and simultaneously provide still deeper roots for particularly valuable components of our people."[73]

Within a week the Labor Minister was complaining in a Cabinet session about unauthorized agencies concocting building schemes and the following day wrote to Hitler rebuking Ley for announcing construction plans without consulting the ministry.[74]

Shortly thereafter Ley created the DAF Settlement Office (Heimstättenamt) and linked it in personal union with the Comissioner for Settlement on Hess's staff. Head in both cases was a man named Ludovici. The DAF lost little time going into action. Soon the new office was planning construction of a huge settlement in the heart of the Aachen coal area.[75] By 1936 at the latest, Ley was claiming the same authority from the Führer to create a settlement program for the German worker as he had for the field of vocational education.[76] The stage for another battle royal with the ministries was set.

Ley's activities in Berlin, then, in a number of important socioeconomic areas were intended to challenge the ministries and business and create a kind of Nazi "super-agency" which would preside over the Nazification of German society, including its most recalcitrant class, the workers.

But for a man who proclaimed that no one was to have a private life in Germany any more except in his sleep, Ley was not one to confine himself to jurisdictional fencing in Berlin. He reached out as well with his bureaucratic tentacles to create a decisive presence in the lives of every gainfully employed German, whether at work or at play. It is appropriate, then, that we turn now to what might be called the microcosmic activities of the DAF.

In a speech to the International Leisure Congress in 1936 Ley said, "We must gradually come to the realization that we must organize leisure anew. This means not only the hours after work but the total man from morning to night; above all in the plants and workshops."[77]

73. See *Völkischer Beobachter*, January 20, 1934, p. 1.

74. See Chefbesprechung of January 26, in *Akten der Reichskanzlei*, vol. 1, p. 1098; also Seldte to Hitler of January 27, in BAK, NS10/123 pp. 75ff.

75. See Marrenbach, *Fundamente*, p. 216.

76. See Ludovici to Ley of February 20, 1936, in BAK, NS22, vorl. 671.

77. Quoted in Laurence van Zandt Moyer's excellent study "The Kraft durch

It was not only leisure which Ley tried to organize in the workshops but almost everything else as well. The average German worker might have been pardoned if he got the impression that the DAF and its *Walter* were ubiquitous. Ley's organizational gigantomania brought the DAF into plants and factories in an impressive way. And the larger the factory, the more extensive the DAF organization. For a plant of over 1,600 workers, for example, Ley had a DAF staff which included, among others, functionaries in charge of career counseling, health, youth, women, press and propaganda, sports, settlement, job protection, and of course, the "Strength through Joy" leisure organization, which developed its own bureaucracy.[78] The DAF Obmann, who was in charge of all these people, himself played an important role, keeping the workers under surveillance on the one hand, but also often trying to function as their go-between on the other. Whether authorized or not, the factory Obmänner (usually in conjunction with the DAF Kreiswalter) often conducted plant inspections and could use the authority of the party to put pressure on the factory owner, although the small entrepreneur was more vulnerable to this pressure than the large industrialist.[79] The DAF top leadership was often ambivalent about interference on the part of the grass-roots functionaries. Occasionally, the DAF papers *Arbeitertum* and *Angriff* would launch campaigns against recalcitrant employers who were not living up to their responsibilities vis-à-vis their "retinues," and would announce crackdowns, arrests, and occasionally, incarceration in concentration camps for asocial employers. "The DAF watches over unsocial plants," read one headline in *Arbeitertum*; "With an iron broom" read another threateningly. "The DAF begins factory inspections," trumped the *Angriff* on another occasion.[80] These campaigns cannot but have whetted appetites at the local level. On the other hand, aware of its obligations under the AOG, the DAF also tried to establish regulations and rein in too-enthusiastic functionaries. Inspections should only be carried out with the cooperation of the plant leader, Selzner had to caution on many occasions, and only

---

Freude Movement in Nazi Germany 1933–1939", unpublished dissertation, Northwestern University, Chicago, Illinois, 1967.

78. See chart "Die DAF-Organisation im Betrieb," in BAK, NS22, vorl. 216.
79. See Martin Broszat, *The Hitler State* trans. John Hiden (New York, Longman, 1981), p. 150.
80. The articles are respectively from isues dated December 15, 1934, p. 28, July 1, 1937, and May 10, 1937.

certain functionaries were authorized to take part at all.[81] On other occasions, top leadership seemed itself unsure as to what was permissible and what not. Mende, head of the Sozialamt, had to caution local functionaries not to demand written protocols of "trust council" meetings from employers. But he then went on to suggest that such intervention was justifiable if the council could not handle a dispute or when specific evidence of violations of wage schedules and so on were present.[82]

One of the ways in which the DAF could have an impact on the lives of individual workers — part of its *Betreuung* function — was through the dispersal of emergency funds. Carrying out a responsibility inherited from the defunct trade unions, the DAF was authorized to disperse special aid to Germans who were temporarily unemployed, invalided, injured on the job, or otherwise struck by calamity. Burial benefits were also available. But these were not benefits to be offered to Germans across the board; nor was there any legal right to receive them. Instead, the dispersal of these funds was "politicized" in the sense that the amount of money one could receive in a given case was pegged directly to how long one had been a dues-paying member of the DAF. Unemployment or illness compensation, for example, was only available to those who had been members of the DAF for at least one year, and the amount of payment hinged on how many months the petitioner had paid his DAF dues uninterruptedly. This was even true for death benefits, for which the deceased was only eligible if he had been a member for 36 months! That minimum time brought 30 marks for the funeral; 72 months' membership brought 60 marks; 120 months, 100 marks; 180 months, the maximum of 125 marks. Thus did Ley make out of what was essentially a private party insurance system, a recruiting device for his Labor Front.[83]

Even more valuable in providing the DAF opportunity to influence conditions in factories were two devices associated with its "educational" function: the schooling courses (*Schulungskurse*) and the Labor Committees (*Arbeitsausschüsse*). The former were designed for the more active DAF members, particularly the 10 percent which carried out leadership functions, usually on a part part-time basis (*ehrenamtlich*). The DAF usually tried to get both employers and

81. See, for example, circular letter no. 24/34 of October 8, 1934, in NS51, vorl. 256.
82. See circular letter of October 10, 1935, in ibid.
83. See DAF Schatzamt, "Unterstützungseinrichtungen der DAF," dated December 5, 1936, in BAK, NS22, vorl. 655.

employees to attend the courses, in order to foster the *Betriebsgemeinschaft* which was a central part of Nazi plant ideology. The course content was frequently non-specific and amounted to pep rallies to develop the correct ideological and social "attitudes" in both workers and bosses. Always, the concept of totality was emphasized, again underscoring the universal claims of the DAF in factory life. "Schooling is a total educational task," the DAF ideologist emphasized, "it is not limited to imparting a specific body of knowledge, but grasps the total person and thereby demands a uniform influencing of soul, body, and spirit in the person to be schooled."[84] It is some indication of the scope of this activity that in the year 1938 alone 46,838 such courses were held with 2,479,621 participants, including 38,850 "plant leaders."[85]

More specific — and therefore more effective in establishing DAF influence in the factories — were the labor committees. Formed in the wake of the Leipzig compromise between Ley and business and the ministries, these committees were composed in equal measure of DAF Obmänner and "plant leaders" — the "men of practice," as the Nazis called them.[86] The point was for both groups to consult on problems which had been encountered in factories but which were of a broad enough nature that they could not be readily solved at the individual plant level, problems having to do with holidays, pay for those attending weekend military maneuvers, protecting pregnant women, and so on. By early 1936 over 1,300 of these committees had been formed all over Germany. The DAF tried very hard to convey the impression that these committees bore no relation to the "arbitration committees" (*Schlichtungsausschüsse*) of the Weimar period, but in fact at the lower levels that is exactly what many DAF Obmänner tried to make out of them, as the DAF itself had to admit years later. Records are very scanty concerning the grass-roots activities of the labor committees, but the 1938 annual report of the DAF Gau office in Regensburg would have been typical. The report notes ninety different labor committee meetings during the year dealing with subjects ranging from protective clothing to heightened protection for the pregnant woman to special arrangements for sick pay.[87] As Timothy Mason has observed, these committees assumed increasing importance as the years went on as a method for the DAF to penetrate industry in a sociopolitical manner and "to impose its

84. See Marrenbach, *Fundamente*, p. 53. 85. Ibid., p. 69.
86. For the Nazi concept of these committees, see ibid., pp. 101–5.
87. See "Jahresbericht" of the Gau Bayerische Ostmark in BAK, NS5I/62, p. 75921.

conception of 'National Socialist common law' in factory social policy."[88]

It is some indication of how far one could stretch the concept of "schooling" that Ley organized the so-called "industrial brigades" (*Werkscharen*) in 1935. These brigades started out as a catalyst for injecting into the factories the martial spirit of which Ley (and Arnhold) had so often spoken. This was a crucial task from Ley's perspective "since any martial impulse had been stifled and made despicable in the plants by the class struggle and by a pacificism knowingly engendered by the Jews."[89] Indeed, the very ethos of the "plant community" was to be a martial one. "The example for that community had always been the soldier for us National Socialists," wrote Ley. "His obedience, his comradeship, and his self-sacrifice are indispensable for building the plant community. Without soldierliness every community becomes a club in which complaining, cowardice, hypocrisy, and bourgeois humanitarianism, which one believes will earn heaven, romp with one another."[90] Accordingly, candidates for the brigades would be drilled and marched around like new army recruits until, after a six-month trial period, they were accepted and given their dark blue uniforms. They would then set about instilling martial spirit into the rest of the plant "retinue."

To this task Ley gradually added another: to "activate" virtually all of the DAF and "Strength through Joy" campaigns and tasks in the factory. This meant that the brigades had to become the moving spirit and organizational impetus behind a host of activities, including plant celebrations and ceremonies, the formation of sport groups and glee clubs, the organization of after-work activities, and so on, all of which had to be imparted with the proper spirit. As Ley put it, the brigades would "as shock troops bring all the virtues into the factories."[91]

In March 1938 the *Werkschar* activities were extended even further as Ley, creating a new DAF office, "Werkschar und Schulung," conferred on the brigades the main responsibility for "schooling" in the factories — not by conducting classes and seminars but by setting a proper example. "They do not 'school,' but set the example."[92]

88. In Mason, *Sozialpolitik*, p. 196.
89. See Ley Anordnung No. 29/38 of May 1, 1938, in BAK, NS22, vorl. 649.
90. See his words in "Die Werkschar," undated in US National Archives, Microcopy T-81, Roll 69, Frame 78934.
91. In a speech at Ordensburg Sonthofen on August 6, 1938, in *Deutsches Nachrichtenbüro*, no. 1237, in BAK, R43II/530 p. 199.
92. Marrenbach, *Fundamente*, p. 72; see also Ley Anordung no. 35/38 in BAK, NS22, vorl. 649.

Finally, in May of the following year, just three months before the outbreak of war, Ley integrated the brigades into the leadership cadres of the NSDAP, thus underscoring their final, and for the war, most important task: the political surveillance and mobilization of the working population in the factories.[93]

For Ley the brigades came to represent the most important element of DAF presence in the factories. They were, in his words, "the combat troops of social responsibility in German economic life in all areas," and without them no *Werkgemeinschaft* could be realized.[94] Indeed, for Ley the brigade was the heart and soul of the "plant community." Occasionally, his dreams of classnessess went so far that he saw the brigades as a vehicle for radical social leveling. As he put it in July 1937: "Businessmen and workers, plant leader and plant [DAF] *Obmann* should march in the same column of the brigade. As the highest level of recognition for the plant leader, I will decorate him with the brigade uniform." This led the far less utopian Göring to respond, "You cannot expect, Dr Ley, that the plant leader stand in the fifth row and let himself be ordered around by his workers."[95]

There is perhaps one other light in which Ley viewed the brigades: as his own personal, uniformed militia which he could order about the way Lutze did the SA and Himmler the SS.[96] If this was originally the case, then Ley had to back off and make his compromises; indeed, the many organizational "homes" which the brigades inhabited might well reflect this backing-off process. Certainly, the brigades aroused the suspicions of other top Nazis, remembering, as they did, Roehm and the pre-June 1934 SA. Hess, for example, felt that the brigades represented unnecessary duplication of effort that would draw off people and energy from the party itself and that "one should not organize new [organizations] for the sake of newness, but out of necessity."[97] Himmler thought that the brigades were being infiltrated with communists and refused to let his SS people join.[98] (See Plate 4.)

93. See Ley Anordnung no. 19/39 of May 4, 1939, in NA, T-580, Roll 549, Ordner 694; see also Reichhardt, "DAF," p. 129.
94. Quoted in Reichhardt, "DAF," p. 131.
95. Both men quoted in Schweitzer, *Nazifizierung*, p. 146.
96. Schumann makes this case in *Nationalsozialismus und Gewerkschaftsbewegung*, p. 154.
97. See pages 6–7 of "Stellungnahme zu den Werkscharen" as enclosure with letter from Friedrichs (Hess's staff) to Simon (ROL) of August 27, 1935, in BAK, Schumacher Sammlung, 282.
98. See circular letter from Müller (Gestapo) to Staatspolizeileitstellen, November

As a result of these pressures, Ley sought several organizational "homes" for his brigades. Initially, through a compact with Lutze, they were to be trained by the SA, which also had a right to nominate brigade leaders to Ley.[99] Later, the brigades were integrated into the party leadership cadres. What Ley did not achieve, however, if that was part of what he wanted, was a personal, uniformed *Hausmacht*. Whatever their organizational position, the *Werkscharen* were not allowed to become a nationally based, *hierarchical* organization, but remained at the plant level. They also remained relatively small, reaching a prewar peak in 1939 of 9,500 brigades with 340,000 members.[100] Ley himself had occasional doubts about the efficacy of the brigades and saw the danger in their becoming "a lot of nice talk which exhausted itself in *Bierabende* and distributing cigarettes."[101]

Because the DAF was often limited in its ability to act as an "honest broker" on behalf of its labor membership and because its standing among the workers was always tenuous, particularly in the case of older, formerly unionized people, Ley and the regime put a great deal of emphasis on trying to raise the status of labor generally. The goal was to eradicate the class consciousness which, the Nazis thought, had kept the worker out of the national community and to integrate labor into the larger *Volksgemeinschaft*. One concept which was supposed to further this goal was that of the "court of social honor." This concept had already been given institutional form in the AOG, which provided an "honor court" for each of the seventeen Trustee districts with an appeal court in Berlin. The reasoning was that not only employers had honor, so did employees. And the boss was supposed to recognize the fact and gear his behavior accordingly. Hence, both workers and bosses who failed to live up to their social obligations vis-à-vis one another could be hauled in front of an honor court and reprimanded, fined, or even dismissed.[102] Mirror-

---

17, 1936, in BAK, R58/265, p. 73; also report of *SS-Oberf.* Zenner (Oberabschnitt Ost) of January 15, 1936, in BAK, Schumacher Sammlung, 287.

99. See Sommer (DAF Amt Information) circular letter no. 34/36 October 15, 1936, in BAK, R58/265, p. 74.

100. These were DAF figures. See Marrenbach, *Fundamente*, p. 60. *Freies Deutschland* estimated that only 5 percent of workers were involved, and many of these were young men who were lured by bonuses, advancement, and so on. December 23, 1938, p. 11.

101. Quoted in Mason, *Sozialpolitik*, p. 191.

102. Documentary evidence is very slim on these courts. The Nazis claimed that more employers than employees were prosecuted, but there is not sufficient evidence to bear that out. The courts did represent, however, something that

ing this institution, Ley created his own honor courts within the DAF to function as a watchdog in the factories. These "honor and disciplinary courts," were founded on October 19, 1935, with Ley as Oberster Gerichtsherr (Supreme Judge). The courts were introduced to create "an orderly appeal route in the [DAF] and to protect the *Walter*, *Warte*, and other colleagues in the [DAF] from arbitrariness by use of disciplinary proceedings." It also had the purpose "in emergency cases of eliminating dirty elements from the leadership corps."[103] These courts were not part of the regular legal system and had very limited jurisdiction. To the extent that they discoverd real crimes, these cases would be turned over to the state's attorney. What they did claim jurisdiction over was offenses against the honor of *Volksgenossen* which might make an individual ineligible to be a member of the DAF or occupy a leadership position within it. In this sense, if a person had already been convicted under the regular courts system, they might also be dealt with by the DAF court to the extent that their crime had also violated the honor of the community. Ley's courts did not have the power to imprison or to levy fines. All they could really do was to issue reprimands, prevent people from holding office in the DAF, or exclude them entirely from that organization — something that Ley, in his social insecurity, thought to be a very severe form of ostracism from the *Volk* community. One might smile at the prospect of being thrown out of an organization which one might have been pressured to join in the first place. But such exclusion could have serious consequences, for either worker or, especially, small employer, against whom the DAF could bring pressure in so many other ways. In 1937, 29,000 cases were brought before the DAF courts; in 1938, 17,400 cases, a drop which the DAF attributed to a lower crime rate and better *Betreuung*.[104] The few records extant do reveal a picture of penalties shaped not so much by the original infraction itself but mitigated (or sharpened) by the political past, current social position of the individual, as well as how the original crime related to what the Nazis considered to be a dishonor to the *Volk* community.[105] Within the legal realm, Ley

might ultimately have evolved into a National Socialist common law. See C. W. Guillebaud, *The Social Policy of Nazi Germany* (New York, Howard Fertig, 1971), pp. 33–6; also Wallace Deuel, *People under Hitler* (New York, Harcourt, Brace, & Co., 1942), pp. 324–31; and Mason, *Sozialpolitik*, p. 119.

103. See Marrenbach, *Fundamente*, pp. 31, 36, 42, and 46 respectively.

104. Ibid., p. 46.

105. For examples of people brought before the DAF courts who had already been

created one other institution as well which brought a DAF presence into the lives of workers: the legal advisory offices (*Rechtsberatungsstellen*). These offices were analogous to the "trust councils" in the sense that both replaced older institutions which the Nazis could not abolish outright, but in such a way as to undermine their original purpose. The *Vertrauensrat* replaced the *Betriebsrat*. The legal advisory offices were designed as a middle man between the individual and the labor courts, which the Nazis had also not dared to abolish. The purpose was to see to it that more and more complaints were handled unofficially so that they would not need to be brought formally to a labor court. There were several hundred *Rechtsberatungsstellen*, separate ones for employers and employees, and Ley liked to brag that while the employer had to pay for his legal council, the worker received his *gratis*, courtesy of the DAF. He pointed out on one occasion, by the way of example, how in Dresden 1,300 cases were handled in a single month, with only sixty taken to a labor court. He did not say how they were handled, however, merely that the offices had done much to smooth industrial relations.[106]

But all of the above taken together — the many DAF functionaries and their chosen specialties, the schooling courses, the labor committees, the factory brigades, the courts of honor and the legal advisory offices — did not have the impact or popularity of the most successful of Ley's experiments in education and *Betreuung*: the "Strength through Joy" (KdF) organization. The KdF was the most successful and popular of all Ley's efforts with the great mass of the people. It also illustrated several important points: the continuity from *Kampzeit* to Third Reich; the Nazi propensity to borrow ideas from others and then adapt them to their own purposes; and the lack of proportion typical of Ley and his gigantomania.

Although Ley pioneered the idea of organizing leisure time during the Nazi regime, the idea was not originally his own. By his own admission, he borrowed the idea in part from the Belgian leisure theorist Henri de Man, but mostly from the Italian Fascist After-Work-Organization (*Dopolavoro*).[107]

As early as 1929 Ley joined the other Nazi members of the

---

convicted of "real" crimes, see October 15, 1936, report of the "Oberste Ehren- und Disziplinarhof der DAF" to lower courts in BAK, NS5I/198.

106. See Ley, *Rede zum Reichsparteitag 1934*, p. 9; also Reichhardt, "DAF," pp. 156–9.

107. See Ley's speech of November 27, 1933, announcing the KdF in Robert Ley, *Durchbruch der sozialen Ehre*. 7th edn. (Berlin, Zentralverlag der NSDAP), pp. 23–4.

Prussian Diet in a junket to Italy hosted by the Italian Finance Ministry to observe the "achievements of Italian Fascism."[108] In late 1932, on the eve of Hitler's coming to power, Ley was publicly recommending that the Italian After-Work program be adopted in Germany.[109] After Hitler's accession to power, Ley brought up the idea again on July 1, after the unions had been smashed. On September 16 he announced plans for its implementation and on November 17, as part of the refashioning of the DAF, he formally established the organization.[110] Indeed, the original designation — a literal translation from the Italian — was to be "Nach der Arbeit"; but Ley's usual gigantomania set in and he began to envision the KdF as far more grandiose than the Italian equivalent. As he put it just a week before announcing KdF, "We must fashion all free time after work into a gigantic undertaking. It will perhaps be the greatest thing that this revolution produces."[111]

Ley's motives in founding the KdF were complex. Most clearly, it was to be a means of raising the productivity of the German worker by making optimum use of his leisure hours to prepare him for ever higher performance. "Since time on the job demands high and peak performance from the worker," Ley said, "one must offer the best of the best in his free time to nourish soul, spirit, and body."[112] The program was also designed to further the integration of the German worker into German society and to improve his self-image. This was to be achieved by offering him all kinds of leisure time, vacations, and other amenities which in the past had been reserved for the middle and upper classes in Germany. At the same time, the ceaseless organization of free time promised to allay Ley's deep-seated fears of the dangers lurking in masses of people who were allowed too much spontaneity in their private lives. "This organisation is [meant] to ban boredom," he announced. "From boredom spring stupid, heretical, yes, in the end, criminal ideas and trains of thought. Gloomy dullness makes people complain; gives them a feeling of homelessness; in a word, the feeling of absolute superfluity. Nothing is more

108. See Italian embassy to Ley of March 18, 1929, and Ley to Hess of April 3, 1929, in Berlin Document Center: File Ley.
109. See *Arbeitertum*, December 22, 1932, p. 25.
110. See Moyer "KdF," p. 78; for full text of Ley's speech proclaiming opening of the KdF on November 27, 1933, see *Deutsches Nachrichtenbüro*, nos. 3039–41, in BAK, R43II/557, pp. 2–9.
111. See his speech to NSBO functionaries on November 20, 1933, in BAK, NS51, vorl. 256, p. 21.
112. Remarks in DAF, *Kraft durch Freude* (Berlin, 1940), p. 6.

dangerous to the state than that."[113]

And so the KdF set up shop — ironically, in the same building, initially, which had housed the leading Socialist newspaper, *Vorwärts*.[114] Convinced from the outset of the importance of this movement within the DAF, Ley assigned his best men to its operation. At first the KdF was run through the Organization Office under Claus Selzner. The all-important Office for Travel, Hiking and Vacation functioned under the skilled administrator Bodo Lafferentz. Brinckmann handled the money; Biallas, the publicity. And perhaps one of the most talented administrators in Germany, Albert Speer, handled the office which was intended to transform the workers' surroundings, the "Beauty of Work" Office.[115] And, like the rest of the DAF, the KdF bureaucracy burgeoned. By 1937 it had 10,000 employees nationwide.[116] The KdF bureaucracy was fashioned to deal with five areas of working people's lives. Firstly, it was to make more pleasant and attractive the work surroundings. This included the related activity of beautifying villages, which were viewed as the workplaces of the peasants. Secondly, it was to structure leisure time at home through radio, art, and forklore. Thirdly, it was to dominate the area of adult education and hobbies. Fourthly, it was to oversee sport activities and finally, to organize vacation travel in Germany.[117]

Perhaps the best publicized and most successful of these endeavors was that of vacation travel. Most workers had never had a vacation away from home. That was an experience reserved for the middle and upper classes. Ley determined to change this, in order to demonstrate that the Nazi regime was breaking down the old class barriers. Especially popular were one-day and weekend trips, for with KdF subsidies these were financially well within the range of the ordinary worker. These could range from a Rhine cruise to several days on a North Sea Beach. Ultimately, 85 percent of German workers took advantage of the short jaunts.[118] More expensive, even with KdF subsidies, were the longer eight-day vacations. They represented up to one week's wage for a skilled laborer, and for that

113. In Ley, *Durchbruch*, p. 27.
114. See *Der Deutsche*, June 17, 1934, p. 16, quoted in Moyer, "KdF," p. 72.
115. See Lothar Kutsch, "Die NS-Gemeinschaft 'Kraft durch Freude' innerhalb der 'Deutschen Arbeitsfront' 1933–1939," unpublished manuscript in the Institut für Sozialgeschichte, Bonn, p. 163; also Ley, *Durchbruch*, p. 163.
116. See Moyer, "KdF," p. 83.
117. For an overview of KdF activities, see ROL, *Organisationsbuch der NSDAP*, 7th ed. (1943), pp. 210–12.
118. See Moyer, "KdF," p. 127.

reason Ley instituted the special savings plan through the BdA. These trips were the much publicized prestige vacations, where workers could practise "status emulation," imitating the leisure habits of their social superiors: they included sailing, yachting, polo, hunting, and above all, sea cruises — all traditional upper class recreations. Ley put special emphasis on the romance for the high-sea cruise. Already in 1935 the KdF had bought the ship *Der Deutsche* from Hamburg-America lines for 42 million marks and refitted it. Soon it was joined by seven others. In 1936, the KdF began building its own ships, first the *Wilhelm Gustloff* (named after an assassinated Swiss Nazi) and then, in 1938, the *Robert Ley*.[119] The latter ship was especially constructed to reflect every amenity for its 1,700 passengers. It was 204 meters long by 24 meters wide, had 5,000 square meters of deck space, and was propelled by electric motors powered by diesel. It was equipped with a theater, three dining halls, sports facilities, reading rooms, and a library. Forty baths, 100 showers, and 145 toilets served the passengers, while two doctors and a dentist stood by in case of emergency. Hitler himself launched the ship with the words: "Now we are in the process of launching the 'Bremen' of the German worker and I want to give this ship the name of my greatest idealist, the name of my old fellow combatant and party comrade, Robert Ley."[120] (See Plates 9, 10, 11.)

By the outbreak of the war the KdF had twelve ships totalling 200,000 BRT. Favorite destinations were the Norwegian Fjords and the Madeira Islands, as well as various Italian ports. In fact, Ley kept up his Italian connections. He became friends with his counterpart, Tullio Ciannetti, President of the Industrial Workers Confederation, and in 1937 concluded an agreement providing for an exchange of vacationers between the two countries.[121] Despite the high cost of the cruises, Lafferentz's office was soon receiving ten requests for every space available. In 1935 alone, 135,000 took part in cruises. Not satisfied with giant floating hotels, Ley also envisioned land-bound ones. In 1936 on the island of Rügen, the KdF began construction of a gigantic resort complex which would have accommodated 20,000 people! The war halted construction, however, as it halted many of Ley's grandiose projects.[122] In this connection, we should also remember that the Volkswagen was envisioned as part

119. Ibid., pp. 122, 128–30, 135.
120. See Marrenbach, *Fundamente*, p. 358.
121. See *Arbeitertum*, August 1, 1939, p. 6.
122. See Reichhardt, "DAF," p. 185.

of this giant vacation empire, and, in fact, was officially designated the "KdF-Wagen."

Thus the DAF added another component to its business empire: travel agency. The KdF earned considerable sums from the modest fees paid for its various trips. In 1939, for example, it earned seven million marks on a turnover of 107 million marks, (if the war had not intervened, thus cancelling 8,000 trips, the 1939 turnover would have been 137 million marks).[123] All this activity, of course, brought protests from the legitimate travel industry, but in vain. Ley announced that: "The tourist agencies must accommodate themselves to the great idea of the KdF. The earlier they do this, the better it will be for them."[124] (See Plate 12.)

After the worker returned from his vacation, he might well see that another branch of the KdF had been busy in the factory in his absence, the "Beauty of Work." This, interestingly enough, was one of the only projects for which Albert Speer, who otherwise could be quite contemptuous of the ROL, gave Ley any credit. He later discussed the etiology of this office and best described its activities:

> After January 30, 1934, at the suggestion of Robert Ley a leisure-time organization was created. I was supposed to take over the section called Beauty of Labor; the name had provoked a great deal of mockery, as had the title Strength through Joy itself. A short while before, on a trip through the Dutch province of Limburg, Ley had seen a number of mines conspicuous for their neatness and cleanliness and surrounded by beautifully tended gardens. By temperament Ley tended to generalize, and he now wanted to have all of German industry follow this example. The project turned out to be an extremely gratifying one, at least for me personally. First we persuaded factory owners to modernize their offices and to have some flowers about. But we did not stop there. Lawn was to take the place of asphalt. What had been wasteland was to be turned into little parks where the workers could sit during breaks. We urged that window areas within factories be enlarged and workers' canteens be set up. What was more, we designed the necessary artifacts for these reforms from simple, well-shaped flatware to sturdy furniture, all of which we had manufactured in large quantities. We provided educational movies and a counselling service to help businessmen on questions of ventilation and illumination. We were able to draw former union leaders and some members of the dissolved Arts and Crafts society into this campaign. One and all devoted themselves to the cause of making some improvements to

123. Ibid., pp. 183–4.
124. Quoted in *Angriff*, November 5, 1935, p. 13.

the workers' living conditions and moving closer to the ideal of a classless People's Community. However, it was somewhat dismaying to discover that Hitler took hardly any interest in these ideas."[125]

Initially, the SdA people concentrated on plant inspections to put pressure on factory owners to beautify the workplace. In April 1934 Speer and his team inspected 400 plants and found only 10 percent to be satisfactory.[126]

The result was a flurry of articles in *Arbeitertum* sketching violations in great detail and often naming plants and employers who had been reported to the Gestapo for their recalcitrance. Typically, an owner was first approached for his cooperation. If he refused he was talked to at length. Then, given continued non-compliance, his name was published and/or a sign was affixed to his plant labelling it a "tumbledown shanty" (*Bruchbude*) or something of the sort. As a last resort, the SdA claimed the right to deny the owner the right to be "plant leader," although it was not clear if in such cases the DAF was actually threatening expropriation, which would have been difficult except in the case of very small enterprises.[127] These methods soon brought howls of protest from businessmen. The Interior Ministry insisted that inspections only be carried out in cooperation with "plant leaders." The result was that by the end of the year Ley was compelled to change tactics somewhat. Adopting a number of ideas which had been espoused for years by plant psychologists, efficiency experts, middle-class reformers, and trade-union leaders, Ley packaged them as major aesthetic steps toward creating a true *Volksgemeinschaft* and launched a series of major propaganda actions.[128]

These large-scale actions began in early 1935 and followed upon one another over the next three years. Each *Aufklärungsaktion* had a particular slogan. "Sun and greenery to all gainfully employed," was the first. There followed "Struggle against noise," "Good light — good work," "Clean people in a clean plant," "Healthy air in the workplace," and "Warm meals in the plant." In each case DAF functionaries and their experts swarmed through the factories bring-

125. See Albert Speer, *Inside the Third Reich* (New York, Macmillan, 1970), p. 57. For a description of the activities of the SdA, see Ley Anordnung no. 4/35, in *Amtliches Nachrichtenblatt der [DAF]*, Berlin, 1/1935, p. 19.
126. Moyer, "KdF," pp. 113–14.
127. See Annegret Walesch, "Das Amt 'Schönheit der Arbeit,' " unpublished manuscript at Institut für Sozialgeschichte, Bonn, p. 37.
128. See Reulecke, "Fahne," p. 248.

ing pressure to bear on the owners to live up to whatever theme that particular action was devoted to. In "Good light — good work," for example, hosts of DAF people equipped with light meters tested plant after plant for sufficient illumination.[129] Each campaign went a bit further than the last in concretely rearranging the internal configuration of the factories, and each was coordinated to reflect national economic priorities, especially after the Four-Year Plan was announced. For example, Operation "Warm meals" had the goal of drastically reducing fat consumption, given the shortages of that product. New office decor and even offices themselves, while ostensibly designed for comfort and convenience, had the additional purpose of conserving scarce raw materials, for example using earthenware to replace metal and developing standard designs to avoid duplication. In 1937, Ley created the post of "Gau Architect" to make use of talented and politically reliable architects to create modern, standardized designs for the DAF.[130] All in all, the SdA organization was designed, at a time when wages were frozen, to replace higher wages with a wide range of social services and amenities, many of them intangible but psychologically important.

Ever the budding "educator," Ley also built an important educational component into the KdF organization. Particularly after mid-1936, he concentrated further attention on "schooling," both within the DAF and within the larger party organization itself. The result in the KdF structure was what Ley termed the "Deutsches Volksbildungswerk" (German People's Education Enterprise) under Fritz Leutloff. This ambitious project was designed to reach people politically through their hobbies and other interests in order, as Ley put it, "to turn these comrades away from their special interests, then to influence gradually their political attitudes to the point where they become participants in a politically oriented *Gemeinschaft*".[131] By 1939 the Volksbildungswerk was offering courses in everything from stamp collecting and foreign languages to amateur photography, in 325 adult education centers all over Germany. Indeed, adult education itself became a preserve of the DAF. More ominously, this particular project illustrated on a very personal basis close to home (what is more personal than one's hobbies?) a process which the DAF was pushing on a massive scale: the destruc-

129. See Kalesch, "SdA," pp. 44ff, for a brief description of these actions.
130. Ibid., pp. 69, 74–6.
131. Quoted in Moyer, "KdF," p. 209; see pp. 210–18 for detailed discussion of the Volksbildungswerk.

tion of any vestiges of the old pluralistic society. Between September 1936 and March 1938 many private federations, including the National Chess Federation, National Philatelic Association as well as the associations of coin collectors, amateur photographers, and so on, were absorbed, occasionally against their will, into the Volksbildungswerk. The rich legacy of German *Vereinsleben* was being systematically dismantled and reconstructed within a Nazi context. Not even the traditional local saint's day festivals (*Kirmes*) were inviolate. When, in 1939, the Remscheid *Schützenverein* set about organizing their local Kirmes festival, as it had done since time immemorial, the local KdF stepped in and took over. By 1938 Ley's adult-education empire involved no less than 6,330,000 people, one-third of them in hobby groups.[132] This whole operation, parenthetically, also opened up a new area of jurisdictional rivalry for Ley, since it encroached upon territory which had long been staked out by Alfred Rosenberg and his National Socialist *Kulturgemeinde*.

Two final areas of KdF activity were operation *Feierabend* and sports. The former focused on providing inexpensive "culture" to the masses, including concerts, plays, opera performances, and so on. There was even a ninety-piece KdF orchestra which traveled to remote areas.[133] And should the worker have had any energy left after surviving all the other demands made upon him by work and DAF, he could take part in a variety of sport activities, which the KdF, largely for budget reasons, organized within the factories themselves. This program even had the advantage, as Ley admitted, of providing a modest amount of job creation — for physical education teachers, who had been unemployed in large numbers during the Depression.[134] Once again, Ley was treading on jurisdictional toes, and a three-way rivalry ensued between him, Lutze, the SA leader, and von Tschammer und Osten, who was Reich Sports Leader (see Plates 8, 14).

In the end millions of Germans took part in "Strength through Joy" activities: in 1938, 9.2 million used its vacation and travel facilities; 8.1 million went to theater performances and concerts; 8.3 million took part in sport activities; 6.3 million in adult education; and 54 million in some aspect of the full panoply of amusements and

132. See *Freies Deutschland*, no. 31, of August 3, 1939, p. 5.
133. See Deuel, *People under Hitler*, p. 322.
134. See Ley's remarks in *Deutschland ist schöner geworden*, p. 81, n. 13. Useful in tracing the sports rivalry is Hajo Bernett, "NS Volkssport bei 'KdF,' " in *Stadion*, vol. 5 (1979), pp. 89–146.

diversions. By 1939 a German worker could take part in a different activity every night of the week without doing the same thing twice.[135]

Whether trying to transform his DAF into a socioeconomic "super-agency" in Berlin or reaching out with dozens of bureaucratic tentacles to "grasp" the German worker at home or in the factory, Robert Ley was frenetic and relentless in his activities. He was always coming up with new ideas or spotting new jurisdictions to conquer. "We will always discover new things," he proclaimed. "We'll never get to the end of it. . . . And so tomorrow we'll find something new and the day after something new again. Every year and every day we'll find something new."[136] This relentless drive was, to be sure, in part ideological fanaticism. But it also reflected Ley's bottomless social insecurity and desperate need to be participating in meaningful social activity. Again and again this fact comes out in his public remarks and is aptly illustrated in his announcement of one of the more crackpot of his ideas: the factory roll-call (*Betriebsappell*). Convinced that punching a time clock was demeaning, Ley tried to substitute a military-like morning roll-call. "It is a short way," he announced somewhat plaintively, "from [being a] number to [being a] zero. There is nothing more degrading and humiliating for a person than when he recognises that he has no worth in human society."[137] But Ley did not have many hours to reflect on such matters. His activities soon conjured up a whole array of enemies, in state, party, and business, and it is to the ensuing jurisdictional struggles that we must now turn.

135. See Moyer, "KdF," pp. 232 and, for the statistics, 238.
136. See *Deutschland ist schöner geworden*, pp. 208f.
137. See Ley, *Rede zum Reichsparteitag 1934*, p. 13.

CHAPTER 8

The Competitive Nightmare

Given Ley's inflated ambitions, the powerful and well-funded organization at his disposal, the tremendous pressures from within and from below for jurisdictional imperialism, and the generally normless, competitive nature of the Nazi regime, it was a foregone conclusion that the Labor Front would soon find itself on a collision course with government ministries, business associations, and party agencies. All felt challenged by the activities and claims of Ley and his people, and all responded by trying to protect their own turf.

The battles were fought out in ways typical of the Third Reich: newspaper announcements and speeches which unveiled sudden *faits accomplis*; detailed position papers which subtly undermined the opponent's position by advancing political or financial arguments against his proposals; a flood of correspondence among opponents in which expressions of desire to cooperate alternated with veiled threats; attempts on the part of all protagonists to acquire that magic "Führer order"; and even occasional personal feuds which nearly led to violence. And, of course, at the grass-roots level, the endless and massive depredations of the DAF functionaries. As Timothy Mason has put it, "With time it became in fact possible for the DAF leadership by means of organizational virtuosity to develop initiatives in so many different areas at once, that government officials and business associations scarcely had an overview of the sphere of operations anymore."[1] Friedrich Syrup, a high official in the Labor Ministry, who experienced many of the battles with the DAF, himself allowed as much when he later wrote, "Again and again and frequently with success the Labor Front tried to wrest areas of sociopolitical tasks away from the state administration and

1. Timothy Mason, *Socialpolitik im Dritten Reich*, 2nd edn (Opladen, Westdeutscher Verlag, 1977), p. 175.

to arrange them according to the political point of view of the party by means of its organs."[2] The struggle between Ley, who was always trying to broaden this jurisdiction and blur normative distinctions, and his government opponents, who were trying to narrow his prerogatives and observe and establish legal conventions, was a real social and political Donnybrook. But it was masked by the fact that all sides had to use jargon of National Socialism as the battles ensued. It was, as one observer has put it, like men fighting under a blanket and helps to explain the faintly unreal quality of these serious squabbles.

Ley's major opponents in the governmental and business sectors resided in the Ministries of Labor and Economics, on whose turf he was treading most of the time, and in the related organizations of business and industry (Organisation der gewerblichen Wirtschaft). His most consistent opponent was Franz Seldte, who was Labor Minister for the entire period of the Third Reich. Seldte, a prosperous chemical manufacturer, had been a decorated soldier in the war, losing his left arm in combat. At the end of the war, he founded the "Stahlhelm," a nationalistic veterans' organization, which would become the largest such organization during the 1920s and which contributed to the decline of the Weimar Republic. After Hitler's accession to power, Seldte obligingly dissolved the Stahlhelm and assumed leadership over a *gleichgeschaltet* Nazi veterans' organization.[3] Seldte was a stubborn opponent to Ley, but his attentions were divided between his ministry and leadership of the veterans' organization, which left much of the brunt of day-to-day combat on the shoulders of his talented assistants, men like Ministerialrat Dr Wernert Mansfeld, who largely drafted the AOG and State Secretary Dr Johannes Krohn, whose defense of the Labor Ministry's prerogatives would nearly involve him in a duel with Rudolf Schmeer, Ley's liaison man for the Four-Year Plan. In fact, Seldte asked Krohn "to bother him as little as possible with the business of the ministry" in order that he might "be able to devote himself to the 'Stahlhelm' and general high-level politics."[4] Once challenged,

2. See Julius Scheuble and Otto Neuloth (eds.) *Friedrich Syrup. Hundert Jahre staatlicher Sozialpolitik 1839–1939 aus dem Nachlaß* (Stuttgart, Kohlhammer, 1957), p. 403.
3. See Robert Wistrich, *Who's Who in Nazi Germany* (New York, Macmillan, 1982), p. 284.
4. See Karl Teppe, "Zur Sozialpolitik des Dritten Reiches am Beispiel der Sozialversicherung," *Archiv für Sozialgeschichte, vol. XVIII* (1977), p. 209. Biographical information on Krohn can be found in BAK, R41, vol. 2, Nachlass Krohn.

however, Seldte backed his people in combating Ley.

Initially, Ley did not find such stubborn opposition in the Economics Ministry — nor such continuity. Alfred Hugenburg, the press czar, who was Hitler's first Economics Minister, soon lost that post in June 1933 to Kurt Schmitt. Schmitt, a Nazi jurist and general director of the Allianz insurance company, represented the interests of big business in the party and resisted those like Otto Wagener who advocated collectivist economic programs. But he was not really the kind of political in-fighter of the sort needed to combat the constant challenges mounted by Ley. Rather, he was a "correct, reserved man equipped with an excellent outward demeanor, but hardly a born fighter."[5] Moreover, Schmitt was also a sick man, whose heart trouble already caused him to make way in June 1934 — after a year in office — to a successor, although he remained officially Economics Minister until January 1935.

His successor, however, was another story entirely. Hjalmar Horace Greeley Schacht, the "financial wizard" of the Third Reich was entirely a match for Ley and his people. Schacht had long experience in banking and industry, going back to executive positions in the Dresdner Bank as early as 1903. During Weimar he gravitated politically to the right, combining economic services to the government (he largely ended the 1923 inflation with his *Rentenmark*) with efforts to overthrow it (he joined the Harzburg Front in 1929 and tried to get Hindenburg to appoint Hitler Chancellor in 1932). His reward for such activities once Hitler came to power was appointment as Reichsbank President in March 1933 and, in July 1934, appointment as provisional Economics Minister, a position which became officially his in January 1935. He soon became indispensable in his capacity to develop new and imaginative ways to finance Hitler's rearmament (Mefo bills, etc.).[6] He would also pose a major roadblock to Ley's ambitions. The two men became deadly enemies and were in their goals, natures, and values diametrically opposite natures. Against the unprincipled, open-ended jurisdictional thievery of Ley, Schacht represented a bastion of jurisdictional clarity and viewed his ministry as a "tower of law" (*Turm des Rechtes*).[7] His advantages in the struggle with Ley included

5. See Willi A. Boelcke, *Die deutsche Wirtschaft 1930–1945. Interna des Reichswirtschaftsministeriums* (Düsseldorf, Droste, 1983), p. 68.
6. See Wistrich, *Who's Who*, pp. 268–9.
7. Boelcke, *Wirtschaft*, p. 82.

his experience and expertise, which were unrivaled; his determination, which could border on ruthlessness; his policy of protecting his subordinates and sheltering them from the worst vagaries of the system; and his unification of the Reich and Prussian Economics Ministries into one bureaucratic structure, which gave him financial resources second only to the Wehrmacht among the various ministries. Still, the struggle would not be an easy one, for Ley was an inexorable and tireless opponent. Nor was he Schacht's only enemy. The Economics Minister also ran foul of the SS and a number of Gauleiter and, in fact, as a representative of the old bourgeoisie, was never fully trusted by any of the Nazi leadership.

Despite the "treaty" which brought businessmen into the DAF at the end of 1933 and the AOG of early 1934, government and industry remained suspicious of Ley and his organization. This suspicion would grow during the course of the year as the DAF gradually altered its nature and Ley's jurisdictional ambitions unfolded. Variously, Ley's enemies saw in his burgeoning Labor Front a massive union, a quasi-government agency, a well-financed business empire and a party propaganda machine. It was like the old story of the blind beggars and the elephant, only in this case all the beggars were correct in their surmises.

At a Cabinet meeting at the end of the year 1933, Economics Minister Schmitt already pointed to the danger posed by the DAF, not only because of its ostensible role as worker advocate but also through its business enterprises as well: "The Labor Front should no more own business enterprises than [it should be a trade union]; otherwise we would have to reckon with such an expansion of its economic apparatus that it would smother the rest of the economy."[8]

Several months later, in February 1934, von Krosigk, the Finance Minister was emphasizing the need to get control of the DAF funds, which, thanks to its inflated dues structure, posed the danger of financing incursions into the jurisdictional territory of others. The quasi-governmental nature of the DAF also did not escape his attention. "The dues demanded by the DAF," he warned, "are much too high and, by being graduated, assume the nature of a tax." There is no reason to amass funds like that, "rather income which flows from that kind of inflated dues poses the danger of all too munificent a use of the means as well as of encroachments on extraneous areas of jurisdiction." He then bade the Labor and Economics Ministers join

8. See meeting of December 1, in BAK, R43II/531.

him in trying to lower the DAF dues.[9] In fact, the Economics Ministry had already produced a *Denkschrift* showing how the constant demands on the part of various Nazi organizations for money were putting a burden on the population.[10] Approached at a reception for the German Industry and Trade Association, Hitler himself stated that dues collected by private organizations might be excessive, but that that was not the case with the party. He did allow, however, that the DAF might be able to achieve some relief with regard to dues. Nothing more came of the matter however.[11]

In the meantime, reservations about DAF finances paled next to ongoing complaints about the activities those finances permitted. Through much of 1934 — at least until the Röhm purge of June 30 and subsequent purging of NSBO people — business focused mainly on the dangers of the DAF as a potentially radical union and as interloper on the turf of the Trustees of Labor, despite Ley's efforts to reassure businessmen.[12] During the summer both the Economics and Traffic Ministers had occasion to complain to Ley about both wage demands raised by the DAF as well as incursions into the jurisdiction of the Trustees.[13] The War Minister went to Hitler in June to complain that DAF wage propaganda was awakening desires for better living conditions which only threatened the rearmament program.[14] About that same time, Ruhr magnate Fritz Thyssen felt constrained to go to the Reich Chancellory with his catalogue of complaints against Ley. After the TdA in the Ruhr had decided on the basis of the AOG to reduce vacation pay for the

9. Von Krosigk to Seldte, February 7, 1934, in BAK, R43II/561, pp. 109–12. A copy was sent to the Reich Chancellory along with a copy of the DAF dues structure.
10. See "Die Belastung der Wirtschaft insbes: der Arbeiterschaft durch Spenden und Beiträge," a copy of which also went to the Reich Chancellory, See BAK, R43II/561, pp. 113–22.
11. See *Vermerk* of February 17, 1934, in BAK, R43II/348, pp. 46–7.
12. See comments of Pietzsch at a meeting of the Socioeconomic Committee of the Reichsgruppe Industrie on February 1, 1934, in which he claims that Ley gave him reassurances, among other things, that the NSBO would not try to name the Trustees of Labor. In BAK, R121/266. Several months later Ley put up his own candidate, an NSBO leader, as Trustee for Labor in Silesia. Although he lost, the matter cannot have reassured Pietzsch. See Seldte to Reich Chancellory, May 23, 1934 (documents on the NSDAP Chancellory) in Helmuth Heiber et al. (eds.), *Akten der Partei-Kartei der NSDAP*, (Munich, Vienna, Oldenbourg, 1983), microfiche no. 117 044950.
13. See Mason, *Sozialpolitik*, p. 193.
14. See Bernice A. Carroll, *Design for Total War: Arms and Economics in the Third Reich* (Den Haag, Mouter 1968), pp. 88f.

miners by 30 percent, Thyssen contended, Ley came along and promised in the name of the DAF to restore the pay. Moreover, he continued, the DAF Reichsbetriebsgruppen were undercutting the committees of experts used by the TdA for advice, while the DAF legal advice offices were improperly functioning as referees in labor disputes. All this was only driving a new wedge between employer and employee.[15]

But it was Ley's announcement of Hitler's decree on the DAF of October 24, the decree on which the Labor Front leader would stake his claims to "totality," which really set off the alarm bells in business and government circles. In a long memorandum to Lammers, Rüdiger von der Goltz, former TdA in Pomerania and Hitler's choice as commissar to reorganize the chambers of commerce, bewailed all that the DAF had been doing during the past months — all of it in contravention of the law.[16]

Goltz was very unhappy about the fact that, whereas Hitler had assured him in July that the DAF was not to play a role in economic and social policy, in fact the opposite was the case. Ley, it seemed clear, could not resist pressures from his own organization to re-enter those forbidden areas. (In fact, the DAF had never left them in the first place.) Goltz referred to a meeting in Berlin at the end of September, where DAF functionaries had complained bitterly about being limited to educational matters, with the result that workers were losing faith in the Labor Front. Ley responded, Goltz continued, by announcing that: "The Labor Front would once again take charge of the sociopolitical settlement, whereupon one of the participants applauded the fact that the socioeconomic struggle would be taken up again, and — after Ley interrupted 'Not struggle, settlement' — added, 'Well, all right then, settlement.' " Moreover, Ley had also issued a proclamation on October 1 announcing that the DAF would be the 'honest broker' for labor. All this caused Goltz to look up Claus Selzner to inform him that such claims were in violation of the law. Selzner was scarcely reassuring. He replied that, "Over and above the law, the party had to point out the facts that had to be changed and to create a situation in which they could be changed. Ley's proclamation had therefore been politically necess-

15. See report of June 12, 1934, to Lammers in BAK, R43II/527b, pp. 62–7.
16. See Vermerk memo of October 26, 1934, in BAK, R43II/530, pp. 68–79; Martin Broszat also deals at some length with this memo in *The Hitler State*, trans. John Hiden (New York, Longman, 1981), pp. 150–3.

ary, since Dr Ley had a very fine instinct for what was politically necessary and had never yet made a mistake." This conversation with Selzner and Hitler's October 24 decree caused the gravest misgivings in Goltz and the business community. Goltz went on to describe how at the local level the DAF people vastly outnumbered the TdA and their staffs; how DAF speeches were mostly directed against businessmen with the intent of demeaning them as a group; how DAF Amtswalter arrogated unto themselves the right to enter factories at will at any time to investigate complaints and to intimidate businessmen, with the authority of the party behind them; how the provisions of the AOG were being systematically undermined. "It must be said openly," Goltz concluded, "that this development means the danger of a union of incredible dynamic which is being loosed in the land and whose development, once underway, cannot be stopped." A second conversation with Selzner held on the "neutral ground" of a café left Goltz with his concerns intact. At the end Selzner said, "Dr Ley will under no circumstances abandon the right of the Amtswalter to inspect factories. . . . Moreover," Selzner repeated, "Dr Ley has a fabulous political instinct, just like the Führer. Ley always knows what to do politically at the right moment. For this reason he has acted, and up to now he has always acted correctly."

Goltz's memorandum was supported by massive complaints from businesses, especially smaller ones, about DAF activities. One noted plaintively how "for months now industry has been so encumbered by a flood of new directives, reports, orders, commands, instructions and meetings . . . that plant leadership is being subject to serious interference in handling the most important question: creating bread and work for the plants."[17]

Ley's challenges provoked more than just memoranda, however. The acting Economics Minister, Schacht, was one who took decisive action. On November 27, 1934, Schacht issued a directive which blocked any organization of the economy based on corporativist schemes and instead created his own organization. A new "Reichswirtschaftkammer" (Reich Economic Chamber) under the aegis of the Economics Ministry served as an umbrella organization for seven new entities which encompassed virtually the entire economy. These *Reichsgruppen* (industry, commerce, trade, banking, insurance,

17. See August Reissmann Aktiengesellschaft, Maschinenfabrik and Eisengiesserei to vaious DAF offices of October 27, 1934, in BAK, R43II/531.

energy, and tourism) were set up, in turn, on a decentralized basis so as to assure Schacht's goals of relative business autonomy and a separation of private economic function from state power. As one observer put it, "All of industry was thus directed into the public-legal sector to a certain extent, but at the same time granted by Schacht more autonomy [*Selbstverwaltung*] through the decentralization of public/legal functions."[18] Schacht thus hoped to forge a close alliance between government and business in resisting encroachments from the party, but not so close as to allow government to smother free enterprise.

As we have seen, the Labor Ministry had also not been inactive in the face of Ley's initial challenges. After co-opting Ley and several DAF people on a committee on which they were outnumbered, the Labor Ministry officials succeeded in producing several laws in the area of social insurance which were designed to block the grand proposals being floated by Ley and the party. These laws — the so-called *Sanierungsgesetz* (Stabilization Law) of December 7, 1983, and the *Aufbaugesetz* (Construction Law) of July 5, 1934 — were cast in the language of National Socialism, but in reality completed a process of reorganization begun during the Weimar Republic. Both laws were designed to block both increasing demands on the part of the DAF for a leveled *Einheitsversicherung* (unitary insurance) and any opportunity the DAF might want to exploit in order to get its hands on the huge reserves involved with pension funds.[19] Despite this tactical success in one area, Seldte was still being pressed hard in others. In a conversation with Hitler's economic adviser, Wilhelm Keppler, Krohn agreed that the AOG law was flawed in not giving the TdA more of a bureaucratic structure and in centering so much authority at the plant level. Both only worked to the advantage of the DAF at a time when its own publications were characterizing the TdA as only a "social judge" who was to act only when absolutely necessary and when local entities and the DAF were stymied.[20] Nor did the Labor Ministry cease drawing attention to the unsalubrious effects of the DAF investment program. At a meeting on work creation on January 10, 1935, there was general consensus "that the uncontrolled use of DAF funds up to now was undesirable and could

18. See Boelcke, *Wirtschaft*, p. 97.
19. For an extended analysis of these laws, see Teppe, "Sozialpolitik," pp. 212–24.
20. See Krohn memo of October 31, 1934, n BAK, R41 (Krohn)/5009; Richard Steinle, "Die Treuhänder der Arbeit in der [NS] Sozialordnung," undated, but 1934 in BAK, NSD/136.

lead to economically nonviable investments. Above all, a considerable lowering of dues was necessary."[21]

Often during the Third Reich the protagonists in unresolved struggles tried to create temporary truces and working compromises. Given the dynamic of the system, these truces seldom held for long. Usually they were aspired to by government agencies anxious to establish some sort of norms in a juridically kaleidoscopic situation. One such truce was the so-called Leipzig Agreement of March 1935. It was the brainchild of Schacht, who wanted to define as clearly as possible the jurisdictional line between the economic organization he had created in July of the previous year (Organisation der gewerblichen Wirtschaft, the OgW) and the Labor Front. Hitler put his imprimatur on the agreement in the form of a decree signed on March 21. The decree and the details of the agreement were then announced several days later at a meeting of 5,000 DAF Amtswalter in Leipzig. All three signatories, Ley, Schacht and Seldte, addressed the throng. Basically the agreement had the purpose of dividing responsibility between the DAF and the OgW. Both were to be equal partners, with the latter handling "economic" questions and the former "social" problems. To ensure cooperation, several steps were taken. The OgW joined the DAF as an institutional member; the head of the Reichswirtschaftskammer, whose responsibility it was to handle economic questions, became head of the DAF Economic Office. He remained, however, responsible to Schacht. In addition, the agreement foresaw the erection at the Reich and district level of "labor and economics councils" (*Arbeits- und Wirtschaftsräte*), on which DAF and business would have equal representation and whose task it would be to discuss common problems and possible solutions. In specific situations, though, the TdA would still have the final say. The agreement also called for the creation at the local level on the initiative of the DAF of "labor committees" (*Arbeitsausschüsse*) composed equally of "plant leaders" and "retinue," the purpose of which it was to discuss technical problems of a sociopolitical nature which did not lend themselves easily to being solved at the plant level.[22]

21. See *Chefbesprechung über Arbeitsbeschaffung*, in BAK, R41/24, p. 6.
22. For the text of the agreement, including Hitler's edict, see *Deutsches Arbeitsrecht*, no. 4 (April 1935), pp. 85–91; for general treatments of the agreement, see Mason, *Sozialpolitik*, pp. 194–6; Arthur Schweitzer, *Big Business in the Third Reich* (Bloomington, Indiana University Press, 1964), p. 363; Hans Joachim Reichhardt, "Die Deutche Arbeitsfront," (FU Berlin), pp. 92ff; Otto Marrenbach,

Schacht saw in the agreement a tool to keep the DAF out of economic affairs. As he put it later, "The Leipzig Agreement deprived Ley of any influence over economic leadership, in that I brought the economy as a whole into a purely formal relationship with the Labor Front with the provision that any effect the Labor Front might have on economic leadership would have to go through the Economics Minister, but that any direct influence be prohibited."[23] Ley, on the other hand, saw the agreement as just a foot in the door. He hoped to use its provisions eventually to seize control of the OgW entirely. Far from representing a true compromise, then, the Leipzig Agreement soon became just another bone of contention with both sides defining their terms to buttress their own position. The Reichswirtschaftskammer, dominated by Schacht, met without inviting DAF leaders. Many of the district councils, shunned by business, especially in the Ruhr, were dominated by the DAF.[24] Ley, himself, soon swung into action to exploit the agreement. Noting the non-participation of business, he soon increased the number of district labor councils from eighteen to thirty-one, thus making them contiguous with the Gaus. This broke the principle of parity with business and gave the DAF Gauwalter additional leverage in trying to take over social and economic policy in the gaus.[25] He also established a special office to carry out the provisions of the agreement "in his sense" and put the reliable Selzner in charge.[26] Finally, he undertook, as we have seen, to create DAF dominated labor committees in large numbers as yet another means of penetrating the factories economically. These committees, to which we will devote some attention, became a major tool at the local level and represented one of several "fronts," including handicrafts and vocational education, social insurance, and wage policy on which the war between Ley on the one hand and Schacht and Seldte on the other, was fought. Let us look, in turn, at each of these "fronts," recalling that each occurred simultaneously and often dovetailed

---

Fundamente des Sieges, 2nd edn (Berlin 1940), pp. 100–13.

23. See letter from Schacht to Reichhardt of August 12, 1955, in Reichhard, "DAF," pp. 92f.
24. See Reichhardt, "DAF," p. 94, n. 19.
25. See Arthur Schweitzer, *Die Nazifizierung des Mittelstandes Bonner Beiträge zur Soziologie* (Stuttgart, Ferdinand Enke Verlag, 1970), vol 9, p. 148.
26. This office became the DAF Amt "Soziale Selbsverantwortung" in 1936. See Marrenbach, *Fundamente*, p. 100; also *Amtliches Nachrichtenblatt der DAF*, no. 10 of April 1935, in BAK, R12I/274.

with the others.

The labor committees represented an important part of Ley's grass-roots campaign to gain economic influence in the factories. These committees were first organized after the 1935 Leipzig Agreement and emerged just as Ley was fashioning a number of institutions, such as the Werkscharen, the "honor- and disciplinary courts" and the SdA "enlightenment" program, all designed to gain entrée into the factories. The local labor committees tended to spring up through grass-roots initiative and eventually numbered 3, 637 nationwide.[27]

The DAF had already begun to fashion the labor committees when Claus Slezner addressed a combined group of DAF *Walter* and businessmen on August 12, 1935, in Ludwigshafen.[28] He characterized the new committees in ways which made business nervous from the outset: "Through this new institution German labor leadership would be assured," he said. Moreover, "I am thinking that a complete reform, if not to say, a revolution must occur. All questions which touch upon the common interests of businessmen and workers are be dealt with in these bodies." Selzner also made it clear that the guidelines for these committees, on which business and labor were to have parity and share a revolving chairmanship, would be forthcoming from the DAF alone.

Even more ominously, Selzner's description conjured up the image of a vast expansion of the Labor Front itself. "According to statistical count," Selzner went on, "there are 36,000 wage contracts in Germany, and therefore 36,000 wage areas. There, where necessary, we shall have to divide the committees into 'labor,' 'main' [gau], and 'subsidiary' [*Kreis*] committees, reflecting the branches and sub-branches of industry [*Reichsbetriebsgemeinschaften*]. In case of need, we'll open fully staffed offices." Here the threat was clear at the outset. Just as the well-financed DAF bureaucracy could threaten the Trustees of Labor, who lacked sufficient staff and therefore vital data for their work, so now Selzner was proposing subcommittees of committees and fully staffed offices which businessmen, already

27. Documentation on these committees is very scanty. However, one valuable source is the records of the Reichsgruppe Industrie, part of Schacht's OgW. Discussions carried out within the Socioeconomic Committee of the association about its relationship with the DAF are very revealing of DAF methods and the response of business. BAK/R12I is the source; figure on number of committees from *Berliner Tageblatt*, March 11, 1938.

28. See copy of paraphrase of Selzner's talk "Die Durchführung der Leipziger Vereinbarung im Gau Pfalz-Saar," in BAK R12I/274.

sufficiently preoccupied with running their firms, could not spare people to share in running. This gave the DAF people, who had nothing else to do but participate in such activities, powerful leverage.

Finally, in a particularly astute political move, Selzner announced that the first committees were being formed in Gau -Saar-Pfalz, that is an area part of which had just joined the Third Reich and was thus more likely to respond with enthusiasm to DAF programs than areas which had been part of the regime since the beginning. Moreover, Selzner also had tactical consideration in mind in carefully targeting the next areas in which committees were to be organized, namely Hesse-Nassau, Württemberg, Bavaria, Pomerania, and East Prussia, all provinces where industry was weakest.[29] Selzner then passed out his guidelines and left.

The Reichsgruppe Industrie, while willing to cooperate, was not at all happy with Selzner's guidelines and saw a number of problems: initiative for naming members of the committees lay with the DAF, there was no clear answer as to *who* would manage the proposed "offices", the definition of the term "bringing about a just social settlement," the ostensible goal of the committees, was open-ended and provided an obvious opportunity to implement the DAF "totality" policy. Most seriously, the fear persisted that the committees would begin to play the role of referees in the factory disputes, which, despite Selzner's denials, turned out precisely to be the case.

As the committees took shape in various parts of Germany, it became clear that the DAF was taking the initiative, that there was a great deal of confusion as to the purpose and jurisdiction of the committees, and that some of the committees were already tackling some very sensitive topics — piece work wage rates, for example.[30]

The Socioeconomic Committee of Reichsgruppe Industrie, to which a growing number of letters of protest were being directed, finally had its first meeting in October. Present among others were the director of the Reichsgruppe Industrie, Ernst Trendelenburg,

29. Some of this information is from the protocol of a follow-up meeting at Neustadt a.d. Haardt on August 14, where Kern, Selzner's man, elaborated on his boss's speech of two days before. The protocol became part of the discussion on the Socioeconomic Committee of the Reichsgruppe Industrie. BAK, 121/274.

30. See, for example, letters to the central office of Reichsgruppe Industrie from Bezirksgruppe Niedersachsen of July 22 and Bezirksgruppe Hessen of July 29, 1935. BAK, R12I/274.

former State Secretary in the Labor Ministry; Pietzsch, director of the Reichswirtshaftskammer; Pietzsch's deputy Lohmann; and Karl Seeliger, leader of the Economic Group Printing and Papermaking.[31]

Seeliger reported to the committee on the practical results of the Leipzig Agreement to date. He expressed hope that the interlocking of OgW and DAF would prevent friction, but also underscored the need for continued independence on the part of business. He made clear what business thought the labor committees should do: they should be tools for the Trustees of Labor — the "long arm of the Trustees," as he put it. As such, they should have narrow jurisdiction and infrequent meetings. The DAF, Seeliger went on, in contrast to Selzner's promises, was setting up committees to handle specific problems in the plants.

An "animated discussion" followed Seeliger's report, with general agreement that factory questions be settled in the factories and not on the committees; that committees be purely advisory and consultative, with Trustees making the real decisions; and that pedagogical and not material questions should form the agenda of the committees.

It was also reported that businessmen had had very mixed experiences with the committees. In Bavaria they had started out fairly well, while in Silesia business had been practically ignored in constituting the committees. One speaker pointed out that since the DAF was ignoring businessmen, "plant leaders" would just have to be more vigorous in inserting themselves into the process, although, given their business obligations, they were at a disadvantage vis-à-vis the full-time DAF functionaries. Moreover, they had to expect far more cooperation from the DAF than had been the case. As for Selzner, it was observed that while he was preaching harmony and cooperation as front man for the DAF, he was also ignoring a myriad of local initiatives which violated the Leipzig Agreement.

Not long after this meeting Lohmann met with Selzner to voice the willingness on the part of business to cooperate if the DAF would come halfway, especially at the local level. Selzner was conciliatory, admitting that his initial directives, which he had subsequently withdrawn, had caused a lot of confusion. He added that Ley and Schacht would take to the road in December to plump for the realization of the Leipzig Agreement.[32]

31. For the protocol of this meeting of October 18, see BAK, R12I/266. for background on Trendelenburg, see Boelcke, *Wirtschaft*, pp. 16–18, 41, 109.
32. See Lohmann memo of October 31, 1935, in BAK R12I/266.

A second meeting of the Socioeconomic Committee on December 13 witnessed Selzner as guest. He was very conciliatory, saying this time what the executives wanted to hear. Yes, the committees should function as the "lengthened arm" of the Trustees. No, not even protocols of the committee meetings should be kept, lest the impression of labor "negotiations" be created as grist for the mill of agitators. But he did keep a foot in the door as far as DAF influence on *economic* policy was concerned.

The committees should represent primarily the opportunity for "plant leaders" and "retinue" to forge personal contracts and discuss technical questions: "Engagement with actual material questions takes second place to this and should happen only after a personal relationship of trust has been established." But, the point was, it *should* happen.

From the fall of 1935 until early 1938 a myriad of letters of complaint flowed into the central offices of the Reichsgruppe Industrie, illustrating just how far apart in conception business and the DAF were with regard to the committees and just how aggresive the DAF was in imposing its definition in practice. From Brandenburg came word that Selzner was giving instructions to name committees without consulting district officials of business organizations.[33] In Schleswig-Holstein 185 committees had been formed and in Hamburg eighty-two, without business having been consulted once as to who the members should be. Nor was business informed who the members were after they had been appointed.[34] From Westphalia came the word that, while the DAF Gauwalter were being cooperative, there was confusion owing to the fact that so many people had to be named for so many committees and that there were no clear directives stipulating that business had the right to appoint the "plant leaders" to those bodies.[35] In Silesia, one report indicated, the DAF was viewing the labor committees as virtually its own organs, with DAF Amtswalter convening the committees at will and choosing the themes to be discussed.[36] A letter from Bavaria bemoaned the fact that despite all good intentions, the business side

33. See Bezirksgruppe Brandenburg of the RGI to Lohmann, November 26, 1935, in BAK, R12I/274.
34. See Bezirksgruppe Nordmark to RGI, November 26, 1935, ibid.
35. See report entitled "Bildung der Arbeitsausschüsse im Wirtschaftsbezirk Westfalen," from Bezirksgruppe Westfalen of the RGI to Lohmann of January 21, 1936, BAK, R12I/274.
36. See "Bericht über die Einführungssitzung der Arbeitsausschüsse der Gaubetriebsgemeinschaft 'Stein und Erdé-Schlesien" of December 1935, in ibid.

was seriously disadvantaged by lacking both the territorial and technical bureaucratic edifice enjoyed by the DAF.[37]

Dominating the formation of the committee also allowed the DAF to dominate the agendas. In the Kurmark, for example, the DAF set up a labor committee for the sugar industry without consulting the industry's business representatives, and installed three members whose names it did not bother to reveal. Then the committee met for two days, "reinterpreted" that section of the law which dealt with protection against illness, and then demanded that "plant leaders" subscribe to that reinterpretation by hanging signs to that effect in their factories.[38]

The Wirtschaftsgruppe Bauindustrie raised a familiar complaint that basic economic questions were being discussed in labor committees in the construction industry, including the awarding of contracts. That was clearly, the complaint went, not within their jurisdiction.[39]

In Bavaria the Labor Trustee complained that the DAF was compelling "plant leaders" to incorporate labor committee decisions into their plant regulations. Reports began to come in to the effect that the DAF was even demanding that firms put their records at the disposal of the labor committees as "data." This obviously violated necessary confidentiality.[40] As late as February 1939 the Economic Chamber for East Prussia lamented the fact that if it wanted to know what was going on in the labor committees, it had to go ask the DAF *Walter*.[41]

It was against the background of these almost constant complaints that the Reichsgruppe Industrie tried to contend with the DAF challenge, usually by reaction rather than action. To make that reaction more difficult, Ley himself issued a set of procedural rules (*Geschäftsordnung*) for the labor committees which strengthened the *de facto* dominance of the DAF. After reading those rules Seeliger wrote to Lohmann: "You are completely right. There is not a trace of common endeavor between the OgW and the DAF in these rules. . . . But it is also clear to me that one cannot undertake anything against these rules at the moment. For any move against

37. See Bezirksgruppe Bayern of the RGI to RGI of April 16, 1936, in BAK, R12I/275.
38. See Wirtschaftsgruppe Zuckerindustrie to RGI of July 14, 1936, in BAK, R12I/274.
39. In a letter to RGI of March 30, 1937. BAK, R12I/278.
40. See monthly report of the TdA of October 1937 in BAK, R43II/528; also Reichsgruppe Stein und Erden to RGI of May 23, 1936, in BAK R12I/275.
41. In a letter to RGI of February 3, 1939, in BAK, R12I/278.

these rules would immediately reach the political level and be scarcely possible in light of the fact that Dr Ley issued them personally." In light of Ley's political power, then, it was impossible to attack his rulings head on. All that was really possible, concluded Seeliger, was to place the best people they could onto the committees and orient the DAF people on the nature of the OgW. They might also "school" the "plant leaders," he noted, but that might be misinterpreted by the DAF. A pale response, indeed![42]

The lack of firm response on the part of this component of Schacht's empire demonstrated just how political the whole question had become and how the only thing men like Seeliger and Lohmann could do was to encourage their local affiliates at the grass-roots level and support the Economics Minister, Schacht, in his struggle against Ley at the highest level. This was particularly true during the years 1936 and 1937, when the Ley–Schacht battles over *Handwerk* and vocational education were at their peak.[43]

Indeed, given the one-sided initiatives of the DAF since at least early 1936 — which included the SdA activities in metal works, Ley's arbitrary rules for labor committees, his equally arbitrary guidelines for "trust council elections" (which never took place), as well as a number of local "agreements" concluded by the DAF over the heads of "plant leaders" — it was decided to form a special committee at the higher level of the Reichswirtschaftskammer, Schacht's own umbrella organization. This so-called Pietzsch Committee (after its chair) was empowered to enter into direct negotiations with Ley and his men, Selzner and Hupfauer, to "clarify" matters. As a result, the Socioeconomic Committee of the RGI fell into what Lohmann called a "Sleeping Beauty sleep."[44] It was clear that the battle with Ley could only be joined at a higher level.

But the level was apparently still not high enough for Ley. Ensuing discussions got nowhere because Ley would not allow himself to be placed on a level with Pietzsch, who was "only" director of the Reich Economic Chamber. Only Schacht would do as an opponent. As it was, Pietzsch and his committee found themselves entangled in the same old party-state thicket as everyone else.[45] In

42. See letter of February 11, 1936, in BAK, R12I/274.
43. General agreement on these points emerges from the correspondence. See, for example, Guth (RGI) to Lohmann of July 29 and Seeliger to Bieske, n.d. but after September 1936, in BAK, R12I/267.
44. Lohmann to Guth, n.d. but early 1937 R12I/267.
45. See Pietzsch report to a subcommittee of the Socioeconomic Committee of February 2, 1937 in BAK, R12I/267.

fall 1937 Seeliger announced the dissolution of the Socioeconomic Committee entirely. At its last meeting he bemoaned the fact that the OgW did not occupy the position it should within the regime, because it simply lacked the right political contacts. Moreover, business also did not put forward a united front, which was disastrous since tensions at the upper levels of party and government, particularly as they had been manifested in Ley's Performance Competition, were likely "to be fought out on the backs of businessmen. This would mean serious damage to our prestige."

What, if any, were the solutions to these problems? Several were presented in the ensuing discussion, including forging political contacts, unfolding propaganda activity, restoring discipline to business ranks, and not leaving progressive social measures "to the other side" — meaning the DAF. But even these were compromised by admonitions for caution. In the end these business leaders were remarkably bereft of ideas. As one of them put it, little of a practical nature could be done other that "setting up a staff of wandering preachers in the land to enlighten the plant leaders as to their rights and duties" — so powerful was the political momentum of the DAF during its "populist years."[46]

One year later, soon after Ley presented his sensational 1938 law drafts, Pietzsch sent a long memorandum to Lammers in the Reich Chancellory with a request for a conversation with Hitler. It revealed with surprising frankness business's position vis-à-vis the DAF.[47] Basically, the memo was an analysis of the German economy and the roles that business, government and the party should play in it. The Third Reich, he argued, was not a system of state socialism; the state should limit itself to directives and controls. To do so, however, demanded an economic apparatus — comprised of autonomous business organizations and run by an "economic czar," who himself should be a businessman. (This was essentially Schacht's position as well.) Within the context of this proposal, Pietzsch turned to the DAF as a major fly in the ointment. The DAF, he wrote, was "neither an organization of self-administration [i.e. business] nor an official administrative office [i.e. government], but rather an apparatus with its own sovereignty." It was all right

46. See Aktennotiz of September 30, 1937, on the last meeting of the committee on September 16 in BAK, R12I/268.
47. See letter of June 22, 1938, with memo entitled, "Wirtschaftslenkung durch den Staat," in BAK, R43II/547, pp. 143–167.

for the DAF to play a social role by constructing *Volk* communitarian institutions like the KdF. "However, insofar as the DAF lays claim to influencing the shaping of the terms of labor and production, it is interfering in the technical tasks of political economy."

Pietzsch pointed in particular to the labor committees, which he denied were true organs of self-administration, "because the representatives of management and retinue in a given branch [of industry] are not brought together there." Rather, he continued, "it is a matter of individuals which the DAF itself has appointed." What Ley really had in mind was for the conducting of social policy to be in the hands of his Amtswalter, "namely the members of the labor committees who meet in secret session." In light of this, it was vital that the relationship between the DAF and the state be clarified and that that part of the DAF which dealt with social policy be brought under the control of the state.

Pietzsch concluded his report by again referring to the sovereign nature of the Labor Front:

> Resulting from that is a persistent turmoil in all offices which have any connection with the DAF, who do not know if they are dealing with a representative of the party, of an agency, an autonomous business organization or the representative of all those who labor in the German economy, because the DAF appears in all these forms depending on what a given [DAF] office decides is expedient.

Lammers showed the memo to Hitler who, according to Lammers, "considered the solution to the problem 'Labor Front' to be urgent" and asked Lammers to get in touch with Hess, Göring, and Funk.[48] None of this deterred Ley, however, from continuing to use the labor committees to infiltrate the business world. In fact, on November 1, 1938, Dr Miltrup of the DAF office in charge of the committees, announced that those committees, which now numbered 4,000 were to be charged with four tasks: "raising economic performance through measures in the plants"; vocational training and education of adults; general health maintenance; and labor integration of German women. He promised a close look at the whole labor system and then "by means of the DAF to show the 'plant leaders' how they can make their firms more viable." Typi-

48. See internal memo accompanying letter of July 6, 1938, from Lammers to Pietzsch, ibid., pp. 168–9.

cally, the plan was announced first through the press.[49]

The experience which one part of Schacht's empire had with the DAF illustrated several important points. First, that the labor committees were an important mechanism by which the DAF tried to infiltrate the factories and bend the business world to its will. Secondly, that business took these depredations with deadly seriousness and was quite intimidated — almost to the point of paralysis — especially at the middle and lower levels. This was not the case perhaps with the great Ruhr barons, but these men were a small fraction of businessmen in general. Thirdly, DAF successes were blunted because the organization lacked an intelligent concept as to what it really was up to other than (1) controlling and pleasing the worker and simultaneously (2) aggrandizing its own power in the areas of economic and social policy. All the language of *Volksgemeinschaft* in the world could not get around this basic defect. This lack of concept was exacerbated by the often mind-boggling incompetence at the lower levels of the DAF. The local DAF Walter might have been an aggressive, opportunistic fanatic, but he usually lacked anything approaching expertise in anything having to do with business.

All this is beautifully illustrated in one of those many letters which were directed to Seeliger and the RGI from Max Renker, a small businessman in the Ruhr.[50] Renker wrote about how businessmen were intimidated by the DAF and how their "hearts sunk into their shoes" when confronted by a DAF functionary, and how they must be enlightened to have self-confidence and "backbone." However, he said, turning to the DAF itself:

> On the other side it must be said that everything is not as it should be with the DAF either, particularly at its lower echelons. The human material which staffs these offices is in every way inadequate. What's knocking about there is for the most part very young people between 20 and 30 without any experience in factory, never mind sociopolitical, matters. If a useful man appears among them, he's soon pulled out, because he is needed more in a more important post. Their intellectual armory consists of memorized phrases which, because they haven't been worked through, remain unconvincing. Independent ideas, or even the inkling of an independent understanding of things, are not in evidence. The result is that these people are not taken seriously by either plant

49. See *Berliner Tageblatt*, no. 517, November 1, 1938, with story entitled "DAF plant Betriebslenkung."
50. See Max Renker to Seeliger of August 29, 1936, in BAK, R12I/274.

leaders or retinue, that the strong words they use 'ring false' in peoples's ears and that they are only successful in pushing through their directives because they have the great power of the Labor Front behind them.

While the widespread formation of labor committees represented one "front," where the initiative was particularly apparent on the grass-roots level, action on the two closely related "fronts" of vocational education and the trades stemmed mostly from Ley, armed with his all-purpose October 24, 1934 decree, which gave the DAF the right to dominate vocational education as well as the formidable apparatus of Carl Arnhold and his Dinta, now incorporated into the DAF itself.[51]

Ley's tactics were clever. Initially, the DAF called for a division of labor, with the chambers and business handling the technical side of vocational education and the DAF assuming responsibility for *Betreuung* and *Menschenführung* (human leadership). In principle this was an arrangement which the trades and industry could readily accept. After all, the DAF had valuable information and expertise to offer and its ideological appeal to workers promised to create both a more compliant and a more productive labor force. The problem came in defining terms. It was an old Ley (and Nazi) technique to use vague terminology which lent itself to a wide range of interpretations. Indeed, *Menschenführung* had a very elastic meaning which soon was stretched to encompass Ley's claims to totality. What he really had in mind was a jurisdiction which included "the ideological and vocational-technical and hygienic *Betreuung* of the laboring person" — inside and outside the plant.

Soon DAF local people were proceeding on just this assumption. And soon complaints were flooding into the office of Albert Pietzsch, head of the Reichswirtschaftskammer, and — more importantly — across the desk of Schacht himself. Pietzsch, continually suspicious of the DAF, asserted that any takeover of vocational education by that organization would "for certain be condemned to failure."[52] Schacht, for his part, left no doubt as to his position. Vocational education should be left in the hands of business and government.

Unfortunately for Schacht, Ley had already got a foot in the door.

51. Important for the following material are Theo Wolsing *Untersuchungen zur Berufsausbildung im Dritten Reich* (Kastelbaum, Aloys Henn Verlag, 1977); Rolf Seubert, *Berufserziehung und Nationalsozialismus* (Weinheim and Basel, Beltz Verlag, 1977); and Schweitzer, *Nazifizierung*.

52. Wolsing, *Untersuchungen*, p. 710.

As early as February 9, 1934, he issued a proclamation calling upon businesses to enrol more apprentices and offering the Dinta program as a basis for training.[53] Schmitt, the Economics Minister at that time, inattentively responded in a directive on February 21 promising action and foolishly calling upon the DAF (and the Hitler Youth) to contribute toward alleviating the shortage of labor.[54] Ley leaped at the opportunity to use the Dinta as his opening wedge to get into vocational education and hence into the plants. Soon DAF "advisers" were interfering in a wide variety of plants, chambers, guilds, and other organizations, activities which, in part, would lead to the Leipzig Agreement of March 1935. Schacht, whose idea the agreement had been, was much more determined than his predecessor to stop Ley. In September 1935 he tried to counter the Dinta campaign by officially designating another organization, the Datsch, as his official pedagogical advisory body for technical education.[55] Undeterred, Ley redoubled his efforts in 1936. On July 26, inundated with complaints from business, Schacht felt constrained to complain to Ley about the activities of the DAF Office for Vocational Education and Plant Leadership, which was trying to "completely grab for itself" the task of vocational education and "to raise the claim of totality in this area, which I must reject decisively." Schacht even suggested that the Arnhold office, as the embodiment of the DAF's "efforts toward exclusivity", be dissolved. Ley feigned a readiness to cooperate.[56] In his response two days later he said, "I want to work with you! Because of that I also want to negotiate with you! I am at your disposal at any time and I have no more anxious desire than that clarity finally be achieved."[57]

Ley's lack of sincerity in this plea became apparent at the beginning of September, when Ley issued yet another order, based on the by now notorious October 1934 Hitler decree, reasserting Ley's claim to exclusivity in vocational training.[58] This training he defined as "everything which is necessary to enable the working person to fill his position in the sense of the performance community and the furtherance of performance."

53. See *Der Deutsche*, no. 33.
54. See Seubert, *Berufserziehung*, p. 103.
55. Ibid., p. 107.
56. See BAK, R41 (Krohn)/5009.
57. In BAK, NS22, vorl. 561.
58. Quoted in Schweitzer, *Nazifizierung*, p. 190; also Seubert, *Berufserziehung*, pp. 106–7.

But Schacht was a determined opponent who was not about to take Ley's claim to totality lying down. He was well aware that this was a critical front in the general battle to keep the DAF from becoming a major force in the economy. He knew that control of vocational education and apprenticeship programs would give the DAF entrée into the vital area of wage policy and the economy in general. He was, to be sure, ready to compromise at all times, as he assured Ley early in 1937. He had no objection to DAF involvement in vocational education as long as it was limited to "ideological-political education." But Ley would accept no such limitation.[59]

As the competition between the two men heightened in 1937, both had recourse to the court of last resort: Hitler. Schacht's complaints to Hitler resulted in April in a Hitler decree commissioning the Economics Minister to produce as soon as possible a draft law on vocational education in trade and commerce, drawing on other ministries and party organizations, including the DAF, for consultation. In the meantime, there was to be no public discussion of the matter.[60]

Undeterred, Ley produced his own report to Hitler. In glowing colors he described in detail all the various ways in which the DAF had been active in vocational education since the Nazi takeover. Most impressively, he bragged of the 5,000 teaching engineers who had been trained by the DAF and who were now themselves training apprentices in 881 workshops all over the land. "A generous program of vocational education," Ley tried to convince Hitler, "is inconceivable without the powerful organization of the German Labor Front and its motor force." Accompanying Ley's report was the draft of a law on vocational education.[61]

Ley's initiative produced a "battle of the law drafts" between the DAF and Schacht which lasted into the fall until the latter's resignation in November, with Ley trying to get a general law passed which gave DAF control and Schacht drafting complex legal documents which would have left control in the hands of business and industry. Ultimately, neither side won. No comprehensive law on vocational education was ever promulgated (although one was finally drafted in 1942). More decisive in the end were the exigencies

59. See Schacht to Ley, March 25, 1937, in BAK, R43II/274a.
60. See Adolf Hitler decree of April 26, 1937, in BAK, R43II/274a.
61. On this letter see Wolsing, *Untersuchungen*, pp. 718–19; also Schweitzer, *Nazifizierung*, p. 167.

posed first by the Four-Year Plan and then the war itself, which acted to change the emphasis of DAF activities and bring it closer to business and government.[62] In the meantime, the battle over vocational education merged with the other "front" in the Ley–Schacht struggle: that for the control of the trades in Germany.

Middle-class business and trades organizations — above all the Kampfbund under von Renteln — had been among the strongest supporters of the Nazi movement during the early 1930s and fully expected the new regime to favor middle-class small business. This entailed closing department stores, allowing crafts and small business a greater autonomy, particularly in pricing, honoring and favoring crafts and small business in governmental economic policy, and in general terms, giving substance to the corporativist spirit which animated these organizations.

After some initial successes, however, it became clear that the trades and small business lacked the clout of big industry. Besides, continuing modernization and rationalization in the economy made many of their ideas seem hopelessly antediluvian. Government and the party responded accordingly, each trying to absorb trades. Ley took over the Kampfbund, for instance, in August 1933 and replaced it with NS-Hago and NS-GHG. Like the NSBO, however, these two organizations also soon became moribund after Ley turned against corporativism as a guiding idea. Ley did, however, keep his finger in the trades pie by creating the "Reichsbetriebsgemeinschaft" (later Fachamt), "German Handicraft," in the DAF. His interest stemmed in part from the fact that handicraft played an important role in training skilled labor, but also as a springboard for playing an important role in the general economy. After a brief, abortive attempt in the summer of 1935 to create chambers of labor as a parallel to the business chambers of commerce, Ley turned his attention to trades.[63]

In the meantime, the traditional guild organizations, now dominated by Nazis, tried to accommodate themselves to the new regime. January 26, 1934, for example, was proclaimed the "historic day" of German labor. Schmidt-Wiesbaden was appointed Reich Handicraft Leader (as well as head of the DAF RBG "Handwerk") and Heinrich Schild as general secretary of the Estate of Handicraft.

62. Wolsing, *Untersuchungen*, deals with the twilight struggle over vocational education, pp. 723–39.

63. See Schweitzer, *Big Business*, p. 147.

Both men would soon be caught in the force-field between party and state.

Schacht, aware of the importance of the handicraft organizations, gradually drew them into his OgW, creating, as one of the twelve Reichsgruppen, "Handwerk." Within this context, Schacht, using existing law, established a hierarchical system of trades guilds with compulsory membership, civil service criteria, and powers of discipline. He also established trades chambers as instruments for controlling the guilds.[64] Ley was not long in responding and quickly a DAF Amt "Deutsches Handwerk" paralleled Schacht's Reichsgruppe Handwerk.[65] One of the first skirmishes came over the firing by Schacht of Schild, who in a plaintive letter to the Reich Chancellory indicated that he had "stumbled into the eternal dilemma between state leadership, party leadership, and Labor Front leadership."[66]

During the ensuing months the DAF busily infiltrated the trades organizations with an eye to taking them over. Indeed, at the national conference of the trades organizations in Frankfurt in June 1936, the DAF pretty much dominated the proceedings. Shortly after the meeting, Ley gave Schmidt-Wiesbaden a set of plans for integrating the guilds into the Labor Font. (The man refused and eventually resigned all his offices.)[67] Schacht reacted sharply to Ley's pressures. In a letter to the DAF leader he warned that Ley's public remarks during the trades conference to the effect that "the trades are increasingly being absorbed into the DAF" could easily be misunderstood. Moreover, Schacht went on, talk of an "agreement" with the Reichshandwerksmeister (Schmidt-Wiesbaden) by which the tasks of Reichsgruppe Handwerk would be taken over by the DAF, were "empty rumors," since no one under Schacht's authority had the authority to make agreements with anyone. In the meantime, Ley's moves were creating great turmoil in trades circles "making the fulfillment of my economic and political tasks considerably more difficult."

Schacht continued by denying the legal viability of what he termed Hitler's "expression" of October 24, 1934 (the decree on which Ley was basing his claim to totality), but kept the door open to cooperation "with the provision that there can be no talk about

64. See law of January 18, 1935, in Broszat, *The Hitler State*, pp. 162–3.
65. See Mason, *Sozialpolitik*, p. 197.
66. See Schild to Willuhn of July 24, 1934, in BAK, R43II/273, pp. 129–30.
67. See Schweitzer, *Big Business*, p. 148.

[DAF] exclusivity and that the prevailing institutions of industry, trades, and chambers under all circumstances retain their effectiveness."[68]

Ley's response was to raise the leadership question. Schmidt-Wiesbaden, he said, was both Reichshandwerksmeister and, through co-option, head of the DAF RBG "Handwerk," in which latter capacity he was Ley's subordinate. So that "Just as you demand that he carry out your orders, I demand that he carry out mine; and when you say that you would, if necessary relieve him of his duties, then I can say the same thing. You must realize, Dr Schacht, that this state is run by National Socialists."[69]

This exchange led to another brief truce between the two men, by which they agreed, given the urgency created by the newly proclaimed Four-Year Plan, to cooperate and to jointly observe the stipulations of the Leipzig Agreement.[70]

But the truce did not last long. Early in 1937 Ley launched a major offensive in the area of trades. On February 4, after a conversation with Schacht, Ley wrote the Economics Minister a letter hinting at a major step. He made a recommendation:

> I would dissolve the 16,000 local guilds, because they are totally worthless and only pose a stumbling block to our mutual cooperation; because — this is completely clear — these local guilds have no tasks whatever, neither sociopolitical nor economic. They are totally caught up in outdated customs . . . and, by the way, represent the last islands where our opponents, critics, and carpers can carry out their destructive work.

He also pointed out critically how Schacht's subordinates were always falling back on the laws, as if the law prevented the DAF from "taking care of" the trades. One of them even referred to a law from the year 1870! "Well, I am of the opinion that the Führer's order of October 24, 1934, is at least as valid as such outdated laws."[71]

Several weeks later, on February 20, Ley went public with his offensive in the usual manner — a proclamation in the press; first, in one Berlin newspaper, then all over Germany. He announced what amounted to a complete takeover of the trades. All masters, journey-

68. See Schacht to Ley of June 26, 1936, in BAK, R41 (Krohn)/5009.
69. See Ley to Schacht of July 20, 1936, in BAK, NS22, vorl. 561.
70. See announcement of November 5, 1936, in BAK, R43II, vorl. 649.
71. See Ley to Schacht of February 4, 1937, in BAK, NS10/64, pp. 26–9.

men and apprentices would now be encompassed in the DAF organization "Deutsches Handwerk." The DAF would now supervise training and testing, partly via the mechanism of the Skills Competition. It would open vocational schools in the various crafts; already it was about to take over the famous Reich Baker's School. It would supervise all public occasions involving trades and develop new ceremonies to celebrate advancement up the ladder to master. It would incorporate the building trades into the DAF housing and settlement plans. It would design new flags and symbols to replace the old guild ones. It would reintroduce the tradition of "wandering apprentice" and build hostels to accommodate them.[72]

Schacht reacted, first by writing to Hess, Ley's party rival, urging him to counter an order by Ley to the Gauleiter to expel any artisan from the party who refused to lay down his guild office at the behest of the DAF.[73]

Getting no response from Hess, Schacht used his powers as Economics Minister. Since Ley's virtual takeover was in violation of the law — the government was in charge of administering trades training, testing, and licensing — Schacht asked the *Reichsstatthalter* to intervene with the police![74]

This even caught Hitler's attention. In an audience with Schacht a week later the Führer assured his Economics Minister that he really had the authority granted to him under the law.

Ley apparently disagreed, for he was in the process of organizing mass meetings in various cities to demonstrate against the existing trades legislation. In Berlin the Grand Master of guilds was instructed to send graduating apprentices to the DAF ceremony — not to that of the trades chambers which traditionally presided. Schacht also reported this to Hitler.[75]

But Hitler played his usual role of referee. In a letter to both men he urged them to compose their differences and find a mutually acceptable solution.[76] This only intensified the rivalry. Both men continued to bombard the Reich Chancellory with memoranda justifying their own positions. Despite Hitler's decree to the contrary, both also went public, seeking to bring their message to the broadest possible audience.

72. Text in Schweitzer, *Nazifizierung*, p. 160.
73. Schacht to Hess of March 3, 1937, in BAK, R43II/274a.
74. See Schweitzer, *Nazifizierung*, p. 161.
75. See Schacht to Hitler of March 18, 1937, in BAK, R43II/274a.
76. See Lammers to Schacht and Ley of March 23, 1937, in ibid.

It was within this context that the conflict between the two men reached its apogee in early May 1937. On May 11 the Chambers for Industry and Commerce as well as for Trades were to stage a combined meeting at the Sportpalast in Berlin, on the occasion of which thousands of apprentices would receive their journeymen certificates. The ceremony was cleverly timed, for Ley was traveling in Italy and thus ostensibly could not interfere. Schacht meant to address the meeting, because, as he put it, "In light of the depicted conflict it was clear that my presence would have a demonstrative importance against the German Labor Front." But Ley heard about the meeting and prevailed upon Hitler to prohibit it, which Schacht found out about just the evening before the rally was to take place. The next morning he rushed to the Reich Chancellory to get Hitler to change his mind. The dictator refused initially, claiming that Ley predicted unrest at the meeting. Schacht replied that the only unrest would come from the DAF. Finally, under the threat of Schacht's resignation, Hitler relented and reinstated the meeting at the last minute.[77]

For the rest of the year, until Schacht's resignation in November, the struggle continued in what might be called the "battle of the legal drafts," as both Ley and Schacht had their staffs draw up complex, paragraph-rich drafts of laws for Hitler's approval.[78]

As usual, Ley also fought out the struggle on the local and regional basis. In many parts of the country local DAF functionaries called meetings to announce the takeover of the trades organizations.[79] Ley himself put strong pressure on the state trades leaders to practise their own *Gleichschaltung*. A good example of this was the case of the Landeshandwerksmeister Schramm of Schleswig-Holstein. Under pressure, Schramm had promised Ley in the summer of 1936 that he would bring the trades organizations of his state into the DAF. Schramm apparently did not keep his promise and later denied that he had made it in the first place, perhaps because he had become Schacht's choice to replace Schmidt-Wiesbaden as Reichshandwerksmeister. This infuriated Ley, who also believed

77. See Hjalmar Schacht, *Abrechnung mit Hitler* (Hamburg, Michaelis Verlag, 1949), p. 52; Wolsing, *Untersuchungen*, p. 715; Seubert, *Berufserziehung*, p. 113.
78. For details, see Wolsing, *Untersuchungen*, pp. 717–25.
79. See, for example, complaint from Fachgruppe Lederwaren und Kofferindustrie, Hessen-Nassau to Wirtschaftsgruppe Lederindustrie of June 10, 1937, in BAK, R12I/275.

that Schramm had been informing to the Economics Ministry. The case led to a personal altercation between Schacht and Ley in which Ley expressed surprise that the Economics Minister availed himself of spies in his (Ley's) meetings. Schacht replied coolly that he had no spies, rather that "creatures from the party brought him these things."

In a long letter to Hitler, Ley related this incident and spoke out against Schramm's candidacy as Reichshandwerksmeister. Schramm had disobeyed his commands, had spread lies, and was an adherent of Othmar Spann's corporativist ideas. Although Ley had had his own candidate, now "after mature reflecion," he decided that the Führer be asked to appoint no one to the post. "The leadership of the trades has been assured through the DAF. The DAF has gradually conquered such a leadership position in German trades that today a Reichshandwerksmeister can be regarded as completely superfluous."[80]

In the end, however, Ley did not triumph in this area either. As with several other "fronts" in his battles with the ministries, the exigencies of the Four-Year Plan and preparation for war undermined his efforts and diverted his drives. And it did not help that Ley had overreached himself. At just about the time when Schacht was about to resign in late 1937, Ley's other party problems caught up with him. Hess finally, months after the fact, acquiesced in Schacht's request that he issue instructions to the Gauleiter to stop disciplinary proceedings against leaders of the trades organizations who had resigned from the DAF on Schacht's orders. This deprived Ley of one weapon. At the same time, Schwarz, the party treasurer, began proceedings against a number of DAF functionaries for corruption and embezzlement, which finally gave Schwarz a foot in the door as far as auditing Ley's books were concerned. It was also a personal rebuke of a sort for Ley, that Göring, the head of the Four-Year Plan, named Schramm Reichshandwerksmeister after all in January 1938. But most importantly, the preparations for war proved the viability of the traditional system of vocational education, which was then integrated into the war economy. The DAF would still have an important role to play in this area, but not the dominating one. Under Göring's influence the new Economics Minister, Walter Funk, issued a proclamation in February 1939 basically leaving training, testing, and licensing in the hands of the

80. See Ley to Lammers of February 10, 1937, in BAK, NS10/64, pp. 20–5.

"plant leaders" and the OgW.[81] It was symptomatic of this development that in 1941 the DAF Office for Vocational Education and Plant Leadership would be absorbed by a Reichsinstitut under the direction of the Economics Ministry. Arnhold himself briefly left his DAF position to take over an office in the Economics Ministry. He briefly returned to the DAF, but in 1942 in the wake of differences with Ley, he retired from all his posts.[82]

The labor committee, trades and vocational education battles represented three "fronts" in a much larger theater of war between Schacht and Ley, that is one to determine whether or not the DAF would succeed in achieving its goal of "totality" in seizing control of social and economic policy in Germany. Both men understood clearly what was at stake, a fact which emerges from their correspondence, despite the polite assurances and expressions of desire to cooperate. Though their exchanges usually focused on the specifics of vocational education or trades, always lurking in the background were Schacht's fear of Ley's "totality" claims and Ley's attempts to "interpret" the Leipzig Agreement in such a way as to further his gigantomania.

As early as summer 1935, Schacht was so angry with Ley's attempt to call a meeting of the Reich Labor and Economic Council, a body which Schacht hoped to dominate, that he wrote committee members that "the convening is meaningless, because the Reich leader of the DAF by himself has no authority to do so." He went on to ask them to "in the future consign all communications of the Labor Front to the files without response" unless they had to do with a person's individual membership in the DAF or unless they had been countersigned by Schacht.[83]

In a particularly acid exchange between the two men in summer 1936, Schacht characterized DAF activities in trade and industry relative to vocational training as an attempt "to raise the claim of totality in this area, which I must reject with decisiveness." After reciting infractions, Schacht went on to say: "After all these developments I must emphatically request that you see to it that in DAF circles subordinate to you attacks against the [OgW] and the invasion of my area of responsibility be stopped completely."

To Ley's claim that the OgW was not really necessary and represented a clique of reactionaries, Schacht observed that the

81. For details, see Schweitzer, *Nazifizierung*, pp. 165ff., 172.
82. See Seubert, *Berufserziehung*, pp. 117–18; Wolsing, *Untersuchungen*, p. 34.
83. Schacht letter of August 21, 1935, in BAK, R41 (Krohn)/5008.

OgW was "an absolute necessity in order for the Economics Minister to carry out his assigned tasks . . . and that this kind of organization of businessmen was indispensable to a war economy."[84]

In his reply, Ley asserted that "secret forces" from the old employers' associations and from circles around Othmar Spann (Ley's favorite scapegoat) "in a word, all enemies of Young Germany" were trying to fashion OgW into "an instrument against the German Labor Front." Moreover, what Schacht had called Hitler's "expression" of October 24, 1934, was to Ley an order which was "just as sacred and irrevocable as any law that the Führer signed."

Ley went on to suggest that Schacht originally agreed with him that the "Leipzig Agreement was viewed by you as by us all as a step on the way to integrating the OgW into the DAF." He again attacked the OgW: "I object to the fact . . . that in your OgW the old employers associations with their tendency to class conflict are reviving"; and then in a threat which conjured up the old spectre of DAF as union: "If there is to be an organization of employers, then one must also tolerate an organization of employees. What that means you can judge for yourself. The economic battles of the former Marxist-liberal system would be the purest child's play next to the economic battle that would break out between the German Labor Front and the OgW."

In conclusion, Ley observed that Schacht had inadvertently sent him a copy rather than the original of his letter, which revealed that many offices and individuals were in on the correspondence. "I myself don't like to fight out differences in front of a large public, but your methods compel me to make available a copy of my reply to you to the same circles."[85]

Both men acted as well as snarled. Schacht countered Ley's big initiatives in the area of Skills and Performance Competition by issuing a [futile] decree prohibiting all factories from taking part unless the OgW could at least share the right to establish criteria and set standards.[86] The central offices of the Reichsgruppe Industrie phoned its branch offices alerting them that the guidelines for carrying out the Performance Competition "aroused concerns about the future," while Pietzsch tried to foil the competition entirely by telling his offices that the report deadline had been postponed.[87]

84. Schacht to Ley of June 26, 1936, in BAK, R41 (Krohn)/5009.
85. Ley to Schacht of July 20, 1937, in BAK, NS22, vorl. 561.
86. See *Sopade*, 1937, p. 1282.
87. Hupfauer to Ley of August 6, 1937, in BAK, NS22, vorl. 838.

During his tenure of office, Schacht rather successfully, at least at the top level, defended the prerogatives of his office and prevented a DAF victory in the areas of trades and vocational education — but these areas had indeed been vulnerable. And only the formidable power of government and big business, both of which Schacht represented, was sufficient to frustrate Ley's ambitions to get virtual control of social and economic policy.[88] Schacht indeed had been "Ley's most embittered opponent, the most consistent critic of DAF efforts to have a say in all areas of economic and social policy."[89]

On November 26, 1937, Schacht resigned after serious difficulties with the regime. He did not want to overheat the economy with all-out defense spending, nor did he agree with the regime's goal of autarky. Rather, he wanted a stable currency and an export-oriented economy geared to the world market.[90] With that, Ley's most important opponent was gone and Schacht's departure may have encouraged the DAF leader to take the most daring step of all with the DAF draft laws of early 1938. But before we examine that démarche, it is important to examine briefly the other "fronts" — between Ley and the Labor Minister, Seldte.

As we have seen, the war between Ley and Schacht involving important aspects of socio-economic policy was fought out on specific fronts vulnerable to Ley's attacks: the trades, vocational education, and the labor committees. Likewise, the Ley–Seldte rivalry, which involved related and overlapping issues, had its dramatic fronts, the two most dramatic, as we have seen, being wage policy and general incursions into the jurisdiction of the Trustees for Labor (and thus the Labor Ministry) and social insurance. Like the Ley–Schacht struggle, this one also reached its apogee during the radical years 1936 to 1938, and was fought with the same weapons.

As we have noted, Ley, with the huge union pension funds under his control, had been casting a covetous eye from the outset on public funds and had developed an ideological rationale for putting these funds under DAF control: the "unitary" insurance plan for all Germans. After initially being outmaneuvered by Seldte in 1933 and 1934, Ley struck back dramatically in December 1935. On December 4 he made a speech in which he said, "We must demand that

88. See Adelheid von Saldern, *Mittelstand im 'Dritten Reich' Handwerker-Einzelhändler-Bauern* (Frankfurt, New York, Campus Verlag), p. 30.
89. Mason, *Sozialpolitik*, p. 248.
90. See Broszat, *The Hitler State*, p. 300.

social insurance in its current form with respect to its social commitment to the individual be recast and built completely anew. Reforms will not help any, since that which we have today is completely broke and bankrupt. It has no value any more."[91] Ley slyly linked his program to raising the workers' living standards by suggesting that while formal wages were not supposed to be raised, that real wages would go up, since his social insurance plan could do the job with lower premiums. To demonstrate this, he produced a plan worked out in his Institute for Labor Science.[92]

This represented a direct challenge to Seldte and the Labor Ministry (RAM), and Seldte responded several days later with a protest to Hitler which characterized Ley's plans as "unreasonable in form and highly dangerous in substance." As usual, Hitler declined to intervene and instructed the two to compose their differences.[93]

The two sides came together on March 5, 1936, in a conversation involving Ley, Seldte, and Krohn. Seldte complained again about Ley's speech, and the DAF leader replied that he had not meant it as an attack, rather he "just wanted to keep the ball rolling." Ley then presented his own simplified "unitary" plan, which he contended would lower premiums by 20 per cent. Neither officials reacted to the substance of the plan but did warn Ley that his prediction of the bankruptcy of social insurance would cause great unrest among the workers. "Two years ago government and party had emphasized to the workers that social insurance had been rescued by the intervention of Adolf Hitler's government. Now Dr Ley is announcing that it is broke. What should the worker believe?" Apparently, Ley had no reply. He quickly changed the subject and laid out his housing and settlement plans. In a clumsy attempt to drive a wedge between the two ministries, Ley suggested that Schacht was willing to provide funds for the program.[94]

Over the next year, Ley continued his agitation to get his insurance plans accepted, pressing RAM from several directions. One of them involved an attempt to play Trojan horse, a favorite trick in Nazi Germany. Selzner tried in vain to get himself appointed

91. Quoted in Teppe "Sozialpolitik", p. 238.
92. See Erdmann (RAM) internal office memo of December 5, 1935, in BAK, R41 (Krohn)/5014.
93. See Seldte to Hitler of December 10 in BAK, R43II/401; and Lammers to Seldte of December 24 in BAK, R41 (Krohn)/Akte DAF, vol. 1.
94. See two office memos: Engel's of March 5 and Krohn's of April 9, 1936 in BAK, R41 (Krohn)/5009.

Ministerial Director in RAM in order to better "coordinate" the activities of DAF and the ministry. The ministry, hard-pressed, defended its prerogatives. In memo after memo it tried to demonstrate the impracticability of Ley's schemes. These made little impression on Ley whose interests were political and not actuarial or fiduciary.[95]

The struggle continued through 1938 and into the last prewar year with many a discussion between Ley and ministry officials to no avail. Krohn sought help where he could, even turning to Bormann and Hess for help. Bormann was no friend of Ley's, but his position did not coincide with that of Seldte either, so that he was little comfort. Indeed, the request only infuriated Ley, who accused Krohn of "playing off one party office against another."[96]

In early 1939 the struggle took a turn which benefited Ley and the DAF: Göring, head of the Four-Year Plan, who had frustrated Ley in trades matters, empowered him now to form a committee which would concern itself with "health care and old-age insurance" and develop a plan to that end. This was a breakthrough. Never before had a party man — rather than a high government official — chaired such a committee. Ley was quickly at hand with his comprehensive plan — already printed — which he called "Der deutsche Volksschutz" (German People's Protection), and he presented it at the first meeting of the committee on March 16.[97] The plan was so outside the realm of financial feasibility that the ministry officials present listened half incredulously, half angrily. Ley would not even permit discussion but demanded written responses instead.

Krohn sent a cost analysis of Ley's plan in great detail, but received no answer. He also mobilized insurance companies and business and got them to reject Ley's plan and stand behind the position of the ministry, which was communicated to Ley in mid-May 1939. Basically, it rejected Ley's plan because it rested on a "foundation of false estimates" and was "full of deficiencies."[98]

Ley responded in kind. "I assume," he wrote to Seldte, "that you yourself did not compose the report included with your letter and

95. See, for example, memo from Dobbernack of January 1, and Krohn of May 3, 1937, in ibid.
96. See Krohn memo of June 29, 1937, in ibid.; Teppe relates the story, in "Sozialpolitik," p. 241.
97. See Teppe, "Sozialpolitik," p. 242–3.
98. See "Stellungnahme zu dem Vorschlag von Staatsrat Dr Robert Ley 'Der Deutsche Volksschutz," in BAK, R41 (Krohn)/5012; Teppe, "Sozialpolitik," p. 243.

were not informed about the negotiations which preceded [it]. Otherwise, you could not have made such errors as crop up in the report." Ley went on to defend his plan, which was originally presented, he indicated, in very tentative form, but in the meantime had been worked out in detail. The Labor Ministry did not know this, he suggested, because Krohn had shown such a lack of interest that Ley had stopped inviting him to working sessions. Moreover, Seldte and his ministry had "rejected any renewal in this area."[99]

Seldte angrily denied the charge: "How you can make such an assertion is beyond me!"[100] But Ley clearly had the weight of initiative on his side. That very summer, at the behest of Ley, who had been after him for years, and Göring, Krohn was relieved of his duties. For years he had not been a party member; he had become one only in January 1938 as a result of a Hitler decree; but in the end even Hitler's reservations about firing such a valuable official were not up to Ley's and Göring's pressure.[101] As the "front" between Ley and Seldte over social insurance continued in late summer, the war broke out. The debate would continue into the war, with a Ley victory; but under very different circumstances than in peacetime.

If Ley's social insurance plans were, in part, an indirect way to resolve the price–wage problem, the solution of which was so important in preserving the credibility of the DAF, the DAF leader did not hesitate to tackle that situation directly either, as his aforementioned letter of August 15, 1935, to Hitler illustrated. It was in 1936 and subsequent years, however, that Ley posed the most direct challenge to Seldte and his ministry in this area. On the local level, the DAF functionaries through their incursions into the plants were constantly challenging the authority of the Trustees of Labor, and hence that of Seldte as well. It is against the background of these constant, daily activities that Ley mounted a sustained attack on the Labor Ministry, casting doubt on its authority in matters of social policy and trying to rob it of its jurisdiction.

Typical was Ley's letter of September 5, 1936, to Seldte.[102] Opening with a criticism of RAM's failure to keep rents down, Ley launched into a general critique of wage policy, particularly the failure to improve wage income. The DAF had taken the lead in this area, Ley contended, in the form of vacation pay, Christmas

99. Ley to Seldte of May 29, 1939, in BAK, R41 (Krohn)/5012.
100. Seldte to Ley of June 12, 1939, in BAK, R41/22.
101. See Teppe, "Sozialpolitik," p. 241.
102. In BAK, R41/22a.

bonuses, and so on: "But mostly it turned out that the Reich Labor Ministry follows these efforts with great hesitation." In fact, Ley contended, RAM was a "pacemaker for a wage rollback."

In the meantime, Ley issued a directive to his Amtswalter in which, interpreting the October 24, 1934 Hitler decree, he appeared to give their activities on behalf of better wages legal sanction. Mansfeld (RAM) called it "a downright clever interpretation of the Führer's decree and carefully considered coupling of party and state powers." He went on, "The wage negotiations [of the DAF] under the aegis of its functionaries, which are increasingly being observed, confirm the fear that, despite the absence of a lawful foundation, the directive is being obeyed as legal." Ley was flouting the wage freeze law without appearing to break it.[103]

On September 26 Seldte, who had only received Ley's letter on the 21st — the annual Nuremberg party day had come in the meantime — threw Ley's "critique" back in his face. He urged the DAF leader to fall into line with the government's wage policy and hinted that Ley could better be spending his time stopping union-like methods throughout the land, a reference to the DAF wage negotiations. As far as rents were concerned, Seldte went on, it was one of the "shining successes" of price policy to have almost completely sheltered the workers from higher rents. Then Seldte, who was obviously furious (he had drafted an even angrier letter without sending it) wrote, "It has not been easy for me to answer you, despite the fact [*sic*] that the tone of your letter vis-à-vis a Reich Minister is impossible. That you manage to drop a term like 'pacemaker for a wage rollback,' which is an insulting term for me and my ministry, fills me with indignation." He was only replying at all in the interests of collaborating with the DAF, some of whose offices had been cooperative. "That I have not always been in a position to accept your often questionable suggestions or positions, in fact have frequently had to combat them, you know."[104]

At the same time, Seldte turned to Hess. Pointing out how conscientiously RAM was carrying out the rigid-wage policy decided upon by the regime and supported in the past by Hess himself, "despite all the difficulties created for me in every aspect of societal life by the irresponsible promises of the Labor Front and its functionaries," Seldte asked just who represented the wishes of the party

103. Mansfeld to Krohn of September 5, 1936, in BAK, R41 (Krohn)/5009.
104. For the actual letter and unsent draft, see BAK, R41/22a.

vis-à-vis his ministry. He took his orders from the Führer, Seldte went on, "but I cannot tolerate it that a high functionary of the party [he meant Ley, or course] expresses the supposed desires of the party to me in this form or in the form of commentaries or other 'directives' as ultimatums, especially when these wishes are in crass opposition to the policy as indicated by the Führer."[105]

Seldte apparently got little satisfaction from Hess, for the Labor Minister and Ley continued to fight a trench war over wage policy simultaneous with that over social insurance, with Ley representing himself as the spokesman of the party. Krohn and Selzner were their frequent proxies in these battles, and a series of discussions between the two men demonstrated the complete lack of trust (despite calls for cooperation) which existed between the DAF and RAM.[106]

As 1936 turned into 1937, the battle escalated. Out in the factories the DAF began a concentrated campaign to grab as part of its jurisdiction the settling of disputes and altering of wage settlements — a clear violation of the functions of the Trustees of Labor. In one particularly crass example, a local functionary convened the "trust council" in the absence of the "plant leader," presented a plan for a whole new wage scale, then called on the "plant leader" to convene a meeting of the same committee to discuss the plan.[107]

And even when officials of the Labor Ministry were able to proclaim measures which workers might find favorable, the DAF, with its huge propaganda system and access to the press, would jump in and take full credit itself.[108]

In May, 1937, Seldte wrote to his Trustees bemoaning the fact that again and again workers "had turned to offices outside the plant for the purpose of mediation, without previously having attempted a solution inside the plant. This behavior can in no way be squared with the basic principles of the new German social order." He made it clear that these were DAF offices and that Trustees should take cognizance of this and remind employers to call the Trustee in directly when disputes could not be settled in the factory. Taking a leaf from Ley's book, Seldte lanced his letter into the press as a "directive."[109]

105. Seldte to Hess of September n.d., 1936 in R41/22a.
106. For examples of Selzner–Krohn discussions, see Krohn office memos of November 6 and 14, 1936, and July 2, 1937, in BAK, R41 (Krohn)/5010.
107. See draft of "trust committee" meeting in Alsdorf on October 30, 1936, as reported to RAM in BAK, R41 (Krohn)/5009.
108. See RAM internal memo of January 21, 1937, in ibid.
109. See Seldte to Reichstreuhänder of May 19, 1937, in BAK, R43II/530, p. 226.

But Ley was not to be deterred. On June 8 he issued yet another "directive" — this time interestingly enough as ROL. He was again underscoring his role as *the* party spokesman, reminding all DAF offices once again of the October 24, 1934 decree, especially paragraph 7, which recognized the right of the DAF to assure labor peace by creating understanding among "plant leaders" for the legitimate interests of their "retinue."[110] Then he responded to Seldte's directive to the Trustees: "I do not want to fail to tell you that your position awakened great astonishment in me." The directive did not further cooperation between the Trustees and the DAF; it would cause unrest in the plants, and— of course— it was the object of a commentary by Radio Moscow! Most importantly, Ley went on, by directing the Trustees to strengthen their staffs, Seldte was violating the AOG, which stipulated that the Trustees were to function solely as "supreme social judges" and invading the rightful jurisdiction of the DAF as established by the Führer decree, which proscribed the formation of any organization other than the DAF in the area of preserving labor peace.[111]

Seldte replied, denying that he had broken the law: the Trustees were operating legitimately within the framework of the AOG. He retreated from his position of having alluded to DAF interference in his orders to the Trustees; the order, he indicated, was not related to DAF activities, although he could not deny that such intereference existed. As for the Radio Moscow commentary: "*I* did not listen to the station. Anyway, I can just prevent its comments on my order about as much [as you can] in its dealings with you." Seldte concluded by saying that he resented Ley's having intruded into his Ministry by calling one of the department heads on the carpet for *his* (Seldte's) directive. He, Seldte, bore the responsibility for the directive.[112]

Krohn turned to Bormann for help. (This was the same occasion on which he also sought the party's help in the social insurance question.) Bormann did indicate that, as far as the wage problem was concerned, he would ask (Reich Press Chief Otto) Dietrich and the Gauleiter to keep wage propaganda out of the press, but he did not see much chance of influencing the DAF, particularly its lower ranks.[113]

110. Quoted in *Freies Deutschland*, no. 23 of June 17, 1937.
111. Ley to Seldte of June 21, 1937, in BAK, R43II/530, pp. 227–8.
112. Seldte to Ley of July 15, 1937, in ibid., p. 229.
113. Krohn Vermerk, June 29, 1937, in BAK, R41 (Krohn)/5009: Bormann was

The struggle between Seldte and Ley over the authority of the Trustees and wage policy generally would go on. In January 1938 in an internal memo the Labor Ministry catalogued and lamented the ongoing interference of the DAF in the factories; its attempts to shortcircuit the work of the Trustees and elbow them out; its use of labor committees to put businessmen under psychological pressure; its direct altering, at will, of factory regulations; and so on.[114] Correspondence between Ley and RAM also continued throughout 1938 and into 1939; Ley tried once more to insinuate his own man, this time Mende, into the ministry; he and Seldte continued to bicker over turf; both parties still signed "treaties" right up to the eve of the war; newspapers continued to announce DAF efforts.[115]

And these struggles were accompanied by strong personal animosities as well. It is some indication of the bitterness and hostility on both sides that the altercations very nearly led to a duel between Schmeer, Ley's liaison to the Four-Year Plan, and Krohn. The immediate background was Krohn's contention that he had shown Schmeer the text of the June 22, 1938, directive on wages before its promulgation. The directive was important because it gave the Trustees broad new powers to control wages. Schmeer saw Krohn at the Nuremberg party day celebration in September and denied he been shown the directive, calling Krohn a liar. Krohn, now a party member, challenged Schmeer to a duel. The two now were "deadly enemies" with Schmeer claiming that "it would be a pleasure anytime to shoot a hole in Dr Krohn's stomach in a duel." Since dueling was forbidden, the matter was taken before the party court in late 1938, after Hess's office had been unable to mediate the quarrel, and settled by compromise so that both men saved face.[116]

Unlike the area of social insurance, Seldte was able to gain ground in the matter of wages in the last two years prior to the war. The

---

scarcely kindly disposed toward the RAM anyway, which, in his opinion, had far too few party members in it (only five of thirty-eight high officials) and needed to be purged. See Bormann to Lammers of January 12, 1938, in BAK, R43II/1138.

114. Undated, but probably January 1938, in BAK, R41/22, pp. 8–13.

115. See Ley to Seldte of August 12, 1938, supporting Mende as "liaison," BAK, R41/22, pp. 44–5; Ley to Seldte of February 1, 1939, on division of jurisdiction, in ibid., pp. 71–2. See "treaty" sent to Syrup (RAM) by Mende (DAF Sozialamt) of August 14, 1939, in BAK, R43II/529, pp. 95–105; see story in *Angriff* of February 12, 1939, on labor committees settling disputes in plants.

116. Extensive documentation on the affair is in BDC: File Schmeer. Quote is from November 19, 1938, deposition of Schmeer "Vernehmungswerk," signed by Oexle.

need to keep a lid on wages, as the Four-Year Plan got into high gear, strengthened Seldte's position and undermined that of Ley. Indeed, Seldte sought Göring as an ally.[117] In addition, a series of reforms also strengthened the hands of the Trustees. In June 1938 their staffs were enlarged. In January 1939 the office of Plenipotentiary (*Beauftragte*) of the Trustee was created with fifty-four district offices. In August 1939 the directors of the labor offices were also made into commissioners and vested with considerable powers. Thus the Trustees acquired a badly needed bureaucratic substructure.[118]

In the meantime, two developments marked 1938 as the peak year of Ley's peacetime aspirations for the DAF as a "populist" organization: one was the emergence of the Four-Year Plan under Göring; the other was Ley's advancement of four draft laws, which, if enacted, would have made the DAF the most powerful entity in Germany.

The discharge of Schacht in November 1937 marked the real emergence of Göring as economic czar, for, in addition to his title as Plenipotentiary for the Four-Year Plan, he also temporarily became Economics Minister. For Ley, Göring's emergence as an economic power was a mixed blessing. On the positive side, Schacht's departure meant the disappearance of a major opponent; Walter Funk, whom Göring would soon appoint as "his" Economics Minister, would never be as skilled an opponent as Schacht. In addition, Göring was, after all, a Nazi, an old fighter, who might ostensibly view the world through the same National Socialist lenses as Ley himself and thus lend the DAF leader his support. Indeed, in some ways this proved true. Goering did support such DAF endeavors as the NS Model Factory Competition and did aid Ley against some of his enemies, as the case of Krohn's retirement demonstrated.

On the other hand, Göring, precisely because he was a powerful Nazi who had Hitler's confidence, broke the virtual monopoly which Ley had had as the party's leading figure in socioeconomic affairs. Moreover, the way in which Göring organized the Four-Year Plan and the priorities he introduced were bound to put him at odds with Ley's ambitions. Eschewing forming a state planning bureaucracy, Göring created in *ad hoc* fashion "business groups" and co-

117. See Seldte to Göring of January 12, 1938, in BAK, R41 (Krohn)/5009.
118. See Timothy Mason, *Arbeiterklasse und Volksgemeinschaft* (Opladen, Westdeutscher Verlag, 1975), p. 800.

opted ministerial state secretaries for an apparatus which would concentrate on certain areas of the economy deemed critical to war production, such as iron and steel, chemicals, transport, and so on. Working through a supreme coordinating body, the General Council for the Four-Year Plan, Göring focused as well on important areas of social policy such as price controls and labor allocation. In doing so, he weakened the power of precisely those ministries which had been Ley's major antagonists: Labor and Economics.[119] This should theoretically have worked to Ley's advantage. But the opposite was the case, for precisely the men who had been his enemies, now became Göring's men within the framework of the Four-Year Plan: Syrup (RAM) became president of the Reich Institute for Labor Allocation and Unemployment, while Mansfeld (RAM) now became director of the Geschäftsgruppe Arbeitseinsatz of the Four-Year Plan.[120] Moreover, Göring's priorities of higher production and wage stability tended to work against Ley's populist support of higher wages and general perks for the workers. Under the pressure of Göring, then, the DAF evolved after 1938 increasingly into an agency for the mobilization and social control of labor and less and less its advocate. The war would complete the transformation.

Göring could also be critical of Ley. In a remark before military leaders in July 1938, Göring hinted that some of the money Ley was using to make workers' lives more pleasant might better be used for building arms. "The Labor Front should make more strength," Göring said, "and less joy."[121]

If 1938 marked the increasing acceleration of war production and the need for stricter controls on labor, it also witnessed, partly because of that development, the high watermark of Ley's "populist" ambitions. At the beginning of the year Ley submitted drafts of four laws, which, had they been enacted, would have made the DAF the most powerful social, economic and political entity in Germany, independent of party and state; would have raised it to the status of the very socioeconomic "super-agency" to which Ley had aspired all along.

The time must have seemed propitious to Ley to undertake such a dramatic move. Virtually all the programs operated by the DAF

119. Specifically on this aspect of the Four-Year Plan, see Broszat, *The Hitler State*, pp. 330ff.

120. See Marie Recker, *Nationalsozialistische Sozialpolitik im Zweiten Weltkrieg* (Munich, Oldenbourg, 1985), pp. 20–1.

121. See Mason, *Sozialpolitik*, p. 253.

were in high gear. The Skills and Performance Competitions were turning out to be great successes, despite the passive resistance of business.[122] The number of DAF *Schulungskurse* and labor committees were at an all-time high. The activities of the *Werkscharen* were being expanded. The "Strength through Joy" tours were growing rapidly, demonstrating this part of DAF activities to be perhaps the most popular of any of the regime's activities. And the vast Volkswagen plant was nearing completion, holding out the popular vision of a German people on wheels. What is more, Ley's most implacable enemy, Schacht, has just recently resigned. All of this represented tremendous — and for Ley encouraging — momentum. Also influential in Ley's decision might have been the perceived need to make the DAF virtually impregnable at precisely the time when the wage and production priorities of the regime were undermining the populist thrust which he had always deemed critical to "legitimizing" his Labor Front in the eyes of the workforce.

Whatever combination of motives was involved, Ley made his move at the beginning of February.[123] The first law "on the DAF" widened the compulsory membership base of the organization to all gainfully employed Germans, not just those in business and industry. Now peasants and government officials alike would be included. It also would have broadened the jurisdiction of the DAF to include the "intellectual, physical, and professional training of all working Germans," a very sweeping mandate. In addition, the DAF Reichsleiter was placed directly under Hitler, and his offices were to take a direct part in shaping legislation. This would have eliminated Hess and, in effect, the party itself, from any meaningful role.

The second law "on Labor-Political Self-administration," also known as the "Labor Chamber Law" raised the status of the DAF labor chambers and labor committees to make them organizations on a part with the Trustees of Labor. They would have been both control and advisory bodies. This law would have greatly strengthened the DAF position in socioeconomic affairs vis-à-vis the government.

122. On DAF successes despite resistance, see Hupfauer to Ley of August 6, 1937, in BAK, NS22, vorl. 838.

123. For copies of the drafts, see BAK, R43II/530a; see also Mason, *Sozialpolitik*, pp. 257ff.; Schweitzer, *Nazifizierung*, pp. 170–2; many of the letters written in response to Ley's drafts are reprinted in Gerhard Beier, "Gesetzentwürfe zur Ausschaltung der Deutschen Arbeitsfront im Jahre 1938," *Archiv für Sozialgeschichte*, vol. 17 (1977), pp. 297–335.

Thirdly, the "Economic Chamber Law" would have created "Gau economic chambers" which would have given the DAF a major tool to invade the power and jurisdiction of the OgW. This draft also proposed that the Economics Ministry should require the consent of the DAF for decrees and guidelines bearing on technical education. This was further spelled out in the fourth law "on Technical Education and Technical Training in Trade and Commerce."

In all cases the wording was sufficiently vague (as were the concepts; the laws were not coordinated with one another) to allow the DAF plenty of opportunity for "organizational imperialism." In fact, with these drafts Ley had come close to his dream of making the DAF virtually contiguous with the entire society. Had the drafts become law and had Ley realized their potential in full, then he might have had his conflict-free society under a gigantic DAF umbrella.

But Ley had vastly overreached himself. He had taken on state *and* party simultaneously. The response was quick and overwhelmingly negative. Hess turned down the proposals indicating that "according to the draft the [DAF] would be *the* decisive factor in the life of the nation as well as in the life of the individual German."[124] R. Walther Darré, Agricultural Minister and head of the Reichsnährstand (Reich Food Estate), whose rural jurisdiction Ley had been trying to invade for years, responded particularly sharply. If he lost his independence to Ley, it would lead to "a sheer panicked paralysis of the desire to produce in farming."[125]

Interior Minister Frick warned, among other things, that the draft meant "placing the Labor Front over all offices of state and party" and also the virtual dissolution of business organizations, as the DAF "laid claim to leadership of all social and economic policy."[126] Himmler, in his initial response, warned that the tasks proposed for the DAF would give it "the fulness of power which previously state and party have had .... The state in the form of its ministries will be degraded to a handmaiden of the Labor Front, while the party does not even have this helping function."[127]

124. Hess to Lammers of February 15, 1938, in BAK, R43II/529, p. 14.
125. Darré to Hitler, February 15, ibid., pp. 27–8.
126. Frick to Göring, February 17, in ibid., pp. 38–46.
127. Himmler to Hess, February 17, in ibid., p. 51.

According to Seldte, who weighed in with his complaints, the laws had the purpose of "freeing the leader of the [DAF] in all areas of social and, therefore, economic life of any ties to party and state and put him in a position of being able himself to determine social and economic events."[128]

Only Funk, the new Economics Minister, a drinking buddy of Ley's, who had lost much of his authority to Göring and hoped to get some of it back by robbing Seldte of some of his, responded at all favorably to the drafts.[129]

In the end Ley failed to gain acceptance for his legal draft laws; he had too clearly overreached himself, had allowed his gigantomania free rein, and threatened the power position of practically every office in party and state in what was a colossal act of misjudgment. His drafts had provoked almost instant reaction and debate.[130] They were certainly the high point of his prewar aspirations. But if he had been defeated in his bid, it was not so much just through the negative reactions of the other *Machtträger*, as it was by the events which formed the backdrop of his endeavor. His drafts were soon forgotten in the flush of foreign policy successes. March, the month he submitted them, witnessed the *Anschluss* with Austria. Within six months, the Sudeten crisis would bring the world to the brink of war. In the meantime, Hitler concentrated on his West Wall, fairly oblivious to power struggles on the domestic scene. Indeed, the DAF would test its mobilization skills in being assigned an important role in the construction of the West Wall, a preview of its wartime activities. It was the political, economic, and ideological preparation for war then, which ultimately weakened the populist thrust of the DAF and brought to the fore its control and mobilization component.

128. Seldte to Göring, February 18, in BAK, R41/22, p. 26.
129. Funk to Göring, February 16, in BAK, R43II/529, pp. 35–7; Funk and Ley may have discussed the "surprise" drafts in advance. See Mason, *Sozialpolitik*, p. 259.
130. Years later in 1942 Gauleiter Röver, looking back, wrote, "Had the party not headed off four new DAF laws in 1938, the DAF would have had the power to dissolve the party altogether." US National Archives Microcopy T-81, R7, F4722–41.

CHAPTER 9

Götterdämmerung

The outbreak of war in September 1939 reawakened in Robert Ley much of the spirit of the *Kampfzeit*: a sense of the confrontation between good and evil; a crusading spirit; a renewed emphasis on the Jew as the ultimate enemy and of National Socialism as a religious faith. This time the struggle was not for power in Germany; it was global and universal, which lent a further apocalyptic dimension to it. Ley's wartime speeches began to sound once again like his earlier campaign tirades. His *Our Socialism: The Hate of the World*, published in 1940, is saturated with pseudo-religious fears and hopes, animated by apocalyptic vision:[1] "The National Socialist knows that all skilled craftmanship and all the cleverness of the mind mean nothing, or in the last analysis must dry up, if they are not impelled, elevated, and driven by the holy fire of faith, of faith in the necessary ideals of *Volk* and nation." He returned to his old theme of two worlds colliding — one good, one evil. The evil one — here he attacked capitalism as one tentacle of the Jewish enemy — is plutocracy, "the dominance of money and gold, the repression and enslavement of people, the reversal of all natural values and exclusion of reason and insight, the mystical darkness of superstition . . . the meanness of human carnality and brutality." Between this dark world and that of good "there is no compromise and no settlement. Whoever wants one, must hate the other. Who gives himself to one, must destroy the other."

As the war went on, especially after the invasion of Russia in June 1941, Ley included Bolshevism as the other Jewish tentacle: "Become fanatic haters in the face of the Jews, who gave birth to the Bolsheviks, who bred the wild Bolshevik beasts and unleashed them

1. "Unser Sozialismus: der Hass der Welt," copy in BAK, NSD50/13, following quote from pp. 16–17.

on European culture," Ley admonished the Germans.[2]

Whether plutocrat or commissar, then, the main enemy remained the Jew, and only by destroying the Jews could the earthshaking struggle be prosecuted and won. In a speech to potential party leaders at the Ordensburg Croessinsee, Ley announced:

> Among our enemies, the Jew is in first place. Not just because the Jew has a crooked nose and other various outward and inner features of a peculiar nature. And we certainly aren't fighting him because of what he believes. The Jew can believe whatever he wants. We are only fighting him because he molests us, molests us fatally . . . all our principles are threatened by the Jew. The Jew wanted to lead us into a world which was not only foreign to us, but which would have destroyed us in short order. In that moment we declared the Jew our enemy . . . If we tolerate the Jew among us, we will never be able to fight against the opponent's world.

But mixed with his hatred for the Jew as the ultimate enemy who had to be destroyed in this Armageddon-like struggle, were also suggestions of a German social revolution amounting to ushering in the millenium. Traditional religion was not to survive this war. The *Volk* itself Ley elevated to Godhead as the core of a new NS-religion, while his sharp rejection of the Catholic Church suggested what the fate of Christians might have been had Germany prevailed in the war. "Where there is a spy network," he suggested, " a Jew, a half-Jew or a priest is definitely involved. We must free our *Volk* of these creatures . . . . I am animated by a deep hatred against the seduction of the German people which the religious institutions perpetrate through lies and deceit." He urged party members to "cross the Rubicon." "Whoever wants to lead in our party must burn his bridge behind him, for our world claims him completely and totally."[3]

Nor did he intend traditional capitalism to survive the war. Winning German freedom meant "Destruction of capitalism: rooting out of plutocracy and with that [creating] the prerequisite to building a socialist Germany."[4] By "socialist Germany" Ley meant

2. From Ley's speech "Die grosse Wende", n.d. but immediately after Stalingrad debacle. US National Archives Microcopy T-580, Roll 9, Ordner 123.
3. Speech of May 17, 1943. Text in Archives des Centre de Documentation Juive Contemporaine, Paris, Document no. CXLII-277, quotes from pp. 6–7 and 11–12, respectively.
4. From "Unser Sozialismus," p. 24.

the core of the Nazi social revolution: an equal-opportunity revolution whereby ordinary Germans might become upwardly mobile in a society purged of the old class and caste differences, with their way paved via government action, while at the same time being protected from many of the vicissitudes of life through an elaborate welfare system. It would be the harmonious, conflict-free society Ley had always dreamed of — a consumer's paradise. But it rested on the basis of vast exploitation of peoples considered inferior by Nazi ideology: peoples outside the world of "equal opportunity" in very unequal situations. And to exploit these people — above all the Slavs to the East — meant first winning the war. And that meant sacrifices.

These dreams were greatly encouraged by the dramatic victories over Poland and in the West during 1939 and 1940. They were given vast impetus by the initial successes of German arms in the Russian campaign of summer 1941. Those successes opened up enormous vistas which were perceived, among others, by Ley's planners in the DAF Institute for Labor Science (AWI). In the flush of victory, the AWI turned out a number of reports detailing the possibilities which the natural resources, the labor potential, and enormous spaces of the eastern territories provided. As with Ley's speeches, these reports were also infused, despite their technical format, with an almost apocalyptic sense of opportunity. One began with the words: "The expansion of the German power sphere to cover large parts of Russian territory will be of earth-shattering importance for European culture, greater than anything since the breakthrough of the Arabs into the Mediterranean basin." But these reports, interestingly enough, also firmly linked the conquest and exploitation of the East with revolutionary changes at home. The same report continued, "In light of such an elemental event [conquest of the East] not only will the German concept of territory [*Raumbegriff*], frozen for a millenium, experience a revolution, its social thinking will as well. In the face of recent events, the goals and methods which arose in the days of Central European small states look like a toy next to a cathedral." The report strongly suggested that exploitation of the East might be used to overcome the prior inequalities in German society and provide opportunities for upward mobility for those fortunate enough to belong to the dominant race. Referring to past social inequalities in Germany, the report concluded:

> National socialism found these differences already existing and could not

> eliminate them in the early year of its rule. Social policy since 1933 has had to limit itself basically to eliminating the worst hardships without its being possible, given the narrowness of *Lebensraum*, to cure the evil root and branch . . . . The push to the East must be bound up with a directly perceptible social ascent.[5]

Thus, as I have suggested, the war, as viewed by Ley and the DAF, provided not only the opportunity to extend German power, it also represented, more importantly, an Armageddon-like struggle to destroy the Jews and thus create the basis for a German social utopia based on exploitation of peoples considered inferior. As Ley put it in his usual pithy way, "Within ten years, the German worker will look better than an English lord today."[6] And Ley's great social plans for the German people, his *Sozialwerk* to which we will shortly turn, must be seen in this light. They represented not just a set of promises made to cement war-torn morale but also a serious post-war social agenda. If the populist thrust of the DAF, so clearly apparent in the years down to 1938, was blunted by the exigencies of war, its spirit remained in the utopia plans expressed in Ley's speeches and in the AWI think tank.

Already before outbreak of the war, the DAF had become harnessed to preparations for that conflict. As early as 1935 it created a liaison office with the Wehrmacht; and the DAF *Betreuung* of workers building the West Wall in 1938 provided experience for the war.[7] Once the war itself broke out, the DAF had to focus its endeavors more and more on heightened productivity and performance which also meant (without dampening Ley's jurisdictional enthusiasms) closer cooperation with government and industry as well as the acceptance, occasionally with great reluctance and under protests, of government measures such as labor regulations, wage freezes, temporary abolition of overtime bonuses, lengthening of standard workday, and so on, which the DAF would have fought

5. Quotes are from "Raum formt Sozialpolitik," in BAK, NS25/1679, pp. 5, 12, 33, respectively; see also "Erwägungen zur Nutzung der eroberten Gebiete durch das deutsche Volk," ibid., which envisions an area as far as as the Urals settled within a century by Germans to the same density as currently by Russians (p. 95). Ironically, both reports were dated November–December 1941, just at the point where the Germans were about to be stopped in front of Moscow.
6. In a speech to foreign journalists on September 15, 1940, quoted in Marie Recker, *Nationalsozialistische Sozialpolitik im Zweiten Weltkrieg* (Munich, Oldenbourg, 1985), p. 98.
7. See Hans-Gerd Schumann, *Nationalsozialismus und Gewerkschaftsbewegung*, (Hannover, Frankfurt, Norddeutsche Verlagsanstalt, 1958), pp. 158–9.

tooth and nail in peacetime years. Even here Ley still offered ideas from time to time as to strategies which would not place undue inequities on the German of modest income, such as his plan to levy a special tax on non-rationed luxury goods which were not articles of daily use. He also pleaded successfully for a restoration of overtime pay for the ninth and tenth hours. In a narrow sense, his generous social plans were meant to be a kind of compensation for the ordinary worker for his wartime material sacrifices.[8]

As for the DAF itself, the organization found itself being drawn increasingly into cooperation with business and industry with respect to heightening war production, and although one cannot talk in terms of complete harmony — jurisdictional rivalries prevented that — nevertheless, signs that the war demanded more cooperation among party and state agencies were abundant. For one thing, war preparations in many respects remained the preserve of traditional state agencies. Government ministries drafted a number of contingency measures *(Schubladen-Gesetze)* without the DAF being involved in the negotiations.[9] For another, the DAF softened its position in a number of areas where government primacy had been demonstrated. A dramatic example here was vocational education, an area of great jurisdictional conflict prior to the war. Now the DAF recognized "that the state must determine the minimum standards for vocational education . . . This schooling is to proceed according to state guidelines. The training of masters, and so on, therefore is the responsibility of the plants and the OgW."[10] The DAF also had to modify some of its ideological points as a result of the exigencies of war, the emphasis of the single-family home, for example, underscored so often by the DAF Homestead Office, now shifted under the austerities of a war economy, to greater attention to urban apartments. This had administrative consequences: Ludovici was replaced as head of the Heimstättenamt; his successor felt constrained to say, "One cannot overlook the fact that large sections of the

8. For a thorough discussion of government wage policy in the first year of the war, see Recker, *NS-Sozialpolitik*, pp. 26–53. On Ley's special tax, see AWI paper "Absaugung der Kaufkraft," November 4, 1939, in BAK, R2/24248. For restoration of overtime pay, see Ley to Syrup, May 18, 1940, in BAK, NS22, vorl. 976. On the link between social plans and compensation for sacrifices, see Ley to Hitler, December 28, 1939, in BAK, R2/24248.
9. See Timothy Mason, *Arbeiterklasse und Volksgemeinschaft* (Opladen, Westdeutscher Verlag, 1975), pp. 981–2.
10. See Hupfauer memo of November 7, 1939, to this effect and agreement between Ley and Funk of February 5, 1940, in BAK, R11/730, pp. 145–50.

population do not appreciate the small rural settlements. The majority of laborers prefer apartments in cities."[11] Even the correspondence between the DAF and its erstwhile rivals lost some of its tension and reflected added areas of agreement.[12]

There was also a subtle shift, even with Ley, away from the carrot and toward the stick. As the DAF leader, who in the spring of 1940 had heard that labor discipline had been slackening in many Gaus, wrote to his *Gauobmänner*, "Where it is necessary, I demand, that when all educational and *Betreuung* measures fail, you take drastic measures with ruthless severity, with the employment of the Secret State Police."[13]

As the war dragged on, and particularly after the turning point at Stalingrad, an increasingly desperate situation drew the DAF deeper into cooperation. Extensive discussions developed between the DAF and business leaders in the Ruhr on how to remove stumbling blocks to higher productivity.[14] Even Albert Speer, after 1942 Minister for Armaments and War Production, and no great respecter of Ley, had an occasional good word for DAF activities, for example in the swift removal of air-raid damage.[15]

But more than a shift in emphasis with regard to carrot and stick and to party-state relations, the war brought changes to the Labor Front itself with regard both to its structure and to its activities. For one thing, the DAF underwent yet another bureaucratic reorganization, designed to streamline it for its wartime duties. It was divided into four so-called "war main working areas" (*Kriegs-Hauptarbeitsgebiete*), under Ley's old standbys, Marrenbach, Hupfauer, Lafferentz, and Simon. The first included personnel, organization, propaganda, and the *Werkscharen*. The second encompassed most of the social responsibilities and *Betreuung* on the job as well as the *Fachämter*, the vocational competition as well as the AWI. The

11. Quoted in Arthur Schweitzer, *Big Business in the Third Reich* (Bloomington, Indiana University Press, 1964), p. 217.
12. See, for example, Pietzsch (Reich Economic Chamber) to Ley, March 20, 1940, praising the cooperation between DAF and OgW, in BAK, R12I/268; also see Otto Marrenbach, *Fundamente des Sieges*, 2nd edn (Berlin, Verlag der DAF, 1940), p. 393, which highlights wartime cooperation between the DAF and OgW (although this must be taken in part with a grain of salt as propaganda).
13. Circular letter of May 10, 1940, in BAK, NS22, vorl. 976.
14. See Ley to *Betriebsführer* and *Betriebsobmänner des Bergbaus und der Eisenschaffenden Industrie* of January 27, 1944, in US National Archives Microcopy T-81, Roll 69, Frames 79233–44.
15. See Albert Speer, *Infiltration* (New York, Macmillan, 1981), p. 74.

third dealt with the areas of entertainment and adult education (and since these two activities were vital to the troops, the KdF-liaison office to the *Wehrmacht* was also included). The fourth handled finance and business.[16]

This ostensibly streamlined Labor Front was assigned seven areas of responsibility as its wartime role. They included (1) general social *Betreuung* as before; (2) assuring social peace in the plants; (3) assisting the state to preserve and raise labor performace; (4) continued use of KdF to organize free time (and the furloughs of soldiers); (5) *Betreuung*, in close cooperation with OgW and state authorities, of labor caught up in the economic shifts occasioned by the war economy; (6) providing provisions for war plants (*Werksküchen*), and (7) kindergartens for those same factories.[17] There was still the old combination of carrot and stick here, but emphasis had subtly shifted toward a command organization in a war economy.

Within the framework of these guidelines, most of the old DAF activities continued, but with a different slant. Thus much of DAF *Betreuung* now dealt with soldiers. This was particularly true of the KdF. Its pleasure liners now became hospital ships; its recreation areas were reserved for soldiers on furlough or for high-priority armament workers and miners; Volkswagen vehicles now became staff cars. One estimate was that 80 percent of KdF activities were now military-oriented.[18] The "Beauty of Work" organization, which had busied itself with beautification campaigns during the 1930s, now erected sleeping quarters for workers trapped in factories by air raids and tried to assure adequate lighting during blackouts. The Volksbildungswerk devoted its time to war propaganda, sponsoring lectures which, among other things, celebrated martial attitudes and the "heroic life principle." Functionaries of the Feierabend office strained their imaginations thinking of evening diversions that would not compromise the blackout.[19]

But most important were the programs which served to raise

16. For details, see DAF Central Office, "Entwurf über Organisation und Aufbau der nachgeordneten Dienststellen der DAF in Kriege," US National Archives Microcopy T-81, Roll 70, Frames 80540–50; also Marrenbach, *Fundamente*, pp. 391ff.
17. Marrenbach, *Fundamente*, p. 390.
18. See Schumann, *NS und Gewerkschaftsbewegung*, p. 159. In 1942 for example, the DAF claimed to have staged 585,000 events attended by 190 million participants from the Wehrmacht. "Gesamtrechenschaftsbericht 1943," BAK, NSD50/21, p. 123.
19. Marrenbach, *Fundamente*, pp. 400–2.

production in a situation where, as the war went into its fourth and fifth year, the need for obtaining and/or creating skilled labor against the background of massive conscription, became critical.[20] Here the DAF office for Performance Training, Vocational Education, and Plant Leadership (Leistungsertüchtigung, Berufserziehung und Betriebsführung, or LBB) under Herbert Steinwarz was considered by the DAF to be particularly important. Under its aegis, for example, war wounded were retrained or retooled to enter the production process. The Vocational Competition continued as well, with 2.5 million participants during 1943. The Performance Competition of German Plants was initially stopped upon the outbreak of war but revived as the War Performance Competition, to which in 1944, Ley added on a limited, experimental basis a new *Herausforderung* or "challenge" competition.[21] Also important were the Gau *Einsatz-Stäbe*, task forces which oversaw provisioning the plants, organizing help for bombed-out workers, overseeing and disciplining foreign labor in barrack settlements, as well as trying to train new skilled labor to replace that being conscripted.

The DAF office for "Health and People's Protection" played a particularly important role in keeping up production quotas among people who had to work long hours, frequently under conditions of privation and lowered rations. This office supervised a number of health "campaigns," including the "Vitamin-Action," the "Detergent-Action," the "X-Ray Examination-Action," the "Miner's-Action," and so on, and claimed to have provided all important war factories with "plant doctors," 6,500 in all.[22] Here is one clear case of the dovetailing of *Betreuung* and social control. The doctors were cer-

20. For an excellent discussion of wartime labor allocation, see Recker, *NS-Sozialpolitik*, pp. 155–93.

21. See Ley to Speer, April 7, 1944, in BAK, NS22, vorl. 900.

22. Information on these DAF activites, particularly during the last three years of the war, has been distilled from the following documentation: DAF, "Gesamtrechenschaftsbericht zum Zehn-Jahrestag der Machtübernahme" (January 1943), in BAK, NSD50/21, gives a good overview of the expansion of DAF programs and activities from 1933 to 1943; "Die deutsche Arbeitsfront im 5. Kriegsjahr," USNA Microcopy T-81, Roll 69, Frames 79362–425, is an opposition report which carries quotes from the German press with critical commentary. It points out the failures of the DAF but does not deny its successes, particularly in the *Betreuung* of those who were bombed out or evacuated. Useful also as a summary of activities is a February 23, 1944, speech by Marrenbach entitled "Kriegsarbeit der DAF," in BAK, NS18/194, pp. 63–6. See also Ley's Rundschreiben to "plant leaders" of June 23, 1942, announcing the third annual "Vitamin-action of the DAF." By special arrangement with Hitler's physician, Dr Morell would provide the pills, a brand called "Vitamultin." BAK, NS22, vorl. 976.

tainly there to provide health care. But they had another role as well: to prevent what had become sizable absenteeism by quickly ascertaining the legitimacy of sick calls. The physicians thus became a weapon against malingerers (*Bummelanten*).[23]

Other DAF activities included distribution of ration cards and work clothes, developing monthly slogans to keep up morale, aid in coordinating ration amounts with levels of hard labor and even putting suggestion boxes in war plants, which produced over 180,000 "suggestions" by the end of 1942.[24]

Of particular importance, especially in light of the fact that for the regime the war was conducted, especially in the East, as one of racial repression and annihilation, was the DAF role in the exploitation of foreign labor. This activity deserves attention, because here rational and ideological considerations appear in particularly clear contrast.

The DAF tried to involve itself from the start in the foreign labor question, and brought with it the usual racial biases in this area. Distinctions were always made between foreign workers who were racially desirable and/or were from allied countries, e.g. Italians, and the racially "inferior" *Ostarbeiter*. In an AWI 1940 report on Polish workers in the Ruhr, for example, the usual stereotypes appear: Poles lacked personal independence, were labile personalities, were dirty and tended toward criminality, played an important role in importing infectious diseases, and so on.[25] The DAF was also involved preliminarily in the discipline of foreign workers through *Aufklärung und Erziehung*, but increasingly this role was taken over by the police authorities, particularly the Security Police. As one scholar put it, " 'Social Policy' vis-à-vis foreign labor became more and more in Nazi Germany the task of the Security Police."[26]

As usual in the Third Reich, the jurisdictional question appeared in this area as in all others. A whole host of agencies tried to involve themselves, including RAM, RWM, Todt's organization, the army, the Four-Year Plan, even individual firms, along with the DAF. Typically, Ley was the first to suggest a centralization of control of foreign labor, first to the Reich Chancellory itself, to which he

23. See Recker, *NS-Sozialpolitik*, p. 274.
24. See Herbert Steinwarz report, "Das betriebliche Vorschlagswesen als nationalsozialistische Führungsinstrument," in BAK, NSD50/44.
25. See Ulrich Herbert's recent study *Fremdarbeiter: Politik und Praxis des "Ausländer-Einsatzes" in der Kriegswirtschaft des Dritten Reiches* (Berlin Bonn, Dietz, 1986), pp. 52–3.
26. Ibid., p. 115; also pp. 90–1, 96–105.

proposed a "central command office" (*zentrale Kommandostelle*), and then to Foreign Minister Ribbentrop, to whom Ley expanded his proposal to suggest an actual "Commissar for the Engagement of Foreigners" (*Kommissar für den Ausländereinsatz*).[27] Ley met with stiff resistance from other authorities, however, so that Hitler only tentatively began centralizing the task in the hands of Todt, RAM, and Wehrmacht, while Göring took a hand on behalf of the Four-Year Plan with respect to Russian labor. Ley still had hopes, but these were dashed when Hitler finally named Fritz Sauckel, the Gauleiter of Thuringia, as "General Plenipotentiary for the Mobilization of Labor" in 1942. Sauckel, Speer as Todt's successor, and Himmler's police system would dominate the exploitation of foreign labor. The DAF would play a subordinate role, which was at least more than Seldte, the ostensible "Labor" Minister got. He was frozen out entirely.[28]

The DAF did get to "*betreuen*," however, and this raised some interesting problems which put ideology into conflict with economic exigencies. Despite its rather firm ideological attitudes about "inferior" races, the DAF was also concerned about productivity. In the debate during early 1942, for example, on whether to treat Ukrainians and Russians as primitive people, virtually as slave labor (the position taken by Himmler and Heydrich), or whether to exploit latent anti-communism and potential pro-German feelings, the DAF took the latter position. In fact, the DAF, which had worked closely with the SS in the past, was in this case reluctant to "surrender its claim to leadership in *Betreuung* work to public organs.[29]

The DAF position here (technological questions taking precedence over ideological ones) actually ran against Ley's own predilections. To treat foreign labor better in order to heighten productivity was a step in the direction of integration — and that violated the whole Ley concept of war as instrument of social change to the exclusive betterment of the *German* working man. The SS realized this, which was one reason it fought hard precisely *not* to integrate *Ostarbeiter* too much into the economy.

During the last two years of the war, however, as large numbers of German laborers were drafted, foreign labor had to fill the gap, and

27. Ley to Lammers, October 31, 1941, ibid., p. 150; Ley to Ribbentrop, November 4, 1941, in BAK, NS22, vorl. 976.
28. Herbert, *Fremdarbeiter*, pp. 153–4.
29. Ibid., p. 155.

that meant raising the skill levels of these people, whatever their racial qualifications. The DAF, concerned primarily with raising productivity, found itself more and more drawn away from ideology and towards a rather rational consideration of quality. In May 1943 the AWI, after research, concluded that Soviet workers could produce at levels of between 70 and 80 percent of that of German workers. The report also made a connection between higher productivity and working conditions, including wages, room and board, clothing, hygiene, and even "mutual understanding."[30]

Indeed, the DAF began a program in which it combined demands for better working conditions for *Ostarbeiter* with serious efforts to raise their skill levels through systematic vocational instructions.[31] The DAF even enlisted modern psychology in its task. A DAF Institute for Work Psychology and Work Pedagogy, founded in 1941, linked up with the so-called Goering Institute, to develop aptitude tests to assess the potential of individual foreign laborers. These tests tended to undermine racial stereotypes as did experiences with *Ostarbeiter* who, the DAF had to admit were "often an excellent, industrious, and decent labor force."[32]

The DAF thus extended its *Betreuung* even to those laborers which its own leader and the regime considered to be the very "human material" which Nazi Germany would exploit in order to make the German worker clearly a part of the "master race."[33] But even in doing so, the DAF remained schizophrenic. The apparent perception in the interest of desperately needed higher production that labor, after all, was labor, regardless of nationality, never triumphed completely over racial ideology and political exigency. Distinctions were always made, even with regard to the most sympathetic and vulnerable of human beings, the pregnant woman. Here, the DAF ordered that women from Bulgaria, Italy, Croatia, Slovakia, Spain, and Hungary should enjoy the same protection as German women

30. See "Arbeitseinsatz der Ostarbeiter in Deutschland," in BAK, R41/274, pp. 61–84.
31. See DAF, Amt LBB, "Richtlinien für die Ausbildung der deutschen und fremdvölkischen Arbeitskräfte," May, 1943, in BAK, R3/1820, pp. 462ff; also Herbert, *Fremdarbeiter*, pp. 263ff.
32. See "Meldungen aus dem Reich," October 7, 1943, in BAK, R58/159, pp. 75f.; Geoffrey Cocks, *Psychotherapy in the Third Reich* (Oxford, Oxford University Press, 1985) pp. 196–202; Herbert, *Fremdarbeiter*, pp. 263–4.
33. According to Richard Grunberger, *The 12-Year Reich* (New York, Holt Rinehart, & Winston, 1971), p. 200. Timothy Mason claimed that the DAF entertained migrant labor "lavishly," although it is not clear *which* laborers were so treated.

under the "*Mutterschutzgetz*," whereas *Ostarbeiter* got only "minimal protection." The tension often appeared even in the same paragraph. "Just as any other group of workers, *Ostarbeiter* cannot be treated as captives or slaves," one DAF report read. "Nevertheless, treatment should be strict. We must intervene quickly, severely and ruthlessly in cases of offenses and encroachments by the *Ostarbeiter*."[34]

Indeed, even behind concessions made to workers to make life more bearable, there lurked "racial" considerations. In 1941 the DAF set up its own company, the "House and Barracks Company," to provide brothels for foreign labor — largely as a prophylactic against the "ethnic-political dangers" (*volkspolitische Gefahren*) of possible sexual contact with German women.[35]

Through all this, the Labor Front continued its bureaucratic growth. Membership went from 22.4 million in 1939 to 25.1 million in 1942, largely the result of new territories brought under Nazi control. With larger membership came additional wealth: dues, which brought in 539 million marks in 1939, were running at 677 million marks in 1942.[36] This monetary growth allowed Ley also to expand the business holdings of the DAF, especially outside the *Altreich* proper. Hirtenberger Munitions Works in Austria and the Thrakische Mining Company in Sofia, Bulgaria, were added to the DAF holdings, as were several shipbuilding firms. The DAF also took over the consumer cooperatives in 1941.[37] Indeed, with respect to its business enterprises, the Labor Front demonstrated no less dynamic and expansive drive than in the peacetime years, something which Economics Minister Funk, a supporter of private industry, felt constrained to criticize severely in a letter to Ley.[38]

But even as the Labor Front evidenced the apogee of its growth and activities, it was being undermined by the war. Most of its better-trained and experienced functionaries, the men who had

34. See DAF, "Beschäftigung von ausländischen Arbeitskräften," in BAK, NSD50/413, BVIII4, p. 1, and NSD50/412, AIVb, p. 26.
35. Herbert, *Fremdarbeiter*, p. 127.
36. See DAF, "Gesamtrechenschaftsbericht 1943," BAK, NSD50/21, pp. 123–6, 144.
37. See Schumann, *NS und Gewerkschaftsbewegung*, p. 159; also article on DAF enterprises in *Berliner Börsenzeitung*, no. 465, October 4, 1941. On the consumer cooperatives, see Ley to Funk, April 18, 1940, in BAK, NS22, vorl. 976.
38. See Funk to Ley, June 3, 1941, in which Funk mentions, among other things, the "nearly unrestrained push to expand" of the Bank of German Labor, BAK, R43II/3526, p. 133.

infused the organization with much of its dynamic, were called to the colors. At the same time, the DAF found itself having to defend so many unpopular measures — by the end of the war, a 72-hour work week — that it lost much of its steam as populist worker advocate and became another command and control mechanism in the total war efforts of the Third Reich.[39] By 1944 the Labor Front was forced to recognize with resignation that it had not been successful everywhere in realizing the National Socialist "plant community," because too many businessmen had simply not become real "plant leaders" in the NS sense.[40] Ley himself was conscious, even as he was issuing order after order, that the DAF had changed under the impact of war. In his order on mobilizing plant reserves in August 1944, the DAF leader wrote what everyone already knew: "It is a requirement of war that the measures taken by us cannot always be in the nature of *Betreuung*; but rather often represent hard and most difficult demands upon all those working in our war economy with respect to labor allocation and performance."[41]

All the additional activities which the exigencies of war mandated for the Labor Front notwithstanding, Ley lost none of his drive to expand his already gigantic empire. Despite the advantage which business and government gained as a result, first, of gearing for war, then from the war itself, Ley never gave up his jurisdictional hunger; indeed, he won several clear, if pyrrhic, victories during the first three, largely victorious, war years. These victories were in part a result of Hitler's tendency, intensified by the war, to turn over large areas of economic and social responsibility to "General Plenipotentiaries," who then began their tasks at the expense of powers which had been exercised by government ministries.[42] Sauckel's appointment as General Plenipotentiary for the Mobilization of Labor in 1942 is a good example. It was this tendency on Hitler's part which Ley hoped to exploit in a final effort to make the DAF into a colossal super-agency. Here Ley put together a jurisdictional "package" which in many ways embodied the postwar agenda which the Labor Front leader had envisioned becoming reality — under his control. The "package" also represented areas which the DAF had been

39. Johnpeter Horst Grill, "The Nazi Party in Baden, 1920–1945", unpublished dissertation (University of Michigan, Ann Arbor, 1975), p. 308, underscores this fact for Baden.
40. See Hans Joachim Reichhardt, "Die Deutsche Arbeitsfront" (FU Berlin), p. 112.
41. See DAF Directive 25/44 of August 4 in BAK, NS5I/190, p. 6.
42. See Recker, *NS-Sozialpolitik*, p. 298.

involved in for years and which had been bones of contention between the DAF and government. Ley termed his package the *Sozialwerk des Deutschen Volkes* ("The Social Program of the German People"). It included several large areas of jurisdiction: social security, including national health; wage and labor allocation, including Vocational Education and National Housing.[43]

As usual, these areas were not really coordinated with each other and, as usual, Ley's competitive success varied from one to another. Each represents a final effort in activities begun, in some cases, very early in the regime, and deserves, for that reason, a final look. More importantly, the content of this variegated "package" indicates where the regime might well have gone had it won the war. It is here, rather than in the attainment of specific and concrete power, that Ley's ultimate pyrrhic victory lay: in Hitler's recognition that his "greatest idealist" should have the authority to set up the post war German social agenda and, with his DAF, see to its realization.

In the area of social insurance and social security, Ley was pushing Seldte to the wall as the war broke out, as indicated by rumors in circulation that Ley would soon succeed Seldte as Labor Minister, as well as probes by Göring as to what areas of jurisdiction RAM might turn over to the DAF as cost-cutting measures.[44] No doubt encouraged by German battlefield successes, Ley now reverted to the same tactics he had in 1934 and "procured" for himself another Führer decree. The decree of February 15, 1940, commissioned Ley with the task of working out plans for a comprehensive retirement plan (*Altersversorgung*).[45] Given all the trouble the October 24, 1934, decree had caused over the years, it is not quite clear why Hitler let himself be talked into another "elastic" order — partly, perhaps, because he saw in the promises suggested in such a plan one means of stabilizing the home front; more likely because he and Ley saw eye to eye on what National Socialism intended to do after a victory that seemed quite near.[46]

Ley went right to work with his usual verve and his usual perception of the elasticity of any order he received from the Führer.

43. Recker, ibid., develops this theme at some length, pp. 82–145.
44. See Teppe, "Zur Sozialpolitik," p. 243.
45. The decree is published in Marrenbach, *Fundamente*, p. 20; also in BAK, NS22/655.
46. Ley had suggested to Hitler implementing an *Altersversorgung* plan precisely as a means both to provide a postwar promise and as a means during the war to soak up purchasing power (through a percentage withholding premium). See Ley to Hitler, December 28, 1939, BAK, RR22/24248.

Altersversorgung soon expanded to become a general pension plan (*Versorgungswerk des Deutschen Volkes*) which included the disabled and families generally. Clearly, Ley meant to deprive both government and the insurance industry of their authority, as the later slogan, "Versicherung oder Versorgung" (Insurance or Care) suggested.[47] As if this were not enough, he also expanded his mandate into the area of health care and proposed in a *Gesundheitswerk* a new public health system for the future as well. As usual, Ley, rather than trying to implement his plans quietly and step by step, announced his programs prematurely in dramatic public announcements which suggested achieved reality when, in fact, they were only plans. "The retirement plan is finished," trumpeted the *Völkischer Beobachter* as Ley announced in September 1940 in his old Gau "that the enterprise is completed and nailed down in all detail."[48]

All this, once again, only provoked the resistance of the ministries. This time, however, loath to create once more the impression of non-cooperation, the ministries, instead of rejecting Ley's plans outright, fell back on convincing financial arguments about the costs of such plans in wartime.[49] Moreover, by drawing health care into his system, Ley made himself another powerful enemy, *Reichsgesundheitsführer* Leonardo Conti and the medical establishment.[50] Nor did the party, which Ley had neglected to prepare for his measures, respond positively. Both Bormann and Karl Fiehler, head of the Party's Office for Municipal Politics, felt Ley's plan to be too general and not well thought out.[51] Ley himself, in additon to his precipitate and incautious activities, also made the mistake of resisting efforts on the part of Seldte to raise current social security benefits, fearing, correctly, that the reality of concrete, specific improvement would undermine his grandiose, but vague, future plans.[52]

In the end, as both sides continued at loggerheads, Hitler intervened without depriving Ley of any of his mandate; he simply ordered in January 1942 that the matter should not proceed any

47. See Ley's draft law of early November 1940, BAK, NS25/1120. The slogan was the title of an AWI manuscript of October, 1942 in IfZ, MA253.
48. See *Völkischer Beobachter*, September 23, 1940.
49. See undated memo within Finance Ministry entitled "Die Aufbringung der Mittel für das Versorgungswerk des Deutschen Volkes," BAK, R2/18541.
50. For this aspect, see Recker, *NS-Sozialpolitik*, pp. 121–7.
51. See Bormann to Fiehler, April 6, 1940, and Fiehler's 51-page reply of May 29, in BAK, NS25/1120.
52. See Ley to Seldte, September 10, 1941, in BAK, R41/28; also Recker, *NS-Sozialpolitik*, pp. 208–9.

further while the war was going on. Until the Führer made a final decision, it was to be understood that "content, execution and reciprocal relations between the (pension, health, and social programs) are still completely open and for the time being not to be determined.[53] It is ironic, in light of the fact that Ley expected the war to usher in a social revolution, that the exigencies of that war put a stop to his implementation of precisely the social plans he expected to be the content of that revolution. His "victory" in getting the authority from Hitler was a hollow one.

Ley did not fare remarkably better in the area of wage and labor allocation, for much the same reason. If he fared better at all, it was because in practice he had to move ideologically away from the radical populist position of the late 1930s and into cooperation with business and government.[54] Part of his long-term planning, as we have seen, was to dominate vocational education as well as develop a whole new basis for wages (*Lohnordnung*), which had the *Volksgemeinschaft* rather than just market forces as its foundation. Prior to the outbreak of war, he had lost a great deal of ground in both areas as government and industry clearly demonstrated their efficacy, especially in vocational training. The war, however, gave Ley a second chance of sorts. The constant drain of skilled labor to the Wehrmacht; the urgent need to train or retool unskilled and semi-skilled labor, including foreign workers, caused the authorities to drop some of their objections to DAF involvement in this area. Authorities now drew in the DAF, made use of its ideas, employed its engineers. This development was facilitated by the fact that Sauckel as labor czar was more open to DAF involvement than Seldte.[55] A reopened door; a weakened RAM: these would have been decisive advantages for a prewar radical DAF. Under wartime circumstances, however, any potential radical activity was diverted into a push for higher productivity. This was especially clear with the wage question. Prior to the war, any inroads which the DAF might have made into vocational training would invariably have been accompanied by loud demands for a new National Socialist

53. Lammers to Ley, January 11, 1942, in BAK, R41/28; also Recker, *NS-Sozialpolitik*, p. 127; and Karl Teppe, "Zur Sozialpolitik des Dritten Reiches an Beispiel des Sozialversicherung," *Archiv für Sozialgeschichte*, vol. XVIII (1977), p. 248.

54. The whole area of labor allocation and wage structure, including DAF involvement, is treated extensively in Recker, *NS-Sozialpolitik*, pp. 58–74, 82–98, 155–242, 265–85.

55. Ibid., pp. 96–7.

wage structure. Again, the war made the difference. The imposition of a wage freeze at the beginning of the now largely stifled *public* discussion of such a fundamental departure — and *public* pronouncements had been one of Ley's main propaganda weapons in the jurisdictional struggle before the war. When Ley did raise the question of a new *Lohnordnung* during the war, it was quietly and within the framework of enforced cooperation with the RAM and the RGI, rather than as an open, all-out struggle.

This is best illustrated by wage plans introduced by the DAF Fachamt Eisen und Metall (Iron and Metal)[56] for workers in this critical branch of war industry. These plans, which gave expression to Ley's old idea of a *Leistungslohn* based on prior training and on-the-job performance, conflicted with those of the RGI, which largely accepted the status quo. Seldte, of course, backed the RGI. In the course of the debate, Ley once again opened the whole question of a new *Lohnordnung* and called for a "radical departure from the [currently] valid wage structure." Seldte fell back on the argument that there was no room for experiments during the war: "Such a reordering will have to await a future time that is more placid economically and less agitated in foreign policy."[57] Ley also tried to revive the by now moribund labor committees and attach them to the Reich Labor Trustees as expert advisory committees.[58] Even this very much tamed activity of the once-radical labor committees did not work. When it came to actual negotiations between the DAF and the RGI to develop a "wage catalog" for iron and steel, things, of course, did not go smoothly. The RGI tried to do as much of the work "internally," while Ley tried to undercut the RGI by reviving his old Gau "labor chambers" and rallying businessmen who were not members of the RGI. But in the end, the needs of war productivity were paramount. Under prodding from Speer, DAF and RGI did develop a "wage catalog" in 1943 and 1944 which was intended as a model for all industry.[59]

Ley recognized, finally, the futility of pursuing his plans too far during wartime. On August 8, 1944, he issued instructions that all planning for a new *Lohnordnung* was to be stopped to the extent that "they did not directly and demonstrably in their effects contribute to

56. Ibid., pp. 234–42.
57. See Ley to Seldte, December 11, 1941, and Seldte's reply of January13, 1942, in BAK, R41/57.
58. Ley to Pietzsch, March 16, 1940, in BAK, R12I/268.
59. See Recker, *NS-Sozialpolitik*, pp. 228, 234–5, 242–7.

a heightening of armaments production."[60]

Perhaps Ley's greatest triumph during the war came in an area where the DAF had also been active for years — housing and settlement. Here Ley achieved a clear and important area of jurisdiction with his appointment as Hitler's Plenipotentiary for Housing. More importantly, with this appointment, unlike most of the others, Ley was actually given real power and the opportunity to demonstrate how effectively he could use it. This was a particularly important area, ideologically and practically. Before the war, manipulation of housing offered the opportunity, as we have seen, to eliminate the older, urban working-class communities — and with them, presumably, a class identity — and to create the foundation for a new National Socialist society. Controlled housing also opened the door to creating the optimum circumstances for large families. This dream remained as part of Ley's postwar thinking. Moreover, housing and construction also represented, and continued to represent, an important part of the DAF business empire. And finally, the war itself, by taking a terrible toll on existing German housing stock, particularly in urban areas, both created an area of immediate and urgent need and "cleared the decks" for a totally new beginning after cessation of hostilities. None of this escaped Ley's attention, and he incorporated the AWI plan for housing into his larger *Sozialwerk* package.

In Ley's mind, the task of "carrying out a great settlement operation for the German worker" as a "contribution to solving the social question" had always been a task which Hitler intended for him to carry out.[61] In the years prior to the war, he had involved the DAF increasingly in "social construction," in part, by pouring large amounts of money into DAF companies at the Gau level; in part, by involving other companies via the NS Performance Competition.[62] After the outbreak of the war, Ley staked out a claim, in the name of the party, to leadership in housing and settlement, an area which Seldte had always insisted was his exclusive jurisdiction.[63]

60. Ley quoted in ibid., p. 249.
61. See Ludovici to Ley, February 20, 1936, in which the head of the DAF Heimstättenamt reminds his boss of this task. BAK, NS22, vorl. 671.
62. See Fischer-Dieskau (RAM) memo of December 29, 1938, in BAK, R41 (Krohn)/5018.
63. See Fischer-Dieskau memo of January 29, 1940, on a meeting between RAM officals and DAF functionaries in which the DAF claim was clearly stated, BAK, 41/22, pp. 121–3; see also Seldte's complaint to Hess about Ley's plans, April 30, 1940, BAK, R43II/1007, pp. 3–4.

Despite Seldte's energetic efforts in the summer of 1940 to fend off Ley's demands, Hitler clearly leaned in the direction of his DAF leader. This was partly because the government activities in the area of housing and settlement appeared to many as too cumbersome and bureaucratic, leading influential voices, such as that of Bormann, to call for a special entity to deal with the problem. In addition, Hitler at this point clearly saw housing and settlement as a crucial postwar *volkspolitische* task which his "idealist" Ley could most reliably formulate.[64]

On September 15, 1940, Hitler issued a decree clearly linking population policy and housing in such a way as to reflect DAF plans of long standing.[65] He appointed a committee composed of Ley, Bormann, Fiehler, Speer, Todt, Seldte, and von Krosigk to formulate postwar housing plans which would best enable Germany "through higher fertility to close the gaps left by the sacrifices imposed on the people by the war" and to present him with these plans by November 1. (Hitler expected a quick victory.) He made quite specific minimum stipulations: 80 percent of the dwellings should contain a large kitchen and three bedrooms, as well as a shower and a balcony. Ten percent should have one room more and ten percent one room less. There also had to be an air-raid shelter with sleeping facilities for all. (Hitler obviously anticipated further conflicts.) Reflecting the high priority which Hitler placed in this area, only a minority of the committee was composed of government ministers (Frick, the Interior Minister, was omitted completely to his great chagrin). Even more importantly, Hitler bestowed the chairmanship of the committee on Ley; and when Bormann suggested instead that Lammers, head of the Reich Chancellory, take over that job, Hitler reconfirmed Ley.[66]

Once again Ley was ready. Discussion at the first meeting on September 27, focused on a report prepared by the AWI which addressed Hitler's concerns directly. "Housing policy," it contended, "must become a protective wall against an aging population, infiltration by aliens and social misery."[67] Once again, the

64. Generally on housing as a part of wartime social policy and Ley's *Sozialwerk* in particular, see Recker, *NS-Sozialpolitik*, pp. 128–54, 250–64.
65. Copy of decree in BAK, R43II/1007, pp. 126–8.
66. See Bormann to Lammers, September 17, 1940, along with Killy memo and reply to Bormann of September 21 in BAK, R43II/1007, pp. 136–8; also Recker, *NS-Sozialpolitik*, p. 135.
67. See "Der Wohnungsbau nach dem Kriege," in BAK, NS6/251; on the ensuing committee debate, see Recker, *NS-Sozialpolitik*, pp. 136–42.

DAF plans were grandiose but reflected the racial/political priorities of the regime. The only serious arguments raised against it, as usual by the ministries, were financial; and these carried little weight against the prospect of the unlimited spoils of victory. There was also, as usual, concern about too much power being accumulated in the hands of Ley. As Todt pointed out:

> With this the Labor Front would achieve an all too encompassing place in the life of the people. Labor-Front-owned construction companies, Labor-Front-owned holding companies, Labor-Front-owned provisions companies already are preparing themselves for this impending major program of the DAF. Here is a clear danger of a development toward collectivism, which I perceive with the gravest concern.[68]

In the wake of these deliberations, Ley drafted a Führer decree which Hitler then signed on November 15, 1940.[69] Ley had hoped for complete authority in the sense of a *Reichsbehörde* (ministry), but instead got another one of those "elastic" decrees appointing him as Commissar for the Construction of Social Housing (Kommissar für den sozialen Wohnungsbau). What "social housing" meant was not completely clear, except to Ley, who interpreted it as a foot in the door for control of *all* housing in the postwar period. Since even a conservative interpretation of "social housing" cut deeply into Seldte's jurisdiction, the two men found themselves once again at odds with one another — with Ley's expansive interpretation of Hitler's decree confronting Seldte's restrictive one.[70]

This time inertia and the war worked in Ley's favor. After several abortive attempts in 1941 to get Hitler to change his decree or to issue a new one, Ley finally prevailed in 1942, largely by wearing everybody down. Gradually, Seldte had lost ground and support. Even Speer, the new Munitions Minister, saw little use in such a vaguely defined term as "social housing" and opted for a unified authority.[71] Seldte, having already surrendered much of his author-

68. Todt to Bormann, October 22, 1940, in BAK, NS6/251; Ley did have to give in on several points, including permitting municipalities a greater role in housing. See Recker *NS-Sozialpolitik*, p. 143.
69. For a draft of the decree see BAK, R43II/1007b, pp. 16–20.
70. For a detailed examination of Ley as Housing Commissar, see Recker, "Der Reichskommissar für den sozialen Wohnungsbau: zur Aufbau, Stellung und Arbeitsweise einer führerunmittelbaren Sonderbehörde," in Dieter Rebentisch and Karl Teppe (eds.), *Verwaltung contra Menschenführung im Staat Hitlers* (Göttingen, Van den Hoeck, 1986).
71. For Speer's advocacy of a unified housing authority, see Speer to Lammers,

ity, lost the stomach for a real fight. In fact, just after Ley's first appointment in November, 1940, Seldte wrote an unusually ingratiating letter to Ley, in effect offering the services of his ministry to the new commissar, a gesture which Ley interpreted as "a basic turning point in the mutual relationship between the Labor Ministry and me and my office, and vice versa."[72]

On October 23, 1942, Hitler issued yet another decree, this time appointing Ley Reich Housing Commissar (Reichswohnungskommissar), bestowing on him all the powers which had adhered in the Labor Ministry. As commissar, Ley would have the authority and power of an *oberste Reichsbehörde*, something which has eluded him before and which remained the single area in all his jurisdictions where he had such authority.[73] It was a dramatic victory for Ley. At last he had executive authority. The question was whether he could exercise that authority nearly as well as he could pursue jurisdictions.

Already as commissar of "social housing" Ley had operated in several ways. He issued a constant stream of decrees and directives on a wide range of housing topics, including public housing, housing financing, but above all typology of housing, with detailed specifications down to individual rooms.[74] Contrary to announcements, he also succumbed to his usual gigantomania, both by announcing unrealistic, grandiose goals and by starting a new bureaucratic edifice. Ley's Stabsleiter, Simon, writing in the new, glossy magazine, *Der soziale Wohnungsbau in Deutschland*, announced that "It is not the intention [of Ley] to expand his commissariat into a large administrative authority; on the contrary, the apparatus should be kept as small as possible but be staffed by the best experts in housing

---

August 4, 1942, BAK, R43II/1009a, pp. 79–80. On Hitler's refusal to change his decree, see Lammers to Ley, August 13, 1941, BAK, R43II/1009, p. 150; see also Recker, *NS-Sozialpolitik*, pp. 148–9.

72. See Seldte to Ley, December 10, 1940, and Ley's unusually quick response of December 14, BAK, R41/26, pp. 58–61. Ley was not long in exploiting Seldte's offer. See his *Dienstanweisung* no. 5 of January 25, 1941, ibid., p. 69; Seldte soon regretted his offer. See Seldte to Ley, January 31, 1941, in BAK, R43II/1009, pp. 11–14; but Hitler backed Ley. See decree of February 4, 1941, in BAK, R43II/1174, p. 37.

73. For the text of the "Dritter Erlass über den deutschen Wohnungsbau," see BAK, R41/26, p. 218. In a plaintive letter to Lammers, October 27, Seldte pointed out that the changes meant the "exiting" of his ministry from the circle of ministries. BAK, R43II/1009b, pp. 74–5.

74. For a number of these decrees, see BAK, NS6/252; also *Der soziale Wohnungsbau in Deutschland*, March 3, 1941, Heft 5, which lists the basic housing needs to be fulfilled.

construction."[75] Despite the announcement, Ley's 1941 budget already projected a staff of seventy-seven and costs of 160 million marks. Ley's housing projections were so unrealistic (five million new apartments by the end of 1941) that Goebbels tried to keep them out of the papers.[76]

As widespread bombing began to gut German cities in 1942, however, Ley had to become more practical. Something had to be done quickly to confront the problem of widespread homelessness. That meant close cooperation, above all, with Speer and with the gauleiters, the achievement of which forced Ley to retreat a bit on his wishes to inject the business side of the DAF into the operation.[77] Now Ley really had to face reality: building emergency housing could not really get started until October; winter delayed much construction; materials and skilled labor were scarce; large-scale evacuations had to be organized; and in 1943, the world witnessed bombing on a hitherto unprecedented scale, as the Allied air war really got underway. Almost from the outset, Ley's efforts lagged far behind the urgent needs created by large-scale destruction of urban housing. By mid-summer 1943, Ley's efforts had produced only 300,000 dwellings. This was clearly not enough. Under these circumstances, prodded by Bormann, Hitler began to change his attitude to the extent that he drew away from Ley's grandiose visions of German dwellings and toward a very simple, almost primitive family dwelling which could be produced in far greater numbers.[78] Ley was so instructed and once again went to work scaling up on quantity and down considerably on quality: the new dwellings were to resemble more the garden huts which dotted the outskirts of many German cities (*Schrebergärten*) than the airy family houses which the AWI had postulated. (The dwellings were christened *Ley-Lauben*, or Ley-Arbors.) The whole operation, named *Deutsches Wohnungshilfswerk* (German Housing Aid Operation), was announced in another Hitler decree on September 9, 1943, which

75. See ibid., January 1, 1941, with the introductory article entitled "Der deutsche Wohnungsbau nach dem Krieg."

76. See Lammers to Ley, August 13, 1941, in BAK, R43II/1174a; Also Killy memo of March 22, 1941, which includes information on Ley's budget, BAK, R43II/1174. On Goebbels, see Dietrich Orlow, *The History of the Nazi Party 1933–1945* (Pittsburgh, University of Pittsburgh Press, 1969), p. 286, n. 113.

77. See Recker, *NS-Sozialpolitik*, p. 252.

78. See Bormann memorandum of August 5, 1943, in BAK, NS6/267. Recker analyses the situation in *NS-Sozialpolitik*, pp. 253ff.

gave Ley full power to implement the program.[79] Goebbels observed in his diary:

> The Führer has signed the decree for an emergency housing scheme, with Dr Ley in charge. That gives Dr Ley a chance, for once, to do something with a big assignment. In the past, he has always been concerned about being clothed with authority. He fought energetically for authority. Once obtained, however, he would fail to use it, but would start another fight for authority.[80]

This time there was no escape. The need was too urgent. Ley had to get underway building the countless *Behelfsheime* (makeshift housing) which became more necessary by the day. In doing so, he ran into the same difficulties the government ministries had always faced: cost and material problems; labor bottlenecks; suspicious municipalities; recalcitrant Gauleiter; a stingy Speer; the whole polycratic system. In the end, he failed and failed miserably. Instead of the million dwellings which Ley had expected to build annually, by the eve of June 1944, with Allied troops already on European soil and German towns and cities facing another ten months of intensive bombing, only 53,000 *Behelfsheime* had been completed, with another 23,000 under construction.[81]

To be sure, much of the problem lay in the above-mentioned difficulties; it is unlikely that anyone could have achieved anything like the projected goals. On the other hand, Ley's poor administrative techniques by this time did not represent a negligible factor either. As one observer commented, "By reason of the constant personnel and organizational changes in the office of the Reich Housing Commissar . . . there [can] be no talk of uniform direction."[82]

Ley's failure to master the concrete task of providing sufficient housing for bombed out Germans was just one symptom of a general decline which set in for him during the last years of the war. His once dynamic DAF, riddled with corruption, decimated by conscription, but still bloated with wealth, lumbered on during the war years through inertia and from the tasks thrust upon it as a result of the war, largely bereft of its once dynamic populism. His dreams of

79. See Hitler decree "Uber die Errichtung des Deutschen Wohnungshilfswerkes," in *Reichsgesetzblatt* 1943, p. 535.
80. Entry of September 15, 1943, p. 515.
81. See RGI memo of August 4, 1944, BAK, R12I/258; see also "Die DAF im 5. Kriegsjahr" for details, USNA Microcopy.
82. Götz quoted *ibid.*, p. 264.

using the war as a revolutionary implement to transform German society backfired when the priorities of war largely cut off activities in that direction and aborted even public discussion of the specifics of those dreams. Goebbels had sensed the inappropriateness of Ley's dramatic announcements even before the invasion of Russia:

> Ley has announced the outline of a new old-age pension scheme for after the war. This is psychologically rather maladroit at the moment. We are promising too much, cannot carry it out at the moment, therefore only succeed in stirring up controversy and whetting appetites. The rule should be to confine oneself to basics and keep quiet about the details.[83]

A year and a half later, with the Stalingrad debacle staring him in the face, Hitler had obviously reached the same conclusion. As Bormann noted:

> The Führer emphasized, moreover, the new year would confront us with the most difficult tasks conceivable, and for that reason, the carrying out of any particular social plans, such as those Dr Ley has suggested, for example, would be completely impossible. We could really only have one thought—victory. And therefore, *everything* must be stopped which involves reorganization and therefore added burdens. . . . Even the most attractive and meaningful social plans, by the way, would not be appreciated at this time; for the individual is not in the mood for social plans. He is only moved by reports from the battlefield and that is only correct . . . The Führer wishes that he withdraw his social plans for the time being. At the moment, they are of no concern, for if we were to lose the war, the German nation would be finished anyway. To the extent that the German and the other European nations were not destroyed, they would be mixed with Central Asian peoples on the Russian example.[84]

Here was the dark side of the Armageddon both Ley and Hitler felt they were fighting: not for victory and the postwar German social utopia, but against defeat and racial death.

In the wake of these developments, Ley turned back to his old metier once again: NSDAP party politics. As we have noted, all the while Ley was fighting for added jurisdictions for his DAF,he never abandoned his attempts to recapture, as Reichsorganisationsleiter, the same power within the party as Strasser had once had. Indeed,

83. Entry of 16 June 1941, p. 413.
84. See Bormann *Aktenvermerk* of 25 December 1942 for Friedrichs, Klopfer and Tiessler, NSDAP *Parteikenzlei*, Microfiche 103 22040.

given the DAF and the party hats which he (and many of his subordinates) wore, he often tended to blend DAF and party into one entity in his own mind. He often issued instructions alternately as DAF leader and ROL, and, as we have seen, had he been able to push through his 1938 draft laws, the DAF would virtually have swallowed up the party entirely.

These party ambitions put him on a collision course very early with the Hess–Bormann–Schwarz team. We have alluded from time to time to that conflict as it impinged upon DAF ambitions and activities, but not in detail, since this has been done successfully elsewhere. A brief look at this rivalry will be useful, however, in shedding light on the last power-political spasms of Ley during the war.[85]

The rivalry ran throughout the peacetime years and into the war itself. At issue, to be sure, was power; but equally as important were the differing concepts of what the party should be. Hess and Bormann tended to view the political wing of the party as an élite comand agency, while Ley saw it as he did the DAF, as a mass propaganda/*Betreuung* agency. He stressed this aspect by pouring enormous sums into his party "training" institutions, such as Napola, the *Ordensburgen*, and the Adolf Hitler Schools.[86]

Almost from the beginning, in contrast to his success in building the DAF empire, Ley's authority in the political organization of the party experienced a gradual erosion. This was partly due to his ineptitude and the fact that he spread himself too thinly; partly owing to the clever tactics of Hess and Bormann. In the fall of 1934, for example, in the wake of the Röhm putsch which had caused widespread confusion in both party and DAF ranks, Hess launched a major offensive against Ley's position. He challenged Ley's right to command party cadres and took away his authority over personnel appointments. He also cut the ground out from under Ley's claim to be Strasser's successor by prohibiting further use of the title "Oberste Leitung der PO," since this implied that Ley commanded the entire political wing of the party. Instead, Ley had to content himself with the title, Reichsorganisationsleiter.[87] Hess even

85. Most importantly see Orlow, *Nazi Party*, II; also Diehl-Thiele, *Partei und Staat*, pp. 206–17; for the wartime years von Lang, *Secretary*, pp. 162–6, 233–8.
86. On Ley's various schools see Orlow, *Nazi Party*, II, pp. 85, 183–92, 22 p. 252–3; on contrasting definitions of the party and its role, ibid., pp. 14–15.
87. See Hess to Ley, 10 November 1934, and Ley *Rundschreiben* of 12 November 1934 in NSDAP *Parteikanzlei* Microfich 117 01433 and 117 01477 resp.; also Orlow, *Nazi Party*, II, pp. 130–4.

charged Ley in party court with violating party regulations. On all but this last action, Hess seemed to have Hitler's support.[88]

In early 1935, Hess hoisted Ley with his own petard, using Ley's insistence on the closeness between DAF and the party's political organization to demand involvement in the DAF itself. Here, he did not succeed.[89] In the meantime, party treasurer Schwarz gradually tightened the noose on Ley from another direction, by fighting for the right to audit Ley's books.[90] In the wake of a corruption scandal involving the DAF Bank, Schwarz won that right in fall 1937 and broke the financial hold the DAF had over the party's political organization. In summer 1938 Schwarz also ruled that a party functionary need not be a DAF member, thus helping to loosen the ties between the party and its overgrown affiliate.[91] Schwarz also took a very dim view of Ley's expensive party schooling and all but forbade his functionaries from attending.[92]

Hess had several advantages in the struggle. His own position in the party gave him a strong position in influencing legislation. Moreover, Bormann came to have almost complete charge of Hitler's personal and financial affairs which helped in the all-important access to the Führer. Moreover, Hess, resisting Ley's centralizing attempts, could often count on help from various other Gauleiter and Reichsleiter.[93]

Ley was unable to prevent this gradual erosion of his power base within the political organization of the party, although he did strike back with some offensives, most dramatically in 1936 and 1938. In late 1936 Ley published his *Organisationsbuch der NSDAP*, which embodied a thoroughgoing reform of the party. The vastly complicated book, full of details on such subjects as uniforms for all occasions, was in reality an attack on Ley's enemies and an attempt to rescue his power position in the political organization of the

88. See Walter Buch *Verfügung* of 23 October 1934 opening the case against Ley in *NSDAP Parteikanzlei* Microfiche 307 03435; also McKale, *Nazi Party Courts*, pp. 131–2; see Hitler to Ley, 29 November 1934, *NSDAP Parteikanzlei* Microfiche 117 00914; Hitler did not want party and DAF 'Kreisleiter' to be identical either. Bormann to Ley, 25 February 1935, in USNA Microcopy T-580, 549, 746.
89. See Hess to Ley, 16 January 1935, *ibid.*
90. See Schwarz to Ley, 26 July and 7 Aug 1935, and Bormann to Schwarz, 25 July 1935 in BAK, NS22/ vorl. 670.
91. See Orlow, *Nazi Party*, II, pp. 207–9; also Lükemann, 'Reichsschatzmeister', pp. 111–13, 120, 126–131.
92. So *Ressortbesprechung* 7/39, 8 March 1939, in USNA Microcopy T580, 842, Box 267, frame 347.
93. Orlow, *Nazi Party*, II, pp. 130–3.

party. Ley laid out a new organizational schema which, while it ostensibly did not violate Hitler's formal delegation of authority to Ley's rivals, actually diminished their power considerably, partly by laying out in great detail the exact limits of their jurisdictions and partly by developing a new bureaucratic flow chart which reached its apex in Robert Ley. Thus Hess would have found himself limited to party-state affairs, Schwarz to minor administrative powers, Rosenberg to the publishing of the Nazi journal. Ley, on the other hand, would have regained control of administration, organization, personnel, and in-service training.[94]

Ley's attempt failed, in part because he did not succeed in rallying enough Gauleiter to his cause, but mainly because the polycratic nature of the system did not lend itself to exact definitions of jurisdictions. Ley had got where he was by blurring distinctions and seeking "elastic" decrees, not by sharply defining lines of authority. He, of all people, should have known this.[95] Typically enough though, Ley's *Organisationsbuch* remained the ostensible standard, although its real importance is reflected in Gauleiter Kaufmann's characterization of it as "Robert Ley's Fairy Tales." Ley's other great offensive, as we have seen, came in late winter 1938, with his infamous draft laws, which were an attempt, in reality, to subordinate the political wing of the party to the DAF itself. This attempt also failed.

Ley did have some successes. Hitler put him in charge of the annual Reich party day in 1936 and seemed to back his training efforts in the party strongly in the two years prior to the war. But this did not disguise the fact that Ley had to suffer major encroachments in his role as ROL, which perhaps helps explain the emphasis he put on expanding his jurisdiction as leader of the DAF. It did not help either that he was locked in running battle with Darré and Rosenberg.[96]

94. On this episode, *ibid.*, pp. 182–8.

95. Hess and Bormann certainly knew this. Hess later characterized his functions, like those of Hitler, as 'limitless'. See Bormann to Ley, 31 August 1939, USNA Microcopy T-380, 549, 746.

96. See Hitler order of August 17, 1936, BAK, NS10/60, naming Ley "Kommandant" of the party day. Ley took great encouragement from a Hitler speech in November 1937 at Ordensburg Sonthofen; see Orlow, *Nazi Party, 1933–1945* p. 221. By 1939 Bormann had almost completely outmaneuvered Ley, whose mistakes only redounded to Bormann's benefit; as in suggesting in 1939 a convening of a meeting of the Gauleiter. This would have been anathema to Hitler, who rebuffed Ley via Bormann. See Bormann to Ley, May 26, 1939, USNA Microcopy T-580, 549, 746. On the rivalry with Rosenberg, see Reinhard Bollmus, *Das Amt Rosenberg und seine Gegner* (Stuttgart, DVA, 1970), esp. pp. 51–74, 85–110, 123–42, 237–75, 294–9.

Ley's final big opportunity to take control of the political organization of the party seemed to have come in the dramatic flight of Rudolf Hess to England on May 10, 1941.[97] Now his main enemy was gone. He would quickly volunteer to fill the vacuum and informed the Führer that, despite his many offices, he was willing to assume the duties of Führer Deputy. Surely Bormann was now finished. How could Hitler replace a traitor with the traitor's deputy? Hitler informed Ley (and Göring, who also warned against Bormann) that he had no intention of replacing Hess with Bormann, or with anyone else either. He would abolish Hess's office entirely and himself take over the political leadership of the party; but Bormann was too useful for Hitler to dismiss him. This move seemed to put Ley and Bormann on a collision course. Many assumed a protracted rivalry, including Himmler, who predicted that the struggle between Bormann and Ley would be "tremendous," with Ley "cashing in during the war on what there was to cash in on."[98] But the great struggle was not to be. With Hitler fully absorbed in the Russian campaign, Bormann began to play that very powerful role of "keeper of the gate" to the Führer, which would make him virtually invulnerable for the rest of the war. Bormann assumed the position of Head of the Party Chancellory, with an "elastic" job description, and firmly cemented his position by early 1942. He was also astute in choosing allies, particularly Fritz Todt, head of armaments, whose rivalry with Ley "was so basic that they could not even agree on who was to manage the workers' canteens at the big construction sites."[99]

Since Ley's correspondence to the Reich Chancellory simply disappeared into Bormann's files, Ley made his attacks public. Many of his articles in the press focused on Todt and his organization. Again this fell into Bormann's hands. He showed copies of Ley's articles and speeches to Hitler, who called Ley in for a tongue lashing.[100] As for Bormann's correspondence with Ley, it gradually took on the tone of commands, always, of course, ostensibly relayed

97. On the Hess mission and its consequences, see Jochen von Lang, *The Secretary. Martin Bormann* (New York, Random House, 1979), p. 157; also Orlow, *Nazi Party, 1933–1945*, pp. 337–9; Albert Speer, *Inside the Third Reich* (New York, Macmillan, 1970), p. 175.

98. See Brandt (SS-Hauptamt) to Berger (RKFDV), August 16, 1941, in USNA Microcopy T-175, Roll 123, Frame 2648461.

99. Von Lang, *Secretary*, pp. 162–6, gives the best account of Bormann's success after Hess's flight; quote from p. 163.

100. Goebbels relates the incident in his diary, entry of February 13, 1942, p. 104: "In my presence the Führer gave Ley a tongue-lashing, and, when the latter

from Hitler himself.[101] When he desired, Bormann could also slyly flatter Ley in his alleged strong points and thereby give him the necessary rope to hang himself. Ley inadvertently revealed being thus taken in, when he once said to Hitler's Youth Leader, von Schirach:

> There is a very curious relationship between Bormann and myself. I get the feeling he is jealous because I am always out making speeches while he sits in headquarters and scribbles. I offered to get him some audiences so he could be more in the public eye. . . . But he said he couldn't do that, he was completely incapable of speaking before a group. That was for me to do. It was my big job in the war.[102]

And Ley proceeded to pull out all the stops in his public remarks, much to the discomfiture, among others, of the master propagandist, Goebbels, who kept track of Ley's gaffes in his diary entries. "As an experiment, I have one of Dr Ley's speeches played to me on a record. Appalling. His amateurism is painfully apparent. Idealism alone is not enough." Or, "Unfortunately, I must complain about Dr Ley. He is conducting a propaganda [campaign] for increasing production that is most inopportune." Or, "The Führer was very angry about the draft of Ley's appeal for May 1. He was especially amazed that the style was like that of a high school sophomore." Or, "Ley delivered a pretty unfortunate speech on the present position of labor in the Mosaic Hall of the Reich Chancellory. The minute he opens his mouth he puts his foot in it."[103]

Eventually, Himmler also became concerned about Ley's verbal excesses and began sending reports to Bormann on the negative public reaction to Ley's speeches.[104] By early 1944 Ley was com-

---

tried to reply, told him that it just won't do for anybody to start things on his own at a time when other departments and other personalities are concerning themselves with the same problem." Ley had been "smashing a lot of china" with his "hysterical articles."

101. See, for example, Bormann, acting in Hitler's name, forbidding Ley to enter into an agreement with Lutze with respect to plant sports. In a letter to Ley of February 22, 1942, *NSDAP Parteikanzlei* Microfiche 117 07592; or a directive to Ley that all correspondence to the Führer go exclusively through Bormann's office, August 2, 1942, ibid., 117 06223; see also Orlow, *Nazi Party, 1933–1945*, pp. 338–9.

102. Quoted in von Lang, *Secretary*, p. 166.

103. Entries of June 5, 1941, p. 396; March 20,1942, p. 161; May 2, 1942, pp. 235–6; May 3, 1942, p. 237.

104. See, for example, Himmler to Bormann, n.d. but June 1943 in USNA Microcopy T-120, Roll 2620, Frames E381732–9.

pelled to send drafts of his speeches to Goebbels and to Bormann in advance, although that did not prevent him from making statements on his own when he felt strongly enough compelled to do so.[105] As late as March 1945 with the end of the Third Reich imminent, Goebbels felt constrained to talk at length with Marrenbach about Ley's leading articles.[106]

Too weak to challenge Bormann on his own, Ley joined Goebbels, Göring, Funk, and Speer in a brief cabal against the "gatekeeper" in February and March of 1943. Ley applauded their plan to revive the moribund Reich Council of National Defense and undermine Bormann by becoming the dynamic force behind mobilization for total war, which in turn, would also revive some of the party's dynamic. Ley was of the opinion that the party had become too inactive because of the "somewhat bureaucratic conduct of party affairs by Bormann. Bormann is not a man of the people," Ley had averred. "He has always been engaged in administrative work and therefore has not the proper qualifications for the real task of leadership."

Bormann, who became officially secretary to the Führer on April 12, easily defeated the group. Göring, sunk in a semi-permanent state of lethargy, allowed himself to be bought off. Goebbels and Speer, sniffing the wind, deserted the plot. This left Ley slowly twisting in the wind.[107]

As usual, Bormann got his revenge quickly. He recorded verbatim a conversation of August 23, 1943, with Ley in which he had, in terse, cutting, and condescending words turned down a series of Ley requests, including an audience with the Führer. He then circulated the memo among his staff.[108]

It was no wonder that Ley had ceased to be a serious political opponent. As the war ground through its last year or so, he became increasingly unstable, drank more and more heavily, and withdrew

105. See Ley to Goebbels, April 7, 1944, in BAK, NS22, vorl. 976; Ley to Bormann, April 9, 1944, in *NSDAP Parteikanzlei* Microfiche 117 00195; for a particularly critical analysis of one of Ley's proclamations, see Sondermann (PROMI) to Goebbels, August 16, 1944, in BAK, R55/625.
106. See Goebbels, *Final Entries*, entries of March 8 and 9, 1945, pp. 97, 111.
107. Von Lang, *Secretary*, describes the plot, pp. 233–4 (quote is from p. 234); as does Speer, *Inside the Third Reich*, pp. 256–66; see also Goebbels' diary entries for March 2, March 6, March 18 and May 22, 1943, pp. 309, 319, 353 and 445–6, respectively.
108. For the text, see USNA Microcopy T-120, Roll 2620; also von Lang, *Secretary*, pp. 237–8.

into a world of illusions. He dreamed of getting back his old Gau, Cologne-Aachen, which had been wrested from him by Strasser.[109] Occasionally, he could still rise to the levels of his old calumny. The officers' plot of July 20, 1944, was one of those occasions. The "treason" of the aristocrats brought out all of Ley's old social resentments. In a radio speech of July 22 and an *Angriff* article the next day, Ley spewed out his hatred for the plotters, behind whom he saw both Jewish Bolsheviks and English lords. "Degenerate to their very bones, blue-blooded to the point of idiocy, nauseatingly corrupt, and cowardly like all nasty creatures — such is the aristocratic clique which the Jew has sicked on National Socialism . . . We must exterminate this filth, extirpate it root and branch . . . It is not enough simply to seize the offensive . . . We must exterminate the entire breed."[110]

These remarks were completely out of place at a time when many aristocrats still filled the ranks of the German officer corps and national solidarity had to take precedence over any renewed talk of class struggle. Goebbels, among others, knew so. Still, these fighting words certainly expressed Hitler's feelings as well as Ley's. Over 5,000 aristocrats did, in fact, pay with their lives in the wake of the plot. Nor did Ley stop with aristocrats. Since some businessmen had also been implicated in the plot, Ley (as well as Himmler) began talking about a "July 20" in industry, by which they meant a purge trial for industrialists and economists.[111]

Among his illusions, then, was the belief that the war might still bring that social revolutionary transformation which he (and Hitler) dreamed about. Certainly, he shrank from nothing in the prosecution of the war. After Stalingrad and then again in the fall of 1944, he (along with Bormann and Goebbels) urged Hitler to use the deadly Tabun nerve gas. Even in the last weeks of the war, he clung to desperate ideas — he suggested combining party activists and the "Volkssturm," a bevy of boys and old men, into an "Adolf Hitler Free Corps" in March 1945. The "Werwolf," a group of fanatical

109. See Goebbels' diary entry for May 9, 1943, pp. 412–13. Ley also repeatedly lost his golden party decoration, presumably while drunk, and had to apply for new ones, as in August 1943, BDC: file Ley.

110. *Angriff* article quoted in Speer, *Inside the Third Reich*, p. 390; radio message quoted in Paul Friedrich Merker, *Deutschland sein oder nicht sein?* (Mexico City, El Libra Libre, 1944), vol. 2, p. 467. For the negative reaction in the Propaganda Ministry to Ley's tirade, see Rudolf Semmler, *Goebbels: The Man Next to Hitler* (London, Westhouse, 1947), p. 140.

111. See Speer, *Infiltration*, pp. 110–11.

fighters who would retreat to the Alpine Redoubt to stop the Americans, was also his idea in April. In all these ideas he got Hitler's support, although those not infused with the Nazi dream could not help but see the huge and growing gap between fantasy and reality.[112]

As Hitler withdrew in the last month of his life, taking his faithful dreamers and fanatics — including Ley, Goebbels, and Bormann — with him, even the faithful, true believer, idealistic Ley began seriously to crumble under the pressure. Goebbels noted in March 27, "Ley has become somewhat hysterical under the impact of recent developments. It shows that he is not a naturally strong personality. He is only strong when there is some external cause to be. Moreover, he oscillates like a windsock when times are serious and critical."[113] The perceptive Goebbels had put his finger on it. For the first time since Ley had disengaged from social reality in 1924 and sought protection and purpose in the brown uniform, he now had to face the complete disintegration of his world, and not even huddling close to his master could change that.

On April 20, Ley saw his Führer for the last time — to wish him a happy birthday. Several days later, as the Third Reich was collapsing into fire and rubble, he set out to the south, presumably to organize final resistance in the Tyrol.[114] Hitler remembered his faithful paladin in his political testament, with a final "elastic" position. In the short-lived Dönitz government, Ley was to be Minister — without Portfolio.[115]

On May 15, 1945, troops from the 101st US Airborne Division captured Ley in a mountain hideaway at Schleching/Kufstein, 45 miles south of Berchtesgaden. He was a wretched figure, dressed in blue pajamas, a green hat, and sporting a four-day growth of beard. From his once portly 200 lb, he had shrunk to 135 lb. He tried to pass himself off as one Dr Ernest Distelmeyer, but at division headquarters to which he was taken after being captured, he was

112. On use of Tabun, see Speer, *Inside the Third Reich*, p. 413, and Joseph Borkin, *The Crime and Punishment of I.G. Farben* (New York, Macmillan, 1978), p. 131. On the "Free Corps" see Hugh Trevor-Roper (ed.), *Final Entries: The Diaries of Joseph Goebbels* (New York, Avon, 1979), entry of March 29, 1945, p. 331; and Semmler, *Goebbels*, April 2, 1945, pp. 189–90; on Werwolf, see Trevor-Roper, *Goebbels: Final Entries*, entry of April 7, 1945, p. 386.

113. Trevor-Roper, *Goebbels: Final Entries*, entry of March 27, 1945, p. 299.

114. See James O'Donnell, *The Bunker* (Boston, Houghton-Mifflin, 1978), p. 250.

115. See Werner Maser, *Hitler's Letters and Notes* (London, Heinemann, 1974), pp. 362–3.

positively identified by his old Nemesis, party treasurer Schwarz, who had also been captured. He had also been trapped by being asked what had happened to Wilhelm Gustloff and replied that he did not know what had happened to that particular *ship*! Trapped, Ley admitted his identity and related that he had been in Linz on the day of the capitulation and had disguised himself in order to visit his children: "I wanted to see my family once more and then I didn't care what the Allies did with me." He had not lost his faith in the Führer though; as he announced to his captors, "Life doesn't mean a damn thing to me; you can torture me or beat me or impale me, but I will never doubt Hitler's acts."[116]

Along with other top Nazis who were scheduled to be tried as war criminals, Ley was transferred to a hotel at Mondorf, Luxembourg. From there, in early August, he and the others were transferred to Nuremberg to await indictment and trial. Ley occupied Cell 45.[117] His captors observed Ley's pronounced emotional instability and poor judgment during the first several months of his captivity. Interrogation revealed the head injury, and the psychiatrists took due note of its possible effects on his behavior, and certainly the collapse of his social dreams also contributed a good deal to his highly labile state. As his interrogators noted in July, "his emotions . . . manifested themselves in tears when he spoke of his and the Führer's blighted hopes of Anglo-German understanding, and again, almost, when he referred to social security plans of his drafting which may never come to fruition and by the side of which 'Beveridge' is very small beer."[118]

The one thing which Ley seemed to have second thoughts about after he had been in captivity for a while, was the very thing in which he had specialized as a rabble-rouser — anti-semitism. This may have simply been a tactical maneuver to get into the good

116. See, "Ley Arrest Record," OSS, Box 31, USNA RG 238, Collection of World War Two Crimes, Justice Jackson File. Quotes from *New York Herald Tribune*, May 18, 1945, and *New York Post*, May 17, 1945; see also quote from Burton C. Andrus, *I was the Nuremberg Jailer* (New York, Conrad McCann, 1969), p. 39.
117. Ley kept a calendar on which he kept a record of certain activities like the cleaning of his cell, receipt of tobacco, and so on. He also noted faithfully his mother's birthday on September 2. USNA, Justice Jackson File.
118. That is, the famous Beveridge Report published in the United Kingdom during the war outlining the social welfare state which was to emerge after the war. See USNA Microcopy 679, Records of the Department of State, Special Interrogation Mission to Germany 1945–1946, Roll 2 (In IfZ, Munich under MA 1300/2).

graces of his captors, or it may have been a result of the fact that the other prisoners shunned him (along with the notorious Jew-baiter, Julius Streicher).

Under interrogation, Ley stated:

> I wish to say at this time that the Führer was one of the greatest men there ever was; but I also wish to say that the positive aspect of it, the positive side of our ideas, was one of the greatest things people ever thought. But one thing broke us — not only externally, but within ourselves — that was our Willensethos . . . and our anti-semitism, which were the things that finally undid us.[119]

Although his world had collapsed, Ley tried desperately during the weeks before the indictments were handed down to find some way to reconstruct that world and again be "socially useful." In August he submitted a proposal for the reconstruction of Germany which he would direct using his experience as DAF leader. This was, of course, rejected. He then wrote, but did not post, a letter to Henry Ford (addressed to "Sir Henry Ford, Detroit, USA"), who had always been favorably viewed by the Nazis because of his anti-semitism, reminding the auto magnate of Ley's role in the Volkswagen enterprise and pointing out that he, Ley, had done nothing more than Ford himself had done, namely to have "written essays and books against the Jews." He had not committed any crimes. Now, perhaps, Ford might find work for him, given his experience with VW and the Beauty of Work Program.[120]

Ley also wrote prolifically while in his cell, using pencil and paper. In addition to his "Bauernschicksal," he composed documents on anti-semitism and on Hitler, as well as a political testament, a personal testament to his children, and an imaginary conversation with his dead wife.[121] The political statements, despite the "disclaimers" about anti-semitism, reveal that Ley's *Weltanschauung* remained by and large intact. In his political testament, for example, Ley admitted that anti-semitism was wrong, that German and Jew would have to be reconciled with one another — but, in the

119. See Andrus, *Nuremberg Jailer*, p. 39; also "Ley Arrest and Interrogation Record," September 1, 1945, in USNA, Justice Jackson File.
120. Letter in "Ley Arrest and Interrogation Record"; see also letter to author from John Dolibois of August 27, 1985. Dolibois, currently US Ambassador to Luxembourg, was one of Ley's interrogators. He used the name John Gillen to protect relatives in Germany.
121. Ley's handwritten statements are in USNA, Justice Jackson File, as is the typed

same breath, said that anti-semitism was all right as long as it was only on the defensive, and that now the Jew had won the war. He had clearly not shaken his *Feindbild.* He predicted that anti-semitism would flare up again stronger than before if the Jew sought revenge, that the soldiers of occupation would encounter the "Jewish problem"; indeed, the upcoming "show trials" would only draw the world's attention to this problem. But if the Jew did not seek revenge, then Ley proposed that Germany become their home. He even suggested a plan for setting up a committee of Jews and anti-semites to establish terms for Jews and Germans to live together, and an organization for "schooling and propaganda" to spread these ideas! He had not lost his organizational mania either. But with this grotesque testament he was clearly slipping further from reality. In his statement "Anti-semitism," Ley admits that the war was one against the Jews. "We National Socialists, starting with Hitler, considered the fight which is now behind us a war merely against the Jews — not against the French, English, Americans, or Russians. We believe that they [Frenchmen, etc.] were only instruments of the Jews, and when reading the indictment, I feel inclined to believe that it actually was like that." Yet Ley denies specific acts against the Jews. "I never prosecuted or tortured any Jew or jailed him or dispossessed him. I had no influence with regard to concentration camps. I had no influence with Himmler. I didn't acquire any Jews' fortunes — not a penny. I had reason for using aggressive vocabulary in my writings but I feel sorry about it today." In his "Thoughts on the Führer," Ley characterized Hitler as the "greatest genius of all time" and reaffirmed his loyalty: "I took this position twenty-one years ago in 1924 as I decided for Hitler and have never changed this opinion since then, and I pray God daily that he may give me the strength not to waver even now under this heavy burden."

During this time, there were signs that Ley was beginning to crumble psychologically. In his testament he wrote, "God caused me to fall and God led me into this lonely, cold, and bare cell, caused

---

manuscript "Gedanken an den Führer;" the typed manuscript "Anti-Semitism" is in English translation in "Ley Arrest and Interrogation File." His farewell message, political testament and outline of his defense have been published in Office of the United States Chief of Counsel for Prosecution of Axis Criminality, *Nazi Conspiracy and Aggression* (Washington, DC, Government Printing Office, 1946), vol. 8, Statements XI, XII, and XIII respectively, pp. 740–55.

me to become nothing, humbled me like scarcely any other person." What kept him from crumbling completely was probably the belief, which he shared with the others, that any judicial action would be perfunctory. After all, they had been acting under orders and in the national interest.[122]

What ultimately pushed Ley over the edge, however, was the indictment, which was handed down on October 18. Here he was clearly charged as a war criminal, his corps of "political functionaries" branded a criminal organization. The psychiatrist, Kelly, recalled the impact:

> Immediately after reading the indictment where he was charged with being a criminal, he became violently disturbed, orating and ranting, maintaining his innocence, and swearing that he would never face trial against such charges. In the middle of this tirade, he marched dramatically to the far end of his cell, placed his back against the window, flung out his arms, and cried, "Shoot me! Shoot me now as a German. Do not try me as a common criminal!" After several days, Ley's fear had not abated; asking once again to be shot, and being refused, he said: "All well and good, you are the victors, but why should I be brought before a tribunal like a c-c-c-c-." At this point [Kelly continued] he stammered so severely that he was unable to continue. When I supplied the word 'criminal', he added, "that's it, I cannot even get that word out. I cannot even say it."[123]

In an interrogation, Ley denied the charges against him. "I have nothing to hide. This is all so terrible. I have read this indictment." He denied planning the war. It was not true, he said,

> that I participated in getting the war started . . . I had prepared the party congress in Nuremberg in 1939. I even had arranged for an excursion for workers to the Far East and around the world for that and the following year. I have had no knowledge or information as to the war. It came to me as a surprise, as a hail stone comes to a corn field . . . and that I should have mistreated foreign workers, it is not true. As a matter of fact, I have favored them. I have done everything that was in my power – everything to improve their fate.[124]

Clearly, the indictment was the final straw. Not only had his

122. See Werner Maser, *Nürnberg* (Munich, Droemer Knauer, 1977), p. 53.
123. See Douglas Kelly, *Twenty-Two Cells* (New York, Greenberg, 1947), p. 170.
124. See "Ley Arrest and Interrogation Record," October 18, 1945, USNA, RG 238, Justice Jackson File.

world of "social usefulness" collapsed, now he was threatened with repeating his father's experience of being labelled a common criminal: the very thing which had represented *the* trauma of his early youth. This time he was really not posturing; death seemed preferable to what he now saw as the ultimate social ignominy. The thought haunted him over the next few days: "They may kill me . . . may do with me whatever they like. I accept the victor. I don't suffer from false conceitedness. I accept my fate. However, I am not a criminal . . . I am a National Socialist, but I am no criminal."[125]

Ley went through the motions of preparing his defense, and even requested a Jewish attorney! But his heart was clearly not in it. During the night of October 25, Ley fashioned a noose from the torn hem of a bath towel and tied it to the stand pipe of his corner toilet, the only place where he could not be directly observed. He then stuffed his mouth with rags to stifle any sounds, sat on the toilet with the noose around his neck and leaned forward until he had strangled himself. It was not a pleasant way to die and demonstrated Ley's determination to depart this world at any cost.[126]

In his cell, Ley left a final note:

> Farewell. I cannot stand this shame any longer. Physically, nothing is lacking. The food is good. It is warm in my cell. The Americans are correct and partially friendly. Spiritually, I have reading matter and write whatever I want. I receive paper and pencil. They do more for my health than necessary and I may smoke and receive tobacco and coffee. I may walk at least 20 minutes every day. Up to this point, everything is in order but the fact that I should be a criminal . . . This is what I cannot stand.[127]

After his death, Ley's corpse underwent autopsy; his brain was excised and flown to the United States for pathological examination; his body, wrapped in plain brown butcher's paper, was buried in an unmarked grave in the Nuremberg cemetery. The only reaction to Ley's suicide amongst the other prisoners came from Göring, who said laconically, "It's just as well that he's dead, because I had my doubts about how he would behave at his trial."[128]

125. From his "Anti-Semitism", ibid.
126. See Kelly, *Twenty-Two Cells*, pp. 171–2; also affidavits of Dr Hoch and Dr Fluecker, October 26, 1945, in "Ley Arrest and Interrogation Record," USNA, RG238, Justice Jackson File.
127. "From the papers of Dr Ley", typed, in ibid., (English trans.).
128. See Andrus, *Nuremberg Jailer*, p. 91; also Dolibois letter to author of August 27, 1985.

Conclusion

The political career of Robert Ley and, in particular, his leadership of the German Labor Front, help to underscore some important lessons about the nature of the Nazi regime and to shed light on several recent controversies which focus on the historical role of that regime.

Ley's path to National Socialism illustrates an important but often neglected aspect of the Nazi movement: that in the lives of many of its adherents, it was far more than just a political party. Rather, it functioned as a quasi-religion, a faith with chiliastic and apocalyptic overtones. In fact, it would be no exaggeration to suggest that in this respect National Socialism represented a twentieth-century recrudescence of those medieval millenarian movements which temporarily seized parts of Western Christendom.

Ley did not just join the Nazi Party, he underwent a conversion experience in 1924 in which he quite literally accepted Hitler as his Germanic "savior" and embraced National Socialism with its revealed insights about the racial nature of history, its schema of good versus evil (with the Jew embodying evil) and its world-historical task of creating a racial utopia for the Germans.

Thus, having embraced a new faith, Ley disengaged himself from the ongoing society and, clothed in the brown uniform of the movement, gave himself completely to the tasks outlined by Hitler: to seize power in Germany and then go on to destroy the power of world Jewry and raise the German people to their rightful place as master race. Ley even derived his image of his own role, that of the party and, eventually, of the DAF itself from his religious commitment: to be preacher and *Betreuer* in the sense of tending a flock.

That Ley should have so surrendered himself illustrates another point about the Nazi movement: that it often attracted a certain kind of personality, particularly into its upper ranks. Ley, like many others around Hitler, possessed ambition, drive, intelligence, and ruthlessness, but lacked the autonomy of personality and the ego strength which would have allowed him to function as a sovereign human being. Instead, he was drawn into a dependent relationship with Hitler which became so pronounced that it lasted until the very end — and, in fact, beyond Hitler's own demise. Goebbels, Himmler, and others revealed similar characters; men who, as marginal social beings, were simply unable to function in the social chaos of post-World War One Germany and who had, in effect, lost their social and moral compasses until drawn by the magnet of Hitler and his movement.

A successful polity presumes a certain level of perceived unity and consensus — either real or fictitious. Usually, real ones are apparent — religious orthodoxy, capitalist hegemony, ethnic homogeneity, or foreign domination. In the eyes of many contemporaries, however, the Weimar republic was not a successful polity, in that it did not seem able to engender that broad spectrum of acceptance which would have produced the kind of stability that labile personalities like Ley needed in order to function on a day-to-day basis. In the apparent absence of genuine social consensus, then, Ley and many like him would embrace a fictional one — the radical gnosticism of National Socialism. This was important, because after Hitler came into power, he and Ley would attempt to impose this fictional consensus on Germany — and one of their main devices would be the Labor Front.

Ley's political career, spanning as it did the early days of the movement through to the last days of the Third Reich, also highlights an important aspect of the Nazi Party and its functionaries: the inability to transcend the identity and role developed during the *Kampfzeit* and become a ruling party once in power. Ley, like the Nazi Party, remained throughout what he had always been — a propaganda tool for mass mobilization and a *Betreuer* of those who were targets of that mobilization. Ley's vision of the party confirmed this fact as did his own day-to-day activities during the Third Reich. Even as head of a massive, bureaucratic party affiliate, the Labor Front, Ley traveled and gave speeches incessantly, just as he had during the campaign trail. His constant pursuit of jurisdictions after 1933, often without having any clear concept of what to do with them or how to relate them to one another, resembled, in a sense, the frantic, even mindless, pursuit of power on the part of the movement in the *Kampfzeit*, with little thought of how that power related to specific programs or goals. Indeed, the frenetic activities of the Labor Front and Ley, always coming up with new programs, new opportunities, new ideas which were then trumpeted grandiosely in press and radio, represented a kind of ongoing, relentless political campaign to win the loyalty of the population and thus give legitimacy to the regime, a kind of "daily plebiscite." Even the endless and well-publicized "actions" of the DAF from the "more and better lighting" action of the "Beauty of Work" Organization during the 1930s to the "vitamin" action during the war, smacked of electioneering. Here is a strong element of continuity with respect to Ley and the Nazi Party, particularly its DAF affiliate: whether haranguing new recruits next to an SA soup kitchen in Cologne in 1928, or unveiling the new VW factory as the key to putting the German worker "on wheels" in 1938, or announcing a grandiose postwar social security program in 1940, Ley basically remained the same, did the same things, throughout. He preached, he harangued and provided the carrot (or the promise of it) which invariably accompanied the stick.

By the same token, like the party itself, Ley lacked the talent and inclination which would have allowed him to focus on a long-term, limited, and coherent administrative task and see to its successful completion. He was adept at chasing jurisdictions, bits and pieces of power; but once he had them, rather than giving them a firm foundation, he simply went on to chase others. When finally given a specific and limited administrative task during the war — emergency housing — and the full power to carry it out, he failed. And his failure reflected the larger failure of the party itself and its often inadequate functionaries. Fanaticism in the end was not enough; talent and expertise were more important.

It was not surprising that the party never lost its pre-1933 role; Hitler really did not want it to, for he, like Ley, felt a pronounced insecurity about the legitimacy of the regime, despite its obvious popularity. Both men believed the myth of the "stab in the back" of 1918 and lived in fear that it might recur. This fear governed much of Ley's conduct before and after the takeover, his "testing of the water" on his many junkets around Germany, his incessant drive always to come up with something new in the way of amenities to be bestowed by his Labor Front, his anxious desire to legitimize the DAF in the eyes of the workers as representative of "their" interests; his concern that the burdens of war not fall too hard on the shoulders of the German people. All this betrayed a fundamental insecurity and the fear that, as in an election campaign, if he were to lose momentum or curry widespread disfavor, everything would collapse and he would fall back into the social abyss which tortured his dreams.

Ley's career after the *Machtübernahme* in January 1933 also underscores what by now has become widely accepted as a defining feature of the Nazi political system: its polycratic nature. Ley, both as Reichsorganisationsleiter of the party and, in particular, as head of the Labor Front, was one of the major contenders in that Mafia-like jungle of deadly rivalries, jurisdictional disputes, and impenetrable personal empires which characterized the Third Reich. In this respect, the history of the Labor Front is suggestive. It was a chameleon-like organization which underwent a number of bureaucratic transformations and never occupied a clear legal or power-political position either with respect to party or state. Indeed, its legitimacy rested on the very shaky ground of an "elastic" Hitler decree, which Ley used as a *carte blanche* to steal as many jurisdictions as he could from party and state agencies. The ensuing endless battles, particularly with Schacht, the Economics Minister, and Seldte, the Labor Minister, as well as intraparty strife with the Hess–Bormann team, confirmed the "bureaucratic state of nature" that was the Third Reich. The fact that, once underway, the DAF grew like a metastasizing cancer also illustrated the basic normlessness of the regime and the extent to which bureaucratic entities were the outgrowth of the outsized, indeed omnicompetent, visions of their leaders. Finally, Ley also sought to cash in on a typically Hitlerian administrative technique — to choose a general problem area and invest one man as "plenipotentiary" with the authority to address that problem. It was this proclivity which enabled Ley to win some dramatic, though pyrrhic, victories during the war, among others as Hitler's Housing Commissar.

Though Ley had many titles and sought entrée into many areas of power during the Third Reich, his most important role, almost from the outset, was that of head of the Labor Front. It was a crucial organization, for its main task was to function as a bridge to bring the working class into the Third Reich, to integrate the worker socially into the regime and thereby secure its long-term legitimacy. The DAF attempted to do so in several ways: it attempted, often in indirect ways, to function as the workers' "representative" in a regime which faced the idea of a trade union with something approaching paranoia. It also provided an endless array of services, and in particular, leisure-time activities, in an attempt to curry favor with the worker, but also to heighten his productivity and prevent him from having too much time to himself to ruminate on the state of the nation. The Labor Front also mounted a major, sustained psychological and cultural campaign to raise the self-image of the worker, to underscore the value of work, whether manual or otherwise, and to blur the traditional distinction between blue collar and white collar, between working class and middle class. Again, the purpose was social integration to gain support and legitimacy for the regime, and historical trends since at least the 1920s lent support to Nazi activities in this area. The DAF also tried, in particular through its vocational education programs, to create for the worker a climate of upward mobility, the sense that in the Third Reich a worker could become middle class if he raised his training level, worked harder, and became more efficient. In short, the DAF tried to bring both the virtues and the amenities of the middle class to the worker. Finally, however, it must not be forgotten, that behind the carrot there always lurked the stick. The same apparatus which lavished benefits on the worker also exercised surveillance over him. And Ley did not neglect to cultivate his ties with the SS and police system.

The DAF also represented a new kind of power structure, one frustratingly difficult to define; it often appears to have been a kind of organizational *Luftmensch*. It lacked the executive powers of a government ministry, or of the SS police empire, or even of Göring's Four-Year Plan. It was always seeking to wrest whole areas of social and economic authority from the government, but actually controlled remarkably few of them, although it did take the combined forces of industry and government to fend off Ley. The DAF was always "educating" people, "organizing" people, and "taking care of" people, although it normally could not issue the kind of directives (except internally) which are the real evidence of political or governmental power. But this is deceptive. The DAF wielded a new kind of power — based on information (which it collected endlessly and in enormous detail), service, and wealth. It was a more diffuse kind of power than that which one associates with governments, particularly dictatorships, but real none the less. It was the power to create a societal illusion and then inculcate people with that illusion; it was the power to depoliticize society by replacing normal political discourse with ubiquitous entertainment; it was the power to defuse discontent by ensuring a certain level of affluence infused with psychological perquisites; it was the power to effect cultural transformation by changing the basic vocabulary with which people discussed themselves and their place in society (even the terms "employer" (*Arbeitgeber*) and "employee" (*Arbeitnehmer*) were abolished); it was the power to create a fictional, but none the less effective societal consensus, and it is indicative of that consensus that this time there would be no November 1918, that the German people in their vast majority stayed with Hitler to the end. Those who actively resisted — aristocratic officers, for example — belonged to the group least touched by that consensus. The DAF was, in short, a harbinger for today's "information and service" society. It was modern also in the way in which it reversed the old Prussian dictum of "mehr sein als scheinen" (be more than you appear). Ley was second only to Goebbels, the creator of the "Hitler-myth," in creating appearances that were more important than reality, which, in fact, replaced reality. (Goebbels might well be called the first political "handler," a term once reserved for those who managed prizefighters, but now is unselfconsciously accepted as a term for those who manage presidents.) Ley, with his own information and propaganda edifice within the DAF, tried to create through incessant propaganda the appearance of a *Volksgemeinschaft*, where class and caste differences were rapidly disappearing, although "reality" belied the appearance.

Finally, although many of the activities of the DAF may appear at first relatively benign, indeed salutary, there lurked behind its grasping dynamism a terrible potential which was embodied in a term Ley often used: "its claim to totality." We must remember that the DAF, although it often played the role of workers' advocate, had as its individual members *both* workers and business men; that is, it aspired to include in its ranks *every* gainfully employed German and to confront that German both at his place of work and in his leisure time. Ley was serious when he said that no one had any private life any more save in his sleep. The DAF, then, with its dynamic drive to omnicompetence, strove, in the end without success, to destroy the rich and varied fabric of a pluralistic society, and replace it with a "brown collectivism" by becoming virtually contiguous with society.

This is an important factor in understanding the role of fascism in its radical attempt to transform society into its own image. In any modern society there is a far-reaching process underway in which traditional organic associations (kinship, village, guild) give way to more functional modern ones (trade and manufacturing associations, unions, etc.).[1] Modern society is then carried along, its future to an extent shaped by the interplay of these functional groups with one another and with government. In liberal societies, that is those with a broadly based consensus, this interplay takes place within a normative political and constitutional framework which permits, for the most part, orderly change. In the totalitarian society of Nazi Germany, however, where there existed neither such a normative framework nor the inclination to tolerate the kind of independent functional association typical of pluralistic societies, a new kind of "functional" association sprang up in the form of quasi-independent Nazi bureaucratic organizations which tried, by constantly expanding their areas of jurisdiction, to destroy the non-Nazi functional organizations and usurp their power.[2] Ley's Labor Front was one of these new organizations, and the fierce conflict which ensued between the DAF and business and well as government ministries was one battlefront in a much larger war. It was a war to create a wholly new German society, one which was supposed to realize a hitherto lacking national consensus based on an equal-opportunity revolution. One of the strategies involved in that struggle, as we have seen, was to desociologize politics, that is to pretend that the class struggle had been overcome. Another, paradoxically, was to politicize society, but in such a way as to make popular participation procedural rather than substantive. The DAF was vital in both these strategies. Its activities in raising the level of the worker, both psychologically and materially, as well as its restructuring of the language to replace older social terminology with new, reflected the first strategy. Injecting political themes into such hitherto non-political activities as arts and crafts and sea cruises contributed to the second. Every activity the DAF sponsored was "political," but not so as to give the German people an actual voice in determining the political fate of the nation.

In the end, the Nazis were unable to complete their victory, as the history of Ley and the DAF illustrates. Ironically, the war, which necessitated utilizing most of the large-scale functional organiza-

1. See Sheldon Wolin, *Politics and Vision. Continuity and Vision in Western Political Thought* (Boston, Little, Brown, 1960), Ch. 10; also Theodore Lovi, *The End of Liberalism: Ideology, Policy and the Crisis of Public Authority* (New York, Norton, 1969), pp. 20–5; also Gaetano Mosca, *The Ruling Class*, (New York, McGraw Hill, 1939), Ch. 3.
2. See Ronald Smelser, "Nazi Dynamics, German Foreign Policy and Appeasement" in Wolfgang Mommsen and Lothar Kettenacker (eds.), *The Fascist Challenge and the Policy of Appeasement* (London, Allen & Unwin, 1983), p. 33, for a discussion of this phenomenon with regard to Nazi foreign policy.

tions in German society (except for trade unions; here the Nazi victory had been complete), undercut Nazi attempts to transform German society, although there can be no doubt that, had they won the war, the battle would have been taken up with renewed vigor. The far-reaching plans projected by the DAF "think tank" indicated so.

But what would a transformed German society have looked like? To what extent would it have been "modern"? To characterize the Labor Front as "modern" raises a question which has been the object of considerable historical debate: was it Hitler's purpose, ultimately, to turn the clock back, to reverse the process by which Germany had become an industrial society, so that Germany's continued modernization during the Third Reich was inadvertent? Or did Hitler instead envision the Nazi revolution as a major tool to push Germany forward into a more modern society? Robert Ley's political career, and particularly the tasks with which Hitler entrusted his "greatest idealist," suggest that the latter interpretation is closer to the truth.[3]

If, by 1940, Ley's career had produced many failures, many excesses, many lapses in judgment, many incidents which earned him the title "*Reichstrunkenbold*," nevertheless, Hitler had sufficient faith in his paladin to entrust him with the crucial task of formulating the context of the revolutionary transformation which the war was supposed to bring about. If one looks at Ley's plans, they are, in one sense, thoroughly modern.[4] They consist of producing for the *German* (and *only* for the German) an equal-opportunity, upwardly mobile society purged of the old class and caste differences and encased within the framework of an extensively developed welfare state. Very many of the individual elements in this cradle-to-grave "performance" society are astonishingly progressive and far-

3. Here my findings dovetail with those of Rainer Zitelmann in his study *Hitler. Selbstverständnis eines Revolutionärs* (Leamington Spa, Berg Publishers, 1986), esp. pp. 316–36.
4. These plans are contained in a number of reports turned out by Ley's "think tank," the Institute for Labor Science of the DAF. On a new wage structure, for example, see "Arbeitsprogramm zur Vorbereitung einer Reichslohnordnung," 1941, in BAK, R113/1716; or on social insurance, "Das Versorgungswerk des Deutschen Volkes. Entwurf und Motivierung," BAK, NSD 50/679; or on protective laws for the workplace, "Gesamtrechenschaftsbericht 1943," BAK, NSD 50/21. pp. 71–7. A discussion of the genesis and content of many of these plans can also be found in Marie Recker, *Nationalsozialistische Sozialpolitik im Zweiten Weltkrieg* (Munich, Oldenbourg, 1985), esp. pp. 89–94, 98–106, 121–5. On Ley's housing plans, see Tilman Harlander and Gerhard Fehl (eds.), *Hitler's Sozialer Wohnungsbau 1940–1945* (Hamburg, Hans Christians Verlag, 1986).

sighted. Ley envisioned a new wage structure which guaranteed the right to work; calculated wages on the basis of the actual demands of the job, regardless of craft or place of work; established a system of comparative worth among widely differing jobs and professions; coupled wages to cost of living and productivity; envisioned equal pay for equal work, even for women, and assumed a minimum wage which would support a family of four at a comfortable level. Borrowing freely from the "Taylorism" pioneered by America in the 1920s, the DAF viewed the worker in the production process in modern, rational terms. A great deal of emphasis was placed on testing, on continuing education, and on an advisory system which would steer and retool workers in directions where future opportunities were reputed to lie. There was a clear view that one did not select a job for life, but that a dynamic economy meant the constant evolution of job categories for which people had to be prepared. Protective measures, particularly for women and youths, were advanced, indeed many were realized, during the Third Reich itself.

A new social insurance system was envisioned which anticipated modern developments. Social security was decoupled from premiums paid in over a working lifetime and covered instead by general revenues. It established the concept of a minimum pension based on average earnings during the last ten years on the job and built in inducements to continue working after retirement age. It was also to be a "unitary" system which replaced older separate systems for blue- and white-collar workers. It recognized health care as a national responsibility and stressed heavily the concept of preventive medicine, with people, like machines, being periodically "overhauled" via a system of sanitaria. And, finally, Ley envisioned a postwar housing plan which would both create green suburbs and revitalize urban centers using prefabricated mass housing and ecologically sound principles.

In its capacity as business conglomerate, the DAF was to play a major role in this postwar transformation. Indeed, the DAF presented the potential for developing precisely the politically driven economic model which Hitler wanted as a middle option between free-market capitalism on the one hand and Soviet communism on the other. Here the DAF-run Volkswagen enterprise stood as a pioneering example.

These were not just pipe dreams cooked up by Ley and his DAF think-tank. They corresponded exactly with the kind of transformation which Hitler himself envisioned. Hitler, in fact, underscored his faith in Ley in 1940 with a gift of 1 million marks. Altogether, the plans worked out by Ley for his Führer amounted to a German "Beveridge Report."[5]

But even progressive-sounding measures can lose much of their validity if they are promulgated within a larger context which is corrupt or dangerous. We dare not forget that the many "progressive" measures which were to constitute the Nazi revolution were deeply and inextricably imbedded in a destructive racial ideology which projected basing the future German utopia on the blood and sweat of peoples considered to be of "inferior" race. The transformation, moreover, was to be carried out by means of an Armageddon-like war of racial destruction, which would pave the way for the coming millenium by destroying the major impediment — the Jews. Within a radically destructive, apocalyptic context such as this, the various "progressive" measures envisioned by the Nazis, attractive as they might be alone or in a very different context, lose much of their validity for they are fatally tainted by the system which gave them birth. In the end, National Socialism destroyed itself, along with millions of lives. In the ruins lay most of the "progressive" measures which awaited (and await) possible attainment in a quite different context. With them lay the organization which Ley proposed as vehicle for realizing his grandiose plans — the German Labor Front.

Ley's great dreams thus faded not only on a macrocosmic plane, but on a microcosmic level as well. His dream of transforming his home town, Waldbröl, into a model city by building a "People's Tractor Plant" there dissolved when the war forced termination of construction.[6] Perhaps most tragically, one of the ships, the *Wilhelm Gustloff*, which was to have symbolized the new National Socialist world of workers' luxury vacations — the ocean cruise — was sunk at the end of the war while taking thousands of refugees from East Prussia across the Baltic in front of the Russian advance. It was perhaps the largest single ocean disaster of the century and it punctuated the destruction of the Third Reich in 1945.

Finally, it is hoped that this study of Ley and the German Labor

5. In fact, Ley's plans have been so characterized recently. See Hans-Günther Hockerts' "Sicherung im Alter, Kontinuität und Wandel der Gesetzlichen Rentenversicherung 1889–1979," in Werner Conze and M. Rainer Lepsius (eds.), *Sozialgeschichte der Bundesrepublik, Beiträge zum Kontinuitäts problem* (Stuttgart, Klett-Cotta, 1983), p. 309.
6. See *Der Spiegel*, no. 4 (1955), p. 16.

Front might demonstrate the value of biography to social history. This would be true in any case, but is particularly so with the Third Reich, where political power was derivative and so highly personal. Dietrich Orlow was right in suggesting that the history of the Nazi Party and, one feels, of the Third Reich itself, "must at times read like a series of interwoven political biographies."[7]

7. See Dietrich Orlow, *The History of the Nazi Party, 1933–1945* (Pittsburgh, University of Pittsburgh Press, 1973), p. 7.

Medical Note

Generally, Robert Ley's frontal lobe injury and over-indulgence in alcohol should be regarded as contributing factors in his often erratic behavior, but not as the sole cause. The injury and resulting brain damage must be seen against the background of several major life traumas, including lengthy combat experience, serious injury, frequent surgical invasion, as well as social and political upheaval, which Ley experienced.

The diagnosis produced by the pathologists — chronic diffuse encephalopathy — describes a condition which often (but not always) produces symptoms characteristic of Ley's behavior throughout his political life. These included large swings in mood, poor judgment, and behavior inappropriate to the situation, a failure to sustain mental activity, an incoherence of the reasoning processes, loss of ego strength, inattentiveness, impersistence, and easy distraction by irrelevant data and hyperactivity ("organic drivenness"). The condition and, hence, the behavior pattern is exacerbated by alcohol.[1]

There is a good correlation between Dr Kelly's Rorschach report on Ley and the US Army pathology report. Both suggest brain damage which is "diffuse," that is enough to impair judgment but not so severe as to render it ineffectual. The Nazi movement provided for Ley an outlet for his powerful, but clumsy, emotions which he was unable to control effectively or to fine tune.[2]

1. See Raymond Adams and Maurice Victor, *Principles of Neurology*, 3rd edn (New York, McGraw Hill, 1985), pp. 332–3.
2. I am grateful for discussions with Dr Molly Harrower, expert on Rorschach testing and Dr Walter Reichert, neurologist, for steering me through some of the complexities of Ley's condition.

Bibliography

Books

Barkun, Michael, *Disaster and the Millenium* (New Haven, Yale University Press, 1974).

Bayles, William, *Caesars in Goose Step* (London, Jarrolds, 1941).

Beier, Gerhard, *Die illegale Reichsleitung der Gewerkschaften 1933–1945* (Cologne, Bund Verlag, 1981).

Berger, Thomas (ed.), *Lebenssituationen unter der Herrschaft des Nationalsozialismus: Materialen.* (Hanover, Niedersächische Landeszentrale für politische Bildung, 1981).

Bergschicker, H. (ed.), *Deutsche Chronik, 1933–1945. Alltag im Faschismus* (Berlin, Verlag der Nation, 1982).

Besgen, Achim, *Der stille Befehl. Medizinalrat Kersten, Himmler und das Dritte Reich* (Munich, Nymphenburger, 1960).

Bleuel, Erich, *Sex and Society in Nazi Germany* (New York, Bantam, 1973).

Bludau, Kudo, *Nationalsozialismus und Gewerkschaften* (Hanover, Verlag für Literatur und Zeitgeschehen, 1968).

Boehnke, Wilfried, *Die NSDAP im Ruhrgebeit 1920–1933* (Bonn, Bad Godesberg, 1974).

Boelcke, Willi, *Die deutsche Wirtschaft 1930–1945. Interna des Reichswirtschaftsministeriums* (Düsseldorf, Droste, 1983).

Bollmus, Reinhard, *Das Amt Rosenberg und seine Gegner* (Stuttgart, DVA, 1970).

Borkin, Joseph, *The Crime and Punishment of I.G. Farben* (New York, Macmillan, 1978).

Broszat, Martin, *The Hitler State*, trans. John Hiden (New York, Longman, 1981).

Bry, Gerhard, *Wages in Germany* (Princeton, Princeton University Press, 1960).

Budde, Otto, *Waldbröl wie es wurde, was es ist* (Gummersbach, Verlag Gronenberg, 1981).

Bullock, Alan, *Hitler: A Study in Tyranny* (New York, Bantam, 1961).

Carroll, Bernice A., *Design for Total War: Arms and Economics in the Third Reich* (Mouton, The Hague, 1968).

Clark, Alan, *Aces High: The War in the Air over the Western Front 1914–1918* (New York, Putnam's Sons, 1973).

Cocks, Geoffrey, *Psychotherapy in the Third Reich: The Göring Institute* (Oxford, Oxford University Press, 1985).

Cohn, Norman, *Pursuit of the Millenium: Revolutionary Messianism in Medieval and Reformation Europe and Its Bearing on Modern Totalitarian Movements*, 2nd edn (New York, Harper, 1961).

Conot, Robert E., *Justice at Nuremberg* (New York, Harper & Row, 1983).

Corbach, Gottfried, *Geschichte von Waldbröl* (Cologne, Scriba Verlag, 1972).

Craig, Gordon, *Germany 1866–1945* (New York, Oxford University Press, 1978).

Dahrendorf, Ralf, *Society and Democracy in Germany* (New York, Norton, 1979).

Deppe, F., and Rossmann, W. (eds.), *Wirtschaftskrise, Fascismus, Gewerkschaften. Dokumente zur Gewerkschaftspolitik 1929–1933* (Cologne, Kleine Bibliothek, 1981).

Deuel, Wallace, *People under Hitler* (New York, Harcourt, Brace, 1942).

Deuerlein, Ernst, *Der Aufstieg der NSDAP in Augenzeugenberichten* (Düsseldorf, Karl Rauch Verlag, 1968).

Diehl-Thiele, Peter, *Partei und Staat im Dritten Reich: Untersuchungen zum Verhältnis von NSDAP und allgemeiner innerer Staatsverwaltung 1933–1945*, 2nd edn (Munich, Beck Verlag, 1971).

Diest, Wilhelm, et al., *Das Deutsche Reich und der Zweite Weltkrieg*. Vol. 1: *Ursachen und Voraussetzungen der deutschen Kriegspolitik* (Stuttgart, Deutsche Verlagsanstalt, 1979).

Dietrich, Otto, *Zwölf Jahre mit Hitler* (Munich, Isar Verlag, 1955).

Dlugoborski, Waclaw (ed.), *Zweiter Weltkrieg und sozialer Wandel. Achsenmächte und besetzte Länder.* Kritische Studien zur Geschichtswissenschaft 47. (Göttingen, Vandenhoeck & Rupprecht, 1981).

Eisenwein-Rothe, Ingeborg (ed.), *Die Wirtschaftsverbände von 1933 bis 1945* (Berlin, Duncker & Humbolt, 1965).

Enfield, Glenn, *Hitler's Secret Life* (New York, Stein & Day, 1979).

Erbe, Rene, *Die nationalsozialistische Wirtschaftspolitik 1933–1939 im Lichte der modernen Theorie* (Zürich, Polygraphischer Verlag, 1958).

Fest, Joachim, *Hitler* (New York, Vintage, 1975).

Das Gesicht des Dritten Reiches. Profile einer totalitären Herrschaft (Munich, Piper, 1980).

Fischer, Kurt (ed.), *Politische Bildung in der Weimarer Republik* (Frankfurt, Europäische Verlagsanstalt, 1970).

Focke, Harold, and Uwe, Reimer, *Alltag unterm Hakenkreuz. Wie die Nazis das Leben der Deutschen veränderten* (Frankfurt, Rowohlt, 1979).

Fraenkel, Ernst, *Der Doppelstaat* (Frankfurt/Cologne, Europäische Verlagsanstalt, 1974).

The Dual State (New York, Oxford University Press, 1940).

Genoud, Francois (ed.), *The Testament of Adolf Hitler: The Hitler–Bormann Documents February–April 1945* (London, Cassell, 1961).

Gillingham, John, *Industry and Politics in the Third Reich: Ruhr Coal, Hitler and Europe* (New York, Columbia University Press, 1985).

Gisevius, Hans-Berndt, *Adolf Hitler: Versuch einer Deutung* (Munich, Bertelsmann, 1973).

Grazia, Victoria de, *The Culture of Consent: Mass Organization of Leisure in Fascist Italy* (Cambridge, Cambridge University Press, 1981).

Grunberger, Richard, *The Twelve-Year Reich: A Social History of Nazi Germany 1933–1945* (New York, Holt, Rinehart, & Winston, 1971).

Guillebaud, C.W., *The Social Policy of Nazi Germany* (1940; New York, Howard Fertig, 1971).

Gutowski, A., et al. (eds.), *Hamburger Studien für Wirtschafts- und Gesellschaftspolitik* (Tübingen, JCB Mohr, 1980).

Habermas, Jürgen, *Legitimization Crisis* (Boston, Beacon, 1975).

Hale, Oron J. *The Captive Press in the Third Reich* (Princeton, Princeton University Press, 1964).

Heiber, Helmuth (ed.), *The Early Goebbels Diaries: The Journal of Joseph Goebbels from 1925–26* (London, Weidenfeld, 1962).

Akten der Partei-Kanzlei der NSDAP (Munich, Oldenbourg, 1983).

Heiden, Konrad, *Der Fuehrer: Hitler's Rise to Power* (Boston, Beacon, 1969).

Hennig, Eicke, *Thesen zur deutschen Sozial- und Wirtschaftsgeschichte 1933–1938* (Frankfurt, Suhrkamp, 1973).

Hentschel, Volker, *Geschichte der deutschen Sozialpolitik 1880–1980. Soziale Sicherheit und kollektives Arbeitsrecht* (Frankfurt, Suhrkamp, 1983).

Herbert, Ulrich, *Fremdarbeiter: Politik und Praxis des "Ausländer-Einsatzes" in der Kriegswirtschaft des Dritten Reiches* (Berlin/Bonn, Dietz, 1986).

Hertz-Eichenrode, Dieter, *Wirtschaftskrise und Arbeitsbeschaffung. Konjunkturpolitik 1925/26 und die Grundlagen der Krisenpolitik Brünings* (Frankfurt, Campus, 1982).

Heyen, Franz Josef, *Nationalsozialismus im Alltag Quellen zur Geschichte des Nationalsozialismus vornehmlich im Raum Mainz-Koblenz-Trier* (Boppard, Harald Boldt Verlag, 1967).

Historische Kommission bei der Bayerischen Akademie der Wissenschaften and the Bundesarchiv, *Akten der Reichskanzlei: Regierung Hitler 1933–1938* (Boppard, Harald Boldt Verlag, 1983).

Hoffmann, Dietrich, *Politische Bildung 1890–1933* (Hanover, Hermann Schroedel, 1970).

Homze, Edward L., *Foreign Labor in Nazi Germany* (Princeton, Princeton University Press, 1967).

Horne, Alistair, *The Price of Glory: Verdun 1916* (New York, Penguin, 1962).

Hüttenberger, Peter, *Die Gauleiter. Studie zum Wandel des Machtgefüges in der NSDAP* (Stuttgart, Deutsche Verlagsanstalt, 1969).

Jarausch, Konrad (ed.), *The Transformation of Higher Learning 1860–1930* (Chicago, University of Chicago Press, 1983).

Kater, Michael, *The Nazi Party: A Social Profile of Members and Leaders, 1919–1945* (Cambridge, Mass., Harvard University Press, 1983).

Kele, Max, *Nazis and Workers: National Socialist Appeals to German Labor 1919–1933* (Chapel Hill, University of North Carolina Press, 1972).

Kelley, Douglas, *Twenty-One Cells in Nuremberg* (New York, Greenberg, 1947).

Kershaw, Ian, *Der Hitler-Mythos 1920–1945*, Schriftenreihe der Vierteljahrshefte für Zeitgeschichte (Stuttgart, Deutsche Verlagsanstalt, 1980).

The Nazi Dictatorship: Problems and Perspectives of Interpretation (London, Edward Arnold, 1985).

Popular Opinion and Political Dissent in the Third Reich: Bavaria 1933–1945 (Oxford, Clarendon, 1983).

Kersten, Felix, *The Kersten Memoirs 1940–1945* (New York, Macmillan, 1957).

Kissenkoetter, Udo, *Gregor Strasser und die NSDAP*, Schriftenreihe der Vierteljahrshefte für Zeitgeschichte no. 37 (Stuttgart, Deutsche Verlagsanstalt, 1978).

Koch, Ludwig C.M., *Geschichte des Fußartillerie-Bataillons Nr. 56 im Weltkriege* (Berlin, Oldenbourg, 1926).

Kranig, Andreas, *Arbeitsrecht im Dritten Reich* (Cologne, Bundverlag, 1984).

Krebs, Albert, *Tendenzen und Gestalten der NSDAP Quellen und Darstellungen zur Zeitgeschichte*, vol. 6 (Stuttgart, Deutsche Verlagsanstalt, 1965).

Krosigk, Lutz Graf Schwerin von, *Es geschah in Deutschland* (Tübingen, Wunderlich, 1951).

Kuczinski, Jürgen, *Die Geschichte der Lage der Arbeiter in Deutschland von 1789 bis in die Gegenwart*, vol. II (Berlin, Tribüne Verlag, 1953).

Germany: Economic and Labour Conditions under Fascism (New York, Greenwood, 1968).

Lang, Jochen von, *The Secretary. Martin Bormann: The Man Who Manipulated Hitler* (New York, Random House, 1979).

Lang, Serge, and Schenck, Ernst von, *Portrait eines Menschenverbrechers* (St Gallen, Zollikufer, 1947).

Lärmer, Karl, *Autobahnbau in Deutschland 1933 bis 1945, Zu den Hintergründen*, Forschungen zur Wirtschaftsgeschichte, vol. 6 (Berlin, Akademie-Verlag, 1975).

Leithäuser, Joachim G., *Wilhelm Leuscher. Ein Leben für die Republik* (Cologne, Bund Verlag, n.d.).

Lochner, Louis P. (ed.), *The Goebbels Diaries* (New York, Popular Library, 1948).

Ludecke, Kurt, *I Knew Hitler* (London, Jarrolds, 1938).

Macdonald, Lyn, *Somme* (London, Michael Joseph, 1983).

McGovern, James, *Martin Bormann* (London, Barker, 1968).

Mandell, Richard D., *Sport: A Cultural History* (New York, Columbia University Press, 1984).

Marsden, Walter, *The Rhineland* (New York, Hastings House, 1973).

Martens, Stefan, *Hermann Goering* (Paderborn, Schöningh, 1985).

Maser, Werner, *Nürnberg. Tribunal der Sieger* (Munich, Droemer Knauer, 1977).

Mason, Timothy, *Arbeiterklasse und Volksgemeinschaft. Dokumente und Materialien zur deutschen Arbeiterpolitik 1936–1939*, Schriften des Zentralinstituts für sozialwissenschaftliche Forschung der Freien Universität Berlin, vol. 22 (Opladen, Westdeutscher Verlag, 1975).

Sozialpolitik im Dritten Reich. Arbeiterklasse und Volksgemeinschaft, 2nd edn (Opladen, Westdeutscher Verlag 1977).

Matthias, Erich, and Morsey, Rudolf (eds.), *Das Ende der Parteien 1933* (Düsseldorf, Droste Verlag, 1960).

Matzerath, Horst, *Nationalsozialismus und kommunale Selbsverwaltung* (Stuttgart, Cologne, Mainz, 1970).

Mausbach-Bromberger, Barbara, *Arbeiterwiderstand in Frankfurt am Main. Gegen den Fascismus 1933–1945* (Frankfurt, Röderberg, 1976).

Merker, Paul Friedrich, *Deutschland, sein oder nicht sein?* Vol. 2 (Mexico City, El Libra Libre, 1944).

Miale, Florence, and Selzer, Michael, *The Nuremberg Mind: The Psychology of the Nazi Leaders* (New York, Quadrangle, 1975).

Mitchell, Otis (ed.), *Nazism and the Common Man: Essays in German History (1929–1939)* (Washington, DC, University Press of America, 1981).

Mommsen, Wolfgang, and Kettenacker, Lothar (eds.), *The Fascist Challenge and the Policy of Appeasement* (London, Allen & Unwin, 1983).

Mosse, George, *The Nationalization of the Masses. Political Symbolism and Mass Movements in Germany from the Napoleonic Wars through the Third Reich* (New York, New American Library, 1975).

Nelson, Walter Henry, *Small Wonder: The Amazing Story of the Volkswagen* (Boston, Toronto, 1965).

Niethammer, Lutz (ed.), *"Die Jahre weiß man nicht, wo man die heute hinsetzen soll." Fascismus-Erfahrungen im Ruhrgebiet*, Lebensgeschichte und Sozialkultur im Ruhrgebiet 1930 bis 1960, vol. 1 (Bonn, JHW Dietz nachf., 1983).

Noakes, Jeremy, *The Nazi Party in Lower Saxony 1921–1933* (London, Oxford University Press, 1971).

(ed.), *Government, Party and People in Nazi Germany*, Exeter Studies in History no. 2 (Exeter, Exeter University Press, 1981).

Nyomarkay, Joseph, *Charisma and Factionalism in the Nazi Party* (Minneapolis, University of Minnesota Press, 1967).

O'Donnell, James, *The Bunker* (Boston, Houghton-Mifflin, 1978).

Office of the US Chief of Counsel for Prosecution of Axis Criminality, *Nazi*

Conspiracy and Aggression (Washington, DC, Government Printing Office, 1946).

Oppenheimer-Blum, Hilde, *The Standard of Living of German Labour under Nazi Rule* (New York, New School for Social Research, 1943).

Orlow, Dietrich, *The History of the Nazi Party, 1919–1933* (Pittsburgh, University of Pittsburgh Press, 1969).

The History of the Nazi Party, 1933–1945 (Pittsburgh, University of Pittsburgh Press, 1973).

Overy, R. J. *The Nazi Economic Recovery 1932–1938* (London, Macmillan, 1982).

Paul, Wolfgang, *Der Heimatkrieg 1939 bis 1945* (Essingen, Bechtle, 1980).

Pentzlin, Heinz, *Hjalmar Schacht. Leben und Wirken einer umstrittenen Persönlichkeit* (Berlin, Frankfurt, 1980).

Peterson, Edward, *The Limits of Hitler's Power* (Princeton, Princeton University Press, 1969).

Petri, Franz and Droege, Georg, *Handbuch der historischen Stätten Deutschlands.* Vol. 8: *Nordrhein-Westfalen* (Stuttgart, A. Krömer, 1965).

Petzina, Dietmar, *Autarkiepolitik im Dritten Reich. Der nationalsozialistische Vierjahresplan.* (Stuttgart, Deutsche Verlagsanstalt, 1968).

Peukert, Detlef, *Die KPD im Widerstand. Verfolgung und Untergrundarbeit an Rhein und Ruhr 1933–1945* (Wuppertal, Peter Hammer, 1980).

Volksgenossen und Gemeinschaftsfremde. Anpassung, Ausmerze und Aufbegehrten unter dem Nationalsozialismus (Cologne, Bund Verlag, 1982).

Peukert, Detlef, and Reulecke, Jürgen, *Die Reihen fast geschlossen. Beiträge zur Geschichte des Alltags unterm Nationalsozialismus* (Wuppertal, Peter Hammer, 1981).

Peuschel, Harald, *Die Männer um Hitler. Braune Biographien* (Düsseldorf, Droste Verlag, 1982).

Picker, Henry, *Hitlers Tischgespräche im Führerhauptquartier 1941–1942* (Stuttgart, Seewald Verlag, 1965).

Plato, Alexander von, "*Der Verlierer geht nicht leer aus*". *Betriebsräte geben zu Protokoll* (Bonn, JHW Dietz, 1984).

Preller, Ludwig, *Sozialpolitik in der Weimarer Republik* (Düsseldorf, Athenäum, 1978).

Pridham, Geoffrey, *Hitler's Rise to Power: The Nazi Movement in Bavaria 1923–1933* (London, Harper & Row, 1973).

Raiffeneisenbank Waldbröl, *Aus der Geschichte Waldbröls* (Waldbröl, 1985).

Rebentisch, Dieter, and Teppe, Karl (eds.), *Verwaltung contra Menschenführung in Staat Hitlers* (Göttingen, Van den Hoeck, 1986).

Recker, Marie, *Die Großstadt als Wohn- und Lebensbereich im Nationalsozialismus*, Wolfsburger Beiträge zur Stadtgeschichte und Städtentwicklung (Frankfurt, Campus, 1982).

Nationalsozialistische Sozialpolitik im Zweiten Weltkrieg (Munich, Oldenbourg, 1985).

Redl, Fritz and Wineman, David, *The Aggressive Child* (New York, 1957).

Rhodes, James, *The Hitler Movement: A Modern Millenarian Movement* (Stanford, Hoover Institution, 1980).

Roberts, Stephen, *The House that Hitler Built* (London, Methuen, 1937).

Rosenberg, Alfred, *Das politische Tagebuch Alfred Rosenbergs 1934–35 und 1939–40*, ed. Hans Günther Seraphim (Göttingen, Musterschmidt, 1956).

Letzte Aufzeichnungen. Ideale und Idole der Nationalsozialistischen Revolution (Göttingen, Plesse Verlag, 1955).

Saldern, Adelheid von, *Mittelstand im 'Dritten Reich' Handwerker-Einzelhändler-Bauern* (Frankfurt, New York, Campus Verlag, 1979).

Sachse, Carole, et al., *Angst, Belohnung Zucht und Ordnung* (Opladen, Westdeutscher Verlag, 1982).

Salm, Fritz, *Im Schatten des Henkers. Widerstand in Mannheim gegen Fascismus und Krieg* (Frankfurt, Röderberg, 1979).

Sargant, William, *Battle for the Mind* (Baltimore, Penguin, 1961).

Schaar, John, *Legitimacy in the Modern State* (New Brunswick/London, Transaction Books, 1981).

Schabrod, Karl, *Widerstand gegen Flick und Florian. Düsseldorfer Antifaschisten über ihren Widerstand 1933–1945* (Frankfurt, Röderberg, 1978).

Schabrod, Karl, and Sbosny, Inge, *Widerstand in Solingen. Aus dem Leben antifaschistischer Kämpfer* (Frankfurt, Röderberg, 1975).

Schäfer, W., *Eure Bänder rollen nur wenn wir es wollen* (Hanover, Münden, 1979).

Schaumburg-Lippe, Friedrich Christian Prinz zu, *Zwischen Krone und Kerker* (Wiesbaden, Limes Verlag, 1952).

Dr. G. Ein Porträt des Propagandaministers (Wiesbaden, Limes Verlag, 1963).

Schirach, Baldur von, *Ich glaubte an Hitler* (Hamburg, Mosaik Verlag, 1967).

Schmidt, Matthias, *Albert Speer: The End of a Myth* (New York, St Martin's Press, 1984).

Schneider, Michael, *Das Arbeitsbeschaffungsprogramm des ADGB. Zur gewerkschaftlichen Politik in der Endphase der Weimarer Republik* (Bonn, Bad Godesberg, Neue Gesellschaft, 1975).

Schneider, Ulrich, *Marburg 1933–1945. Arbeiterbewegung und Bekennende Kirche gegen den Fascismus* (Frankfurt, Röderberg, 1980).

Schonberger, Angela, *Die 'neue Reichskanzlei' von Albert Speer. Zum Zusammenhang von nationalsozialistischer Ideologie und Architektur* (Berlin, Mann Verlag, 1981).

Schonfeld, Andrew, *Modern Capitalism: The Changing Balance of Public and Private Power* (New York, Oxford University Press, 1965).

Schumann, Hans-Gerd, *Nationalsozialismus und Gewerkschaftsbewegung. Die Vernichtung der deutschen Gewerkschaften und der Aufbau der 'Deutschen Arbeits-*

front' (Hanover, Frankfurt, Norddeutsche Verlagsanstalt, 1958).

Schweitzer, Arthur, *Die Nazifizierung des Mittelstandes*, Bonner Beiträge zur Soziologie vol. 9 (Stuttgart, Ferdinand Enke Verlag, 1970).

Big Business in the Third Reich (Bloomington, Indiana University Press, 1964).

Semmler, Rudolf, *Goebbels: the Man Next to Hitler*, ed. G.S. Wagner (London, Westhouse, 1947).

Seubert, Rolf, *Berufserziehung und Nationalsozialismus Berufliche Bildung und Berufspolitik*, vol. 1 (Weinheim/Basel, Beltz Verlag, 1977).

Smith, Bradley F., *The Road to Nuremberg* (New York, Basic Books, 1981).

Speer, Albert, *Inside the Third Reich* (New York, Macmillan, 1970).

Spandau: The Secret Diaries (New York, Pocket Books, 1978).

Infiltration (New York, Macmillan, 1981)

Speier, Hans, *Die Angestellten vor dem Nationalsozialismus. Ein Beitrag zum Verhältnis der deutschen Sozialstruktur 1918 bis 1933*, Kritische Studien zur Geschichtswissenschaft 26 (Göttingen, Vandenhoeck 1977).

Stachura, Peter (ed.), *The Shaping of the Nazi State* (New York, Barnes & Noble, 1978).

Gregor Strasser and the Rise of Nazism (London, Allen & Unwin, 1983).

Steiner, George, *In Bluebeard's Castle: Some Notes toward the Redefinition of Culture* (New Haven, Yale University Press, 1971).

Stoddard, Lothrop, *Into the Darkness: Nazi Germany Today* (New York, Duell, Sloan & Pierce, 1940).

Syrup, Friedrich, *Hundert Jahre staatlicher Sozialpolitik 1839–1939 aus dem Nachlaß*, ed. Julius Scheuble and Otto Neuloth (Stuttgart, Kohlhammer Verlag, 1957).

Taylor, Fred (ed.), *The Goebbels Diaries 1939–1941* (New York, G.P. Putnam, 1983).

Teppe, Karl, *Provinz-Partei-Staat. Zur provinziellen Selbsverwaltung im Dritten Reich, untersucht am Beispiel Westfalens* (Münster, Aschendorff Verlag, 1977).

Thies, Jochen, *Architekt der Weltherrschaft. Die 'Endziele' Hitlers* (Düsseldorf, Droste Verlag, 1976).

Trevor-Roper, Hugh (ed.), *The Bormann Letters. The Private Correspondence between Martin Bormann and his Wife from January 1943 to April 1945* (London, Weidenfeld & Nicolson, 1954).

(ed.) *The Diaries of Joseph Goebbels, Final Entries 1945* (New York, G.P. Putnam, 1978).

Turner, Henry A., *German Big Business and the Rise of Hitler* (New York/Oxford, Oxford University Press, 1985).

(ed.), *Hitler: Memoirs of a Confidant* (New Haven, Yale University Press, 1985).

Tyrell, Albrecht (ed.), *Führer befiehl . . . Selbstzeugnisse aus der 'Kampfzeit' der*

NSDAP Dokumentation und Analyse (Düsseldorf, Droste Verlag, 1969).

Voegelin, Eric, *The New Science of Politics* (Chicago, University of Chicago Press, 1952).

Science, Politics and Gnosticism: Two Essays (Chicago, Regnary Gateway, 1968).

Volkmann, Hans Erich, *Wirtschaft im Dritten Reich, Teil I, 1933–1939 Eine Bibliographie*, Schriften der Bibliothek für Zeitgeschichte 20 (Munich, Bernhard & Graefe, 1980).

Vollmer, Bernhard, *Volksopposition im Polizeistaat* (Stuttgart,Deutsche Verlagsanstalt, 1957).

Waltz, Manfred, *Wohnungsbau und Industriesiedlungspolitik in Deutschland*, Aachen dissertation (New York, Campus, 1979).

Weinstein, Fred, *The Dynamics of Nazism: Leadership, Ideology, and the Holocaust* (New York, Academic Press, 1980).

Welch, David (ed.), *Nazi Propaganda: The Power and the Limitations, 1939–1945* (London, Croom Helm, 1983).

Wiedemann, Fritz, *Der Mann der Feldherr werden wolte. Erlebnisse und Erfahrungen des Vorgesetzten Hitlers im l. Weltkrieg und seines späteren Persönlichen Adjutanten* (Velbert, Blick & Bild Verlag für politische Bildung, 1964).

Wolsing, Theo, *Untersuchungen zur Berufsausbildung im Dritten Reich*, Schriftenreihe zur Geschichte und politischen Bildung no. 24 (Kastelbaum, Aloys Henn Verlag, 1977).

Worsley, Peter, *The Trumpet Shall Sound: A Study of 'Cargo' Cults in Melanesia*, 2nd edn (New York, Schocken, 1968).

Wunderlich, Frieda, *German Labor Courts* (Chapel Hill, University of North Carolina Press, 1946).

Young, Peter (ed.), *The Marshall Cavendish Illustrated Encyclopedia of World War One* (New York/London, Marshall Cavendish, 1984).

Zorn, Gerda, *Widerstand in Hannover. Gegen Reaktion und Fascismus 1920–1946* (Frankfurt, Röderberg, 1977).

Articles

Beier, Ehrhard, "Gesetzentwürfe zur Ausschaltung der DAF im Jahre 1938," *Archiv für Sozialgeschichte* 17 (1977): 297–335.

Berghahn, Volker, "NSDAP und 'Geistige Führung' der Wehrmacht 1939–1943," *Vierteljahrshefte für Zeitgeschichte* VII (January 1969).

Bernett, Hajo, "NS Volkssport bei 'KdF,'" *Stadion* 5 (1979): 89–146.

Craig, John E., "Higher Education and Social Mobility in Germany," in Konrad Jarausch (ed.), *The Transformation of Higher Learning 1860–1930*

(Chicago, University of Chicago Press, 1983, pp. 219–44.

Douglas, Donald, "The Nazi Party in Hannover, 1921–1923," *Wichita State University Bulletin Universities Studies* no. 108, vol. LII/3 (August, 1976).

Farrar-Hockley, Anthony, "The Somme Barrage," in Peter Young (ed.), *The Marshall Cavendish Illustrated Encyclopedia of World War One* (New York/London, Marshall Cavendish, 1984), vol. V, pp. 1493–501.

Frye, Charles, "The Third Reich and the Second Republic: National Socialism's Impact upon German Democracy," *Western Political Quarterly* 21 (1968): 668–80.

Gies, Horst, "Aufgaben und Probleme der nationalsozialistischen Ernährungswirtschaft 1933–1939," *Vierteljahrsschrift für Sozial-und Wirtschaftsgeschichte* 66/4 (1979): 466–500.

Gillingham, John, "The Deproletarianization of German Society: Vocational Training in the Third Reich," *Journal of Social History* 19 (spring 1986): 423–32.

Graebing, Helga, "Gewerkschaftliches Verhalten in der politischen Krise der Jahre 1930–1933," addendum to reprint of *Gewerkschaftszeitung 1933* (Berlin/Bonn, Dietz, 1983), pp. 7–47.

Harrower, Molly, "Rorschach Records of the Nazi War Criminals: An Experimental Study after Thirty Years," *Journal of Personality Assessment* 40/4 (1976): 341–51.

Herbst, Ludolf, "Die Krise des nationalsozialistischen Regimes am Vorabend des Zweiten Weltkrieges und die forcierte Aufrüstung: Eine Kritik," *Vierteljahrshefte für Zeitgeschichte* 26/5 (1978).

Horne, Alistair, "Verdun: Nivelle Takes Over," in Peter Young (ed.), *The Marshall Cavendish Illustrated Encyclopedia of World War One* (New York/London, Marshall Cavendish, 1984), vol. V, pp. 1358–9.

Hüttenberger, Peter, "Nationalsozialistische Polykratie," *Geschichte und Gesellschaft* 2 (1976): 417–42.

Jannen, William, "National Socialists and Social Mobility," *Journal of Social History*, 9/3 (1976): 339–66.

Jarausch, Konrad, "Liberal Education as Illiberal Socialization: The Case of Students in Imperial Germany," *Journal of Modern History* 50/4 (December 1978).

"German Students in the First World War," *Central European History* XVIII/4 (December, 1984): 310–29.

Jeschke, Gerhard, "Vom 'neuen Staat' zur 'Volksgemeinschaft'. Unternehmerverbände und Reichspolitik vom Sturz Brünings bis zu den Märzwahlen 1933," *Ergebnisse* 8 (1979): 11–96.

Kahn, Leo, "July 1, 1916 — a Generation Sacrificed," in Peter Young, (ed.) *The Marshall Cavendish Illustrated Encyclopedia of World War One* (New York/London, Marshall Cavendish, 1984), vol. V, pp. 1502–10.

Kelley, Douglas, "Preliminary Studies of the Rorschach Records of the Nazi War Criminals," *Rorschach Research Exchange* X/2 (June 1946: 45–8.

Kluke, P., "Hitler and the Volkswagenprojekt," *Vierteljahreshefte für Zeitgeschichte* VIII (1960).

Koelble, Hartmuth, "Social Stratification in Germany in the 19th and 20th Centuries: A Survey of Research Since 1945," *Journal of Social History* 10/2 (winter 1976).

Krieger, Leonard, "The Idea of the Welfare State in Europe and the United States," *Journal of Modern History* XXIV/4 (October–December 1963).

Lampert, Heinz, "Staatliche Sozialpolitik im Dritten Reich," in A. Gutowski, B. Molitir, and W. Krone (eds.), *Hamburger Jahrbuch für Wirtschafts- und Geselschaftspolitik* (Tübingen, JCB Mohr, 1980), pp. 149–76.

Lange, Dieter, "Fritz Tarnows Pläne zur Umwandlung der faschistischen deutschen [DAF] in Gewerkschaften," *Zeitschrift für Geschichtswissenschaft* 24 (1976): 150–67.

Loewenberg, Peter, "The Psychohistorical Origins of the Nazi Youth Cohort" in *American Historical Review* 76/5 (December, 1971): 1457–502.

Lölhöffel, Dieter von (ed.), "Die Umwandlung der Gewerkschaften in eine nationalsozialistische Zwangsorganisation," in Ingeborg Eisenwein-Rothe (ed.), *Die Wirtschaftsverbände von 1933 bis 1945* (Berlin, Duncker & Humblot, 1965), pp. 1–184.

Mason, Timothy, "Labour in the Third Reich 1933–1939," *Past and Present* 33 (April 1966).

"Zur Entstehung des Gesetzes zur Ordnung der nationalen Arbeit" in Hans Mommsen et al. *Industrielles System und politische Entwicklung in der Weimarer Republik* (Düsseldorf, Droste Verlag, 1975).

Matzerath, Horst, and Turner, Henry, "Die Selbsfinanzierung der NSDAP," *Geschichte und Gesellschaft* 3 (1977): 59–92.

Medical Record. "Robert Ley's Brain," vol. 159 (1946), p. 188.

Merritt, Michael A., "Strength through Joy: Regimented Leisure Time in Germany," in Otis Mitchell (ed.), *Nazism and the Common Man* (Washington, DC, University Press of America, 1981).

Neumann, Franz, "Mobilisierung der Arbeit in der Gesellschaftsordnung des Nationalsozialismus" (1942), in Franz Neumann, *Staat, Demokratie* (Frankfurt, Suhrkamp, 1978), pp. 255–89.

Orlow, Dietrich, "Die Adolf-Hitler Schulen," *Vierteljahrshefte für Zeitgeschichte*, July, 1965, pp. 272ff.

Peball, Kurt, "Gorlice: Turning Point on the Eastern Front," in Peter Young (ed.), *The Marshall Cavendish Illustrated Encyclopedia of World War One* (New York/London, Marshall Cavendish, 1984), vol. III, pp. 929–35.

Rabinach, Anson, "The Aesthetics of Production in the Third Reich," in George Mosse (ed.), *International Fascism*, (London, Sage, 1979), pp. 189–222.

Reulecke, Jürgen, "Die Fahne mit dem goldenen Zahnrad: der 'Leistungskampf der deutschen Betriebe 1937–1939," in Peuker and Reulecke, *Die Reihen fast geschlossen*, (Wuppertal, Peter Hammer, 1980), pp. 245–72.

Ritzler, Barry, "The Nuremberg Mind Revisited: A Qualitative Approach to Nazi Rorschachs," *Journal of Personality Assessment* 42/4 (1978): 345–53.

Rutherford, Ward, "The Somme: Bloody and Futile," in Peter Young (ed.), *The Marshall Cavendish Illustrated Encyclopedia of World War One* (New York/London, Marshall Cavendish, 1984), vol. V, pp. 1608ff.

Salter, Stephen, "Structures of Consensus and Coercion: Workers' Morale and the Maintenance of Work Discipline, 1939–1945," in David Welch, (ed.), *Nazi Propaganda* (London, Croom Helm, 1983), pp. 88–116.

Shand, James, "The Reichsautobahn: Symbol for the Third Reich," *Journal of Contemporary History* 19 (1984): 189–200.

Scholz, Harold, "Die NS-Ordensburgen," *Vierteljahrshefte für Zeitgeschichte* XV (July 1967).

Siegel, Tilla, "Lohnpolitik im nationalsozialistischen Deutschland," in Carole Sachse et al., *Angst, Belohnung Zucht und Ordnung* (Opladen, Westdeutscher Verlag, 1982), pp. 54–132.

Smelser, Ronald, "Nazi Dynamics, German Foreign Policy and Appeasement," in Wolfgang Mommsen and Lothar Kettenacker, (eds.), *The Fascist Challenge and the Policy of Appeasement* (London, Allen & Unwin, 1983), pp. 31–47.

Stachura, Peter, "'Der Fall Strasser': Gregor Strasser, Hitler and National Socialism 1930–1932," in Peter Stachura (ed.), *The Shaping of the Nazi State* (New York, Harper & Row, 1978), pp. 88–130.

Teppe, Karl, "Zur Sozialpolitik des Dritten Reiches am Beispiel der Sozialversicherung," *Archiv für Sozialgeschichte* XVIII (1977): 195–250.

Tubbs, D.B., "Aircraft: Higher, Faster, Lighter," in Peter Young (ed.), *The Marshall Cavendish Illustrated Encyclopedia of World War One*, (New York/London, Marshall Cavendish, 1984), vol. VI, pp. 1860–70.

"The Air War: Tactics and Technology," in Peter Young, (ed.), *The Marshall Cavendish Illustrated Encyclopedia of World War One* (New York/London, Marshall Cavendish, 1984), vol. V, pp. 1440–51.

Tyrell, Albrecht, "Führergedanke und Gauleiterwechsel: Die Teilung des Gaues Rheinland der NSDAP 1931," *Vierteljahrshefte für Zeitgeschichte* 5/4 (1975): 341–74.

Voges, Michael, "Klassenkampf in der 'Betriebsgemeinschaft'. Die 'Deutschlandberichte' der Sopade (1934–1940) als Quelle zum Widerstand der Industriearbeiter im Dritten Reich," *Archiv für Sozialgeschichte* 21 (1981): 329–83.

Wallace, Anthony, "Stress and rapid personality changes," *International*

Record of Medicine 169 (1956): 761–4.
Werner, Wolfgang, "Die Arbeitserziehungslager als Mittel nationalsozialistischer 'Sozialpolitik' gegen deutsche Arbeiter," in Waclaw Dlugoborski, (ed.), *Zweiter Weltkrieg und sozialer Wandel* (Göttingen, Vanden Hoeck, 1981), pp. 138–47.

Dissertations

Buchheim, Hans, "Die Übernahme staatlicher Fürsorgeaufgaben durch die NSV," in *Gutachten des Instituts für Zeitgeschichte* (1966).
Buchholz, Wolfhard, "Die NS-Gemeinschaft 'Kraft durch Freude' Freigestaltung von Arbeiterschaft im Dritten Reich" (Munich, 1976).
Barclay, David, "A Prussian Socialism? Wichard von Moellendorf and the Dilemma of Economic Planning in Germany, 1918–1919" (Stanford, 1974).
De Witt, Thomas, "The Nazi Party and Social Welfare, 1919–1939" (Virginia, 1972).
Gies, Horst, "R. Walther Darré und die nationalsozialistische Bauernpolitik 1930 bis 1933" (Frankfurt, 1966).
Grill, Johnpeter Horst, "The Nazi Party in Baden, 1920–1945" (University of Michigan, Ann Arbor, 1975).
Hanf, Reinhardt, "Möglichkeiten und Grenzen betrieblicher Lohn und Gehaltspolitik, 1933–1939" (Bamberg, 1975).
Lükemann, Ulf, "Der Reichsschatzmeister der NSDAP" (FU Berlin, 1968).
Moyer, Laurence Van Zandt, "The Kraft durch Freude Movement in Nazi Germany 1933–1939" (Northwestern University, 1967).
Reichhardt, Hans Joachim, "Die Deutsche Arbeitsfront: Ein Beitrag zur Geschichte des nationalsozialistischen Deutschlands und zur Struktur des totalitären Herrschaftssystems" (FU Berlin, 1956).
Scheuer, Wolfgang, "Einrichtungen und Maßnahmen der sozialen Sicherheit in der Zeit des Nationalsozialismus" (Cologne, 1967).
Schleicher, Reinhold, "Die Wandlung der Wohlfahrtspflege durch den Nationalsozialismus" (Heidelberg, 1939).
Schneider, Christian, "Stadtgründung im III Reich. Wolfsburg und Salzgitter. Ideologie, Ressortpolitik, Representation" (Munich, 1979).
Siegel, Mark, "The National Socialist People's Welfare Organization — 1933–1939: The Political Manipulation of Welfare" (University of Cinncinnati, 1976).
Stokes, Lawrence, "The 'Sicherheitsdienst' (SD) of the 'Reichsfuehrer' SS and German Public Opinion, September 1939–June 1941 (Johns Hopkins, 1972).

Westhoff, Carl William, "The Role of 'Leibesübung und Sport' in the Third Reich" (Michigan State University, 1978).

Unpublished Manuscripts

Kutsch, Lothar, "Die NS-Gemeinschaft 'Kraft durch Freude' innerhalb der 'Deutschen Arbeitsfront,'" in Institut für Sozialgeschichte, Bonn.

Walesch, Annegret, "Das Amt 'Schönheit der Arbeit' in der NS-Organisation 'Kraft durch Freude' 1933–1939" in Institut für Sozialgeschichte, Bonn.

Contemporary Nazi Publications

Biallas, Hans, and Starcke, Gerhard (eds.), *Leipzig: das Nürnberg der DAF 1935* (Berlin, Verlag der DAF, 1935).

DAF Zentralamt, *Richtlinien über die Mitgliedschaft zur Deutschen Arbeitsfront* (Berlin, Verlag der DAF, 1935).

Arbeiter, Bauern und Soldaten (Berlin, Verlag der DAF, n.d.).

DNB (Deutsches Nachrichtenbüro), *The New Germany Desires Work and Peace* (Berlin, DNB, 1933).

Goebbels, Joseph, *Kampf um Berlin* (Berlin/Munich, Franz Eher Verlag, 1938).

Vom Kaiserhof zur Reichskanzlei (Munich, Zentralverlag der NSDAP, Franz Eher nachf. 1934).

Grohé, Josef, *Der politische Kampf im Rheinlande nach dem Weltkriege*, 3rd edn, Kriegsvorträge der Rheinischen Friedrichs-Wilhelm-Universität Heft 40 (Bonn, Scheuer, 1941).

Kiehl, Walter, *Mann an der Fahne. Kameraden erzählen von Dr Ley* (Munich, Zentralverlag der NSDAP, 1938).

Ley, Robert, *Die Deutsche Arbeitsfront. Ihr Werden und ihre Aufgaben* (Munich, Verlag der DAF, 1934).

Kraft durch Freude. Rede zur Gründung der NS-Gemeinschaft 'Kraft durch Freude' am 27.11.1933 (Berlin, Verlag der DAF, 1934).

Deutschland ist glückicher geworden! Zwei Reden auf dem Reichsparteitag 1935 (Berlin, Verlag der DAF, 1935).

Deutschland ist schöner geworden (Berlin, Mehden-Verlag 1936).

Wir alle helfen dem Führer, ed. Heinrich Simon (Berlin, Zentralverlag der NSDAP, 1937).

Soldaten der Arbeit (Munich, Zentralverlag der NSDAP, 1938).

Durchbruch der sozialen Ehre, 7th edn (Berlin, Zentralverlag der NSDAP, 1939).

Der ständische Aufbau und die Deutsche Arbeitsfront (Berlin, Verlag der DAF, 1933).

Marrenbach, Otto, *Fundamente des Sieges. Die Gesamtarbeit der deutschen Arbeitsfront 1933–1940*, 2nd edn (Berlin, Verlag der DAF, 1940).

NSDAP, *Reichsparteitag 1934* (Berlin, Zentralverlag der NSDAP, 1934).

Offizieller Berich über den Verlauf des Reichsparteitages mit sämtlichen Kongressreden (Munich, Zentralverlag der NSDAP, 1938).

Kreisleitung, Oberberg Kreis, Buch des Oberbergischen Kreises (Cologne, Westdeutscher Beobachter, 1939).

Reichsorganisationsleiter der NSDAP, *Organisationsbuch der NSDAP* (Munich, Zentralverlag der NSDAP, 1943).

Rühle, Gerd, *Das Dritte Reich. Dokumentarische Darstellung des Aufbaues der Nation*, vol. 2 (Berlin, 1934).

Schmidt, P., *Zwanzig Jahre Soldat Adolf Hitlers* (Cologne, Westdeutscher Beobachter, 1941).

Starcke, Gerhard, *NSBO und Deutsche Arbeitsfront* (Berlin, Verlag der Reimar Hobbing, 1934).

Störmer, Helmuth, *Das rechtliche Verhältnis der NS-Volkswohlfahrt und des Winterhilfswerkes zu den Betreuten im Vergleiche zur öffentlichen Wohlfahrtspflege*, NSV-Schriftenreihe 10 (Berlin, Zentralverlag der NSDAP, 1940).

Wilhelm, Oskar von (ed.), *Zehn Jahre Ortsgruppe Leverkusen der NSDAP* (Cologne, Westdeutscher Beobachter, 1934).

Newspapers

Amtliches Nachrichtenblatt der DAF
Angriff
Arbeitertum
Berliner Börsenzeitung
Der Deutsche
Freude und Arbeit
Gewerkschaftszeitung
Kölner Stadtanzeiger
Kölner Jüdisches Wochenblatt
Oberbergische Bote
Oberbergische Volkszeitung
Völkischer Beobachter

Volksstimme, Cologne
Westdeutscher Beobachter

Archives

Bundesarchiv Koblenz (BAK)
R2 — Reichsfinanzministerium
R11 — Reichswirtschaftsministerium
R12 — Reichsgruppen und Wirtschaftsgruppen der gewerblichen Wirtschaft
R22 — Reichsjustizministerium
R36 — Deutscher Gemeindetag
R41 — Reichsarbeitsministerium
R43 — Reichskanzlei
R55 — Reichsministerium für Volksaufklärung und Propaganda
R58 — Sicherheitspolizei und politischer Nachrichtendienst
NS5 — Deutsche Arbeitsfront
NS6 — Stellvertreter des Führers
NS8 — Kanzlei Rosenberg
NS10 — Politische Adjutantur des Führers und Reichskanzlers
NS22 — Reichsorganisationsleiter der NSDAP
NS25 — Hauptamt für Kommunalpolitik
NS26 — Hauptarchiv der NSDAP
NSD50 — printed materials
Schumacher Sammlung
Berlin Document Center (BDC)
Personal files on:
Hans Biallas
Johannes Engel
Max Frauendorfer
Otto Gohdes
Josef Grohé
Erich Klapper
Robert Ley
Otto Marrenbach
Reinhold Muchow
Karl Peppler
Hans Graf Reischach
Rudolf Schmeer
Walter Schumann
Claus Selzner

Centre de Documentation Juive Contemporaine, Paris
Friedrich Ebert Stiftung, Bonn
Institut für Zeitgeschichte, Munich (IfZ)
R. Walther Darré, "Aufzeichnungen 1945–1948" (unpublished manuscript)
Graf Lutz Schwerin von Krosigk, "Politische Erinnerungen" (unpublished manuscript)
Landeshauptarchiv Rheinland Pfalz, Koblenz (LHAK)
Bestand 403 — Oberpräsident der Rheinprovinz
National Archives of the United States
RG238 Collection of World War Two Crimes, Justice Jackson File
Microcopy T-81, T-580
Stanford Institution
NSDAP Hauptarchiv
United States Department of Defense, Armed Forces Institute of Pathology
Reports on clinical and pathological diagnosis and microscopic examination of Robert Ley's brain and correspondence pertaining thereto.
Universitätsarchiv Münster
Philosophische Fakultät prom: 2231

Correspondence

Julius Cieslik
Dieter Corbach
Wolfgang Corsten
John F. Dolibois
Tom Doch
Molly Harrower
Wilhelm Heuser
K.H. Pampus

Index

Of persons, institutions and organizations